John Dryden

FOUR TRAGEDIES

Curtain Playwrights

GENERAL EDITOR
R. C. Bald

John Dryden

FOUR TRAGEDIES

Edited by

L. A. Beaurline and Fredson Bowers

The University of Chicago Press

CHICAGO AND LONDON

Library of Congress Catalog Card Number: 67–26813

THE UNIVERSITY OF CHICAGO PRESS, CHICAGO & LONDON
The University of Toronto Press, Toronto 5, Canada

Preface

This edition aims to present an accurate text of representative serious plays by Dryden, with suitable commentary and other aids to understanding. The selection of *Aureng-Zebe* and *All for Love* was more or less automatic, although it is odd that *Aureng-Zebe* has not been so frequently anthologized as it has been admired. *Don Sebastian* justly claimed a place as one of Dryden's neglected masterpieces. Beyond these three, the choice became difficult. To include *The Spanish Friar*, a well-known and considerable play, would have made all the group drawn from Dryden's middle and late periods, and we had two examples of tragicomedies in the companion to this volume. *The Conquest of Granada* would have required both parts to be very satisfactory. Therefore, *The Indian Emperour* was settled upon, as an illustration of his early heroic plays. The most popular of his plays, it set the vogue in a way that Roger Boyle and Davenant never did, and it shows modern readers more vividly than any other play how heroic drama was related to concepts of ideal primitivism, natural religion, and contemporary politics.

Introductions and annotations have been kept as brief as possible, following the admirable model of G. R. Noyes' editions. I found the task easier, knowing that the University of California Press was publishing an elaborate edition of all the works. Fortunately, the second volume of plays in that set, volume IX, was far enough advanced so that Vinton Dearing could generously allow me to see page proofs before we went to press. I have benefited greatly from his and John Loftis' work on *The Indian Emperour*, but our texts and commentary on *Secret Love* and *Sir Martin Mar-All* were already too far into production to use their edition in any material way.

Mr. Bowers prepared the texts and the textual notes, although I made a few alterations and read the final page proof. The introductions and glosses are largely my work but they rely heavily upon recent discussions of the heroic plays. In particular, Arthur Kirsch's *Dryden's Heroic Plays* and Michael Alssid's essays have influenced my interpretations. Somewhat more original views are expressed here concerning *All for Love* and *Don Sebastian*. In the glosses definitions are generally from the *OED*, except where specified.

I am grateful for help from several of my students, especially from John Pesta. Arthur Kirsch and John Freehafer kindly read the introductions and made valuable suggestions.

L.A.B.

Contents

Abbreviations

Q   quarto

F   folio, *The Comedies Tragedies and Operas* written by John Dryden, 1701

Brower   Reuben Brower, "Dryden's Epic Manner and Virgil," *PMLA*, LV (1940), 119–38

Cibber   *An Apology for the Life of Mr. Colley Cibber*, edited by Robert W. Lowe, 1889

Congreve   *The Dramatick Works of John Dryden, Esq.*, with William Congreve's character of Dryden, 1717

Downes   John Downes, *Roscius Anglicanus; or, An Historical Review of the Stage*, edited by Montague Summers, 1928

Essays   *Of Dramatic Poesy and Other Essays*, edited by George Watson, 1962

Farmer   John S. Farmer and W. E. Henley, *Slang and Its Analogues*, 1890–1904

Gómara   Francisco López de Gómara, *The Conquest of the Weast India (1578)*, edited by Herbert Priestley, 1940

Macd   Hugh Macdonald, *Dryden: A Bibliography*, 1939

Noyes   *Selected Dramas of John Dryden*, edited by George R. Noyes, 1910

OED   *The Oxford English Dictionary*, 1888–1928

S-S   *The Works of John Dryden*, edited by Sir Walter Scott, revised and corrected by George Saintsbury, 1882–93

Summers   *Dryden: The Dramatic Works*, edited by Montague Summers, 1931

W & M   Gertrude L. Woodward and James G. McManaway, *A Check List of English Plays 1641–1700*, 1945

General Introduction

When Dryden adapted Shakespeare's *Troilus and Cressida* for the Restoration stage (1679), he rewrote the curiously muted scene in which Aeneas brings the bad news that Cressida has been traded for Antenor on the very night that Troilus has consummated his love. The magnificent new confrontation scene, III.ii of the adaptation, displays Dryden's talents as a serious playwright, and if we can appreciate what he has done here, we are in the way of understanding the achievement as well as the weaknesses in his tragedies and heroic plays. Every alteration of Shakespeare places more pressure on the characters, heightening their innocence, their delight, and their serious concerns, serving to make the terrible news come as a greater blow. Instead of the blunt Aeneas delivering the message, Hector himself, to whom the "fiery youth" pays an "awful homage," comes to "manage" Troilus. In a way worthy of Shakespeare's theatrical talents, Hector prepares the boy for the shock, postponing the unpleasant truth for over fifty lines and increasing the anxiety. Troilus must first guess what would be the worst possible news, and, of course, he is not even able to conceive that Cressida might be taken away. As Troilus comes closer and closer to guessing the truth,

> It comes like thunder grumbling in a cloud,
> Before the dreadfull break: if here it fall,
> The subtile flame will lick up all my blood,
> And in a moment turn my heart to ashes.
>
> [III.ii. sig. F2, 1679 ed.]

Hector says he did not tell everything at once, "but by degrees and glimpses . . . let it in, lest it might rush upon you / And quite orepower your Soul." Troilus must curb his anger, control his grief, and bear it like a man.

But Troilus cannot hold himself back, and he flatly refuses to give up Cressida; the issue is joined, and a highly charged debate begins between the interests of the "general state" and a single citizen. Since the common safety depends on Antenor's freedom, Troilus' happiness must be sacrificed; indeed, he should, according to Hector, welcome the chance to be the victim, "if parting from a Mistress can procure a Nation's happiness." Even though she be his life, his being, his soul, he should for the public good give her up. In passionate defense, Troilus scorns the people:

I

> And what are they that I shou'd give up her
> To make them happy? let me tell you Brother,
> The publick, is the Lees of vulgar slaves:
> Slaves, with the minds of slaves: so born, so bred:
> Yet such as these united in a herd
> Are call'd the publique: Millions of such Cyphers
> Make up the publique sum: an Eagle's life
> Is worth a world of Crows: are Princes made
> For such as these, who, were one Soul extracted
> From all their beings, cou'd not raise a Man.
>
> [Sig. F2ᵛ.]

But Hector points out that princes would not be great if there were not inferior people to serve and adore them, almost as gods. In reply, Troilus turns his defense and insists that Helen must go if Cressida goes, but Hector reminds him that he has already voted that Helen should stay; indeed, he has pleaded Helen's case and persuaded Hector against his better judgment. The tension rises as argument after argument is beaten down, and the full range of Troilus' loyalties is covered: his respect for his father's authority, his friendship and brotherly feeling for Hector, his budding sense of manhood, his pride in his first sexual conquest, his respect for Andromache, his gratitude to Hector. At the same time Hector goes through a sequence of emotions, from tenderness to sternness, to surprise, anger, indignation, almost contempt. Each man goes too far, but at the last critical moment each is brought back to himself by some residuum of good sense, as when Hector warns Troilus:

> Take heed, young man how you too far provoke me!
> For Heaven can witness 'tis with much constraint
> That I preserve my faith.
>
> [Sig. F4.]

Troilus, too, reveals a division in his soul, some preservation of his old faith in his friend that is separate from his devotion to Cressida. On this faith the two begin to build a confidence, first with elaborate apologies for what they have said, then with pity for the other's feelings, and eventually with renunciation. For at the last moment Hector freely offers to tell Priam that the treaty is canceled and that he will be Cressida's champion. In a counterturn Troilus says,

> It must not be, my Brother!
> For then your errour would be more then mine:
> I'le bring her forth, and you shall bear her hence;
> That you have pitied me is my reward.

Thus the "triumph of kindness" comes at the end of a most charming and tempestuous scene. A whole galaxy of emotions has been displayed in a series of turns and counterturns and depicted in elegant and proper language, unlike most arguments between friends or between husbands and wives. The whole is grandly heightened to a perfection of elemental feelings, clashing with different sorts of loyalty.

Such a sustained pitch of drama, however, creates difficulties and leads to Dryden's most persistent fault—the evenness of his plays. If every scene is almost equally high-pitched, no greater emphasis seems possible. A climax is hard to reach beyond an already devastating episode, for everything stands on one lofty plateau. Dryden seems unable to vary the scale of representation, a mistake that Shakespeare seldom made, for Shakespeare could compress or throw off-stage anything subordinate to his main intent. Dryden sometimes gained a change of pace by interspersing comic and serious scenes, but that was more proper to tragicomedy. He was, therefore, the victim of his own talents, which induced him to develop almost every episode fully. He may have thought he should follow a decorum of epic poetry, less suited to the varying emphasis needed in a drama. The monumental *Don Sebastian,* in which he indulged himself beyond the limits of the theater, grew to staggering proportions, with full scale scenes of eight and nine hundred lines. But he maintained a remarkable quality of writing in each scene; each is a gem, many-faceted and polished, worthy of a master craftsman.

Looking at the debate between Hector and Troilus again, we see that it does not proceed logically, nor do Troilus and Hector make a great show of reason; rather the whole impression comes from our awareness that their words project intense feelings by means of artificial devices, mannered contrasts, and patterned development: the movement from self-centered passion to public-centered compassion. The pattern has almost a life of its own; it is a desirable form by which to depict character and to excite the audience's sympathy, yet we are always conscious of the artifice, the bold turns and counterturns. This sense of disjunction—of the gap between art and nature continually opening and closing but most often being maintained in surprising tension, wherein artifice restrains boldness and boldness itself becomes artificial in order to limit some contrary passion—this is Dryden's most characteristic mode, and it makes him, in modern terms, a distinctly "inorganic" artist.

The organic writer employs imitative form in which manner imitates the thought and feeling, as in Keats's poetry

3

or Ibsen's plays, so that the whole work is permeated with echoes and reechoes of the same central images and attitudes. This produces expressive literature. Inorganic writers, if I may adapt Ivor Winters' convenient term for a broader conception, often use form in a quite different way. In their work they may sometimes use recurrent imagery, as we shall see in *Don Sebastian*, but often their use of form will clash with feeling, resist feeling, or at least be somewhat independent of feeling. Spenser, Dryden, and, to a certain extent, Milton create this kind of art, and although they have been accused of using artifice as a mere ornament, a kind of frosting on the cake, we are coming to see that some powerful effects may be achieved by their more or less self-conscious use of form in tension with matter.

This sense of impassioned design informs most of Dryden's serious plays, from the *Indian Emperour* to *Don Sebastian*. It is less emphatic in his late plays, but it is always present. It may, taken out of context, seem to us extravagant, bombastic, and unreal, in our age of deflated oratory and informality; yet its greatness cannot be denied by those whose critical sense carries them beyond the present conventions. Design existing almost for its own sake and elaborate speech patterns copiously developed can have a special heightened propriety in keeping with strong and genuine feeling, even though they may not imitate feeling.

The outrageous cries of Almanzor, when he discovers that Almahide has infected him with love, have a certain formal propriety in *The Conquest of Granada*, Part I: "I'me pleas'd and pain'd, since first her eyes I saw, / As I were stung with some *Tarantula*. . . . I'm numb'd and fix'd and scarce my eyeballs move; / I fear it is the Lethargy of Love!" (III.i. sig. D2ᵛ, 1672 edition). When heard at the end of an elaborate development of Almanzor's fierce but naturally responsive character, these are not absurd speeches; the audience has witnessed more than an hour of Almanzor's mounting excitement, expressions of his free spirit, his passionate concern for justice, his natural virtue, and his pride. Earlier he has declared that "I alone am king of me, / I am as free as nature first made man." So we look forward to the moment when he might be conquered by a mistress, some representative of the first-made woman. We have been assured that Almahide's beauteous power is godlike, and we have heard her admire Almanzor, almost against her will:

Mark how terrible his Eyes appear!
And yet there's something roughly noble there,

Which, in unfashion'd Nature, looks Divine,
And, like a Gemm, does in a Quarry shine.
[III.i. sig. D2.]

The resulting combination of savage independence, hubris, spiritual sensibility, natural sympathy, great beauty, and the "slavery" of love creates an explosive reaction that is properly depicted in the irregular yet mannered style that Almanzor uses—"wild and daring sallies of sentiment," and "an eccentrick violence of wit" that treads "upon the brink of meaning, where light and darkness begin to mingle; to approach the precipice of absurdity, and hover over the abyss of unideal vacancy."[1] In Dryden's satires, such style conveys mockery, but in the heroic plays it creates a heady grandeur, appropriate to the genre of a heroic play. The rhymed couplet acts as a further distancing device to keep the speeches from toppling over into rant or ridicule, supplying just the right amount of mannered expression so that the passions do not entirely dominate the language. To take another extreme example, the sexual and military rage of Lyndaraxa, who makes a literal identification of her love and her ambition to be a queen, is embodied in some vigorous lines, as she describes her reactions to the distant sounds of battle:

The sound goes farther off; and faintly dies,
Curse of this going back, these ebbing cryes!
Ye Winds, waft hither sounds more strong and quick:
Beat faster, Drums, and mingle Deaths more thick.
I'le to the Turrets of the Palace goe,
And add new fire to those that fight below.
[III.i. sig. D1ᵛ.]

Such turbulence has seldom boiled up in such an elegant kettle. The future author of the St. Cecilia Day Odes here tries his hand at onomatopoeia, where the sound pattern calls attention to the rhymes, intensifying the heavy beat. Nothing could be more conventional and "set" for the occasion. For that matter, the entire scene where Lyndaraxa and Almahide state their counter feelings about the battle is a conventional substitution for off-stage action, going all the way back to Marlowe's *Tamburlaine*, Part I, III.iii, where the two

---

[1] Dr. Johnson's remarks on Dryden's wit, *Lives of the Poets* (1905 edition), I, 460, also cited by Bruce King, *Dryden's Major Plays* (1966), chap. 1, but King interprets it as supporting a comic view of the heroic style. D. W. Jefferson in "The Significance of Dryden's Heroic Plays," *Proceedings of the Leeds Philosophical Society*, V (1940), 125–39, develops a point similar to King's.

queens sit on thrones and rail at each other as their husbands fight off-stage.

In less agitated passages the couplet still lends an austere dignity: "I need not haste the end of Life to meet; / That precipice is just beneath my feet" (*Aureng-Zebe*, IV.51–52). And at other moments it suffuses a speech with haughty contempt, such as the emperor feels for his wife's "clamorous virtue":

> In vain of pompous chastity y'are proud:
> Virtue's adultery of the Tongue, when loud.
>
> [II.i.259–60.]

A brilliant example of cooler language embodying wild thoughts is found at the end of *Don Sebastian*. Here Sebastian tries to say good-bye to his wife Almeyda after having discovered that she is also his sister, and his talk almost breaks out of moral bounds, as he holds back his intense desire. During the speech he creeps closer and closer to incestuous lust, but Dryden has little need to rough up the language, and lawless thought is conveyed in the plain and dignified blank verse.

> We must make hast, or we shall never part.
> I wou'd say something that's dear as this;
> Nay, wou'd do more than say: one moment longer,
> And I shou'd break through Laws Divine, and Humane;
> And think 'em Cobwebs, spred for little man,
> Which all the bulky herd of nature breaks.
> The vigorous young world, was ignorant
> Of these restrictions, 'tis decrepit now;
> Not more devout, but more decay'd, and cold.
> All this is impious; therefore we must part.
>
> [V.i.636–45.]

Both kinds of high style, the heroic and the later restrained style, bring together visceral excitement and conscious artifice in a powerful and incisive unit, joining the two qualities of justness and liveliness. In the larger elements of Dryden's plays we find the same complementary balance and tension; tender womanish feelings and vigorous manly expression, irregular morality and generous self-denial often combine in a character such as Mark Antony or Cortez; and in the heroic play these qualities are projected with a controlled boldness, often conforming to the French rules, but occasionally taking liberties for the sake of the pleasure of variety.[2] This subtle

---

[2] In fact Dryden showed little patience with specific rules of composition, although he believed in the possibility of an orderly, general theory of writing. See Hoyt Trowbridge's illuminating essay, "The Place of Rules in Dryden's Criticism", *MP*, XLIV (1946), 84–96.

and dynamic union demands that we be discerning readers and recognize the silent graces in action, the purity of style, "the clearness of conception and expression, the boldness maintained to majesty and sound of words, not strained into bombast, but justly elevated" (*Essays*, I, 278).

II

Dryden did not always keep an equal balance of artifice and passion, of justness and liveliness in his writing, but no wonder. He wrote plays off and on for over thirty years, satisfied the needs of at least two acting companies, and responded to the critical challenge of the 1670's and the political revolution of the 1680's. In the early years of the Restoration, during the heyday of national satisfaction and of obsession with royalty, he experimented with heroic drama, brought it to the height of perfection, varied it, and abandoned it, just as Shakespeare, in the patriotic days following the defeat of the Great Armada, developed the English history play, varied it, and then set it aside. In the latter part of Dryden's career, pathetic tragedy became more popular, and his accomplishments in the form display his remarkable artistic genius. The foundation of both heroic plays and tragedies, however, rests on his idea of genres, an idea which must be understood at the outset.

The theory was oriented toward a psychology of composition and controlled by a notion of "inverisimilitude"; the purpose of drama was to produce certain emotional and moral effects in the audience. Thus Dryden's theory is firmly within the context of seventeenth-century thought, which placed a new emphasis on epistemology and the theory of the mind and supplied a framework of ideas for theology, science, politics, and poetry. All literary compositions, Dryden said, required imagination or lively fancy, and like fire, fancy is a good servant but a poor master: "if this fancy be not regulated, 'tis mere caprice, and utterly incapable to produce a reasonable and judicious poem" (I, 261). Judgment, the regulating force, exercises conscious choice of genre and understands the significant differences in form, distinguishing high, middle, and low style, observing the level of manners in character, controlling the moral design, permitting liberties of invention, and sometimes consciously departing from ordinary human experience. In the minds of most critics there was a sliding scale of genres, from the highest, the epic, to the lowest, the comedy. Comedy, oddly enough, offered the least liberty to the poet. Since it was closest to life, the audience could be least deluded by a

comic scene which kept close to the lifelike images of sensa-
tion and familiar knowledge. The style had to be conversa-
tional, character morally blemished, events "common."
Heroic poetry, at the other extreme, was the queen of literary
forms, and it required the most active fancy. It was frankly
artificial, for it allowed the most license in style, which was
elevated above common life, and it required the most exalted
persons and permitted miraculous events, which could evoke
intense admiration in its readers.

The heroic play, a heroic poem "in little," was an attempt
to reach beyond the limits of the ordinary drama. Its irregular
but great spirit, embodied by the protagonist, supplied the
main force for evoking admiration. The plays are indeed
"beautiful dreams of magnanimity," as Clifford Leech has
remarked, but like all dreams they were grounded in reality.
The critical theory that Dryden sets forth in his "Defence of
the Epilogue" to *The Conquest of Granada* (1672) comes directly
from Pierre Corneille's plays and his discourses on drama,
especially the concept of *la gloire*. Dryden's plays themselves,
however, often show a debt to Beaumont and Fletcher and
their imitators on the Caroline stage: James Shirley, Philip
Massinger, and Sir William Davenant. The works of courtly
playwrights, William Habington's *The Queen of Aragon* (1640),
Sir John Suckling's *Aglaura* (1638) and *Brennoralt* (ca. 1639),
William Cartwright's *The Royal Slave* (1636), and Sir John
Denham's *The Sophy* (1641?) offer parallels of basic situations
in heroic plays. We should remember that such plays were
revived on the London stage in the 1660's and 1670's as the
stock plays of the major companies. These works were re-
plete with besieged cities, tyrannical monarchs, lecherous
fathers who sought the love of their son's mistresses, generous
rivals, discontented generals who changed sides in war, and
with grand opportunities for confrontation scenes and for
debates of political policy. The persistent themes of many of
these centered upon the difficulties of maintaining private
love under stress from public duty.

Later in life, Dryden regretted some of his early experi-
ments and began to doubt that heroic effects could success-
fully be achieved on the stage, for in a mere three hours a
play could not induce a habit of heroic virtue, as an epic
narrative could. "The shining quality of an epic hero, his
magnanimity, his constancy, his patience, his piety, or whatever characteristical virtue his poet gave him, raises first our
admiration: we are naturally prone to imitate what we admire, and frequent acts produce a habit" (*Essays*, I, 228). A
tragedy may rectify a passion, but not a defect in manners,

he came to believe. But in the heroic plays of the 1660's and early 1670's, he had greater confidence in the powers of drama, and he sometimes succeeded in raising loftier images than were usually found on the tragic stage. As in the magnificent Rubens painting, the "Apotheosis of James I" on the ceiling of the Banqueting House in Whitehall, he used broad brush strokes to depict figures larger than life. And although Montezuma, Cortez, or Aureng-Zebe do not burst into the glowing skies to the accompaniment of cherubim and seraphim, they urge themselves forward with great energy, and they achieve great ends.[3] Even supernatural spirits have their role in the "enthusiastic parts" of the plays. As in viewing a great painting, the audience sees the action from a suitable distance and responds with admiration, a mental state above pity and terror, a kind of rapt contemplation that had been important to drama and poetry for three or four generations of Englishmen. Owen Feltham, for instance, explained the idealizing effects of admiration, betraying its Platonic origins.

Whatsoever is rare, and passionate, carries the soule to the thought of Eternitie. And, by contemplation, gives it some glympses of more absolute perfection, then here 'tis capable of. When I see Royaltie of a State-show, at some onwonted solemnity, my thoughts present me something, more royall then this. When I see the most inchanting beauties that Earth can shew me; I yet thinke, there is something farre more glorious: me thinkes I see a kinde of higher perfection, peeping through the frailty of a face. When I heare the ravishing straines of a sweet-tuned voyce, married to the warbles of the Artfull instrument; I apprehend by this, a higher Diapason: and doe almost beleeve I heare a little Deity whispering, through the pory substance of the tongue. But this I can but grope after. I can neither finde nor say what it is. When I read a rarely sententious man, I admire him, to my owne impatiency. I cannot read some parts of Seneca, above two Leaves together. Hee raises my soule to a contemplation, which sets me a thinking, on more, then I can imagine. So I am forced to cast him by, and subside to an admiration. Such effects workes Poetry, when it lookes to towring Vertues. It gives up a man to raptures, and inradiates the soule, with such high apprehensions: that all the Glories, which this World hath, hereby

[3] A full account of what is here briefly mentioned may be found in Eugene Waith's *The Herculean Hero* (1962), and in chapter 2 of Arthur Kirsch's *Dryden's Heroic Drama* (1965).

appeare contemptible. Of which the soft-soul'd Ovid gives a touch, when he complaines the want. . . .

> That Sacred vigor, which had wont, alone,
> To flame the Poet's noble breast, is gone.[4]

Many critics have discussed the role of admiration in the drama, but the most interesting association with history plays has not been emphasized enough. Thomas Heywood, in *An Apology for Actors*,[5] explains the artistic motives of plays based on English or foreign history, which try to present a pattern of heroic virtue. Heywood says that actions of military heroes can "move the spirits of the beholder to admiration" and

> What English blood seeing the person of any bold Englishman presented and doth not hugge his fame, and hunnye at his valor, persuing him in his enterprise with his best wishes, and as being wrapt in contemplation, offers to him in his heart all prosperous performance, as if the Personater were the man Personated, so bewitching a thing is the lively and well spirited action, that it hath power to new mold the harts of the spectators and fashion them to the shape of any noble and notable attempt.[6]

Heywood also assumes that noble audiences were particularly susceptible to plays about heroes. "Is thy mind Noble? and wouldst thou be further stir'd up to magnanimity? Behold upon the stage thou maist see *Hercules, Achilles, Alexander, Cæsar*" (Sig. F4ᵛ). In effect magnanimity has passed down through the ages in a sort of apostolic succession: Hercules moved by plays about his father Jupiter, Theseus inspired by Hercules, Achilles following Theseus, Alexander taught by representations of Achilles, Caesar by plays about Alexander. "Why should not the lives of these worthies, presented in these our dayes, effect the like wonders in the Princes of our times, which can no way bee so exquisitly demonstrated, nor so lively portrayed as by action" (Sig. B3ᵛ).

[4] Owen Feltham, *Resolves* (1628), frequently reprinted in the century.

[5] First edition, 1612, reprinted as *The Actor's Vindication* (ca. 1658). I used the edition prepared by Richard H. Perkinson (Scholars' Facsimiles and Reprints, 1941).

[6] *Ibid.*, sig. B4. It should be remembered that Dryden saw no significant distinction between historical and epic matter in his preface to *Annus Mirabilis, Essays*, I, 95.

It should not be surprising, then, that Dryden thought his central character was modeled on Achilles, on Tasso's Rinaldo, and on La Calprenède's Artaban, who presents the "highest pattern of human life," a fierce individualist, "who in strength and courage surpassed the rest," but is "of so fiery a temper, so impatient of an injury" that he would huff at kings and would disobey when provoked. But Dryden did not simply imitate his English and continental predecessors, for he made the hero relevant, adapting him to Restoration times and depicting him as a natural man who prized his freedom and self-respect above all things. That strain of primitivism was woven through contemporary libertine thought, and it was manifest in comedies of the age. In *Secret Love* Dryden himself showed the complementary nature of heroic and libertine passion,[7] and Dryden's enemies were quick to point out the contemporary implications of his heroic plays. The facetious recipe for a Dryden tragedy, given by Richard Leigh in *The Censure of the Rota* (1673), makes an explicit connection between Dryden's heroes and the town gallants:

> It is but framing the character of a Huff of the Town, one that from breaking Glass-windows, and combating the watch, starts up an *Heroe*: him you must make very saucy to his superiors, to shew he is of the same stamp with *Achilles* and *Rinaldo*; then tame the savage with the charming sight of the *Kings Daughter* (or wife) whom this *St. George* is to deliver from *Dragon*, or greater dangers: to heighten his character the more, bring in a sheepish King with a Guard of poultrons to be kick't by him as often he thinks fit his Miss. should be a witnesse of his Gallantry: if this be not enough, let him play prizes with Armies, still Tumults with one look, and raise Rebellions with another.[8]

The great free spirit, the natural man, is represented in the plays by means of an unfolding grand design. The plot usually begins with a moral dilemma in which the hero and his associates are confronted by a situation that requires a difficult choice. The caliber of the hero's response reveals his spiritual fiber, the dimensions of his soul. From a modern existential point of view, his choice enhances the value of his manhood and creates the value of his choice. Thus Cortez could crush

[7] See my comments in the introduction to *Secret Love* in this edition. *The Spanish Friar, Marriage a-la-Mode,* and *Don Sebastian* continue to exploit the analogy.
[8] P. 9, cited by Kirsch, p. 44.

Montezuma with his army, in the second scene of *The Indian Emperour*, but he alone of his men appreciates the delicate moral circumstances. Civilized man, as it were, confronts natural man, and Cortez realizes that he, as civilization's representative, is being tested. Because he must show the existence of a code that is higher than the law of beasts or of bestial nations, he generously frees the emperor and his court. The "cruell God" of the Indians has to give way to the "gentle God" of Cortez. The rest of the play offers successive predicaments such as this, and natural love idealized in the person of Cydaria creates the most exciting complication. Love for her lures Cortez into dangerous and paralyzing dilemmas, almost causing him to abandon his dreams of conquest. But each new confrontation exalts him in our esteem, differentiating him more and more from his "civilized" soldiers, until he fulfills his great potential and deservedly wins both the empire and the virtuous maiden. One of the crucial moments illustrates his spiritual power. In the prison scene (IV.i), as he lies chained on the floor, he withstands Almeria's raging lust, pride, and jealousy with magnificent dignity and fortitude. Almeria asks him to break "Cydaria's fetters" before she will loosen his chains, but he resolutely refuses. She is baffled to see that Cortez "cannot feare so faire an Enemy," and she asks "Whence can thy Courage come?" His "innocence" so charms her that she is sure "some Divinitie" holds back her dagger. In the next sixty lines, she gradually reveals that she has been touched by amorous passion; bit by bit she discovers it to herself and to him. Her "disorder'd words" finally show a "distemper'd mind," and she makes an open declaration. To this Cortez gives the gallant reply—in effect— that she would not admire him nearly so much if he were to prove inconstant to another woman, "For Love once giv'n from her, and plac'd in you, / Would leave no ground I ever could be true" (IV.i.95–96). Almeria must grudgingly agree, and she exits, leaving Cortez in despair for his "strange condition," loved by his enemy's mistress, bereft of his military power, isolated from his own mistress. He thinks man can never achieve happiness in desire for pleasure, only in "rest from pain." But the following scenes show the falseness of that quietism and withdrawal (it is clearly not Hobbesian, as some have thought); providential coincidence and generous renunciation repeatedly save Cortez's life, as well as the life of Cydaria, until he achieves the perfect conquest by courage and virtuous love. He wins both power and beauty, demonstrating that independence and truth to an inner code of natural virtue are finally consistent with power and public virtue.

Furthermore, we value the hero and heroine all the more for the price they must pay for their grandeur.[9]

The tissue of confrontations, renunciations, and surprising reversals binds the play together as they lead toward a climactic union of idealized love and political power. In one way or another these themes reappear in various schematized patterns in the rest of Dryden's heroic plays. The ten whirling acts of *The Conquest of Granada* put an emphasis on the freedom of an essentially powerful and natural man and on the incompatibility of a free spirit's serving under a tyrant. *Aureng-Zebe*, as Kirsch suggests, splits the heroic man, giving greater range for the aggressive "irregular" Morat and the supremely kind and reflective Aureng-Zebe. In the end the double blessing of empire and love come to Aureng-Zebe alone. Michael Alssid states succinctly:

> *Aureng-Zebe* marks Dryden's final effort, in the rhymed drama, to represent dramatically the conditions and nature of the triumph of the ideal prince over a variety of physical, emotional, and spiritual obstacles. As something of a "panegyric" in dramatic form, the heroic play, as Dryden saw it, was intended to establish lucidly and emphatically the poet's ultimate ideal, his "mirror" of the great monarch whose private happiness is fused to the public good and who can provide the promise of a productive future for himself as well as for his people.[10]

It should be emphasized that the qualities of heroic virtue were vigorously represented more by strong feeling and passionate expression than by reason. Rational choice or "discipline" plays a very small part, even though we find many speeches of ratiocination. Some critics believe that Dryden's heroes receive mental discipline from their virtuous mistresses: Almanzor from Almahide, Aureng-Zebe from Indamora, and Morat from Indamora. But various evidence in and out of the plays contradicts this opinion. Dryden admired strong passions, even to the end of his life, when his other tastes became more restrained and conservative; he thought the "vehemence" of Homer more "suitable to his temper" than the softness of Virgil. He preferred Homer's continual agitation of spirits, the "violent impetus, full of

---

[9] For a brilliant and detailed analysis of this play along the same lines, see Michael W. Alssid's "The Perfect Conquest: A Study of Theme and Structure in Dryden's *The Indian Emperour*," *SP*, LIX (1962), 539–59.

[10] "The Design of Dryden's *Aureng-Zebe*," *JEGP*, LXIV (1965), 452–69.

fire," the copious invention, Achilles' hot impatience and vengefulness that "set you on fire all at once," over Virgil's feminine, phlegmatic, more confined way of writing (*Essays*, II, 274–76). In the plays themselves, furthermore, sexual passion, not discipline, solves most of the dramatic problems. Love pulls the hero out of his withdrawal and despair at the critical moment, and it fires him with desire as, for instance, when Aureng-Zebe has been convinced that Indamora is loyal to him (IV.i.509–46). In a furious reawakening of physical desire "that marks, so to speak the 'saints' return to the human condition,"[11] he exclaims

> Love mounts, and rowls about my stormy mind,
> Like Fire, that's born by a tempestuous Wind.
> Oh, I could stifle you, with eager haste!
> Devour your kisses with my hungry taste!
> Rush on you! eat you! wander o'r each part, . . .
> Invade you, till my conscious Limbs presage
> Torrents of joy, which all their banks o'rflow!
> [533–41.]

A renewed attack by the enemy prevents immediate gratification, but before he rushes into battle with new heat, he assures everyone that "With Glory, and with Love, at once I burn: / I feel th' inspiring heat, and absent God return" (610–11). His renewed sexual energies, therefore, are directed to protect the nation and the emperor and the public good.

Similarly, the closing speeches in Part II of *The Conquest of Granada* express Almanzor's undisciplined vehemence to the end, when he scorns modesty:

> From a false fear that Modesty does grow;
> And thinks true love, because 'tis fierce, its foe,
> 'Tis but the wax whose seals on Virgins stay:
> Let it approach Loves fire, 'twill melt away . . . .
> I thought to climb the steep ascent of Love;
> But did not think to find a foe above.
> 'Tis time to dye, when you my bar must be,
> Whose aid alone could give me Victory.
> Without——
> I'le pull up all the sluces of the flood:
> And Love, within, shall boyl out all my blood.
> [V.ii. sig. V3–V3ᵛ.]

Almahide, who has secretly burned for him all along, agrees to yield to his desire after a period of mourning. To be sure,

[11] Alssid, "The Design of Dryden's *Aureng-Zebe*," p. 464.

this is not the ambitious sensuality of Lyndaraxa or the morbid uncontrolled incestuous passion of Nourmahal, but it never was. Almanzor and Aureng-Zebe always had great souls, naturally disposed to generous love that could be awakened by a beautiful and chaste woman.

These passionate outbursts are important because they have a special connection with the idea of freedom. Only a great spirit can be free, Dryden suggests; and in society only a king and queen are free from external restraint. It would be inappropriate for a king to be the "servant" of a woman beneath his power, or for a queen to love one of her subjects. And since true love liberates the soul from servitude, a true lover is a potential rebel. If he cannot be king, he occupies an ambiguous place in society, for his naturally royal soul yearns to burst out of its restraints. In *Tyrannic Love*, the love of liberty logically leads to the behavior of Maximin, who resents God. These difficulties may have interested contemporary audiences because of their parallels in the English and French monarchs, who conducted themselves very like Montezuma, Maximin, and the old emperor in *Aureng-Zebe*, and whose courtiers often aspired to the beds of the royal mistresses.

The paradoxes of love and freedom also explain why Alibech and Guyomar refuse to stay under Cortez's benevolent domination. Rather they choose to go together into the wilderness, outside the power of gold and silver and away from the lust for power. In the desert where "Rocks ly Cover'd with Eternal snow" they enjoy "Love and Freedom" in peace. It is not that they lack the ability to assimilate themselves into civilization so much as that they do not wish to be subjugated by conquest. Like Almanzor and Aureng-Zebe, they want perfect freedom and power. If they cannot have power over their destinies in Mexico, they choose to leave, rather than see what they cannot redress.

In both artistic motive and accomplishment, therefore, these plays do more than ring the familiar changes on mere love and honor.[12] Nor should we reduce them to satiric attacks on "Hobbesian morality" or to half-comical attempts to please

[12] Recent discussions of love and honor may be found in Scott C. Osborn's "Heroical Love in Dryden's Heroic Drama," *PMLA*, LXXIII (1958), 480–90, and in Jean Gagen's "Love and Honor in Dryden's Heroic Plays," *PMLA*, LXXVII (1962), 208–20. Both rightly emphasize the diverse ideas that are gathered under the catch-all terms love and honor: sexual passion, love of virtue, justice, fame, ambition, and renunciation. Both, however, take little account of the dramatic function of the ideas.

a debased audience,[13] for they have a high conception of serious and well-articulated themes, relevant to the twentieth as well as to the seventeenth century. After all, many of us believe that personal commitment to justice and freedom often clashes with the law or the national interest. Now that we live under the tyranny of the majority, many of us turn for renewal to the high ideals of social thought born in the seventeenth century, those of Grotius and Locke.

In the Restoration period it may very well be that the plays had general importance, especially for those who remembered the civil war of the 1640's, the regicide, and the role of military heroes: Prince Rupert, Cromwell, and the magnanimous Lord Falkland, for instance. *Aureng-Zebe* in particular reverberates with political issues of the 1670's: the problems of succession to the throne in the latter days of an exhausted and idle king, of efforts to legitimize one of the king's sons to force the rightful heir from his claim, of a rebellious son in command of an army in the outlying provinces, of banishment, and of intrigue by way of mistresses. These might bring to mind the anti-papist feeling against James, Duke of York, and the efforts of the Duke of Monmouth's friends to bring that "Protestant duke" to power. At any rate, a more general relevance of all the heroic plays lies in the contemporary mystique of kingship; it was still thought by many that kings were above the law, enjoying a perfect freedom, and it was a fact that dominion was gained by conquest and advancement by way of female intrigue.

III

For a number of reasons Dryden changed the emphasis of his serious plays between 1675 and 1680. He became "weary of his long lov'd Mistress, Rhyme," and he tried imitating Shakespeare, Milton, and possibly Racine as well. Le Bossu's *Du poème epique* (1675), Rapin's *Reflexions* (1674), and Thomas Rymer's blast at the English theatre in *The Tragedies of the*

---

[13] The search for Hobbesian ideas in the plays has been of limited value. Mildred Hartsock, "Dryden's Plays: A Study in Ideas," *Seventeenth Century Studies*, 2d ser. (Princeton, 1937), pp. 71–176, is the most elaborate but undiscriminating. Louis Teeter, "The Dramatic Use of Hobbes's Political Ideas," *ELH*, III (1936), 140–69, says that only villains are Hobbesians. Various shades of disagreement may be found in John A. Winterbottom, "The Place of Hobbesian Ideas in Dryden's Tragedies," *JEGP*, LVII (1958), 665–83; in Thomas H. Fujimura, "The Appeal of Dryden's Heroic Plays," *PMLA*, LXXV (1960), 868–83; and in Bruce King, *Dryden's Major Plays* (1966).

Last Age (late fall of 1677, dated 1678) shook Dryden's faith in irregular plots and in admiration as an effect of tragedy. Although he outlined a forthright reply in his "Heads of an answer to Rymer," the eventual essay, "The Grounds of Criticism in Tragedy" (1679), was very conciliatory in tone and content. He no longer believed that proper tragedy aroused admiration and compassion, but only the orthodox pity and fear. Poetical justice must be regularly administered, something that Fletcher and Massinger had not done. Dryden still did not insist upon poetic justice as rigidly as Rymer; he thought that a great beauty might countervail some fault in the plot. But the general rule was to imitate Shakespeare and Fletcher only so far as they "have copied the excellencies" of the ancients, "who invented and brought to perfection dramatic poetry." This is a considerable retreat from the more liberal position taken eleven years earlier in "An Essay of Dramatic Poesy." According to Dryden's new views, echoing Bossu's, a work must have an overall "moral" or controlling idea—a precept that the poet should lay down from the start, for " 'tis the moral that directs the whole action of the play to one centre; and that action or fable is the example built upon the moral, which confirms the truth of it to our experience" (*Essays*, I, 248).

Parallel developments seem to have occurred in English comedy after 1675, when the carefree roguish hero began to give way to the good-natured, even sentimental lover. Nathaniel Lee's and Thomas Otway's tragedies came into favor, with their straining rhetoric and tearful heroines. Shakespeare's tragedies were adapted at this time; Nahum Tate would not allow Cordelia to die. Shadwell's *Timon*, although not a sentimental melodrama, supplied Timon with a faithful mistress and implied that his mistreatment of her made his unfortunate end just. Audiences approved, says Downes, because of the "excellent moral."[14] But more than anything, Rymer had destroyed the fabric of artifice in heroic drama when he insisted that the action had to be literally believable. Drama could no longer put its emphasis on *imitation* of nature, for it had shifted to an imitation of *nature*. Literal verisimilitude would not allow the witty turns in debate between Amintor and Melantius in *The Maid's Tragedy*, and a character who is determined to kill, once he has drawn his sword, must continue that "probable" direction of intent. He cannot stop, for men are not often dissuaded from such a bloody resolution. "No simple alteration of mind

---

[14] Cited by Clifford Leech in "Restoration Tragedy: A Reconsideration," *Durham University Journal*, XI (1950), 106–15.

ought to produce or hinder any action in tragedy."[15] This unfortunate dictum shattered the exciting possibilities of debates in heroic plays, and after 1676 Dryden seems to have changed his technique so as to produce more gradual transitions. He reduced surprise and wit in preference for the massive development of one dominant feeling in each scene. The tendency can already be noted before he had articulated the critical theory, for *Aureng-Zebe* (acted in 1675) contains fewer sudden reversals and more evocation of pity than plays before, as Kirsch observed. *All for Love* (acted 1677) and *Troilus and Cressida* (acted 1678) carried the change even farther.

The scene construction of *All for Love* illustrates the change most clearly, for instead of a rapid series of emotional shifts, the whole play covers what would be a typical act in a heroic play. Each segment of the plot is greatly simplified, reduced to a single transition from one emotional state to a second, from one moral claim on Antony to another. Every act yields to such analysis in an orderly progression: Act I, despairing shame displaced by courageous resolution; Act II, resolution undermined by love; Act III, love overthrown by the claims of duty to family; Act IV, duty destroyed by jealousy; and Act V, jealousy transformed into an ecstatic despair. In each episode someone acts or speaks eloquently to move Antony into the next mood, much like a game of musical chairs, and after four shifts of position, brings Antony back to the place where he started. Ventidius obviously works on Antony, when he praises the image of the soldier Antony once was, the model of admiration:

> you, ere Love misled your wandring eyes,
> Were sure the chief and best of Human Race,
> Fram'd in the very pride and boast of Nature,
> So perfect, that the gods who form'd you wonder'd
> At their own skill, and cry'd, A lucky hit
> Has mended our design. Their envy hindred,
> Else you had been immortal, and a pattern,
> When Heav'n would work for ostentation sake,
> To copy out again.
>
> [I.i.403–11.]

By bolstering Antony's pride, scourging his self-pity, and strengthening the manly bond between two old soldiers, Ventidius manipulates his friend, squeezing despair out of his

[15] *The Critical Works of Thomas Rymer*, ed. Curt Zimansky (1956), p. 73; cited by Kirsch, pp. 152–53.

spongy soul and causing it to soak up the love of valor, in an effort to recreate the greatness of Antony's past.

All subsequent scenes move in the same way: Antony at the start screwed up to a pitch just short of breaking; but some contrary feeling always survives, some antithetical memory of great pleasure felt in the past, of great sacrifice made, of great rivalry surmounted. Alexas or Octavia has only to touch the tender spot, the old scar of memory, with a word, a symbol, or a name, and Antony will begin to emote: the "absent Cleopatra bleeds in him" (II.i.180). Indeed, the impression given of human character agrees with Dolabella's comment on the unconscious impulses of men, whose appetite drives them on,

> And yet the Soul, shut up in her dark room,
> Viewing so clear abroad, at home sees nothing.
>
> [IV.i.46–47.]

By the fifth act we may have some difficulty believing that Antony is worth enough to deserve pity, that he and Cleopatra are a great enough loss, or that the world is important enough to regret losing.[16] The apparent emptiness may come from the spareness of the representation, by comparison with Shakespeare, but the trouble may lie elsewhere. We know that Racine was very economical without being penurious. An objection often heard is that Dryden's play fails to show the value of the lost world of Rome or the voluptuousness of Cleopatra for whom it is renounced. The end seems just a matter of exhaustion, when Antony has achieved absolute stasis, indifference to life. It is hard to escape the feeling that the entire action on stage is a last recapitulation of Antony's life, repeating symbolically the various choices he has made in the past in preparation for his present emptiness and despair; but the final effect is a triumph of love.

The severe limitations on the form would have strait-jacketed a lesser playwright; Dryden seems to have turned them into concealed virtues. How much he manages to convey, in these limits, of Antony's heroic and amorous past! By friends' retrospective comment, by set speeches, by anguished contention over past desires, we are ourselves encouraged to remember Shakespeare and Plutarch, to supply the details from familiar history. The rhetoric of dramatic speech, therefore, is his chief instrument, and allusion his method. We who praise modern poems that assume knowledge of Jessie Weston and Sir James Frazer, we "who are

---

[16] See R. J. Kaufmann's provocative introduction to his edition of *All for Love* (1962), vii–xviii, and Bruce King's "Dryden's Intent in *All for Love*," *College English*, XXIV (1963), 267–71.

acquainted with these works will immediately recognize in the poem certain references to vegetation ceremonies," we should not fail to appreciate Dryden's method. Hence it is a mistake to compare *All for Love* with *Antony and Cleopatra*, for Dryden appears to have invited contrast, having deliberately built on our prior knowledge.

The speeches, moreover, do a great deal to create impressions that are set out antithetically: between Ventidius' and Alexas' views of the situation, between cool morning and passionate night, between iron and soft allurement, as Moody Prior has suggested.[17] Characteristically, Antony combines the two attitudes, at one moment seeing Cleopatra as an agent of decay, for in her arms "the World fell mouldering from my hands each hour" (II.i.296), at another moment remembering her continually refreshed beauty:

> There's no satiety of Love in thee;
> Enjoy'd, thou still art new; perpetual Spring
> Is in thy armes; the ripen'd fruit but falls,
> And blossoms rise to fill its empty place;
> And I grow fresh by giving.
>
> [III.i.24–28.]

The world lost was one of pomp, sceptered slaves, morning chambers filled, menial kings, and the rest of the symbols of empire. Antony rejects it with superb contempt as early as Act II:

> Give, you Gods,
> Give to your Boy, your *Cæsar*,
> This Rattle of a Globe to play withal,
> This Gu-gau World.
>
> [II.i.442–45.]

At the end of Act V, the most interesting quality of the speeches lies in the doubleness of the tone, of waste and ruin combined with triumph. We are left with the sense that Antony is stripped of his divinity but exalted by his suffering because he has made the right choices and has shown himself resolute, within his human limitations.

Dryden's later work amplified and reshaped what he tried in *All for Love*, *Oedipus*, and *Troilus*. Pity and sorrow remain the dominant effect, scenes continue to be made with gradual emotional development, great reverses are massively prepared for, and dialogue is elevated but not elaborately pointed. The stately *Cleomenes* (1692) offers a clear example. Some plays throw back to his earlier interest in mixed forms. The

---

[17] *The Language of Tragedy* (1947), 192–211.

impressive tragicomedy, *The Spanish Friar* (1681), with its double plot, mixes bawdy and profound interests with remarkable facility, and *Don Sebastian* (1690) combines a burst of rich and daring language with earthy prose—a philosophic main plot with some outrageous foolishness in the underplot. The art of *Secret Love* and *Marriage a-la-Mode* returns in more heightened form and more serious intent.[18] *Don Sebastian*, of all his plays, requires a sympathetic reading and an undaunted effort, but it rewards us.

H. S. Wilson made the usual comment on the play:

> It is all very sad; but perhaps the saddest fact is that, by a trick, Dryden turned a rousing villain melodrama into a pathetic tragedy. The moral of the play seems to be (as Moses discovered on Mount Sinai): "That unrepented crimes of parents dead, / Are justly punished in their children's head."[19]

This rests on the opinion that pathetic tragedy is something inferior to rousing melodrama. Another critic thinks the play is only concerned with "distressed nobility," aiming at theatrical excitement instead of representation of men "as they are." Clifford Leech urged that pathetic tragedy, including *Don Sebastian*, *All for Love*, and Otway's *Venice Preserved*, along with a half-dozen lesser plays, presents "an anthropocentric view of things, which shows men struggling without avail against decrees of Fate." It arouses in us "a sense of pride that man can do so well" when he is caught in life's trap. This attitude depends on a contradiction "that man is a puppet and yet can be admirable." It is not "rational," therefore it is "inconsistent with orthodox belief."[20] The "tragic idea," Leech thinks, was best understood by Dryden, but when clearly stated it "is too easily recognized for the platitude that it is."

We may make two inferences from these remarks. They mean that even though he understood the "tragic idea" Dryden should not have stated it so clearly, for that very explicitness takes the mystery out of tragedy. Or we might decide that all pathetic tragedy, in so far as it shows understanding of its form, is inferior. Both opinions seem mistaken, for few of us care to dispense in this fashion with *Romeo and Juliet*, *Saint Joan*, *Antigone*, and *Oedipus at Colonus*. Their main thrust comes from a recognition of man's smallness and his nobility. And when Joan utters the anguished cry, "O God

[18] It has been said that this is a return to the heroic play, but the analogies with tragicomedy seem more interesting.

[19] *A Preface to Restoration Drama* (1965), p. 114.

[20] "Restoration Tragedy: A Reconsideration," pp. 106–15.

that madest this beautiful earth, when will it be ready to receive thy saints? How long, O Lord, how long?"—when we reflect upon this paradox, we are touched in some of our deepest recesses. Such plays combine the sense of man's grandeur, his debasement, and God's inscrutability. Because of the gap between justice and personal worth, between fortune and human responsibility, the world is, in fact, irrational. It is probably an "unorthodox" view, but what requires that tragedies be orthodox? Shades of Thomas Rymer!

By the irrational view of life, our aspirations and our just pride seem to be inexplicably entwined with guilt and ignorance, forcing us to do the wrong thing for the right reasons. *Don Sebastian* embodies that tragic idea, and although the play may not deserve to be ranked with the best examples of pathetic tragedy, it deserves high esteem.

The disjunction of providence and virtue emerges in the first scene when the three heroes draw lots for their execution. The note is struck of "suff'ring Majesty," for even the corrupt emperor sees Sebastian "secure of Death, superior Greatness, / Like *Jove* when he made Fate, and said thou art / The slave of my Creation" (I.i.314–16). His soul can take any punishment because fate is not his nor is he fate's. Consequently he has impudent greatness and extravagant bravery; here is the man truly made in his Maker's image. Nevertheless fortune cuts him down cruelly. Thus far, the situation may evoke Leech's platitudes, but complications appear in the following act, when Sebastian's love of Almeyda becomes the central concern. His every movement brings unexpected consequences, as his pleas to the emperor come back "like Wild-fire thrown against the Wind, returns / With double force to burn" (II.i.432–33). The only reason he continues to "drag his being" is his love for Almeyda, yet his misery has somehow been brought on by his taking up her "fatal Cause" (II.i.509). He scoffs at oracles who prophesied incest and, oddly enough, a long, holy life, but Almeyda feels the dark portents. Her desire and her "fatal Beauty," she seems to realize, draw her to Sebastian against her better judgment. She thinks hers is "chast as sister's love," but after one night of marriage she speaks of it in highly erotic terms. And when Sebastian leads her off to the priest, Almeyda admits that she goes somewhat willingly:

> I go; with Love and Fortune, two blind Guides,
> To lead my way: half loath and half consenting . . .
> Forgive me Heav'n; and all ye Blest above,
> Excuse the frailty of unbounded Love.
>
> [II.i.629–733.]

Almost everyone in the play shares Almeyda's predicament, half motivated by desire and half forced unwillingly, they plunge ahead into the uncertainties of life and death. Antonio meets the unexpected with a jaunty equanimity, Alvarez meets it with patience and fortitude, Dorax with angry resentment. They eventually find that they have willingly chosen what is to be, and they cannot escape some guilt. "Were I to choose again, and know my fate, / For such a night I would be what I am," says Sebastian (III.i.180–81). Love is an essential part of our being, and we cannot evade it, the play suggests. Is it a devil or a king? Whatever it may be, it speaks unknown within, pushing us on by force, desired and resisted at the same time.

Love, in these terms, is a kind of magnificent original sin, not just part of the flesh but of the soul itself, as Alvarez says:

Know King, your Father had like you, a Soul;
And Love is your Inheritance from him.
Almeyda's Mother too had eyes, like her,
And not less charming, and were charm'd no less
Than yours' are now with her, and her's with you.

[V.i.316–20.]

By virtue of his soul, at the center of his identity, Sebastian commits incest. It is part of him, and he openly admits, in Act V, that if he looks upon Almeyda he knows he will commit it again, his soul is so little his own and so much hers. The divided soul yet one soul, beauty that only Sebastian deserves yet sins to enjoy: this is the spiritual abyss. At the end, although he cannot understand the full meaning, Sebastian refuses to conceal his guilt. "O, palliate not my wound," he says. "When you have argu'd all you can, 'tis Incest," and when he sees Almeyda, he sins in thought and expression, using Dryden's favorite pun: "Heav'n has inspir'd me with a Sacred thought, / To live alone to Heav'n: and dye to her" (V.i.554–55). Aureng-Zebe's renunciation of love and power lead ultimately to his possession of both, whereas in *Don Sebastian*, as in Sophocles' *Oedipus the King*, consummated love and royal power must be renounced because they are poisoned by human ignorance and desire.

The fascinating ambivalence of these scenes comes out in the language as well, emphasizing countless times the power of natural forces and the presence of spiritual abysses. The emperor expresses them in the first few acts, and in the last three Almeyda and Sebastian pick up the same images. Resistless passion is a "spring," "a torrent," a "tempest," a "rising storm." Man would endure vast deserts to satisfy it, and one might as well "Go bid our moving Plains of Sand lye still / And stir not, when the stormy South blows high" (III.i.5–6). Thwarted love is destructive, as the emperor shows:

> I will engender Poyson with thee;
> Joyn Hate with Hate, add Venom to the birth;
> Our off-spring, like the seed of Dragons Teeth,
> Shall issue arm'd, and fight themselves to death.
>
> [I.i.464–67.]

Yet gratification is a "deeply plunged" joy, and its guilt lies in the dark recesses of the soul, the abyss of minds (III.i.136 and 159). Such a night as Sebastian has enjoyed lies in his memory, behind eternity, "Hid in the treasure of the past," but "bles'd remembrance" brings it hourly back (III.i.182–85). As a consequence he would plunge himself into the deep, but when Dorax leads him to the edge of the abyss (i.e., his damnation by suicide, V.i.220 and 539), he draws back. Such metaphors do, indeed, confound Hell and Elysium, and they help create the sense of the ultimate irrationality of the world and the mystery of life.

The role of Dorax effectively illustrates the theme in an oblique mode. He scathingly resents Sebastian and in the same breath praises him. His satiric speeches, containing some of Dryden's best poetry, attack the very foundations of civil and religious power, but he too learns how his choices have helped to mold his destiny. The social outcast protests that had he been Enriquez, the favorite, he would have stood by the king, and had Enriquez been tempted as he, "so had he fall'n" (IV.ii.822–23). As Dorax, he feels his soul is that of a regicide; as Alonzo he is someone else.

> *Alonzo* was too kind a name for me
> Then, when I forgot and conquer'd with your Arms,
> In that blest Age I was the man you nam'd:
> Till rage and pride debas'd me into *Dorax*
> And lost like *Lucifer*, my name above.
>
> [IV.ii.895–99.]

Dorax, the divided man, is one of the most fiery and complex characters in the play. Malcontent, erratic but not corrupt, intelligent, proud, he left his "foolish Faith," Christianity, because it required that he forgive Sebastian (II.i.237–38). Dorax's soldiers idolize him, and the emperor trusts Dorax with the castle, "the Key of all his Kingdom" (II.i.285). He becomes the key to the entire play, as well, when at the end he appears to be the devil and does the angels' work

(V.i.514–44). In one of the best passages in the play, he seems to urge Sebastian to suicide, only to save him. So the "patch'd work of fate" generously brings Sebastian to think for a moment, and his thought somehow saves him. But he is saved only for a solitary life of contrition in the desert.

Obviously the concluding lines of *Don Sebastian* are more ceremonial than significant, for they express the dark meaning of the play no more than the simple comment by the chorus at the close of *Oedipus the King*. The full meaning of *Don Sebastian* is meshed in the intricacies of thought and feeling evoked by the characters as they face their undeserved misfortunes, recognizing their guilt, enjoying the illusion of free choice. They willingly embrace their choices to fulfill their fate. This is suffering majesty.

The Text of This Edition

This edition presents a critical, old-spelling text of the plays on the plan of *The Dramatic Works in the Beaumont and Fletcher Canon* (Cambridge, 1966), with a few modifications for a reading edition. The first editions of all but *The Indian Emperour* provide the copy-texts, since they were the only ones set from manuscript. The collation of all seventeenth-century quartos, as well as the folio of 1701, revealed no new authority except in a few isolated readings. Consequently, there was no great difficulty in editing three of the plays, and it did not seem necessary to print a complete historical collation. The apparatus is thus considerably reduced to include only departures from copy. Substantive departures are noted at the foot of the page, above the commentary, and emendations of accidentals along with press variants are listed at the end of each play. Silent alterations are the same as in the Beaumont and Fletcher, notably modernized *i, j, u, v*, and long *ſ*; correction of turned letters, expanded abbreviations, normalized spelling of proper names, capital letters at the beginnings of sentences, full stops at the ends of speeches, and italicized proper names in the dialogue. In addition, an apostrophe has been silently supplied before an *s* in elisions of *is* and before *s* in genitive singular nouns when no other orthographic change is required. Bracketed notations in stage directions are supplied by the editor. Prefaces, prologues, and epilogues as they appear in the first edition are included, but dedications and lists of actors have been regularly excluded. When these have significance they are mentioned in the brief introduction or in the commentary.

The Indian Emperour, however, presents such complex problems owing to Dryden's frequent revisions and to the uncertainty about the authority of the first edition and the Cambridge manuscript that it has been treated differently. The headnote to the play outlines some of the difficulties and the procedure.

For a detailed account of the method, the reader should consult *The Dramatic Works in the Beaumont and Fletcher Canon*, I, ix–xxv, along with Sir Walter Greg's "The Rationale of Copy-Text," *Studies in Bibliography*, III (1950–51), 19–36; Fredson Bowers' "Textual Criticism," in *The Aims and*

Methods of Scholarship in Modern Languages and Literature,
edited by James Thorpe (1964); and Bowers' "Current
Theories of Copy-Text, with an Illustration from Dryden,"
Modern Philology, XLVIII (1950), 12–20.

Dryden's Tragedies and Heroic Plays

*with dates of first performance
and publication*

The Indian Queen (with Howard), 1664 (1665)
The Indian Emperour, or, the Conquest of Mexico, 1665 (1667)
Tyrannick Love, or the Royal Martyr, 1669 (1670)
The Conquest of Granada by the Spaniards: In Two Parts, 1670–71 (1672)
Amboyna, 1673 (1673)
The State of Innocence, and Fall of Man, an opera, unacted (1677)
Aureng-Zebe, 1675 (1676)
All for Love, or, the World Well Lost, 1677 (1678)
Oedipus (with Lee), 1678 (1679)
Troilus and Cressida, or, Truth Found too Late, 1679 (1679)
The Duke of Guise (with Lee), 1682 (1683)
Albion and Albanius, an opera, 1685 (1685)
Don Sebastian, King of Portugal, 1689 (1690)
King Arthur: or, the British Worthy, an opera, 1691 (1691)
Cleomenes, the Spartan Heroe, 1692 (1692)

The Indian Emperour

Dryden and Robert Howard's *Indian Queen*, acted in 1664, was mounted with at least five elaborate and expensive painted sets: the front scene of open country, the soldiers' camp with a prospect of tents, the enchanter's cell, the prison, and the Temple of the Sun. Although the play was in the process of losing its appeal, it was still "so beautified with rich Scenes as the like had never ben seene here as happly . . . on a mercenarie theater" (Evelyn, *Diary*, February 5, 1664). For costumes there were "Habits" of feathers and "glorious wreaths for their Heads, Necks, Arms, Legs." Aphra Behn says, "I had a set of these presented to me, and I gave 'em to the King's Theater; it was the Dress of the Indian Queen, infinitely admir'd by Persons of Quality; and was inimitable."[1] Obviously the equipment had to be used again, and Dryden obliged, preparing *The Indian Emperour*, his first unaided heroic play, to open after Easter in 1665. The devastating London plague raged so intensely by early summer that theaters closed, not to open until late 1666, after the great fire. Those who could afford it fled to the country, and there Dryden worked on *An Essay of Dramatic Poesy* and *Secret Love*. About the same time he revised *The Indian Emperour*, probably before the performance of January 15, 1667. It was an immense success and from that year until about 1737, the play continued to be excellent box office, with at least fifteen known performances and twelve editions before 1700. The Duchess of Monmouth, to whom the published play was dedicated, enhanced its reputation by acting in a much-talked-about amateur production. On January 13, 1668, four "persons of quality," probably including the Duke of Monmouth, entertained a select group, but "not any woman but the Duchess of Monmouth and Mrs. Cornwallis did anything but fools and stocks . . . . Captain O'Bryan spoke and did well but above all things, did dance most incomparably" (Pepys, *Diary*, January 14, 1668).

The military events in the play could have come from any number of sources, romances and histories of the Spanish conquest of Mexico and Peru, in which the Indians were generally cast in the role of noble savages. The invaders were civilized brutes, with the notable exception of Cortez.[2] He

[1] *Plays, Histories, and Novels of Mrs. Aphra Behn* (1871), V, 77.
[2] Surveyed by Dougald MacMillan, "The Sources of Dryden's *The Indian Emperour*," *The Huntington Library Quarterly*, XIII (1950), 353–70;

was traditionally the courageous and resourceful soldier, an independent spirit who frequently disobeyed superiors and took his own course, a handsome dashing man known to have huffed an emperor. An anecdote, first recorded by Voltaire, typifies the popular conception of Cortez: in later life when Cortez accosted Emperor Charles V and Charles asked "Who are you?" Cortez replied, "I am a man who has given you more provinces than your ancestors left you cities."[3] Dryden enhanced the military story by emphasizing the contrast between Montezuma's natural reason and the Spaniard's greedy and oppressive spirit. Montaigne's essay "Of Coaches," as John Loftis has shown, supplied arguments for the torture scene (V.ii), where Montezuma defends natural religion against bigotry. The idealized view of the Indians may also owe a debt to Montaigne's "Of the Canibales," one of the sources of Shakespeare's *Tempest*, and curiously the high priest in the Cambridge manuscript of *The Indian Emperour* is consistently named Caliban. Some connection also existed with Davenant's "entertainment" *The Cruelty of the Spaniards in Peru* (1658) and *The History of Sir Francis Drake* (1658), included in *The Playhouse to be Let* (1663).

The theme of cultural relativism has an important emotional effect upon *The Indian Emperour*, for it puts Cortez's forces in a bad light and offers a strong appeal for primitivism and the toleration of religions other than Christianity. The final withdrawal of Guyomar and Alibech reminds us of the yearning for the simple, free, and natural life, even though Cortez in Mexico has succeeded in uniting natural feeling with civilized exercise of power. In so far as we sympathize with Cortez, our feeling arises most from his association with natural virtue. And Thomas Fujimura quite rightly suggests that the ideal primitivism here accounts for some of the play's popular appeal.[4] It came to the stage at the beginning of the era of cultural self-criticism, representing Montezuma as a sort of "Citizen of the World," who, as John Loftis noted, looks objectively at European civilization as do Montesquieu's Persian, Swift's King of Brobdingnag, Voltaire's Micromégas, and Goldsmith's Chinaman. But that thematic emphasis does not make Montezuma the central character, for he is not

---

supplemented by John Loftis in *The Works of John Dryden*, IX (1966), 306–18.

[3] Voltaire, *Essai sur les mœurs et l'esprit des nations*, ed. René Pomeau (1963), II, 353.

[4] "The Appeal of Dryden's Heroic Plays," *PMLA*, LXXV (1960), 37–45. I do not agree that Dryden's outlook here should be described as "naturalistic."

on stage enough and he functions mostly as a contrast to Cortez. Montezuma is the natural man degraded and almost destroyed by lust, whereas Cortez is a civilized man who saves himself by the exercise of natural virtue and idealized passion. On the other hand, most of us do not find Cortez enough of a Herculean or "irregular" hero to make him a sufficiently commanding figure.

Dryden, in the dedication to the first quarto, implies that he too was more interested in Montezuma than in Cortez, when he writes to the Duchess of Monmouth:

> Under your Patronage *Montezuma* hopes he is more safe than in his Native *Indies*: and therefore comes to throw himself at your Grace's feet; paying that homage to your Beauty, which he refus'd to the violence of his Conquerours. He begs only that when he shall relate his sufferings, you will consider he is an *Indian Prince*, and not expect any other Eloquence from his simplicity, then that, with which his griefs have furnished him. His story is, perhaps, the greatest which was ever represented in a Poem of this nature; (the action of it including the Discovery and Conquest of a New World.) In it I have neither wholly follow'd the truth of the History, nor altogether left it: but have taken all the liberty of a Poet, to adde, alter, or diminish, as I thought might best conduce to the beautifying of my work. It being not the business of a Poet to represent Historical truth, but probability. But I am not to make the justification of this Poem, which I wholly leave to your Grace's mercy. 'Tis an irregular piece if compar'd with many of *Corneille's*, and, if I may make a judgement of it, written with more Flame then Art; in which it represents the mind and intentions of the Author . . . .

A manuscript, in a pretty scribal handwriting, inscribed with the date "1665," survives in the Trinity College, Cambridge, Library (R.III.10) that contains an early version of *The Indian Emperour*. The Stationers' Register bears an entry by the publisher Henry Herringman, May 26, 1665, but the first printing of a revised text did not appear until October, 1667, Q1 (Macd. 69a, W & M 414). There followed Q2 1668 prefaced by "A Defence of An Essay of Dramatic Poesy" which was suppressed in all later editions, Q3 1670 (W & M 417a, Bowers' correction), Q4 1670 (Macd. 69c, W & M 417), Q5 1670 (Macd. 69d, W & M 418), Q6 1681, Q7 1686, Q8 1692, Q9 1694, Q10 1696 (W & M 425), Q11 · 1696 (W & M 424), Q12 1696 (W & M 423). Since Dryden

revised and corrected for Q1, Q2, and Q3, the authority of
the substantives in Q3 is greatest, except for a few readings
in the manuscript and a few in Q1 and Q2 that retain the
purer text. Consequently the present edition follows most of
the substantives in Q3.

The copy-text, however, must be chosen for its "accidentals"
—spelling, capitalization, and other nonsignificant features.
Since printers impose their system of accidentals more and
more thoroughly every time a text is reprinted, Q2 and Q3
are obviously of less authority than Q1. The problem remains
to decide whether Q1 or the Trinity College manuscript is
closer to Dryden's lost manuscript. Both represent an earlier
form of the play, but the manuscript is dated two years before
Q1. Mr. Bowers has suggested that the manuscript and the
quarto were both copied from Dryden's papers and that the
manuscript preserves more of Dryden's known spelling habits.[4]
He distinguished between "major" and "minor" spellings and
concluded that in the "overwhelming majority" of cases the
manuscript agrees with Dryden's holograph letters. Vinton
Dearing, using a computer, tried to determine more exactly
what Dryden's habits were in 1664–65, based on the same holograph letters that Bowers used, and he tried to include more
authorial spellings.[5] By some unexplained statistical methods,
he concluded that slightly more authorial spellings are found
in Q1. The discrepancy in their data may be explained partly
by the nature of the evidence, for, although sixty-two letters
survive, they offer scant data for Dryden's habits before 1682.
Only six letters are earlier: three written in 1673–77 and three
before 1667. The two letters from 1664–65 total just thirty-six
lines in C. E. Ward's edition, and the one from 1653 has fifty-
seven lines. It does not seem proper, as Dearing has done, to
project backwards from Dryden's later habits, to fill in the
gaps in evidence. Rather we should place most weight upon
the outstanding features of Dryden's spelling that persist
from early to late letters.   When his habits changed, as they
did in the use of *hee*, *shee*, and *bee*, we should give more
weight to the early spellings. In this way, our data are based
on the solid evidence, not on mathematical projections from
letters written in the 1670's or 1680's. On these assumptions
Bowers is right to choose the manuscript. Dearing, on the
other hand, attempts to be more precise than the evidence will

[4] "The 1665 Manuscript of Dryden's *Indian Emperour*," *SP*, XLVIII
(1950), 738–60.
[5] "The Use of Computer in Analysing Dryden's Spelling," *Literary
Data Processing Conference Proceedings, September 9, 10, 11, 1964* (IBM,
1964), pp. 200–210.

allow, and he seems mistaken at several points. He misunderstands the criteria for the spellings *haveing, giveing, doeing,* and *takeing,* that retain a final *e* of an infinitive made into a present participle. He calculates the ratio of Dryden's use of *hee, shee, bee* to *he, she, be* at ten to one, whereas it is much closer to three to one in the letters before 1667. He also counts abbreviations, which would normally be modernized in a sound critical text, and his figures on the use of apostrophe in elided past participles are probably meaningless, because the letters are in prose and the play in verse. He claims to be "purely quantitative," causing him to give equal emphasis to distinctive and non-distinctive spellings. If we look for the obvious archaic features of Dryden's spelling (the *-eing* ending, doubled consonants, final *-e* after consonants, *hast* for *haste,* final *-yes* for *-ies, loose* for *lose,* and the frequent use of *hee, shee, and bee*), the manuscript is clearly more representitive than the quarto.

The present text therefore is based on photographs of the Trinity College manuscript. The seven known American copies of Q1 (1667) have been directly collated against each other as follows: William A. Clark, Folger Shakespeare, Henry F. Huntington, Boston Public, Harvard, Yale, and Texas. The prologue, epilogue, and note on connexion are supplied from this Q1 text revised from Q2–3. The following six copies of Q2 (1668) have been collated against each other: Clark, Folger, Huntington, Yale, Michigan, and Texas. Six copies of Q3 (1670) were collated against each other from the holdings of Clark, Harvard, Yale, Texas, and Folger (Dobell, bound; Dobell, unbound). "A Defence of An Essay of Dramatic Poesy" is omitted here because it makes few specific comments on *The Indian Emperour,* although it states some of Dryden's theories of drama more clearly than in the original essay it defends.

A detailed account of the method may be found in "Current Theories of Copy-Text, with an Illustration from Dryden," *MP,* XLVIII (1950–51), 12–20. Press variants and the order of editions have been discussed in Bowers' "Variants in Early Editions of Dryden Plays," *Harvard Library Bulletin,* III (1949), 278–88, and *A Supplement to the Woodward & McManaway Check List* (1949); in J. M. Osborn's "Macdonald's Bibliography of Dryden," *MP,* XXXIX (1941), nos. 1, 2, 3; in James S. Steck's "Dryden's *Indian Emperour*: The Early Editions and their Relation to the Text," *Studies in Bibliography,* II (1949–50), 139–52; and in Vinton Dearing's textual notes to the play, *Works,* IX (1966), 381–86.

The song, "I look'd and saw within the Book of Fate," in Act III was set by Purcell and is printed in *The Banquet of*

Musick (1691), VI, 14–15. And the other song, "Ah fading joy, how quickly art thou past?" is found with music in *Choyce Ayres, Songs, & Dialogues* (1675), I, 70–71. Two manuscripts of the song are in Bodleian MS Rawl. poet. 65, and in Folger MS V.a.226. The Folger MS is copied from one of the early quartos, but the Bodleian MS seems to descend from an unknown source: it has two couplets not found elsewhere. As Dearing notes, after line 2 it reads "And what too soon would dye / Help to destroy." After 12 it reads "For vain doth natures bounteous hands supply / What peevish mortalls to themselves deny."

The apparatus of this edition has been abbreviated to avoid an unusually long list; the record of Dryden's revision may be seen in Dearing's text, *Works*, IX, 386–420. The notes here record only substantive departures from Q3.

THE

Indian Emperour,

OR,

THE CONQUEST OF

MEXICO

BY THE

SPANIARDS.

Being the Sequel of the *Indian Queen*.

By JOHN DRYDEN Esq;

Dum relego scripsisse pudet, quia plurima cerno
Me quoque, qui feci, judice, digna lini. Ovid.

LONDON,
Printed by *J. M.* for *H. Herringman* at the Sign of the *Blew Anchor*
in the Lower walk of the *New Exchange,* 1667.

Title Page of the First Quarto, Folger Library Copy.

Dum . . . lini.] When I read it over I am ashamed of my work because I note many things that
en in my own, the maker's judgment, deserves to be erased (Ovid, *Epistolae ex Ponto*, I.v.15–16;
odern editions read *Cum* for *Dum*).

Connexion of the *Indian Emperour*,
to the *Indian Queen*

The Conclusion of the *Indian Queen*, (part of which Poem was writ by me) left little matter for another Story to be built on it, there remaining but two of the considerable Characters alive, (*viz.*) *Montezuma*, and *Orazia*; thereupon the Author of this, thought it necessary to produce new persons from those two; and considering that the late *Indian Queen*, before she lov'd *Montezuma*, liv'd in clandestine Marriage with her General *Traxalla*; he has rais'd from them a Son and two Daughters, supposed to be left young Orphans at their Death: On the other side, he has given to *Montezuma* and *Orazia*, two Sons and a Daughter; all now supposed to be grown up to Men's and Women's Estate; and their Mother *Orazia* (for whom there was no further use in the story) lately dead.

So that you are to imagine about Twenty years elapsed since the Coronation of *Montezuma*; who, in the Truth of the History, was a great and glorious Prince; and in whose time happened the Discovery and Invasion of *Mexico* by the *Spaniards*; under the conduct of *Hernando Cortez*, who, joyning with the *Tlaxcallan-Indians*, the inveterate Enemies of *Montezuma*, wholly Subverted that flourishing Empire; the Conquest of which, is the Subject of this *Dramatique* Poem.

I have neither wholly followed the story nor varied from it; and, as near as I could, have traced the Native simplicity and ignorance of the *Indians*, in relation to *Europæan* Custumes: The Shipping, Armour, Horses, Swords, and Guns of the *Spaniards*, being as new to them as their Habits and their Language were to the Christians.

The difference of their Religion from ours, I have taken from the Story it self; and that which you find of it in the first and fifth Acts, touching the sufferings and constancy of *Montezuma* in his Opinions, I have only illustrated, not alter'd from those who have written of it.

In *The Rehearsal*, I.ii, Bayes says "I have printed above a hundred sheets of paper, to insinuate the Plot into the Boxes." There is no other evidence that this prefatory note was circulated in the theater.

20 *Tlaxcallan*] Taxallan (not to be confused with Traxalla, father of Orbellan). Q1 reads *Taxallan*, and Dryden may be responsible for the change to *Tlaxcallan* in Q2, bringing it into agreement with the usual spelling in Gómara. If so, he neglected to change it in the dialogue, perhaps deliberately neglected it to avoid difficulty of pronunciation for the actors.

The Names of the Persons Represented

Indians, Men,
{
Montezuma, Emperour of *Mexico*.
Odmar, his Eldest Son.
Guyomar, his Younger Son.
Orbellan, Son to the late *Indian* Queen by *Traxalla*.
High Priest of the *Sun*.
}

Women,
{
Cydaria, *Montezuma*'s Daughter.
Almeria ⎱ Sisters; and Daughter to the late *Indian*
Alibech ⎰ Queen.
}

Spaniards,
{
Cortez, the *Spanish* General.
Vasquez ⎱ Commanders under him.
Pizarro ⎰
}

[Christian Priest.]
[Ghosts of *Acacis*, *Traxalla*, and the *Indian* Queen; an Earthy Spirit; *Kalib*, another spirit.]
[Spanish soldiers, Mexican Indians, Taxallan Indians, Priests, Messengers, Guards.]

The Scene *MEXICO* and two Leagues about it

The Names of the Persons] the original cast, according to Downes: *Montezuma*, Michael Mohun; *Odmar*, William Wintershall; *Guyomar*, Edward Kynaston; *Priest*, William Cartwright; *Cydaria*, Mrs. Ellen Gwyn [probably not in the earliest cast, for Pepys says she was put in, August 22, 1667; he also said it was "a great and serious part" which Nell did "basely"]; *Almeria*, Mrs. Anne Marshall; *Alibech*, Mrs. Elizabeth Weaver? [not mentioned by Downes. Pepys said that Mrs. Knipp took Mrs. Weaver's place on January 15, 1667]; *Cortez*, Charles Hart; *Vasquez*, Nicholas Burt.

12 *Pizarro*] In fact Pizarro took no part in Cortez's operations, but his reputation for cruelty made him a convenient foil to Cortez.

37

Prologue

Almighty Critiques! whom our *Indians* here
Worship, just as they do the Devil, for fear.
In reverence to your pow'r I come this day
To give you timely warning of our Play.
5   The Scenes are old, the Habits are the same,
We wore last year, before the *Spaniards* came.
Our Prologue, th'old-cast too ——————
For to observe the new it should at least
Be spoke, by some ingenious Bird or Beast.
10 Now if you stay, the blood that shall be shed
From this poor Play, be all upon your head.
We neither promise you one Dance, or Show,
Then Plot and Language they are wanting too:
But you, kind Wits, will those light faults excuse:
15 Those are the common frailties of the Muse;
Which who observes he buyes his place too dear:
For 'tis your business to be couz'ned here.
These wretched spies of wit must then confess
They take more pains to please themselves the less.
20 Grant us such Judges, *Phœbus* we request,
As still mistake themselves into a jest;
Such easie Judges, that our Poet may
Himself admire the fortune of his Play.
And arrogantly, as his fellows do,
25 Think he writes well, because he pleases you.
This he conceives not hard to bring about
If all of you would join to help him out.
Would each man take but what he understands,
And leave the rest upon the Poet's hands.

7–9 Our Prologue . . . Beast.] Q1; *omit* Q2–3

5–6 *The Scenes . . . came.*] See the introduction to this play for comment on the sets and costumes.

7–9 *Our Prologue . . . or Beast.*] attacking some forgotten theatrical gimmick, perhaps so little noted that Dryden omitted the lines in Q2–3.

The Indian Emperour

ACT I. SCENE I

The Scene a pleasant Indian *Country.*

Enter Cortez, Vasquez, Pizarro, *with* Spaniards *and*
[Taxallan] Indians *of their party.*

Cortez. On what new happy Climate are wee throwne,
    Soe long kept secret, and soe lately knowne;
    As if our old world modestly withdrew,
    And heere, in private, had brought forth a new!
Vasquez. Corne, Wine, and Oyle are wanting to this
        ground,   5
    In which our Countryes fruitfully abound:
    As if this infant world, yet unarray'd,
    Naked and bare, in Nature's lapp were layd.
    Noe usefull Arts have yet found footeing here;
    But all untaught, and Salvage, does appeare.   10
Cortez. Wild and untaught are termes which wee alone
    Invent, for fashions diffring from our owne:
    For all their Customes are by Nature wrought,
    But wee by Art, unteach what Nature taught.
Pizarro. In *Spaine* our Springs, like old men's children, be 15
    Decay'd and witherd from their Infancy:
    Noe kindly Show'rs fall on our barren earth
    To hatch the Seasons, in a timely birth.
    Our Summer such a russet Livery weares
    As in a Garment often dy'd appeares.   20
Cortez. Here Nature spreads her fruitfull sweetnesse round,
    Breaths on the Aire and broods upon the ground.
    Here days and Nights the only Seasons be,
    The Sunne noe Clymate does soe gladly see:
    When forc'd from hence, to view our parts, he mournes: 25
    Takes little Journeys, and makes quick returnes.
Vasquez. Mee thinks wee walke in dreames on fayry Land,
    Where golden Oare, lies mix'd with Common Sand;
    Each downfall of a flood the Mountains pou'r
    From their rich Bowells, Rolls a Silver Shower.   30
Cortez. Heaven from all ages Wisely did provide
    This wealth, and for the bravest Nation hide,
    Who with foure hundred Foot and Forty Horse,
    Dare boldly goe, a new found World to force.

10 *Salvage*] i.e., savage.

39

Pizarro. Our men, though valliant, wee should find too
35   few,
    But *Indians* joyne, the *Indians* to subdue.
    Taxallan, shooke by *Montezuma's* pow'rs,
    Has to resist his forces, calld in our's.
Vasquez. Rashly to arme against soe great a King
40   I hold not safe, nor is it just to bring
    A Warr, without a faire defiance made.
Pizarro. Declare wee first our Quarrell: then invade.
Cortez. My selfe, my King's Ambassadour, will goe;
    Speake *Indian* guide, how farre to *Mexico*?
45 *Indian.* Your Eyes can scarce soe farre a prospect make,
    As to discerne the City on the Lake.
    But that broad Cawswey will direct your way,
    And you may reach the Towne by noone of day.
Cortez. Command a partie of our *Indians* out,
50   With a strict charge not to engage but Scout;
    By noble wayes wee Conquest will prepare.
    First offer peace, and that refus'd make Warr.

                                 Exeunt.

[ACT I.] SCENE 2

*A Temple, and the high Priest with other Priests appeareing
in it. To them an* Indian.

Indian. Hast holy Priest, it is the King's command.
High Priest. When sets hee forward?
Indian.   Hee is nere att hand.
High Priest. The Incence is upon the Altar plac'd,
    The bloody Sacrifice allready past.
5   Five hundred Captives saw the riseing Sun,
    Who lost their light ere halfe his race was run.
    That which remaines wee here must celebrate;
    Where farr from noyse, without the Citty gate,
    The peacefull pow'r that governes Love repayres,
10   To feast upon Soft vows, and Sylent Pray'rs.
    Wee for his Royall presence only Stay,
    To end the rites of this soe Solemne day.

                                 Exit Indian.

0.1 *appeareing in it*] MS; *omit* Q1–3

47 *Cawswey*] a stone causeway to the south, five miles long
between two lakes (Gómara, p. 195).

Enter Montezuma, *his eldest Sonne* Odmar, *his Daughter*
   Cydaria: Almeria, Alibech, Orbellan, *and traine.*
       They place themselves.

High Priest. On youre birth day, while wee sing
   To our Gods, and to our King,
   Her, among this beautious Quire,   15
   Whose perfections you admire,
   Her, who fairest does appeare,
   Crowne her Queen of all the yeare.
   Of the yeare, and of the day,
   And at her feet your Garland lay.   20
Odmar. My Father this way does his lookes direct,
   Heav'n graunt he give it not where I suspect.

   Montezuma *rises, goes about the Ladies, and at length*
        stayes at Almeria, *and bows.*

Montezuma. Since my *Orazia's* death I have not seen
   A Beautie soe deserving to be Queen
   As faire *Almeria.*
Almeria (*to her Brother and Sister aside*).
           Sure hee will not knowe   25
   My birth I to that Injur'd Princesse owe,
   To whom not only he his Love deni'd,
   But in her Sufferings tooke unmanly pride.
Alibech. Since *Montezuma* will his Choice renew,
   In dead *Orazia's* Roome electing you,   30
   'Twill please our Mother's Ghost that you succeed
   To all the glories of her Rivall's Bedd.
Almeria. If news be carried to the shades belowe,
   The *Indian* Queene will be more pleas'd, to knowe
   That I his scornes on him, who scorn'd her, pay.   35
Orbellan. Would you could right her some more noble way.
        She turns to him who is kneeling all this while.
Montezuma. Madame this posture is for Heav'n design'd
   And what moves Heav'n I hope may make you kind.
Almeria. Heav'n may be kind, the Gods uninjur'd live,
   And crimes below cost little to forgive.   40
   By thee, Inhumane, both my Parents dy'd;
   One by thy sword, the other by thy pride.
Montezuma. My haughty mind noe fate could ever bow,
   Yet I must stoope to one who scornes mee now:
   Is there noe pitty to my Suffrings due?   45
Almeria. As much as what my Mother found from you.

  18 her] MS, Q1–2; the Q3
   15 *Quire*] i.e., choir.

Montezuma. Your Mother's wrongs a Recompence shall meet,
I lay my Scepter at her daughter's feet.
Almeria. Hee, who does now my least commands obey,
50   Would call mee Queen, and take my pow'r away.
Odmar. Can hee heare this, and not his Fetters breake?
Is Love soe pow'rfull, or his Soule soe weake?
Ile fright her from it! Madame, though you see
The King is kind, I hope youre modestie
55   Will knowe, what distance to the Crown is due.
Almeria. Distance, and modestie, prescrib'd by you?
Odmar. Almeria dares not thinke such thoughts as these.
Almeria. Shee dares both thinke, and Act, what thoughts shee please.
Tis much belowe mee on his Throne to sitt;
60   But when I doe, you shall Petition it.
Odmar. If, Sir, *Almeria* does your bed partake,
I mourne for my forgotten Mother's sake.
Montezuma. When parents Loves are order'd by a Sonne,
Let streames prescribe their fountaines where to runne.
65 *Odmar.* In all I urge, I keep my duty still,
Not rule youre reason, but instruct your will.
Montezuma. Small use of reason in that Prince is shown,
Who followes others, and neglects his owne.

      Almeria *to* Orbellan *and* Alibech, *who are this while whispering to her.*

Almeria. No, hee shall ever love, and allwaies bee
70   The Subject of my Scorne and crueltie.
Orbellan. To prove the lasting torment of his life,
You must not be his Mistresse, but his Wife.
Few knowe what care an husband's peace destroyes,
His reall greifes, and his dissembled joyes.
Almeria. What marke of pleaseing vengeance could be
75   shown,
If I to breake his quiet loose my owne?
Orbellan. A Brother's life upon youre love relyes,
Since I doe Homage to *Cydaria's* Eyes.
How can her Father to my hopes be kind
80   If in youre heart, hee noe example find?
Almeria. To save youre life I'll suffer any thing,
Yet I'll not flatter this tempestuous King;
But worke his stubborne Soule a Nobler way,
And if hee love, I'll force him to obey.
85   (*To* Montezuma) I take this Garland, not as given by you.

55 *distance*] deference.

42

But as my merit, and my beauties due.
As for the Crowne that you, my slave, possesse,
To share it with you would but make mee lesse.

Enter Guyomar *hastily.*

Odmar. My brother *Guyomar*! me thinks I spie
  Hast in his Stepps, and wonder in his Eye.   90
Montezuma. I sent thee to the Frontiers, quickly tell
  The cause of thy returne, are all things well?
Guyomar. I went in Order, Sir, to your Command,
  To view the utmost limitts of the land:
  To that Sea shore, where noe more world is found,   95
  But foameing Billowes breakeing on the ground.
  Where, for a while, my Eies noe object mett
  But distant Skies that in the Ocean sett:
  And low hung clouds that dipt themselves in raine
  To shake theire fleeces on the Earth againe.   100
  At last, as farr as I could cast my Eyes
  Upon the Sea, somewhat mee thought did rise
  Like blewish mists, which still appeareing more,
  Tooke dreadfull Shapes, and mov'd towards the Shore.
Montezuma. What formes did these new wonders repre-
    sent?   105
Guyomar. More strange then what your wonder can invent.
  The Object I could first distinctly view
  Was tall straight Trees which on the Waters flew.
  Wings on their sides in stead of Leaves did growe,
  Which gather'd all the breath the Winds could Blowe: 110
  And at their rootes grew floating Pallaces,
  Whose out-bow'd bellies cutt the yeilding Seas.
Montezuma. What divine Monsters, O yea Gods, are these
  That flote in aire and fly upon the Seas!
  Came they alive or dead upon the shore?   115
Guyomar. Alas! they liv'd too sure, I heard them roare:
  All turn'd their sides, and to each other spoke,
  I saw their words breake out in fire and smoake.
  Sure tis their voice that thunders from on high,
  Or these the younger Brothers of the skie.   120
  Deafe with the noise I tooke my hasty flight,
  Noe mortall courage can support the Fright.
High Priest. Old Prophesies foretell oure fall at hand,
  When bearded men in floating Castles land.
  I feare it is of dire Portent.
Montezuma.   Goe see   125
  What it foreshows, and what the Gods decree.
                  [*Exit* High Priest.]

Meane time proceed we to what Rites remaine;
Odmar, of all this presence does containe,
Give her your wreath whom you esteeme most faire.

130 *Odmar*. Above the rest I Judge one Beautie rare,
And may that Beautie prove as kind to mee
As I am sure faire *Alibech* is shee.

> *He gives* Alibech *the wreath*.

Montezuma. You *Guyomar*, must next performe your
part.
Guyomar. I want a Garland, but I'll give a heart:

135 My Brother's pardon I must first implore,
Since I with him faire *Alibech* adore.
Odmar. That all should *Alibech* adore tis true,
But some respect is to my Birthright due.
My claime to her by Eldership I prove.

140 *Guyomar*. Age is a Plea in Empire, not in love.
Odmar. I long have stai'd for this Solemnitie
To make my Passion publick.
Guyomar.   Soe have I.
Odmar. But from her birth, my Soule has been her Slave,
My heart receiv'd the wounds which first she gave:

145 I watch'd the early glories of her Eyes,
As men for day breake watch the Eastern skies.
Guyomar. It seems my Soule then mov'd the quicker pace,
Youres first set out, mine reach'd her in the race.
Montezuma. *Odmar*, your choise I cannot disapprove;

150 Nor justly *Guyomar*, can blame your love.
To *Alibech* alone referre youre Sute,
And let her sentence finnish youre dispute.
Alibech. You thinke mee Sir a Mistresse quickly won,
Soe soone to finnish what is scarce begun:

155 In this Surprize I can no Judgment make,
Tis answering Riddles ere I'm well awake:
If you obleige mee suddenly to choose,
The choise is made, for I must both refuse.
For to my selfe I owe this due regard

160 Not to make Love my guift, but my reward.
Time best will show whose services will last.
Odmar. Then judge my future service, by my past.
What I shall be, by what I was, you knowe:
That Love tooke deepest roote, which first did growe.

165 *Guyomar*. That Love which first was set will first decay,
Myne of a fresher date will longer Stay.
Odmar. Still you forgett my Birth.

139 *Eldership*] precedence of birth.
148 *Youres . . . race*] an allusion *Aeneid*, V, 294-361 (Brower).

44

Guyomar.   But you, I see,
  Take care still to refresh my memorie.
Montezuma. My Sonn's, let your unseemly discord cease,
  If not in freindship, live at least in peace.   170
  Orbellan, where you love bestow your wreath.
Orbellan. My Love I dare not, ev'n in whispers breath.
Montezuma. A vertuous Love may venture any thing.
Orbellan. Not to attempt the Daughter of my King!
Montezuma. Whether is all my former fury gone?   175
  Once more I have *Traxalla's* chaines put on,
  And by his children am in triumph ledd,
  Too well the liveing have reveng'd the dead!
Almeria. You thinke my Brother borne youre Enemy,
  He's of *Traxalla's* bloud, and soe am I.   180
Montezuma. In vaine I strive: ———
  My Lyon-heart is with Love's Toyles besett,
  Struggling I fall still deeper in the nett.
  Cydaria, your new Lover's Garland take,
  And—use him—kindly, for youre father's sake.   185
Cydaria. Soe strong a hatred does my nature sway,
  That spight of duty I must disobey.
  Besides you warn'd mee still of loveing two:
  Can I love him allready loveing you?

                Enter a Guard hastily.

Montezuma. You looke amaz'd, as if some suddaine feare   190
  Had seiz'd your hearts, is any danger neare?
1. Guard. Behind the covert where this Temple stands,
  Thick as the Shades, there Issue swarming Bands
  Of Ambush'd men, whom, by their Armes and dresse,
  To be *Taxallan* Enemies I guesse.   195

                Another Enters.

2. Guard. The Temple, Sir, is almost compas't round.
Montezuma. Some speedy way for passage must be found.
  Make to the Citty by the Postern gate,
  I'll either force my victory, or fate;
  A glorious death in Armes Ile rather prove,   200
  Then stay to perish tamely by my Love.
                          Exeunt omnes.

    An Alarm within, Enter Montezuma, Odmar,
    Guyomar, Alibech, Orbellan, Cydaria, Almeria
            as pursu'd by Taxallans.

  195 *Taxallan*] MS; *Taxcallan* Q1–3
  201.1 *Exeunt omnes.*] MS; *omit* Q1–3
  194 *Ambush'd*] i.e., lying in ambush.

                        45

Montezuma. No succour from the Towne?
Odmar.   None, none is nigh.
Guyomar. Wee are inclos'd, and must resolve to dye.
Montezuma. Fight for revenge now hope of life is past,
205   But one stroake more, and that will be my last.

  Enter Cortez, Vasquez, Pizarro, *to the* Taxallans,
  Cortez *stays them, just falling on.*

Cortez. Contemn'd? my orders broke even in my sight!
 (*To his* Indians) Did I not strictly charge you should
  not fight?
Indian. Your Choller, Generall, does unjustly rise,
 To see youre freinds pursue your Enemies;
210   The greatest and most cruell foes we have
 Are these whom you would Ignorantly save;
 By Ambush'd men, behind their Temple laid,
 Wee have the King of *Mexico* betray'd.
Cortez. Where, bannish'd virtue, wilt thou shew thy face
215   If treachery infects thy *Indian* race!
 Dismisse your rage, and lay youre weapons by:
 Know I protect them, and they shall not dy.
Indian. O wondrous mercy showne to foes distrest!
Cortez. Call them not soe, when once with odds opprest,
220   Nor are they foes my clemency defends,
 Untill they have refus'd the name of freinds:
 (*To* Vasquez) Draw up our *Spaniards* by themselves,
  then fire
 Our Gunns on all who doe not straight retire.
Indian. O Mercy, Mercy, at thy feete wee fall,
          Indians *kneeling.*
225   Before thy roareing Gods destroy us all;
 See wee retreat, without the least reply,
         The Taxallans *retire.*
 Keepe thy Gods silent, if they speake, wee dye.
Montezuma. The fierce *Taxallans* lay their weapons downe,
 Some miracle in our releife is showne.
230   *Guyomar.* These bearded men, in shape and collour be
 Like those I saw come floating on the Sea.
        Montezuma *kneeles to* Cortez.
Montezuma. Patron of *Mexico*, and God of Warrs,
 Sonne of the Sun, and Brother of the starres———
Cortez. Great Monarch, youre devotion you misplace.
Montezuma. Thy actions showe thee borne of Heav'nly
235   Race.

 223 who] MS; that Q1-3
 236 *cruell God*] Huitzilopotchli, god of war.

If then thou art that cruell God, whose Eyes
Delight in bloud, and humane sacrifice,
Thy dreadfull Altars I with slaves will store,
And feed thy nostrills with hot reeking gore;
Or if that mild and gentle God thou be,   240
Who dost mankind below with pitty see,
With breath of Incense I will glad thy heart,
But if like Us, of Mortall seed thou art,
Presents of rarest fowles and fruites I'll bring,
And in my Realmes thou shalt be more then King.   245
Cortez. Monarch of Empires, and deserveing more
   Then the Sun sees upon youre Western shore;
   Like you a man, and hither led by fame,
   Not by constraint but by my choice I came;
   Ambassadour of peace, if peace you choose,   250
   Or Herrald of a Warr if you refuse.
Montezuma. Whence or from whome dost thou these offers
      bring?
Cortez. From *Charles* the Fifth, the World's most potent
      King.
Montezuma. Some petty Prince, and one of little fame,
   For to this houre I never heard his name: 255
   The two great Empires of the world I know,
   That of *Peru*, and this of *Mexico*;
   And since the Earth none larger does afford,
   This *Charles* is some poore tributary Lord.
Cortez. You speake of that small part of Earth you know, 260
   But betwixt us and you, wide Oceans flow,
   And Watry desarts, of soe vast extent
   That passing hither, foure full Moons we spent.
Montezuma. But say, what news, what offers dost thou
      bring
   From soe remote, and soe unknowne a King?   265
      While Vasquez *speaks,* Cortez *spies the Ladies and goes
      to them entertaining* Cydaria *with Courtship in dumb show.*
Vasquez. *Spain's* mighty Monarch, to whom Heav'n thinks
      fitt
   That all the Nations of the Earth submitt,
   In gracious Clemency, does condiscend
   On these condicions to become youre freind.
   First that of him you shal your Scepter hold,   270
   Next, you present him with your useless gold:
   Last, that you leave those Idolls you adore,
   And one true Deitie with prayers implore.

240 *gentle God*] Quetzalcoatl, associated with a lost golden age. The
Mexicans longed for his eventual return.

Montezuma. You speak youre Prince a Mighty Emperour,
275   But his demands have spoke him proud, and poore;
    Hee proudly at my freeborn Scepter flies,
    Yet poorely beggs a mettall I despise.
    Gold thou mayst take, what ever thou canst find,
    Save what for Sacred uses is design'd:
280   But, by what right pretends your King to bee
    This Soveraigne Lord of all the World, and mee?
Pizarro. The Soveraigne Preist
    (Who represents on Earth the pow'r of Heav'n)
    Has this youre Empire to our Monarch given.
285 *Montezuma.* Ill does he represent the Pow'rs above,
    Who nourishes debate, not preaches love;
    Besides, what greater folly can be shown?
    He gives another what is not his own.
Vasquez. His pow'r must needs unquestion'd be below,
290   For hee in Heav'n an Empire can bestow.
Montezuma. Empires in Heav'n he with more ease may
      give,
    And you perhaps would with less thanks receive;
    But Heav'n has need of no such Viceroy heere,
    It selfe bestow's the Crowns that Monarchs weare.
295 *Pizarro.* You wrong his pow'r as you mistake our end,
    Who came thus farr Religion to extend.
Montezuma. Hee who Religion truly understands
    Know's it's extent must be in men, not lands.
Odmar. But who are those that truth must propagate
300   Within the Conffines of my Father's State?
Vasquez. Religious men, who hither must be sent
    As awfull guides of Heav'nly Government;
    To teach you pennance, Fasts, and abstinence,
    To punnish bodies for the Soul's offence.
Montezuma. Cheaply you sinne, and punnish crimes with
305   ease,
    Not as th'offended but th'offenders please.
    First Injure Heav'n, and when its wrath is due,
    Youre selves prescribe it how to punnish you.
Odmar. What numbers of these holy men must come?
310 *Pizarro.* You shall not want, each village shall have some;
    Who, though the Royall dignity they owne,
    Are equall to it, and depend on none.
Guyomar. Depend on none! you treat them sure in state,

274 *speak*] describe.
276 *flies*] attacks.
299 *propagate*] a possible play on the Congregation for Propagation of the Faith.

For tis their plenty does their pride create.
Montezuma. Those Ghostly Kings would parcell out my
    pow'r,   315
    And all the fattnesse of my land devoure;
    That Monarch sitts not safely on his Throne,
    Who beares within a pow'r that shocks his owne.
    They teach obedience to Imperiall sway,
    But thinke it sinne if they themselves obey.   320
Vasquez. It seems then our Religion you accuse,
    And peacefull Hommage to our King refuse.
Montezuma. Your gods I slight not, but will keep my owne,
    My Crown is absolute, and holds of none;
    I cannot in a base subjection live,   325
    Nor suffer you to take, though I would give.
Cortez. Is this your Answere, Sir?
Montezuma.   This as a Prince,
    Bound to my people's and my Crown's defence,
    I must returne, but, as a man by you
    Redeem'd from death, all gratitude is due.   330
Cortez. Honour requir'd that Act, ev'n from a Foe,
    But what I did were I againe to doe,
    That reason which inclin'd my will before
    Would urge it now, for Love has fir'd it more.
    Is no way left that wee may yet agree?   335
    Must I have Warre, yet have no Enemy?
Vasquez. Hee has refus'd all termes of peace to take.
Montezuma. Since we must fight, heare Heav'n what
    pray'rs I make,
    First, to preserve this ancient State and mee,
    But if your doome the fall of both decree,   340
    Grant only hee who has such honour showne,
    When I am dust, may fill my empty throne.
Cortez. To make mee happyer then that wish can doe,
    Lies not in all your Gods to grant, but you;
    Let this faire Princess, but one minute stay,   345
    A looke from her will your obleigements pay.
Montezuma (to Cydaria). Your duty in your quick return
    be shown,
    (*To his Guards*) Stay you, and wait my Daughter to the
    Town.
        Exeunt Montezuma, Odmar, Guyomar, Orbellan,
                        Almeria, *and* Alibech.
Cydaria *is goeing but turnes and lookes back upon* Cortez,
    who is lookeing on her all this while.
Cydaria (aside). My Father's gone and yet I cannot goe;
    Sure I have something lost or left behind!   350

Cortez (*aside*). Like Travellers who wander in the Snow,
    I on her beautie gaze till I am blind.
Cydaria [*aside*]. Thick breath, quick pulse, and heaving of
    my heart,
    All signes of some unwonted change appear:
355   I find my selfe unwilling to depart,
    And yet I know not why I would be here.
    [*To him*] Stranger you raise such Stormes within my
        breast,
    That when I goe (if I must goe againe)
    Ile tell my Father you have robb'd my rest,
360   And to him of youre Injuries complaine.
Cortez. Unknowne, I sweare those wrongs were which I
    wrought,
    But my Complaints will much more just appear,
    Who from another World my freedom brought,
    And to youre Conquering Eyes have lost it heere.
Cydaria. Where is that other World from whence you
365   came?
Cortez. Beyond the Ocean, farr from hence it lyes.
Cydaria. Your other world, I feare, is then the same
    That Soules must goe to when the body dies.
    But what's the cause that keeps you here with mee,
370   That I may know what keeps me here with you?
Cortez. Mine is a love which must perpetuall be,
    If you can be so just as I am true.

Enter Orbellan.

Orbellan. Your Father wonders much at your delay.
Cydaria. Soe great a wonder for soe small a stay!
375 *Orbellan*. Hee has commanded you with mee to goe.
Cydaria. Has hee not sent to bring the stranger too?
Orbellan. If hee to morrow dares in fight appear,
    His high plac'd love, perhapps may cost him deare.
Cortez. That word was never spoke to *Spaniard* yet,
380   But forfeited his life, who gave him it.
    Hast quickly with thy pledge of safetie hence,
    Thy guilt's protected by her Innocence.
Cydaria. Sure in some fatall houre my love was borne,
    Soe soone orecast with absence in the morne!
385 *Cortez*. Turne hence those pointed Glories of your Eyes,
    For if more charmes beneath their Circles rise,
    (Soe weake my vertue; they so strong appear)
    I shall turne Ravisher to keepe you here.
Exeunt severally.

ACT II. [SCENE 1]

SCENE, *The Magician's Cave.*

Enter Montezuma, High Priest.

Montezuma. Not that I feare the utmost fate can doe,
  Come I th'event of doubtfull Warr to know,
  For life and death are things indifferent,
  Each to be chose as either brings content;
  My search does from a nobler motive spring,   5
  Love rules my heart, and is your Monarch's King;
  I more desire to know *Almeria's* mind,
  Then all that Heav'n has for my State designed.
High Priest. By pow'rfull charmes which nothing can
    withstand,
  I'le force the Gods to tell what you demand.   10
              Charme.
Thou Moone, that aidst us with thy Magick might,
And yea Small Starres (the scatt'red seeds of light,)
Dart your pale beams into this gloomy place,
That the sad Pow'rs of the infernall race
May read above what's hid from humane Eyes,   15
And in youre walkes, see Empires fall and rise.
And yea immortall Soules, who once were men,
And now resolv'd to Elements againe,
Who wait for mortall frames in depths below,
And did before what wee are doom'd to doe;   20
Once, twice, and thrice, I wave my sacred wand,
Ascend, Ascend, Ascend at my Command.

    An Earthy Spirit rises.

Spirit. In vaine, O mortall men youre Pray'rs implore
  The aid of pow'rs below, which want it more:
  A God more Strong, Who all the Gods Commands,   25
  Drives us to Exile from our native Lands;
  The Aire swarms thick with wandring Deities,
  Which drowsily, like humming Beetles rise,
  From their lov'd Earth, where peacefully they slept,
  And farre from Heav'n, a long possession kept.   30
  The frighted *Satyrs* that in Woods delight,
  Now into Plains with prick'd up Ears take flight;
  And scudding thence, while they their horn-feet ply,
  About their Syres the little *Silvans* cry.
  A Nation loveing Gold must rule this place,   35

12 *yea*] ye.

Our Temples ruine, and oure rites deface:
To them, O King, is thy lost Scepter given,
Now mourn thy fatall Search, for since wise Heav'n
More ill then Good to mortalls does dispence,
40 It is not safe to have too quick a sense.   *Descends.*
Montezuma. Mourne they who thinke repineing can
    remove
The firme decrees of those who Rule above;
The brave are safe within, who still dare die,
When ere I fall, Ile scorne my destinie.
45 Doome as they please my Empire not to stand,
Ile graspe my Scepter with my dyeing hand.
High Priest. Those Earthy Spiritts black and envious
    are,
I'll call up other Gods of Forme more faire:
Who visions dresse in pleasing collours still,
50 Sett all the good to show, and hide the ill.
Kalib ascend, my faire spoke Servant, rise,
And Sooth my heart with pleaseing Prophecies.

*Kalib ascends to a light ayrie tune, all in white, in the
shape of a Woman, and Sings.*

Kalib. I look'd and saw within the Booke of Fate,
        Where many dayes did lowre,
55   When loe one happy houre
Leap'd up, and Smil'd to save thy Sinking State;
        A day shall come when in thy pow'r
            Thy cruell foes shall bee;
            Then shall thy Land be free,
60   And thou in peace shalt raigne:
But take, O take that opportunitie,
Which, once refus'd, will never come againe.
                                    Descends.
Montezuma. I shall deserve my fate if I refuse
That happy houre, which Heav'n allotts, to use;
65 But of my Crowne thou too much care dost take,
That which I value more, my love's at stake.
High Priest. Arise yea Subtill Spiritts that can Spie
When Love is enter'd in a Female's Eye;
You that can read it in the midst of doubt,
70 And in the midst of frowns can find it out;
You that can search those many corner'd mindes,
Where Woman's crooked Fancie turnes, and windes;
You that can love explore, and truth impart,

52.1 *to a light ayrie tune*] MS; *omit* Q1–3

Where both lye deepest hid in Woman's heart.
Arise. ——— 75

The Ghosts of Traxalla *and* Acacis *arise, they stand still
and point at* Montezuma.

High Priest. I did not for these ghastly visions send,
  Their suddaine comeing does some ill portend:
  Begone. ——— begone. ——— they will not dissappeare.
  My Soule is seiz'd with an unusuall feare.
Montezuma. Point on, Point on, and see whom you can
    fright. 80
  Shame and confusion seize these shades of night;
  Yee thinn and emptie formes am I your sport?
                                          They smile.
  If you were flesh
  You know you durst not use mee in this sort.

The Ghost of the Indian Queen *rises betwixt the Ghosts with
a dagger in her breast.*

Montezuma. Ha! 85
  I feele my haire grow stiffe, my Eye balls Rowle,
  This is the only forme could shake my Soule.
Ghost. *The hopes of thy Succeslesse Love resigne,*
  Know Montezuma, *thou art only mine;*
  For those who heere on Earth their passion show, 90
  By Death for Love, receive their right below.
  Why dost thou then delay my longing Armes?
  Have cares, and age, and mortall life such charmes!
  The Moone growes sickly at the sight of day,
  And early Cocks have summon'd mee away: 95
  Yet I'll appoint a meeting place below,
  For there fierce Winds, ore duskie valleys blow,
  Whose every puffe beares empty shades away,
  Which guideless in those darke dominions stray.
  Just at the entrance of the Feilds belowe, 100
  Thou shal't behold a tall black Poplar growe,
  Safe in its hollow Trunck I will attend,
  And Seize thy Spirit when thou dost descend.   Descends.
Montezuma. I'le seize thee there, thou Messenger of fate:
  Would my short life, had yet a shorter date! 105
  I'me weary of this flesh which holds us here,

75.1 *Ghosts of Traxalla and Acacis*] The husband and son of the Indian Queen, whose deaths were caused by Montezuma.
95 *early Cocks*] as in *Hamlet*, I.i.149–55, a ghost must return to his abode upon the first crowing of the cock.
97 *duskie valleys*] recalling *Aeneid*, VI, 440–74 (Summers).

And dastards manly Soules with hope and feare;
These heats and colds still in oure breasts make warre,
Agues and Feavers all oure Passions are.

Exeunt.

[ACT II.] SCENE 2

[*Enter*] Cydaria *and* Alibech, *Betwixt the two Armies.*

Alibech. Blessings will Crowne your name if you prevent
That bloud, which in this Battle will be spent;
Nor need you feare soe Just a Suite to move,
Which both becomes your duty and your Love.
Cydaria. But thinke you hee will come? their Camp is
5   neare,
And hee already knowes I wait him here.
Alibech. You are too young, you'r pow'r to understand,
Lovers take wing upon the least command;
Already hee is here.

Enter Cortez *and* Vasquez *to them.*

10 *Cortez.* Mee thinkes like two black stormes, on either hand,
Our *Spanish* Army and your *Indians* stand;
This only Space betwixt the Clouds is cleer,
Where you, like day, broke Loose from both appeare.
Cydaria. Those closeing skies might still continnue bright,
15 But who can help it if you'll make it night?
The Gods have giv'n you pow'r of life and death,
Like them to save or ruine with a Breath.
Cortez. That pow'r they to your Father did dispose,
Twas in his choice to make Us freinds or Foes.
20 *Alibech.* Injurious strength would rapine still excuse,
By off'ring termes the weaker must refuse;
And such as these your hard condicions are,
You threaten Peace, and you invite a Warre.
Cortez. If for myselfe to conquer here I came,
25 You might perhaps my actions Justly blame.
Now I am sent, and am not to dispute
My Prince's Orders, but to execute.
Alibech. Hee who his Prince soe blindly does obey,
To keep his faith his vertue throws away.
Cortez. Monnarchs may erre, but should each private
30   breast
Judge their ill Acts, they would dispute their best.
Cydaria. Then all your care is for your Prince I see,

107 *dastards*] makes a coward, terrifies.

Your truth to him out weighs your Love to mee;
You may soe cruell to denie mee prove,
But never after that, pretend to Love.   35
Cortez. Command my life, and I will soon obey,
To save my honnour I my bloud will pay.
Cydaria. What is this Honour which does Love controule?
Cortez. A rageing fitt of Virtue in the Soule;
A painfull burden which great minds must beare,   40
Obtain'd with danger, and possest with feare.
Cydaria. Lay down that burden if it painfull grow,
You'l find, without it, Love will lighter goe.
Cortez. Honour once lost is never to be found.
Alibech. Perhaps hee lookes to have both Passions Crown'd: 45
First dye his honour in a purple flood,
Then Court the daughter in the Father's bloud.
Cortez. The Edge of Warre I'll from the Battaile take,
And spare her Father's Subjects for her sake.
Cydaria. I cannot love you lesse when I'm refus'd,   50
But I can dye to be unkindly us'd;
Where shall a Maid's distracted heart find rest,
If shee can misse it in her Lover's breast!
Cortez. I till to morrow will the fight delay,
Remember you have Conquer'd mee to day.   55
Alibech. This grant destroyes all you have urg'd before,
Honnour could not give this, or can give more.
Our Women in the Foremost Ranks appeare;
March to the Fight, and meet your Mistresse there.
Into the thickest Squadrons shee must runn,   60
Kill her, and see what Honnour will be wonn.
Cydaria. I must be in the Battaile, but I'le goe
With emptie Quiver, and unbended Bow;
Not draw an Arrowe in this fatall strife,
For feare its point should reach your noble life.   65

       Enter Pizarro.

Cortez. Noe more, your kindnesse wounds mee to the
    death,
Honour begone, what art thou but a breath!
I'll live, proud of my Infamy and Shame,
Grac'd with no Triumph but a Lover's name;
Men can but say, Love did his reason blind,   70
And Love's the noblest frailtie of the mind.
Draw off my men, the Warr's already done.
Pizarro. Your Orders come too late, the Fight's begunne,

52 *distracted*] distraught.

The Enemy gives on with fury led,
75 And fierce *Orbellan* Combatts in their head.
Cortez. Hee justly feares a peace with mee would prove
Of ill concernment to his haughtie Love;
Retire, faire excellence, I goe to meet
New Honour, but to lay it at your feet.

> *Exeunt* Cortez, Vasquez, Pizarro.

Enter Odmar *and* Guyomar *to* Alibech *and* Cydaria.

80 *Odmar.* Now, Madame, since a danger does appeare
Worthy my Courage, though below my feare,
Give Leave to him who may in Battaile dye,
Before his death to aske his destinie.
Guyomar. Hee cannot dye whom you command to live,
85 Before the fight you can the Conquest give;
Speake where you'll place it?
Alibech.   Breifly then to both,
One I in secret Love, the other loath;
But where I hate, my hate I will not show,
And hee I love, my Love shall never know;
90 True worth shall gaine mee, that it may be sed,
Desert, not Fancy, once a Woman ledd.
Hee who in fight his Courage shall oppose
With most successe against his Countries foes,
From mee shall all that recompence receive
95 That vallor meritts, or that Love can give:
Tis true my hopes and feares are all for one,
But hopes and feares are to my selfe alone.
Let him not shunne the danger of the strife,
I but his Love, his Countrey claimes his life.
100 *Odmar.* All obstacles my courage shall remove.
Guyomar. Fall on, fall on.
Odmar.   For libertie,
Guyomar.   For Love.

> *Exeunt, the Women following.*

SCENE *Changes to the* Indian *Countrey.*

Enter Montezuma *at the doore behind attended by the*
Indians.

Montezuma. Charge, Charge, their ground the faint
Taxallans yeild,
Bold in Close Ambush, base in open feild:
The envious divell did my Fortune wrong,

101.3 *at the doore behind*] MS; *omit* Q1–3
74 *gives on*] deals a blow, makes an attack or charge on.

Thus fought, thus Conquer'd I when I was young.   105
                                                        Exit.

Allarm: Enter Cortez *bloudy.*

Cortez. Furies pursue these false *Taxallans* flight,
    Dare they be freinds to Us, and dare not fight?
    What freinds can Cowards be? what hopes appeare
    Of help from such, who where they hate show feare!

Enter Pizarro, Vasquez.

Pizarro. The feild growes thinn, and those that now remaine,   110
    Appeare but like the Shaddowes of the Slayne.
Vasquez. The fierce old King is vannish'd from the place,
    And in a Cloud of dust pursues the chace.
Cortez. Their eager Chace disorder'd does appeare,
    (*To* Vasquez) Command our Horse to Charge them in
        the Reare;   115
    (*To* Pizarro) You to our old *Castillian* Foot retire,
    Who yet stand firme, and at their backs give fire.
                                            Exeunt Severally.

Enter Odmar *and* Guyomar *meeting each other in the*
                        Battel.

Odmar. Where hast thou been since first the fight began,
    Thou lesse then Woman in the shape of Man?
Guyomar. Where I have done what may thy envy move,   120
    Things worthy of my Birth, and of my Love.
Odmar. Two bold *Taxallans* with one dart I slew,
    And left it sticking er'e my Sword I drew.
Guyomar. I sought not Honour on soe base a Traine,
    Such Cowards by our Women may be Slaine;   125
    I fell'd along a Man of bearded face,
    His limbes all cover'd with a shining case,
    Soe wondrous hard, and soe secure of wound,
    It made my Sword, though Edg'd with flint, rebound.
Odmar. I kill'd a double man, the one halfe lay   130
    Upon the ground, the other ran away.
                                    Guns go off within.

Enter Montezuma *out of breath, with him* Alibech
                and an Indian.

Montezuma. All's lost.
    Our foes with Lightning and with Thunder fight,

130 *double man*] The Indians believed a rider and his horse to be one
creature (Summers).

My men in vain shunn death by shamefull flight;
135   For deaths Invisible come wing'd with fire,
They heare a dreadfull noise and straight expire.
Take, Gods, that Soule yea did in spight create,
And made it great to be unfortunate:
Ill fate for mee, unjustly you provide,
140   Great Soules are sparkes of your owne heav'nly pride.
That Lust of pow'r wee from your Godheads have,
You'r bound to please those appetites you gave.

Enter Vasquez *and* Pizarro, *with* Spanniards.

Vasquez. Pizarro, I have hunted hard to day,
Into our Toyles the noblest of the prey;
145   Seize on the King, and him your prisoner make,
While I in kind Revenge, my taker take.
    Pizarro *with two goes to attacque the* King, Vasquez *with
        another to seize* Alibech.
Guyomar. Their danger is alike, whome shall I free?
Odmar. I'll follow Love.
Guyomar.   I'le follow pietie.
    Odmar *retreats from* Vasquez *with* Alibech *off the Stage.*
        Guyomar *fights for his father.*
Guyomar. Fly Sir, while I give back that life you gave,
150   Mine is well lost, if I your Life can save.
    Montezuma *fights off,* Guyomar *makeing his retreat,
        stayes.*
Guyomar. Tis more then man can do to scape them all,
Stay, let mee see where noblest I may fall.
    He *runns at* Vasquez, *is seiz'd behind and taken.*
Vasquez. Conduct him off,
And give Command he strictly guarded be.
155   *Guyomar*. In vaine are Guards, death setts the valliant free.
        Exit Guyomar *with* Guards.
Vasquez. A glorious day! and bravely was it fought,
Great fame our Generall in great dangers sought;
From his strong Arme I saw his Rivall runne,
And in a Crowd, th'unequall Combatt shunn.

Enter Cortez *leading* Cydaria, *who seems weeping,
and begging of him.*

Cortez. Man's force is fruitelesse, and your Gods would
160   faile
To save the Citty, but youre teares prevaile;
I'll of my fortune noe advantage make,
Those termes they had once given, they still may take.
Cydaria. Heav'n has of right all Victory design'd,

58

Where boundless pow'r dwells in a Will confin'd;   165
Your *Spannish* honour does the World excell.
Cortez. Our greatest honour is in Loveing well.
Cydaria. Strange wayes you practise there to winn a
   heart,
   Here Love is Nature, but with you tis Art.
Cortez. Love is with us, as naturall as here,   170
   But fetter'd up with Customes more severe;
   In tædious Courtshipp wee declare our paine,
   And ere wee kindnesse find, first meet disdaine.
Cydaria. If Women Love, they needles paines endure,
   Their pride and folly but delayes their cure.   175
Cortez. What you miscall their folly, is their care,
   They know how fickle Common Lovers are:
   Their Oathes and vowes are cautiously beleiv'd,
   For few there are but have been once deceiv'd.
Cydaria. But if they are not trusted when they vow,   180
   What other marks of Passion can they show?
Cortez. With Feasts, and Musick, all that brings delight,
   Men treat their Eares, their Pallates, and their sight.
Cydaria. Your gallants sure have little Eloquence,
   Faileing to move the Soule, they Court the sense,   185
   With pomp and traines, and in a Crowd they woe,
   When true felicity is but in two;
   But can such Toyes your Women's Passion move?
   This is but noise and tumult, tis not Love.
Cortez. I have noe reason Madame to excuse   190
   Those ways of Gallantry I did not use;
   My Love was true and on a Nobler score.
Cydaria. Your Love! alas! then have you Lov'd before!
Cortez. Tis true I Lov'd: but she is dead, shee's dead,
   And I should think with her all beautie fled,   195
   Did not her faire resemblance live in you,
   And by that Image, my first flames renew.
Cydaria. Ah happy Beautie whosoere thou art!
   Though dead thou keep'st possession of his heart;
   Thou makst mee Jealous to the last degree,   200
   And art my Rivall in his memorie.
   Within his memorie! ah, more then soe!
   Thou liv'st and triumph'st ore *Cydaria* too.
Cortez. What strang disquiet has uncalm'd your breast!
   Inhumane faire, to robb the dead of rest!   205
   Poore heart! Shee slumbers in her silent tombe,
   Let her possesse in peace that narrow roome.
Cydaria. Poore heart! hee pitties and bewailes her death:
   Some God, much hated Soule, restore thy breath

210   That I may kill thee, but some ease twill be,
        Ile kill my selfe for but resembling thee.
      Cortez. I dread your anger, youre disquiet feare,
        But blowes from hands so soft who would not beare!
        Soe kind a passion why should I remove?
215   Since Jealousie but shew's how well wee Love.
        Yet Jealousie soe strange I never knewe,
        Can shee who loves mee not disquiet you?
        For in the grave noe passions fill the breast,
        Tis all wee gaine by death to be at rest.
220   *Cydaria*. That shee noe longer loves brings noe releife,
        Your Love to her still lives, and that's my greife.
      Cortez. The object of desire once tane away,
        Tis then not Love, but pitty which wee pay.
      Cydaria. Tis such a pitty I should never have,
225   When I must lye forgotten in the Grave;
        I meant to have obleidg'd you when I died,
        That after mee you should love none beside,
        But you are false allready.
      Cortez.   If untrue,
        By heav'n my falshood is to her, not you.
      Cydaria. Observe (Sweet Heav'n) how falsely he does
230   sweare,
        You said you lov'd mee for resembling her.
      Cortez. That Love was in mee by resemblance bred,
        But show's you cheer'd my sorrows for the dead.
      Cydaria. You still repeate the greatness of your greife.
235   *Cortez*. If that was great, how great was the releife?
      Cydaria. The first Love still the strongest wee account.
      Cortez. That seems more strong which could the first
        surmount:
        But if you still continnue thus unkind,
        Whom I love best, you by my death shall find.
240   *Cydaria*. If you should Die, my death should yours pursue,
        But yet I am not satisfied you'r true.
      Cortez. Heare me, yea gods, and punnish him you heare,
        If ought within the world, I hold so deare.
      Cydaria. You would deceive the Gods and mee, she's dead,
245   And is not in the world, whose Love I dread.
        Name not the world, say nothing is soe deare.
      Cortez. Then nothing is, let that secure your feare.
      Cydaria. Tis time must weare it off, but I must goe.
        Can you your Constancie in absence showe?

226 *obleidg'd*] bound you, put you under an obligation.
233 *cheer'd*] encouraged, animated.

Cortez. Misdoubt my Constancie and doe not trie,   250
  But stay and keep mee ever in your Eye.
Cydaria. If as a Pris'ner I were here, you might
  Have then insisted on a Conqu'rour's right,
  And stay'd mee here; but now my love would be
  Th'Effect of force, and I would give it free.   255
Cortez. To doubt your virtue, or your Love, were sinne;
  Call for the Captive Prince and bring him in.

    Enter Guyomar bound and sadd.

(*To* Guyomar) You looke, Sir, as your fate you could
    not beare,
  Are *Spannish* fetters then so hard to weare?
  Fortune's unjust, shee ruines oft the brave,   260
  And him who should be Victor, makes the Slave.
Guyomar. Sonn of the Sunn, my fetters cannot be
  But glorious for mee, since put on by thee;
  The ills of Love, not those of fate I feare,
  These I can brave, but those I cannot beare;   265
  My Rivall Brother, while I'm held in chains,
  In freedome reaps the fruit of all my pains.
Cortez. Let it be never said, that he whose breast
  Is fill'd with Love, should breake a Lover's rest;
                    [*Unbinds him.*]
  Hast, loose no time, your Sister setts you free,   270
  And tell the King my Generous Enemy,
  I offer still those termes he had before,
  Onely aske leave his Daughter to adore.
Guyomar. Brother (that name my breast shall ever owne,
               He embraces him.
  The name of Foe, be but in Battailes knowne)   275
  For some few dayes all hostile Acts forbeare,
  That if the King Consents, it seeme not feare;
  His heart is noble, and great soules must be
  Most sought and Courted in adversitie.
  Three dayes I hope the wish'd successe will tell.   280
Cydaria. Till that long time.
Cortez.   Till that long time, farwell.
               Exeunt severally.

ACT III. [SCENE 1]

SCENE, *Chamber Royall.*

Enter Odmar *and* Alibech.

Odmar. The Gods, faire *Alibech*, had so decreed,
 Nor could my Vallour, against fate succeed;
 Yet though our Army brought not conquest home,
 I did not from the fight inglorious come:
5 If as a Victour you the brave regard,
 Successlesse courage then may hope reward,
 And I returning safe may justly boast
 To winn the prize which my dead brother lost.

Enter Guyomar *behind him.*

Guyomar. No, noe, thy Brother lives, and lives to bee
10 A wittnesse both against himselfe, and thee;
 Though both in safetie are return'd againe,
 I blush to aske her Love for vanquish'd men.
Odmar. Brother, I'le not dispute, but you are brave,
 Yet I was free, and you it seemes, a slave.
15 *Guyomar.* *Odmar,* tis true, that I was Captive ledd
 As publiquely is knowne, as that you fledd;
 But of two shames if shee must one pertake,
 I think the choice will not be hard to make.
Odmar. Freedome and bondage in her choice remain,
20 Dar'st thou expect shee will put on thy chaine?
Guyomar. Noe, noe, faire *Alibech*, give him the Crowne,
 My brother is return'd with high renowne.
 Hee thinks by flight his Mistresse must be wonn,
 And claimes the prize, because he best did runn.
Alibech. Your Chaines were Glorious, and your flight was
25 wise,
 But neither have orecome youre Enemies:
 My secret wishes would my choice decide,
 But open Justice bends to neither side.
Odmar. Justice already does my right approve,
30 If him who loves you most, you most should Love.
 My Brother poorly from your aid withdrew,
 But I my Father left to succour you.
Guyomar. Her Countrey shee did to her self preferr,
 Him who fought best, not who defended her;
35 Since shee her Interest for the Nation's wav'd,
 Then I who sav'd the King, the Nation sav'd;
 You aiding her, your Country did betray,
 I aiding him, did her Commands obey.

Odmar. Name it no more, in Love there is a time
  When dull obedience is the greatest crime;   40
  She to her Countries use resign'd your sword,
  And you, kind Lover, tooke her at her word;
  You did youre duty to your Love preferre,
  Seeke your reward from duty, not from her.
Guyomar. In acting what my duty did require,   45
  Twas hard for mee to quitt my owne desire,
  That fought for her, which when I did subdue,
  Twas much the easyer taske I left for you.
Alibech. Odmar a more then common Love has shown,
  And *Guyomar's* was greater, or was none;   50
  Which I should choose, some God direct my breast,
  The certaine good, or the uncertaine best:
  I cannot choose; you both dispute in vaine,
  Time, and your future Acts, must make it plaine;
  First raise the Seige, and set your Countrey free,   55
  I, not the Judge, but the reward will be.

    To them, Enter Montezuma *talking with* Almeria
       and Orbellan.

Montezuma. Madame, I thinke with reason I extoll
  The virtue of the *Spanish* Generall;
  When all the Gods our ruine have foretold,
  Yet Generously he does his Armes withhold,
  And offering peace, the first Condicions make.   60
Almeria. When peace is offer'd tis too late to take;
  For one poore losse to stoop to termes like those!
  Were we o're come what could they worse impose?
  Go, goe, with homage your proud Victors meet,   65
  Goe, lye like doggs, beneath your Masters feet.
  Goe, and beget them Slaves to digg their Mines,
  And groane for gold which now in Temples shines;
  Your shamefull Story shall record of mee,
  The men all crouch'd, and left a Woman free.   70
Guyomar. Had I not fought, or durst not fight againe,
  I, my suspected Counsell should refraine:
  For I wish peace, and any termes preferre
  Before the last extremities of Warr.
  We but exasp'rate those wee cannot harme,   75
  And fighting gaines Us but to dye more warme:
  If that be Cowardice, which dares not see
  The Insolent effects of Victorie;
  The Rape of Matrons, and their Children's cries,
  Then I am fearfull, let the brave advise.   80
Odmar. Keene Cutting swords, and Engines killing farr,

Have prosperously begunn a doubtfull Warre;
But now oure foes with less advantage fight,
Their strength decreases with our *Indians* fright.

85 *Montezuma*. This Noble Vote does with my wish Comply,
I am for Warre.
Almeria.   And soe am I.
Orbellan.   And I.
Montezuma. Then send to breake the truce, and I'le take
care
To cheer the Souldjers, and for fight prepare.
                    Exeunt Montezuma, Odmar, Guyomar, Alibech.

Almeria *stays* Orbellan. Guyomar *returns and hears them.*

Almeria (to Orbellan). Tis now the houre which all to rest
allow,

90 And sleep sitts heavie upon every browe;
In this dark silence softly leave the Towne,
And to the Generall's tent, (tis quickly knowne)
Direct your stepps: you may dispatch him straight,
Drown'd in his sleep, and easie for his fate:

95 Besides the truce will make his Guards more slack.
Orbellan. Courage which leads mee on, will bring mee
back:
But I more feare the basenes of the thing,
Remorse, you knowe, beares a perpetuall sting.
Almeria. For meane remorse no roome the valliant finds,

100 Repentance is the virtue of weak minds;
For want of judgment keeps them doubtfull still,
They may repent of good, who can of ill;
But dareing courage makes ill actions good,
Tis foolish pitty spares a Rivall's blood;
You shall about it straight.
                              Exeunt Almeria, Orbellan.

105 *Guyomar*.   Would they betray
His sleeping virtue, by soe meane a way!
And yet this *Spaniard*, is our Nation's foe,
I wish him dead ——— but cannot wish it soe;
Either my Countrey never must be freed,

110 Or I consenting to soe black a deed!
Would chance had never ledd my Steps this way!
Now, if he dies, I murder him, not they.

95 his] MS; the Q1–3
88 *cheer*] encourage, incite.
94 *Drown'd in his sleep*] recalling *Aeneid*, II, 265 (Brower).

———— Something must be resolv'd, ere tis too late,
Hee gave me freedome, I'le prevent his fate.
Exit Guyomar.

[ACT III.] SCENE 2

A Camp.

Enter Cortez *alone in a night Gowne.*

Cortez. All things are hush'd, as nature's self lay dead,
 The mountaines seem to nodd their drowsie head;
 The little Birds in dreams their Songs repeat,
 And sleeping flow'rs, beneath the night dew sweat;
 Ev'n lust and Envy sleep, yet Love denyes   5
 Rest to my Soule, and Slumber to my Eyes.
 Three dayes I promis'd to attend my Doome,
 And two long dayes and nights are yet to come:
Noyse within.
———— Tis sure the noise of some tumultuous fight,
 They break the truce, and Sally out by night.   10

Enter Orbellan *flying in the darke, his sword drawne.*

Orbellan. Betray'd! pursu'd! oh whether shall I fly?
 See, see, the Just reward of Treachery!
 I'me sure among the tents, but knowe not where,
 Even night wants darknes to secure my feare.
Comes neare Cortez *who heares him.*
Cortez.   Stand, who goes there?
Orbellan (*aside*).   Alas! what shall I say!   15
 (*To him*) A poore *Taxallan* that mistook his way,
 And wanders in the terrours of the night.
Cortez. Soldjer, thou seemst afraid, whence comes thy
  fright?
Orbellan. The Insolence of *Spaniards* caus'd my feare,
 Who in the dark pursu'd me entring here.   20
Cortez. Their crymes shall meet immediate punishment,
 But stay thou safe within the Generall's Tent.
Orbellan. Still worse and worse!
Cortez.   Feare not but follow me.
 Upon my life I'le set thee safe and free.
Cortez *leads him in and returnes.*

To him Vasquez, Pizarro, *and* Spanniards *with torches.*

Vasquez. O sir, thanke Heav'n, and your brave *Indian*
  freind
 That you are safe, *Orbellan* did intend   25

65

This night to kill you sleeping in youre Tent:
But *Guyomar*, his trusty Slave has sent,
Who (followeing Close his silent stepps by night
30   Till in our Camp they both approach'd the light)
Cry'd seize the Traytor, seize the Murderer.
The Cruell Villaine fled, I know not where,
But farre hee is not, for hee this way bent.
Pizarro. Th'inraged Soldiers seek from tent to tent,
35   With lighted Torches, and in Love to you,
With bloody Vowes his hated life pursue.
Vasquez. This Messenger does since he came relate,
That the old King, after a long debate,
By his Imperious Mistresse blindly ledd,
40   Has giv'n *Cydaria*, to *Orbellan's* bedd.
Cortez. Vasquez, the trusty Slave with you retaine,
Retire a while, Ile call you back againe.

                    Exeunt Vasquez, Pizarro, *&c.*
          Cortez *at his tent doore.*

Cortez. Indian come forth, youre Enemies are gone,
And I who sav'd you from them, here alone;
45   You hide your face, as you were still afraid,
Dare you not looke on him who gave you aid?

          Enter Orbellan *holding his Face aside.*

Orbellan. Moon slipp behind some Cloud, some Tempest
    rise
And blow out all the Starrs that light the skies,
To shrowd my shame.
Cortez.   In vaine you turne aside,
50   And hide your face, youre name you cannot hide;
I know my Rivall, and his black designe.
Orbellan. Forgive it as my passion's fault, not mine.
Cortez. In youre excuse youre Love does little say,
You might have taken a much nobler way.
55   *Orbellan.* Tis true my passion small defence can make,
Yet you must spare mee for your honour's sake
That was engag'd to set mee safe and free.
Cortez. Twas to a stranger, not an Enemy:
Nor is it prudence to prolong thy breath,
60   When all my hopes depend upon thy death.
———— Yet none shall tax mee with base perjury,
Something I'le doe, both for my selfe and thee;
With vow'd revenge my Soldjers search each tent,
If thou art seen, none can thy death prevent:

42.1 &c.] MS; *omit* Q1–3

Follow my stepps with silence and with hast.   65

They goe out, the Scene changes to the Indian Country,
they returne.

Cortez. Now you are safe, you have my Outguards past.
Orbellan. Then here I take my leave.
Cortez.   *Orbellan,* noe,
  When you returne you to *Cydaria* goe.
  Ile send a Message.
Orbellan.   Let it be exprest,
  I am in hast.
Cortez.   I'le write it in youre breast.   *Draws.*   70
Orbellan. What meanes my Rivall?
Cortez.   Either fight or dye,
  I'le not straine Honour to a point too high;
  I sav'd your Life, now keep it if you can,
  Cydaria shall be for the bravest man;
  On equal terms you shall your Fortune try,   75
  Take this and lay your flint-edg'd weapon by;
                    Gives him a Sword.
  I'le arm you for my Glory, and pursue
  No Palm, but what's to manly Vertue due.
  Fame with my Conquest, shall my Courage tell,
  This you shall gain by placing Love so well.   80
Orbellan. Fighting with you ungratefull I appeare.
Cortez. Under that shaddow thou would'st hide thy feare:
  Thou would'st possesse thy love at thy returne,
  And in her armes my easie virtue scorne.
Orbellan. Since wee must fight, no longer time delay,   85
  The Moon shines clear, and makes a paler day.
    They fight, Orbellan *is wounded in the hand, his sword*
                    falls out of it.
Cortez. To Courage, even of Foes, ther's pittie due,
  It was not I, but Fortune vanquish'd you;
                    Throws his Sword again.
  Thank mee with that, and soe dispute the prize,
  As if you fought before *Cydaria's* Eyes.   90
Orbellan. I would not poorely such a guift requite,
  You gave mee not this Sword to yeild, but fight;
  But see where your's has forc'd its bloody way,
                    He strives to hold it, but cannot.
  My wounded hand my heart does ill obey.
Cortez. Unlucky honour that controul'st my Will!   95
  Why have I vanquish'd, since I must not kill?

82 *shaddow*] dissemblance, concealment.

67

Fate sees thy life Lodg'd in a brittle glasse,
And lookes it through, but to it cannot passe.
Orbellan. All I can doe is frankly to confesse,
100   I wish I could, but cannot love her lesse;
To sweare I would resigne her were but vaine,
Love would recall that perjur'd breath againe;
And in my wretched case twill be more just
Not to have promis't, then deceive youre trust.
105   Know, if I live once more to see the Towne,
In bright *Cydaria's* armes my love I'le Crowne.
Cortez. In spight of that I give thee libertie,
And with thy person leave thy Honour free;
But to thy Wishes move a speedy pace,
110   Or death will soon oretake thee in the Chace.
———— To armes, to Armes, fate shews my love the way,
I'le force the Citty on thy Nuptiall day.

Exeunt severally.

[ACT III.] Scene 3

SCENE, *Mexico*.

Enter Montezuma, Odmar, Guyomar, Almeria.

Montezuma. It moves my wonder that in two dayes space,
This Early Famine spreads so swift a pace.
Odmar. Tis, Sir, the Generall Cry, nor seems it strange,
The face of plenty should so swiftly change;
5   This Citty never felt a Seige before,
But from the Lake receiv'd it's daily store,
Which now shutt up, and Millions Crowded here,
Famine will soone in multitudes appeare.
Montezuma. The more the number still the greater shame.
10   *Almeria*. What if some one should seeke immortall fame
By ending of the Seige at one brave blow?
Montezuma. That were too happy!
Almeria.   Yet it may be soe.
What if the *Spannish* Generall should be slaine?
Guyomar (*aside*). Just heav'n I hope does other-ways
ordaine.
15   *Montezuma*. If slaine by Treason I should mourn his death.

Enter Orbellan *and whispers his Sister.*

Odmar. Orbellan seem's in hast and out of breath.
Montezuma. Orbellan, wellcome, you are Earely here,
A Bridegroome's hast does in your lookes appeare.

68

Almeria (aside to her brother). Betray'd! noe twas thy
  Cowardice, and feare:
Hee had not scap'd with life had I been there.   20
But since so ill you Act a brave designe,
Keep close youre Shame, fate make the next turne mine.

  Enter Alibech, Cydaria.

Alibech. O Sir, if ever pitty touch'd youre breast,
  Let it be now to youre owne blood exprest:
  In teares youre beautious Daughter drowns her sight,   25
  Silent as dews that fall in dead of night.
Cydaria. To your Commands I strict obedience owe,
  And my last Act of it I come to showe;
  I want the heart to dye before youre Eyes,
  But greife will finnish that which feare denyes.   30
Almeria. Your will should by youre Father's precept move.
Cydaria. When hee was young hee taught mee truth in
  Love.
Almeria. Hee found more love then he deserv'd, tis true,
  And that it seems, is lucky too to you;
  Your Father's Folly tooke a headstrong course,   35
  But I'le rule your's, and teach you Love by force.

  Enter Messenger.

1. Messenger. Arme, Arme, o King, the Enemy comes on,
  A Sharp assault allready is begunn;
  Their murd'ring Gunns, play fiercly on the Walls.
Odmar. Now Rivall, lett Us runn where honour calls.   40
Guyomar. I have dischardg'd what gratitude did owe,
  And the brave *Spaniard* is againe my foe.
                Exeunt Odmar *and* Guyomar.
Montezuma. Our Walls are high and multitudes defend;
  Their vaine Attempt must in their ruine end.
  The Nuptialls with my presence shall be grac'd.   45
Alibech. At least but stay till the assault be past.
Almeria. Sister, in vaine you urge him to delay:
  The King has promis'd, and hee shall obey.

  Enter Second Messenger.

2. Messenger. From severall parts the Enemies repell'd,
  One onely quarter to th'assault does yeild.   50

  Enter Third Messenger.

3. Messenger. Some foes are enter'd, but they are so few
  They onely death, not victory pursue.

22 make] MS; makes Q1–3

69

Orbellan. Hark, Hark, they shout!
From virtue's rules I do too meanly swerve:
55   I by my Courage will youre Love deserve.
                             Exit [Orbellan.]
Montezuma. Heere in the heart of all the Towne I'll stay:
And timely succour where it wants, convey.

     A noise within, enter Orbellan *and* Indjans *driven in,*
         Cortez. *after them and one or two* Spanniards.

Cortez. Hee's found, hee's found, degenerate Coward, stay:
Night sav'd thee once, thou shalt not scape by day.
                          Kills Orbellan.
60   *Orbellan.* O, I am kill'd.   *Dyes.*

         Enter Guyomar *and* Odmar.

Guyomar. Yeild Generous stranger, and preserve your life,
                          He is beset.
Why choose you death in this unequall strife?

     Almeria *and* Alibech *seem to weep over* Orbellan's *body.*

Cortez. What nobler fate could any Lover meet?
I fall reveng'd and at my Mistresse feet.

     They fall on him and bear him down, Guyomar *takes his*
                                Sword.

65   *Alibech.* Hee's past recovery, my deare Brother's slaine:
Fate's hand was in it, and my care is vaine.
Almeria. In weake complaints you vainly wast your breath:
They are not tears that can revenge his death.
Dispatch the Villain straight.
Cortez.   The Villain's dead.
70   *Almeria.* Give mee a Sword and let mee take his head.
Montezuma. Though, Madame, for your Brother's losse I
     greive,
Yet let me begg ———
Almeria.   His Murderer may live?
Cydaria. Twas his misfortune, and the chance of Warr.
Cortez. It was my purpose, and I kill'd him faire;
75   How could you so unjust and cruell prove
To call that chance which was the Act of Love?
Cydaria. I call'd it any thing to save your life:
Would hee were living still, and I his Wife;
That wish was once my greatest misery,
80   But tis a greater to behold you dy.

     55.1 *Exit*] MS; *omit* Q1–3   57.1 Orbellan *and*] MS; Orbellan,
     Q1–3   76 which] MS; that Q1–3

Almeria. Either Command his death upon the place,
　Or never more behold *Almeria's* face.
Guyomar (to Montezuma). You by his Vallour, once from
　　death were freed:
　Can you forget so generous a deed?
Montezuma. How Gratitude and Love, divide my breast!　　85
　Both wayes alike my Soule is robb'd of rest.
　But ——— let him dye, ——— can I his sentence give?
　Ungratefull, must he dy by whom I live?
　But can I then *Almeria's* teares deny!
　Should any live, whom shee Commands to dy?　　90
Guyomar. Approach who dares: he yeilded on my Word;
　And as my Pris'ner, I restore his sword;
　　　　　　　　　　Gives his Sword.
　His life concernes the safety of the state,
　And I'le preserve it for a calme debate.
Montezuma. Darst thou rebell! false and degenerate boy,　　95
　That being which I gave I thus destroy.

　　　　Offers to kill him, Odmar *steps between.*

Odmar. My Brother's bloud I cannot see you spill,
　Since he prevents you but from doing ill:
　Hee is my Rivall, but his death would bee
　For him too glorious, and too base for mee.　　100
Guyomar. Thou shalt not conquer in this noble strife:
　Alas! I meant not to defend my life:
　Strike, Sir, you never pierc'd a breast more true:
　Tis the last wound I ere can take for you.
　You see I live but to dispute your Will;　　105
　Kill mee, and then you may my Pris'ner kill.
Cortez. You shall not, gen'rous youths, contend for mee:
　It is enough that I your honour see.
　But that your duty may no blemmish take,
　I will my selfe your Father's captive make:　　110
　When hee dares strike, I am prepar'd to fall:
　　　　　　　Gives his Sword to Montezuma.
　The *Spaniards* will Revenge their Generall.
Cydaria. Ah you too hastily your life resigne,
　You more would love it, if you vallu'd mine!
Cortez. Dispatch mee quickly, I my death forgive,　　115
　I shall grow tender else, and wish to live;
　Such an infectious face her sorrow weares,
　I can beare Death, but not *Cydaria's* teares.
Almeria. Make hast, make hast, they merit death all three:
　They for Rebellion, and for murder hee.　　120
　See, see, my Brother's Ghost hangs hovering there

Ore his warme bloud, that steem's into the aire.
Revenge, Revenge it cries.
Montezuma.   And it shall have;
But two dayes respite for his Life I crave:
125 If in that space you not more gentle prove,
I'll give a fatall proofe how well I love.
Till when, you *Guyomar*, your Pris'ner take;
Bestow him in the Castle, on the Lake:
In that small time, I shall the Conquest gaine
130 Of these few Sparkes of vertue which remaine:
Then all who shall my headlong Passion see,
Shall curse my crimes, and yet shall pitty mee.

Exeunt omnes.

ACT IV. [Scene 1]

SCENE, *A Prison.*

Almeria *and an* Indian *speake entering.*

Indian. A dangerous proofe of my respect I show.
Almeria. Feare not, Prince *Guyomar* shall never know:
While hee is absent let us not delay;
Remember tis the King thou dost obey.
Indian. See where he sleeps.

Cortez *appears Chain'd and laid asleep.*
5 *Almeria.*   Without my comming wait:
And on thy life secure the Prison gate.

Exit Indian.
She plucks out a Dagger and approaches him.
Spaniard awake: thy fatall houre is come:
Thou shalt not at such ease receive thy doome.
Revenge is sure, though sometimes slowly pac'd,
10 Awake, awake, or sleeping sleep thy last.
Cortez. Who names revenge?
Almeria.   Looke up and thou shalt see.
Cortez. I cannot feare so faire an Enemy.
Almeria. No aid is nigh, nor can'st thou make defence:
Whence can thy Courage come?
Cortez.   From Innocence.
15 *Almeria.* From Innocence? let that then take thy part,
Still are thy looks assur'd? ——— have at thy heart.

Holds up the Dagger.
——— I cannot kill thee, sure thou bearst some charme,

Goes back.

0.2 Almeria . . . *entering.*] MS; *Enter* Almeria *and an* Indian *they*
speak entring. Q1–3 [Indian, Q2–3]

Or some Divinitie holds back my Arme.
(*Aside*) Why doe I thus delay to make him bleed?
Can I want Courage for so brave a deed?   20
I've shooke it off; my Soule is free from feare,
                              Comes again.
And I can now strike any where ——— but heere.
His scorne of death, how strangely doth it move!
A mind so haughty, who could choose but love!
                              Goes off.
Plead not a charme, or any God's command,   25
Alas! it is thy heart that holds thy hand!
In spight of mee I love, and see, too late,
My Mother's pride must find my mother's fate.
——— Thy Countries foe! thy Brother's murderer.
For shame, *Almeria*, such mad thoughts forbeare.   30
It w'onnot be, if I once more come on
                              Coming on again.
I shall mistake the breast, and pierce my owne.
                              Comes with her Dagger down.
Cortez. Does your Revenge malitiously forbeare
To give mee death, till tis prepar'd by feare?
If you delay for that, forbeare, or strike,   35
Foreseen and suddain death are both alike.
Almeria (*aside*). To show my Love would but increase his
    pride:
They have most pow'r who most their passions hide,
Spaniard, I must confess I did expect
You could not meet your death with such neglect;   40
I will deferr it now and give you time:
You may repent, and I forget your crime.
Cortez. Those who repent, acknowledg they did ill:
I did not unprovok'd your Brother kill.
Almeria. Petition mee, perhaps I may forgive.   45
Cortez. Who beggs his life, does not deserve to live.
Almeria. But if tis given, you'l not refuse to take?
Cortez. I can live gladly for *Cydaria's* sake.
Almeria. Does shee so wholly then possesse your mind?
What if you should another Lady find,   50
Equall to her in Birth, and farre above
In all that can attract, or keep your love.
Would you so dote upon your first desire
As not to entertain a nobler fire?
Cortez. I think that person hardly will be found,   55
With gracious forme, and æquall vertue Crown'd:
Yet if another could precedence claime,
My fixt desires could find no fairer aime.

73

Almeria (aside). Dull Ignorance! he cannot yet conceive:
60   To speake more plaine, shame will not give mee leave.
    ——— (*To him*) Suppose one lov'd you whom ev'n
      Kings adore:
    Who with your life, your freedom would restore,
    And adde to that the Crown of *Mexico*:
    Would you for her, *Cydaria's* love forgoe?
65 *Cortez.* Though shee could offer all you can invent,
    I could not of my faith, once vow'd, repent.
Almeria [aside]. A burning blush has cover'd all my face:
    Why am I forc'd to publish my disgrace?
    [*To him*] What if I Love? you know it cannot be,
70   And yet I blush to put the case 'twere mee.
    If I could love you with a flame so true,
    I could forget what hand my Brother slew? ———
    ——— Make out the rest, ——— I am disorder'd so
    I know not further what to say, or do.
75   ——— But answer mee to what you think I meant.
Cortez. Reason or Witt no answer can invent:
    Of Words confus'd who can the meaning find?
Almeria. Disorder'd words show a distemper'd mind.
Cortez (aside). Shee has obleidg'd mee so, that could I choose,
80   I would not answer what I must refuse. ———
Almeria. His mind is shook, ——— suppose I Lov'd you,
    speak,
    Would you for mee *Cydaria's* fetters breake?
Cortez. Things meant in Jest, no serious Answer neede.
Almeria. But, put the Case that it were so indeed.
85 *Cortez.* If it were so (which but to thinke were pride)
    My constant Love would dangerously be try'd:
    For since you could a Brother's death forgive,
    Hee whom you save, for you alone should live:
    But I the most unhappy of mankind,
90   Ere I knew your's, have all my Love resign'd:
    Tis my own Losse I greive, who have no more;
    You goe a begging to a Bankrupt's doore.
    Yet could I change (as sure I never can)
    How could you Love so infamous a man?
95   For Love once giv'n from her, and plac'd in you,
    Would leave no ground I ever could be true.
Almeria. You constru'd mee aright ——— I was in Jest:
    And by that offer meant to sound your breast;
    Which since I find so constant to your Love,
100   Will much my vallue of your worth improve.

74 further] MS; farther Q1–3

Spanniard assure your selfe you shall not be
Obleidg'd to quitt *Cydaria*, for mee:
Tis dangerous though, to treat me in this sort,
And to refuse my offers though in sport.

Exit Almeria.
Cortez *solus*.

Cortez. In what a strange Condition am I left!   105
More then I wish, I have! of all I wish bereft!
In wishing nothing wee enjoy still most;
For ev'n our wish is, in possession, lost:
Restlesse wee wander to a new desire,
And burn our selves by blowing up the fire: 110
Wee tosse and turne about, our feav'rish Will,
When all our Ease must come by lyeing still:
For all the happinesse man kind can gaine
Is not in pleasure, but in rest from paine.

Goes in and the Scene closes upon him.

[ACT IV.] SCENE 2
Chamber Royal.

Enter Montezuma, Odmar, Guyomar, Alibech.

Montezuma. My Eares are deafe with this impatient Crowd.
Odmar. Their wants are now growne mutinous, and lowd:
   The Generall's taken but the Seige remaines;
   And their last food our dyeing men susteins.
Guyomar. One means is only left, I to this houre   5
   Have kept the Captive from *Almeria's* pow'r:
   And though by your Command she often sent
   To urge his doome, doe still his death prevent.
Montezuma. That hope is past: him I have oft assayl'd,
   But neither threats, nor kindnesses, have prevail'd;   10
   Hiding our wants, I offer'd to release
   His chaines, and equally conclude a peace:
   He feircely answer'd, I had now no way
   But to submitt, and without termes, obey.
   I told him, hee in chaines demanded more   15
   Then he impos'd in Victory before:
   He sullenly reply'd he could not make
   These offers now; honnour must give, not take.
Odmar. Twice have I sallyed, and was twice beat back:
   What des'prate Course remaines for us to take!   20
Montezuma. If either death or bondage I must choose,
   I'le keep my freedom, though my life I loose.
Guyomar. I'le not upbraid you that you once refus'd
   Those meanes you might have then with honour us'd:

75

25 I'll lead your men, perhapps bring victory:
They know to Conquer best, who know to dy.
Exeunt Montezuma, Odmar.
Alibech. Ah mee! what have I heard? stay *Guyomar*,
What hope you from this Sally, you prepare?
Guyomar. A death with honour for my Countryes good:
30 And to that use your selfe design'd my blood.
Alibech. You heard, and I well know the Townes distresse,
Which sword and famine both at once oppresse:
Famine so feirce, that (what's deny'd man's use)
Ev'n deadly plants, and herbs of poys'nous juice
35 Wild hunger seeks; and to prolong our breath,
We greedily devour our certaine death:
The Soldjer in th'assault of famine falls;
And Ghosts, not men, are watching on the Walls.
As Callow Birds
40 Whose Mother's kill'd in seeking of the Prey,
Cry in their nest, and thinke her long away;
And at each Leafe that stirrs, each blast of wind,
Gape for the Food which they must never find:
So cry the people in their misery.
45 *Guyomar.* And what releife can they expect from mee?
Alibech. While *Montezuma* sleep's call in the foe:
(The Captive Generall your designe may know)
His noble heart, to honour ever true,
Knowes how to spare, as well as to subdue.
50 *Guyomar.* What I have heard I blush to heare: and greive
Those words you spoke, I must your words beleive.
I to doe this! I, whom you once thought brave,
To sell my Country, and my King enslave!
All I have done by one foule Act deface,
55 And yeild my right to you by turnning base?
What more could *Odmar* wish that I should doe
To loose youre Love, then you perswade mee to?
No, Madame, noe, I never can committ
A deed so ill, nor can you suffer it.
60 Tis but to try what virtue you can find,
Lodg'd in my Soule.
Alibech. I plainely speake my minde.
Deare as my Life, my virtue Ile preserve:
But vertue you too scrupulously serve:
I lov'd not more then now my Country's good,
65 When for it's service I employd your blood:
But things are alter'd, I am still the same,
By different wayes still moving to one fame;
And by disarming you I now doe more

To save the Towne, then Arming you before.
Guyomar. Things good or ill by circumstances be,   70
  In you tis virtue, what is vice in mee.
Alibech. That ill is pardon'd which does good procure.
Guyomar. The good's uncertaine, but the ill is sure.
Alibech. When Kings grow stubborn, slothfull, or unwise,
  Each private man for publique good should rise;   75
  As when the Head distempers does endure,
  Each several part must join t'effect the cure.
Guyomar. Take heed, faire Maid, how Monarchs you
  accuse:
  Such Reasons none but impious Rebells use:
  Those who to Empire by dark paths aspire,   80
  Still plead a call to what they most desire;
  But Kings by free consent their Kingdoms take,
  Strict as those sacred tyes which Nuptialls make;
  And what ere faults in Princes time reveale,
  None can be Judge where can be no appeale.   85
Alibech. In all debates you plainly let mee see
  You Love your vertue best, but *Odmar* mee:
  Goe, your mistaken pietie pursue:
  I'le have from him what is deny'd by you:
  With my Commands you shall no more be grac'd,   90
  Remember, Sir, this tryall was your last.
Guyomar. The Gods inspire you with a better mind;
  Make you more Just, and make you then more kind:
  But though from vertue's rules I cannot part,
  Thinke I deny you with a bleeding heart: 95
  Tis hard with mee what ever choice I make,
  I must not merit you, or must forsake:
  But in this streight, to honour Ile be true,
  And leave my Fortune to the Gods and you.

Enter Messenger *privately.*

Messenger. Now is the time; be aiding to youre fate;   100
  From the Watch Tow're, above the Westerne gate,
  I have discern'd the foe securely lye,
  (Too proud to feare a beaten Enemy:)
  Their careless Cheifes to the coole Grotto's runn,
  (The Bow'rs of Kings) to shade them from the Sun.   105
Guyomar. Upon thy Life disclose thy news to none;
  I'le make the Conquest, or the shame my owne.
Exit Guyomar *and* Messenger.

76–77 As when . . . cure.] Q1; Virtue though straight, doth of
loose foles [*i.e.,* folds] consist / which larger Soules can can [sic]
widen as they list. MS; *omit* Q2–3

77

Enter Odmar.

Alibech. I read some wellcome Message in his Eye:
Prince *Odmar* comes, I'le see if hee'll deny.
110   *Odmar*, I come to tell you pleasing news:
I begg'd a thing your Brother did refuse.
Odmar. The news both pleases mee, and greives mee too;
For nothing, sure, should be deny'd to you:
But hee was blest who might Commanded be;
115   You never meant that happinesse to mee.
Alibech. What he refus'd your kindnesse might bestow,
But my Commands, perhaps, your burden grow.
Odmar. Could I but live till burdensome they prove,
My Life would be immortall as my Love.
120   Your wish, ere it receive a name, I grant.
Alibech. Tis to releive your dying Countries want.
All hopes of succour from your armes is past,
To save us now, you must our ruine hast;
Give up the towne, and (to obleidge him more)
125   The Captive Generall's libertie restore.
Odmar. You speake to try my Love, can you forgive
Soe soone, to let your Brother's Murtherer live?
Alibech. *Orbellan*, though my Brother, did disgrace
With treacherous deeds our mighty Mother's race;
130   And to revenge his blood, so justly spilt,
What is it less then to pertake his guilt?
Though my proud Sister to revenge Incline,
I to my Countries good, my own resigne.
Odmar. To save our lives, our freedome, I betray ———
135   ——— Yet since I promis'd it I will obey;
Ile not my shame nor your Commands dispute:
You shall behold your Empire's absolute.
                                        Exit Odmar.
                                        Sola.

Alibech. I should have thank'd him for his speedy grant;
And yet I know not how, fitt words I want:
140   Sure I am growne distracted in my mind,
That Joy this grant should bring I cannot find:
The one, denying, vex'd my Soule before;
And this, obeyeing, has disturb'd mee more:
The one with griefe, and Slowly, did refuse,
145   The other, in his grant, much hast did use.
——— He us'd too much, ——— and granting me so
soone,
He has the merit of the guift undone:

137.2 *Sola.*] MS; *omit* Q1-3

Mee thought with wondrous ease, he swallow'd downe
His forfeit honour, to betray the Towne.
My inward choice was *Guyomar* before,   150
But now his vertue has confirm'd mee more.
——— I rave, I rave, for *Odmar* will obey,
And then my promise must my choice betray.
Fantastique honour, thou hast fram'd a toyle,
Thy selfe, to make thy Love, thy vertues spoile.   155
Exit Alibech.

[ACT IV.] Scene 3

*A pleasant Grotto discovered: in it a Fountaine spouting; round
about it* Vasquez, Pizarro, *and other* Spaniards *lying carelessly
un-arm'd, and by them many* Indian *Women, one of which
Sings the following Song.*

SONG

Ah fading joy, how quickly art thou past?
Yet we thy ruine haste:
As if the cares of Humane Life were few
We seek out new:
And follow Fate which would too fast pursue.   5

See how on every bough the Birds express
In their sweet notes their happiness.
They all enjoy, and nothing spare;
But on their Mother Nature lay their care:
Why then should Man, the Lord of all below,   10
Such troubles chuse to know
As none of all his Subjects undergo?

Hark, hark, the Waters fall, fall, fall;
And with a Murmuring sound
Dash, dash, upon the ground,   15
To gentle slumbers call.

After the Song two Spaniards *arise and Dance a* Saraband *with*

0.1 *discovered . . . .*] Q1–3; discovered a Fountaine spouting
in it, Indian rarities round about. Vasquez, Pizarro and other
Spaniards lying carelessly disarm'd, two Spaniards dancing a Sara-
brand at the end of which Guyomar enters and ere they can recover
their Swords seizes them. MS
154 *Fantastique*] influenced by the imagination.
1–16 *SONG*] See the introduction to this play for additional
lines found in a manuscript miscellany.
5 *And . . . pursue*] Dryden answered criticism of this line by citing
its source in *Aeneid*, XI, 695 (Preface to *Tyrannic Love*, noted by
Loftis).

Castanieta's: *at the end of which* Guyomar *and his* Indian's *enter, and e're the* Spaniards *can recover their Swords, seize them.*

Guyomar. Those whome you tooke without in triumph bring,
But see these straight conducted to the King.
Pizarro. Vasquez, what now remaines in these extreams?
20   *Vasquez.* Only to wake us from our Golden dreames.
Pizarro. Since by our shamefull Conduct we have lost
Freedom, wealth, honour, which we vallue most,
I wish they would our Lives a period give:
They live too long who happines outlive.
                        Spaniards *are led out.*
25   *1. Indian.* See, Sir, how quickly your successe is spread:
The King comes marching in the Armyes head.

       Enter Montezuma, Alibech, Odmar *discontented.*

Montezuma. Now all the Gods reward and bless my Sonne:
                         Imbracing.
Thou hast this day thy Father's youth out done.
Alibech. Just Heav'n all happiness upon him Show're,
30   Till it confesse it's Will beyond it's power.
Guyomar. The Heav'ns are kind, the Gods propitious be,
I only doubt a mortall deitie:
I neither fought for conquest, nor for fame,
Your Love alone can recompence my flame.
35   *Alibech.* I gave my Love to the most brave in Warre;
But that the King must Judge.
Montezuma.   Tis *Guyomar.*
          Souldjers shout, A Guyomar, *&c.*
Montezuma. This day your Nuptialls wee will celebrate;
But guard these haughty Captives till their fate:
Odmar, this night to keepe them be youre care,
40   To morrow for their Sacrifice prepare.
Alibech. Blott not your Conquest with your cruelty.
Montezuma. Fate saies wee are not safe unlesse they dy:
The Spirit that foretold this happy day,
Bid mee use caution, and avoid delay:
45   Posteritie be juster to my fame,
Nor call it murder, when each private man
In his defence may justly doe the same:

30.2 *and sees it*] MS; *omit* Q1–3

16.2 *Castanieta's*] i.e., castanets.
23 *period*] end.
36.1 *A Guyomar*] a war cry.

But private persons more then Monarchs can.
All weigh our Acts: and what ere seems unjust,
Impute not to necessitie, but Lust.   50
    Exeunt Montezuma, Guyomar, *and* Alibech.
                    [*Solus.*]
Odmar. Lost and undone! hee had my Father's voice!
And *Alibech* seem'd pleas'd with her new choice:
Alas, it was not new! too late I see,
Since one shee hated, that it must be mee.
    ——— I feel a strange temptation in my Will   55
To doe an action great at once and ill:
Vertue ill-treated, from my soule is fledd;
I by Revenge and Love am wholly ledd.
Yet Conscience would against my rage rebell ———
    ——— Conscience, the foolish pride of doeing well!   60
Sinke Empire, Father perish, Brother fall,
Revenge does more then Recompence you all.
    ——— Conduct the Prisners in. ———

        Enter Vasquez, Pizarro.

Spaniards you see your owne deplor'd estate:
What dare you doe to reconcile your fate?   65
Vasquez. All that dispaire, with Courage Joyn'd, can doe.
Odmar. An easie Way to Victory I'll show:
When all are buried in their sleep or Joy,
I'll give you Armes, burne, ravish, and destroy;
For my owne share one beautie I designe,   70
Engage your honours that shee shall be mine.
Pizarro. I gladly Sweare.
Vasquez.   And I; but I request
That in returne, one, who has touch'd my breast,
Whose name I know not, may be giv'n to mee.
Odmar. Spaniard 'tis Just; shee's yours who ere shee be.   75
Vasquez. The night comes on: if fortune bless the bold
I shall possesse the beautie.
Pizarro.   I the Gold.
                  Exeunt omnes.

[ACT IV.] Scene 4

A Prison.

Cortez discover'd bound, Almeria *talking with him.*

Almeria. I come not now youre Constancy to prove,
You may beleive me, when I say I love.

68 *buried in their sleep*] See III.i.94.

81

Cortez. You have too well instructed mee before
  In your Intentions to beleive you more.
5 *Almeria.* I'm Justly plagu'd by this your unbeleife,
  And am my selfe the cause of my owne greife:
  But to begg Love! I cannot stoop so low;
  It is enough that you my passion know:
  Tis in your Choice; Love mee, or love mee not,
10   I have not yet my Brother's death forgott.
                    Lays hold on the Dagger.
Cortez. You menace me, and Court me in a breath:
  Your *Cupid* looks as dreadfully as death.
Almeria. Youre hopes, without, are vannish'd into smoake:
  Youre Captaines taken, and your Armies broke.
15 *Cortez.* In vaine you urge mee with my miseries:
  When fortune falls, high Courages can rise.
  Now should I change my Love, it would appeare
  Not the effect of Gratitude, but feare.
Almeria. I'll to the King, and make it my request,
20   Or my Command that you may be releas'd;
  And make you Judge, when I have set you free,
  Who best deserves your passion, I, or shee.
Cortez. You tempt my faith so Generous a way,
  As without guilt might constancy betray:
25   But I'm soe farre from meritting esteem,
  That If I Judge, I must my selfe Condemne;
  Yet having giv'n my worthles heart before,
  What I must ne're possesse, I will adore.
  Take my devotion then this humbler way;
30   Devotion is the Love which Heav'n we pay. ———
                    Kisses her hand.

        Enter Cydaria *and sees it.*

Cydaria. May I beleive my Eyes? what doe I see!
  Is this her hate to him, his love to mee?
  Tis in my breast shee sheathes her dagger now.
  (*To him*) False man! is this the faith? is this the Vow?
35 *Cortez.* What words, deare Saint, are these I heare you use?
  What faith, what vows are those which you accuse?
Cydaria. More cruell then the Tygar ore his spoile!
  And falser than the weeping Crocodile!
  Can you add vannitie to guilt, and take
40   A pride to heare the Conquests which you make?
  Go, publish youre renowne, let it be said
  You have a Woman, and that Lov'd, betray'd.
Cortez. With what Injustice is my faith accus'd?
  Life, freedome, Empire, I at once refus'd;

And would againe ten thousand times for you.   45
Almeria (aside). Sheel have too great content to find him
    true;
    And therefore since his love is not for mee,
    Ile help to make my Rivall's miserie. ———
    (*To him*) Spaniard, I never thought you false before:
    Can you at once two Mistresses adore?   50
    Keep the poore Soule no longer in Suspense,
    Your change is such as does not need defence.
Cortez. Riddles like these I cannot understand!
Almeria. Why should you Blush? shee saw you kisse my
    hand.
Cydaria. Feare not, I will (while your first Love's deny'd)   55
    Favour your shame, and turne my Eyes aside.
    My feeble hopes, in her deserts are lost:
    I neither can such power nor beauty boast:
    I have no tie upon you to be true
    But that which loosend yours, my love to you.   60
Cortez. Could you have heard my words?
Cydaria.   Alas, what needs
    To heare youre words, when I beheld your deeds?
Cortez. What shall I say! the fate of love is such,
    That still it sees too little or too much.
    That act of mine which does your passion move   65
    Was but a marke of my respect, not love.
Almeria. Vex not youre selfe excuses to prepare:
    For one you love not is not worth your care.
Cortez. Cruell *Almeria*, take that life you gave;
    Since you but worse destroy mee, while you save.   70
Cydaria. No, let mee dye, and I'll my claime resigne;
    For while I live, me thinks you should be mine.
Cortez. The bloodiest vengeance which she could pursue,
    Would be a trifle to my losse of you.
Cydaria. Your change was wise: for had shee been deny'd,   75
    A swift revenge had follow'd from her pride:
    You from my gentle Nature had no feares,
    All my Revenge is onely in my teares.
Cortez. Can you Imagine I so meane could prove,
    To save my Life by changeing of my Love?   80
Cydaria. Since death is that which nat'rally we shunn,
    You did no more then I, perhaps, had done.
Cortez. Make mee not doubt, faire Soule, your Constancy;
    You would have dy'd for Love, and so would I.
Almeria. You may beleive him; you have seen it prov'd.   85
Cortez. Can I not gaine beleife, how I have Lov'd?
    What can thy ends, malicious Beauty, be?

Can hee who kill'd thy Brother live for thee?
A noise of Clashing of Swords.
Vasquez within, Indians *against him.*
Vasquez (within). Yeild Slaves, or dy; our Swords shall
force our way.
Indians (within). Wee cannot, though o're powr'd, our trust
90   betray.
Cortez. Tis *Vasquez* voice, he brings mee liberty.
Vasquez (within). In spight of fate, I'll set my Generall free:
Now Victory for Us, the Towne's our owne.
Almeria. All hopes of safety and of Love are gone:
95   As when some dreadfull Thunder clap is nigh,
The winged fire shoots swiftly through the Sky,
Strikes and consumes ere scarce it does appeare,
And by the suddaine ill, prevents the feare:
Such is my State, in this amazeing woe;
100   It leaves no pow'r to thinke, much lesse to doe.
————*(aside)* But shall my Rivall live? shall shee
enjoy
That Love in peace I labour'd to destroy?
Cortez. Her looks grow Black as a Tempestuous Wind;
Some rageing thoughts are rowling in her mind.
105 *Almeria.* Rivall, I must your Jealousie remove,
You shall hereafter be at rest for Love.
Cydaria. Now you are kind.
Almeria.   Hee whom you love is true:
But hee shall never bee possest by you.
Draws her Dagger, and runs towards her.
Cortez. Hold, hold, ah Barbarous Woman! flye, oh
flye!
110 *Cydaria.* Ah pity, pity, is no succour nigh!
Cortez. Runne, runne behind mee, there you may be
sure,
While I have life I will youre life secure.
Cydaria gets behind him.
Almeria. On him, or thee, light vengeance any where:
She stabs and hurts him.
———— What have I done? I see his bloud appeare!
115 *Cydaria.* It streames, it streames, from every vitall part:
Was there no way but this to find his heart?
Almeria. Ah Cursed Woman! what was my designe!
This Weapon's point shall mix that bloud with mine!
Goes to stab her selfe, and being within his reach he
snatches the Dagger.
Cortez. Now neither life nor death are in your pow'r.
120 *Almeria.* Then sullenly I'le wait my fatall houre.

84

Enter Vasquez *and* Pizarro *with drawn Swords.*

Vasquez. Hee lives, hee lives.
Cortez.   Unfetter mee with speed;
  Vasquez, I see you troubled that I bleed:
  But tis not deep, our Army I can head.
Vasquez. You to a certaine Victory are ledd;
  Your men all arm'd, stand silently within: 125
  I with youre freedome, did the worke beginn.
Pizarro. What freinds wee have, and how we came so
      strong,
  Wee'l softly tell you as we march along.
Cortez (*to* Cydaria). In this safe place let me secure youre
      feare:
  No Clashing swords, no noise can enter here.   130
  Amidst our Armes as quiet you shall bee
  As Halcyons brooding on a Winter Sea.
Cydaria. Leave me not here alone, and full of fright,
  Amidst the terrours of a dreadfull night:
  You Judge, alas! my Courage by your owne,   135
  I never durst in darknesse be alone:
  I begg, I throw mee humbly at your feet. ———
Cortez. You must not goe, where you may dangers meet.
  Th'unruly Sword will no distinction make:
  And beautie will not there give wounds, but take.   140
Almeria. Then stay and take mee with you; though to be
  A Slave to waite upon youre victory.
  My heart unmov'd, can noise, and horror beare:
  Parting from you is all the death I feare.
Cortez. *Almeria,* tis enough I leave you free: 145
  You neither must stay here, nor goe with me.
Almeria. Then take my Life, that will my rest restore:
  Tis all I aske for saveing youres before.
Cortez. That were a barbarous returne of Love.
Almeria. Yet leaving it, you more Inhumane prove: 150
  In both extreames I some releife should find:
  Oh, either hate mee more, or be more kind!
Cortez (*to* Cydaria). Life of my Soule do not my absence
      mourne:
  But cheare your heart in hopes of my returne:
  Your noble Father's life, shall be my care;   155
  And both your Brothers I'm obliedg'd to spare.
Cydaria. Fate makes you deafe while I in vaine implore,
  My heart forebodes I nere shall see you more:
  I have but one request, when I am dead
  Lett not my Rivall to youre Love succeed.   160

Cortez. Fate will be kinder then your feares foretell;
Farwell my deare.
Cydaria.   A long and last Farwell!
—— So eager to imploy the cruell sword;
Can you not one, not one last looke afford?

165   *Cortez.* I melt to Womanish teares, and If I stay,
I find my Love my Courage will betray;
Yon Tow'r will keep you safe, but be so kind
To your owne life that none may entrance find.
Cydaria. Then lead mee there.   *He leads her.*

170   For this one minute of youre Company,
I goe me thinkes, with some content to dy.
      Exeunt Cortez, Vasquez, Pizarro, Cydaria.
                                Sola.
Almeria. Farwell, o too much lov'd! since lov'd in vaine!
What dismall fortune does for mee remaine!
Night and dispaire my fatall footsteps guide;

175   That chance may give the death, which he deny'd.
                                      Exit.

Cortez, Vasquez, Pizarro, *and* Spanniards, *returne againe.*

Cortez (to Pizarro). All I hold deare, I trust to youre defence;
Guard her, and on youre life, remove not hence.
                Exeunt Cortez, *and* Vasquez.
Pizarro. I'le venture that.
The Gods are good; I'le leave her to their care,

180   Steale from my post, and in the Plunder share.
                     Stalks off and Exit.

ACT V. Scene I

The Chamber Royall, an Indian Hammock *discoverd in it.*

Enter Odmar *with Soldjers.* Guyomar, Alibech, *bound.*

Odmar (to Alibech). Fate is more just then you to my desert,
And in this Act you blame, Heav'n takes my part.
Guyomar. Can there be Gods, and no revenge provide!
Odmar. The Gods are ever of the Conquering side:

5   Shee's now my Queen; the *Spaniards* have agreed
I to my Father's Empire shall succeed.
Alibech. How much I Crownes Contemn, I let thee see,
Chooseing the younger, and refuseing thee.
Guyomar. Were she ambitious, she'd disdaine to owne

10   The Pageant-Pomp of such a servile Throne:

1 *to* Alibech.] MṠ; *omit* Q1–3

86

A Throne which thou by Paraside dost gaine,
And by a base submission must retaine.
Alibech. I Love'd thee not before, but, *Odmar*, knowe
That now I hate thee, and despise thee too.
Odmar. With too much violence you crimes pursue, 15
  Which if I acted, twas for Love of you:
  This, if it teach not Love, may teach you feare:
  I brought not Sinne so farr, to stopp it here.
  Death in a Lover's mouth would sound but ill:
  But know I either must Enjoy, or Kill. 20
Alibech. Bestow, base man, thy Idle threats else where:
  My Mother's daughter knowes not how to feare. .
  Since, *Guyomar*, I must not be thy Bride,
  Death shall enjoy what is to thee deny'd.
Odmar. Then take thy wish. 25
Guyomar. Hold *Odmar*, hold:
  My right in *Alibech* I will resigne;
  Rather then see her dy, I'll see her thine.
Alibech. In vaine thou would'st resigne, for I will bee,
  Ev'n when thou leav'st mee, constant still to thee: 30
  That shall not save my life: wilt thou appeare
  Fearefull for her who for her selfe wants feare?
Odmar (*aside*). Her love to him shows mee a surer way:
  I by her Love, her virtue must betray. ———
  (*To her*) Since, *Alibech*, you are so true a Wife; 35
  Tis in youre pow'r to save your husband's life.
  The Gods, by mee, your Love and virtue try:
  For both will suffer if you let him dy.
Alibech. I never can beleive you will proceed
  To such a Black and Execrable deed. 40
Odmar. I only threatn'd you; but could not prove
  So much a Foole, to murder what I love:
  But in his death, I some advantage see:
  Worse then it is, I'me sure it cannot be.
  If you consent, you with that gentle breath 45
  Preserve his life: if not, behold his death. ———
                    Holds his Sword to his breast.
Alibech. What shall I doe!
Guyomar.   What, are your thoughts at strife
  About a Ransome to preserve my life?
  Though to save yours I did my Interest give,
  Thinke not when you were his I meant to live. 50
Alibech (*to* Odmar). O let him be preserv'd by any way:

49 *Interest*] concern, with a play on the financial sense of "interest,"
associated with "Ransome" in line 48.

87

But name not the fowle price which I must pay.
Odmar. You would and would not, I'le no longer stay.
                                    Offers again to Kill him.
Alibech. I yeild, I yeild, but yet ere I am ill,
55   An innocent desire I would fulfill:
        With *Guyomar* I one chast kisse would leave,
        The first and last he ever can receive.
Odmar. Have what you aske: that minute you agree
        To my desires, your husband shall be free.
                        They unbind her, she goes to her Husband.
60 *Guyomar.* No, *Alibech*, we never must embrace:
                                    He turns from her.
        Your guilty kindnesse why do you misplace?
        Tis meant to him; hee is your private Choice:
        I was made yours but by the publique voice.
        And now you leave me, with a poore pretence
65   That youre ill Act is for my life's defence.,
Alibech. Since there remaines no other means to try,
        Think I am false; I cannot see you dy.
Guyomar. To give for mee both life and honour too
        Is more perhapps then I could give for you.
70   You have done much to cure my Jealousie,
        But cannot perfect it unlesse both dy:
        For since both cannot live, who stays behind
        Must be thought fearfull, or, what's worse, unkind.
Alibech. I never could propose that death you choose;
                                    Embracing him.
75   But am like you, too Jealous to refuse.
        Together dyeing, we together showe
        That both did pay that faith which both did owe.
Odmar. It then remaines I act my owne designe:
        Have you your wills, but I will first have mine.
80   Assist me Souldjers.
                        They go to bind her, she cries out.

Enter Vasquez, *two* Spaniards.

Vasquez. Hold, *Odmar*, hold! I come in happy time
        To hinder my misfortune, and your cryme.
Odmar. You ill returne the kindnesse I have showne.
Vasquez. Indian, I say dessist.

54 *ill*] evil as suffered or endured; in misfortune.
73 *unkind*] ungenerous as a mistress, and possibly contrary to the
nature of a true lover.
75 *Jealous*] perhaps used as in biblical language where it is attri-
buted to God, who will not endure the love of His creatures to be
transferred from Him, or divided with Him.

Odmar.   *Spaniard*, be gone.
Vasquez. This Lady I did for my selfe designe: 85
   Dare you attempt her honour who is mine?
Odmar. You'r much mistaken; this is shee whom I
   Did with my Father's losse, and Country's buy:
   Shee whom your promise did to mee convey,
   When all things else were made your common prey.   90
Vasquez. That promise made excepted one for mee;
   One whom I still reserv'd, and this is shee.
Odmar. This is not shee, you cannot be so base.
Vasquez. I Love too deeply to mistake the face:
   The Vanquisht must receive the Victor's Laws.   95
Odmar. If I am vanquisht I my selfe am cause.
Vasquez. Then thanke your selfe for what you undergoe.
Odmar. Thus Lawlesse might does Justice overthrow.
Vasquez. Traytors, like you, should never Justice name.
Odmar. You owe your Triumphs to that Traytor's shame.   100
   But to your Generall I'le my right referre.
Vasquez. Hee never will protect a Ravisher:
   His generous heart will soon decide our strife;
   Hee to your Brother will restore his Wife.
   It rests wee two our clayme in Combate try,   105
   And that with this faire Prize, the victor fly.
Odmar. Make hast,
   I cannot suffer to be long perplext:
   Conquest is my First wish, and death my next.
                    They fight, the Spaniards *and* Indjans *fight.*
Alibech. The Gods the wicked by themselves orethrow: 110
   All fight against us now, and for Us too!
                              Unbinds her Husband.
   The two Spaniards *and three* Indians *kill each other,*
      Vasquez *kills* Odmar, Guyomar *runs to his Brother's*
                                                      sword.
Vasquez (to Alibech*).* Now you are mine; my greatest foe
   is slayne.
Guyomar. A greater still to vanquish does remaine.
Vasquez. Another yet!
   The wounds I make but sow new Enemies,   115
   Which from their blood, like Earth borne brethren rise.
Guyomar. Spaniard take breath: some respit I'le afford,
   My Cause is more advantage then your sword.
Vasquez. Thou art so brave ——— could it with honour be,
   I'de seeke thy freindship, more then Victory.   120

105 *rests*] remains to be done.
115-16 *The wounds . . . rise*] referring to the legend of Cadmus
(Ovid, *Metamorphoses*, III, 101-10).

Guyomar. Freindshipp with him whose hand did *Odmar*
    kill!
Base as he was, he was my Brother Still:
And since his bloud has wash'd away his guilt,
Nature askes thine for that which thou hast spilt.
    They fight a litle and breath, Alibech *takes up a Sword*
                                      and comes on.
125   *Alibech.* My weakenesse may help somthing in the strife.
Guyomar. Kill not my Honour to preserve my life:
                                          Staying her.
Rather then by thy aid I'll Conquest gaine,
Without defence I poorely will be slaine.
        She goes back, they fight againe, Vasquez *falls.*
Guyomar. Now, *Spaniard,* beg thy life and thou shalt live.
Vasquez. 'Twere vain to aske thee, what thou canst not
130   give:
My breath goes out, and I am now no more;
Yet her I lov'd, in death I will adore.   *Dyes.*
Guyomar. Come, *Alibech,* let us from hence remove:
This is a night of Horrour, not of Love.
135   From every part I heare a dreadfull noise:
The Vanquish'd Crying, and the Victor's Joyes.
I'll to my Father's aid, and Countryes fly,
And succour both, or in their ruine dy.
                                          Exeunt.

[ACT V.] Scene 2
A Prison.

Montezuma, Indian High Priest, *bound.* Pizarro,
Spanniards *with swords drawn,* a Christian Priest.

Pizarro. Thou has not yet discover'd all thy store.
Montezuma. I neither can nor will discover more:
    The Gods will punnish you if they be Just;
    The Gods will plague your Sacrilegious lust.
Christian Priest. Marke how this Impious Heathen Justifies
    His owne false Gods, and our true God denyes:
    How wickedly he has refus'd his wealth,
    And hid his Gold from Christian hands, by Stealth!
    Downe with him, kill him, meritt Heav'n thereby.
Indian High Priest. Can Heav'n be Author of such Cruelty?
Pizarro. Since neither threats nor kindnesse will prevaile,
    Wee must by other meanes your minds assayle;
    Fasten the Engines; stretch 'um at their length,
    And pull the straightned Cords with all your strength.
        They fasten them to the Rack, and then pull them.

Montezuma. The Gods, who made mee once a King, shall
    knowe   15
  I still am worthy to Continnue soe:
  Though now the Subject of youre Tyranny,
  I'll plague you worse then you can punish mee.
  Know I have gold, which you shall never find,
  No pains, no tortures shall unlock my mind.   20
Christian Priest. Pull harder yet; he does not feele the Rack.
Montezuma. Pull till my veines breake, and my Sinews
  crack.
Indian High Priest. When will you end your Barb'rous
  Cruelty?
  I begg not to escape, I begg to dye.
Montezuma. Shame on thy Priesthood that such pray'rs can
  bring: 25
  Is it not brave to suffer with thy King?
  When Monarchs suffer, Gods themselves beare part;
  Then well may'st thou who but my Vassall ar't:
  I charge thee dare not groane, nor shew one signe,
  Thou at thy torments dost the least repine.   30
Indian High Priest. You tooke an Oath when you receiv'd
  your Crowne,
  The Heav'ns should pow'r their usuall blessings down;
  The Sun should shine, the Earth its fruits produce,
  And nought be wanting to youre Subjects use:
  Yet wee with famine were opprest, and now   35
  Must to the Yoake of cruell Masters bow.
Montezuma. If those above, who made the World, could
  bee
  Forgettfull of it, why then blam'st thou mee?
Christian Priest. Those paines, o Prince, thou suffer'st now
  are light
  Compar'd to those, which when thy Soule takes flight, 40
  Immortall, Endlesse, thou must then endure:
  Which death begins, and time can never cure.
Montezuma. Thou art deceiv'd: for whensoere I dy,
  The Sunne my Father beares my Soule on high:
  Hee lets mee downe a beame, and mounted there, 45
  He drawes it back, and pulls mee through the Ayre:
  I in the Eastern parts, and riseing skye,
  You in Heav'n's downfall, and the West must ly.
Christian Priest. Fond man! by Heathen Ignorance misled!
  Thy Soule destroyeing when thy Bodies dead: 50

39–97] See John Loftis' commentary (*Works*, IX, 311–14) for a discussion of natural religion here debated.

Change yet thy faith, and buy eternall rest.
Indian High Priest. Dy in your owne: for our beleife is best.
Montezuma. In seeking happinesse, you both agree,
　　But in the search, the paths soe diff'rent bee,
55　　That all Religions with each other Fight,
　　While only one can lead Us in the right.
　　But till that one hath some more certaine marke,
　　Poor humane kind must wander in the darke;
　　And suffer paines, Eternally below,
60　　For that, which here, wee cannot come to Knowe.
Christian Priest. That which wee Worshipp, and which you
　　beleive,
　　From nature's Common hand wee both receive:
　　All under various names, Adore and Love
　　One power Immense, which ever rules above.
65　　Vice to abhorre, and virtue to pursue,
　　Is both beleiv'd, and taught, by Us, and you.
　　But here our Worship takes another way. ———
Montezuma. Where both agree, tis there most safe to stay:
　　For what's more vaine then publique light to Shunn,
70　　And sett up Tapers while wee see the Sunn?
Christian Priest. Though Nature teaches whom we should
　　Adore,
　　By Heav'nly Beams we still discover more.
Montezuma. Or this must be enough, or to Mankind
　　One equal way to Bliss is not design'd.
75　　For though some more may know, and some know less,
　　Yet all must know enough for happiness.
Christian Priest. If in this middle way you still pretend
　　To stay, your Journey never will have end.
Montezuma. Howe're, 'tis better in the midst to stay,
80　　Then wander farther in uncertain way.
Christian Priest. But wee by Martyrdome our faith
　　avow.
Montezuma. You do no more, then I for ours do now.
　　To prove Religion true
　　If either Witt or suffrings would suffice,
85　　All Faiths afford the Constant and the Wise.
　　And yet ev'n they, by Education sway'd,
　　In age defend what Infancy obey'd.
Christian Priest. Since age by erring Childhood is misledd,
　　Referr your selfe to oure unerring head.
90 *Montezuma.* Man and not erre! what Reason can you give?
Christian Priest. Renounce that carnall Reason, and beleive.
Montezuma. The light of Nature should I thus betray,
　　T'were to winke hard that I might see the day.

Christian Priest. Condemn not yet the way you do not
  know;
  I'le make your reason judge what way to go.   95
Montezuma. Tis much too late for me new ways to take,
  Who have but one short step of life to make.
Pizarro. Increase their paines, the Cords are yet too slack.
Christian Priest. I must by force Convert him on the Rack.
Indian High Priest. I faint away, and find I can noe more: 100
  Give leave, O King, I may reveale your store,
  And free my self from paines I cannot beare.
Montezuma. Think'st thou I lye on Bedds of Roses heere,
  Or in a wanton Bath stretch'd at my ease?
  Dy, Slave, and with thee dy such thoughts as these.   105
        High Priest *turnes aside and dyes.*

Enter Cortez *attended by* Spaniards, *he speaks entring.*

Cortez. On pain of death kill none but those who fight;
  I much repent me of this bloody night:
  Slaughter grows murder when it goes too far,
  And makes a Massacre what was a War:
  Sheath all your weapons and in silence move,   110
  Tis sacred here to Beauty and to Love.
  Ha —————   *Sees* Montezuma.
  What dismall sight is this, which takes from mee
  All the delight that waits on Victory!
        Runns to take him off the Rack.
  Make hast! how now, Religion, doe you frowne?   115
  Hast, holy Avarice, and helpe him downe.
  Ah! Father! Father! what do I endure
                          Imbracing Montezuma.
  To see these Wounds my pitty cannot cure!
Montezuma. Am I so low, that you should pitty bring,
  And give an Infant's comfort to a King!   120
  Aske these, If I have once unmanly groan'd;
  Or ought have done deserveing to be moan'd.
Cortez (*to* Pizarro). Did I not Charge thou should'st not stir
    from hence?
  But Martiall Law shall punish thy offence.
  (*To the* Christian Priest) And you,   125
  Who sawcily, teach Monarchs to obey,
  And the Wide world in narrow Cloysters sway;
  Set up by Kings as humble Aids of pow'r,
  You that which bred you, Viper like devoure,

---

101 your] MS; thy Q1-3   113 What] Q6; *Cort.* What MS,
Q1-5

93

     You Enemyes of Crownes!

130 *Christian Priest.*   Come let's away,

    Wee but provoke his fury by oure stay.

   Cortez. If this go free, farewel that discipline

    Which did in *Spanish* Camps severely shine:

    Accursed Gold, 'tis thou hast caus'd these crimes;

135   Thou turn'st our Steel against thy Parent climes!

    And into *Spain* wilt fatally be brought,

    Since with the price of Blood thou here art bought.

       Exeunt [Christian] Priest *and* Pizarro.

       Cortez *kneels by* Montezuma *and weeps.*

   Cortez. Can you forget those Crimes they did Com-

    mitt?

   Montezuma. I'll doe what for my Dignity is fitt:

140   Rise, Sir, I'm satisfi'd the fault was their's:

    Trust mee you make me weep to see your teares:

    Must I cheere you!

   Cortez.   Ah Heav'ns!

   Montezuma.   You'r much too blame;

    Youre greife is cruell, for it shews my Shame,

    Does my lost Crown to my Remembrance bring:

145   But weep not you, and I'll be still a King.

    You have forgott that I your death design'd,

    To satisfie the proud *Almeria's* mind:

    You who preserv'd my life, I doom'd to dy.

   Cortez. Your Love did that, and not youre Cruelty.

      Enter a Spaniard.

150 *Spaniard.* Prince *Guyomar* the Combate still maintains,

    Our men retreate, and he their ground regaines:

    But once Encourag'd by our Generall's sight,

    Wee boldly should renew the doubtfull fight.

   Cortez (to Montezuma). Remove not hence, you shall not

    long attend:

155   I'll aid my Souldjers, yet preserve my freind.

        Exit Cortez, *&c.*

   Montezuma. Excellent Man!

    But I, by living, poorely take the way

    To Injure goodnes, which I cannot pay.

      Enter Almeria.

129 *Viper like devoure*] the ancient belief that vipers ate their parents.

135 *climes*] tracts or regions of the earth.

Almeria. Ruinn and death runn Arm'd through every
    Street;
    And yet that fate I seeke I cannot meet: 160
    What Guards misfortunes are and misery!
    Death that strikes all, yet seems afraid of mee.
Montezuma. Almeria's here! oh turne away your face!
    Must you be Wittnesse too of my disgrace?
Almeria. I am not that *Almeria* whom you knew,   165
    But want that pittie I deny'd to you:
    Your Conquerour, alas! has vanquish't mee!
    But he refuses his owne Victory:
    While all are captives, in your Conquer'd State,
    I find a wretched freedome in his hate.   170
Montezuma. Couldst thou thy love on one who scorn'd
    thee loose?
    Hee saw not with my Eyes who could refuse:
    Him who could prove so much unkind to thee,
    I ne'er will suffer to be kind to mee.
Almeria. I am content in death to share your fate;   175
    And dy for him I Love with him I hate.
Montezuma. What shall I do in this perplexing straight!
    My tortur'd Limbs refuse to beare my weight:
            Endeavoring to walk and not being able.
    I cannot goe to death to set mee free:
    Death must be kind, and come him selfe to mee.   180
Almeria. I've thought upon't! I have affaires below,
               Almeria musing.
    Which I must needs dispatch before I goe:
    (*To him*) Sir, I have found a place where you may
    bee
    (Though not preserv'd) yet like a King dy free:
    The Generall left you'r Daughter in the Tow'r,   185
    We may a while resist the *Spaniards* pow'r,
    If *Guyomar* prevaile, ——
Montezuma.   Make hast and call;
    Shee'll heare youre voice, and answer from the Wall.
Almeria. My voice she knowes and feares, but use your
    owne,
    And to gaine entrance, feigne you are alone.   190
               Almeria steps behind.
Montezuma. Cydaria!
Almeria.   Lowder.
Montezuma.   Daughter!
Almeria.   Lowder yet.
Montezuma. Thou canst not, sure, thy Father's voice for-
    gett?

> *He knocks at the door, at last* Cydaria *lookes over the* Zoty.
> *Cydaria.* Since my Love went, I have been frighted so,
> With dismall groanes, and noises from below,
195 I durst not send my Eyes abroad, for feare
> Of seeing dangers, which I yet but heare.
> *Montezuma. Cydaria*!
> *Cydaria.* Sure tis my Father calls.
> *Montezuma.*   Deare childe make hast,
> All hope of succour, but from thee is past:
200 As when upon the Sands the Traveller
> Sees the high Sea come Rowling from afarre,
> The Land grow short, he mends his weary pace,
> While death behind him cover's all the place:
> Soe I by swift misfortunes am pursu'd, ·
205 Which on each other, are like Waves, renew'd.
> *Cydaria.* Are you alone?
>   *Here* Almeria *beckens earnestly to him.*
> *Montezuma.*   I am.
> *Cydaria.*   I'll straight descend;
> Heav'n did you here for both our safeties send.
>   Cydaria *descends and opens the doore,* Almeria *rushes*
>   *betwixt with* Montezuma.
> *Cydaria. Almeria* here! then I am lost againe!
>   *Both thrust.*
> *Almeria.* Yeild to my strength, you struggle but in vaine:
210 Make hast, and shutt, Our Enemies appeare.
>   Cortez *and* Spaniards *appeare at the other end.*
> *Cydaria.* Then doe you enter, and let mee stay here.
>   *As she speakes,* Almeria *over pow'rs her, thrusts her in,*
>   *and shutts.*
> *Cortez.* Sure I both heard her voice, and saw her face;
> Shee's like a vision vanish'd from the place:
> Too late I find my absence was too long;
215 My hopes grow sickly, and my feares grow strong.
>   *Hee knocks a little, then* Montezuma, Cydaria, Almeria
>   *appeare above.*

192.1 Zoty Q1(c); Balcone MS, Q1(u)–3

192.1 *Zoty*] i.e., azotea, a flat roof. *Balcone,* the reading in the MS and uncorrected state of Q1 explains the staging of the scene.

200–205 *As . . . renew'd*] In 1679 Dryden took exception to this grand epic simile. "My Indian potentate was well skilled in the sea for an inland prince, and well improved since the first act, when he sent his son to discover it. The image had not been amiss from another man, at another time: . . . he destroyed the concernment which the audience might otherwise have had for him; for they could not think the danger near when he had the leisure to invent a simile" (*Essays,* I, 257).

Almeria. Looke up, Looke up, and see if you can knowe
  Those whom, in vaine, you thinke to find below.
Cydaria. Looke up and see *Cydaria's* lost estate.
Montezuma. And cast one looke on *Montezuma's* fate.
Cortez. Speake not such dismall words as wound my eare: 220
  Nor name death to mee, when *Cydaria's* there.
  Dispaire not, Sir, who knowes but Conquering *Spaine*
  May part of what you lost, restore againe?
Montezuma. No, *Spaniard,* know, he who to Empire borne,
  Lives to be lesse, deserves the Victor's scorne: 225
  Kings and their Crownes have but one destiny:
  Pow'r is their Life, when that expires they dy.
Cydaria. What dreadfull words are these?
Montezuma.   Name life no more;
  Tis now a torture worse, then all I bore:
  I'll not be brib'd to suffer Life, but dy   230
  In spight of your Mistaken Clemency.
  I was your Slave, and I was us'd like one;
  The Shame Continues when the paine is gone:
  But I'm a King while this is in my hand,   *His sword.*
  He wants no Subjects who can death Command: 235
  You should have ty'd him upp, t'have Conquerd mee,
  But hee's still mine, and thus he setts me free.
                        Stabs himselfe.
Cydaria. Oh my deare Father!
Cortez.   Hast, breake ope the doore.
Almeria. When that is forc'd, there yet remaine two more.
    The Souldiers break open the first door, and go in.
  Wee shall have time enough to take our way,   240
  Ere any can our fatall Journey stay.
Montezuma. Already mine is past: O Pow'rs divine
  Take my last thankes; no longer I repine:
  I might have Liv'd, my owne mishapps to mourne,
  While some would pitty mee, but more would scorne!   245
  For pittie only on fresh Objects stayes:
  But with the tædious sight of Woes, decayes.
  Still less and less my boyling Spirits flow;
  And I grow stiffe, as Cooling mettalls doe:
  Farwell *Almeria* ——   *Dyes.*
Cydaria.   Hee's gone, hee's gone,   250
  And leaves poore me defenceless here alone.
Almeria. You shall not long be so: prepare to dy,
  That you may beare youre Father Company.
Cydaria. O name not death to me! you fright mee soe,
  That with the feare I shall prevent the Blow: 255
  I know your mercies more, then to destroy

A thing so young, so Innocent, as I.

Cortez. Whence can proceed thy cruell thirst of blood,
Ah barb'rous Woman! Woman? that's too good,

260   Too mild for thee: ther's pitty in that name,
But thou hast lost thy pitty, with thy shame.

Almeria. Your Cruell Words have peirc'd me to the heart;
But on my Rivall I'll Revenge my Smart.

                        Going to kill her.

Cortez. Oh stay your hand! and to redeeme my fault

265   I'll speake the kindest Words
That tongue ere utter'd, or that heart ere thought.
Deare ——— Lovely ——— Sweet ———

Almeria.   This but offends mee more,
You Act youre kindness on *Cydaria's* Score.

Cydaria. For his deare Sake let mee my Life receive.

270 *Almeria.* Foole, for his sake alone, you must not Live:
Revenge is now my Joy; hee's not for mee,
And I'll make sure hee ne'r shall be for thee.

Cydaria. But what's my cryme?

Almeria.   Tis loving where I Love.

Cydaria. Your owne example does my Act aprove.

275 *Almeria.* Tis such a fault I never can forgive.

Cydaria. How can I mend, unlesse you let mee Live?
I yet am tender, young, and full of feare,
And dare not dy, but faine would tarry here.

Cortez. If blood you seek, I will my owne resigne:

280   O spare her Life, and in Exchange take mine.

Almeria. The Love you show but hasts her death the more.

Cortez. I'll runn, and help to force the inner doore.

                      Is going in hast.

Almeria. Stay, *Spaniard*, stay, depart not from my Eyes:
That moment that I loose your sight, she dyes.

285   To looke on you Ile grant a short repreive.

Cortez. Oh make your guift more full, and let her live:
I dare not goe; and yet how dare I stay!
Her I would save, I murder either Way.

Cydaria. Can you be so hard hearted, to destroy

290   My ripning hopes, that are so neare to Joy?
I Just approach to all I would possesse:
Death only stands twixt mee and happinesse.

Almeria. Your Father, with his Life, has lost his Throne:
Youre Countryes freedome and Renoune is gone.

295   Honour requires your death: you must obey.

Cydaria. Do you dy first; and shew mee then the way.

263.1 *Going to kill her.*] MS; *omit* Q1-3

98

Almeria. Should you not follow, my Revenge were Lost.
Cydaria. Then rise againe, and fright mee with your Ghost.
Almeria. I will not trust to that, since death I choose,
  I'll not leave you that Life which I refuse: 300
  If death's a paine, it is not lesse to mee;
  And if tis nothing, tis no more to thee.
  But harke! the noise increases from behind,
  They'r neare, and may prevent what I design'd:
  Take there a Rivall's guift ——   *Stabs her.*   305
Cortez. Perdition seize thee for soe black a deed.
Almeria. Blame not an Act which did from Love proceed:
  I'le thus Revenge thee with this fatall Blow;
                Stabs her selfe.
  Stand faire, and let my heart blood on thee flow.
          Cortez *here goes in as to her.*
Cydaria. Stay life, and keep me in the cheerfull light;   310
  Death is too black, and dwells in too much night.
  Thou leav'st mee, Life, but Love supplyes thy part,
  And keeps mee warme by lingring in my heart:
  Yet dyeing for him, I thy Clayme remove;
  How deare it Costs to Conquer in my Love!   315
  Now strike: that thought, I hope, will arme my breast.
Almeria. Ah, with what diffring passions am I prest!
Cydaria. Death, when farre off, did terrible appeare;
  But looks lesse dreadfull as he comes more nere.
Almeria. O Rivall! I have lost the pow'r to kill!   320
  Strength has forsooke my arme, and Rage my Will:
  I must surmount that Love which thou hast shown:
  Dying for him is due to mee alone.
  Thy weaknesse shall not boast the victory,
  Now thou shalt Live, and dead I'le Conquer thee: 325
               Enter Souldjers.
  Soldjers assist mee downe.
   Exeunt from above led by Soldjers, *and enter both led by*
               Cortez.
Cortez (*to* Cydaria). Is there noe danger then?
Cydaria.   You need not feare
  My wound, I cannot dy when you are neare.
Cortez (*to* Almeria). You for my sake, Life to *Cydaria* give:
  And I could dy for you, if you might Live.   330
Almeria. Enough, I dy content, now you are kind;
  Kill'd in my Limbes, reviving in my mind:
  Come neare, *Cydaria*, and forgive my Cryme.
           Cydaria *starts back.*

307 which] MS; that Q1–3   325.1 *Enter* Souldjers.] MS; *omit*
Q1–3

335
You need not feare my rage a Second time:
Ile bath youre wound in teares for my offence:
That hand which made it make this Recompence.
    Ready to joyne their hands, [then] *shoves her back.*
I would have Joyn'd you, but my heart's too high:
You will, too soone, possesse him when I dye.
Cortez. Shee faints, o softly sett her downe.
Almeria.   Tis past!

340
In thy Lov'd bosome let mee breath my Last.
Here in this one short moment that I Live,
I have what ere the longest life could give.   *Dies.*
Cortez. Farewell thou Generous Maid: ev'n victory
Glad as it is, must lend some teares to thee:

345
(*To* Cydaria) Many I dare not shedd, least you beleive
I Joy in you less then for her I greive.
Cydaria. But are you sure shee's dead?
I must embrace you fast, before I know
Whether my Life be yet secure or no:

350
Some other houre I will to teares allow;
But haveing you, can shew no sorrow now.
                     Both kissing.

Enter Guyomar *and* Alibech *bound, with* Souldjers.

Cortez. Prince *Guyomar* in bonds! o freindshipp's shame!
It makes me blush to owne a Victor's name.
              Unbinds him, and Cydaria, Alibech.
Cydaria. See *Alibech, Almeria* lyes there!

355
But doe not thinke twas I that murther'd her.
          Alibech *kneeles and kisses her Dead Sister.*
Cortez (*to* Guyomar). Live and enjoy more then your
   Conquerour:
Take all my Love, and share in all my Pow'r.
Guyomar. Thinke mee not proudly rude if I forsake
Those Guifts I cannot with my honour take:

360
I for my Country fought, and would againe,
Had I yet Left a Country to mainteyne:
But since the Gods decreed it other wise,
I never will on its deare ruines rise.
Alibech. Of all your goodnesse Leaves to our dispose,

365
Our Liberty's the onely gift wee choose:

---

335 wound] MS; wounds Q1–3   336.1 *shoves her back*] MS;
omit Q1–3   351.1 *Both kissing.*] MS; *omit* Q1–3   353.1 *and*]
MS; *omit* Q1–3

353.1 *Unbinds*] "It has not been said that Cydaria was bound.
If it be not a mistaken direction the binding must have been
implied in Almeria's 'overpowering' her," line 211 (Saintsbury).

Absence alone can make oure Sorrowes less;
And not to see what wee can nere redresse.
Guyomar. Northward, beyond the Mountaines we will goe,
  Where Rocks ly Cover'd with Eternall Snow;
  Thinne herbage in the plaines, and fruitless feilds,   370
  The Sand noe Gold, the myne no Silver yeilds:
  There Love and freedome wee'l in peace enjoy;
  Noe *Spaniards* will that Colony destroy.
  Wee to our selves, will all our wishes grant;
  And nothing Coveting, can nothing want.   375
Cortez. First your Great Father's funerall Pomp provide:
  That done, in Peace your Generous Exiles guide.
  While I Lowd thanks pay to the Pow'rs above,
  Thus doubly blest, with Conquest, and with Love.
                                                    Exeunt.
                    FINIS

377 *Generous*] noble-minded, noble in spirit.

101

Epilogue

By a MERCURY

To all and singular in this full meeting,
Ladies and Gallants, *Phœbus* sends me greeting.
To all his Sons by what e're Title known,
Whether of Court, of Coffee-house, or Town;
5   From his most mighty Sons, whose confidence
Is plac'd in lofty sound, and humble sence,
Ev'n to his little Infants of the Time
Who Write new Songs, and trust in Tune and Rhyme.
Be't known that *Phœbus* (being daily griev'd
10 To see good Plays condemn'd, and bad receiv'd,)
Ordains your judgement upon every Cause,
Henceforth be limited by wholesome Laws.
He first thinks fit no Sonnettier advance
His censure, farther then the Song or Dance.
15 Your Wit Burlesque may one step higher climb,
And in his sphere may judge all Doggrel Rhyme:
All proves, and moves, and Loves, and Honours too:
All that appears high sence, and scarce is low.
As for the Coffee-wits he says not much,
20 Their proper bus'ness is to Damn the *Dutch*:
For the great *Dons* of Wit ———
Phœbus gives them full priviledge alone
To Damn all others, and cry up their own.
Last, for the Ladies, 'tis *Apollo's* will,
25 They should have pow'r to save, but not to kill:
For Love and He long since have thought it fit
Wit live by Beauty, Beauty raign by Wit.

20 *Damn the Dutch*] with whom England was at war.

PRESS VARIANTS
Q1, 1667

Sheet B (outer forme)
Corrected: CSmH, CtY, MB, MH, TxU
Uncorrected: CLUC, DFo

Sig. B3
I.ii.75 shown,] shown

Sheet D (outer forme)
Corrected: CLUC, CSmH, DFo, MB, MH, TxU
Uncorrected: CtY

Sig. D1
II.ii.0.1 Alibech] Alibeck
Sig. D3
II.ii.124 on] in

Sheet E (inner forme)
Corrected: CLUC, CSmH, Cty, DFo
Uncorrected: MB, MH, TxU

Sig E3^v
III.ii.19 *Orb.*] omitted

Sheet E (outer forme)
Corrected: CLUC, DFo, MH, CSmH
Uncorrected: TxU

Sig. E2^v
III.i.92 known,] known
Sig. E4^v
III.ii.81 appear.] appear:

Sheet G (outer forme)
Corrected: CLUC, CSmH, DFo, TxU
Uncorrected: MH

Sig. G3
IV.iii.7 In their] In the

Sheet H (inner forme)
Corrected: CSmH, MH, TxU
Uncorrected: CLUC, DFo

Sig. H2
IV.iv.124 *Vasq.*] *Vsq.*

Sheet H (outer forme)
Corrected: CSmH, CtY, MB, MH, TxU
Uncorrected: CLUC, DFo

Sig. H2^v
IV.iv.175.1 Spaniards,] Spaniards
Sig. H3
IV.iv.179 her to] to her
V.i.2 blame,] blame
21 elsewhere:] elsewher

Sheet I (inner forme)
Corrected: CSmH, CtY, DFo, MB, MH, TxU
Uncorrected: CLUC

Sig. 13ᵛ
  V.ii.172 who] that
      173 Him] He
      178.1 *walk and not*] *walk not*
Sig. 14
  V.i.192.1 Zoty] *Balcone*

Sheet I (outer forme)
Corrected: CSmH, CtY, MB, MH, TxU
Uncorrected: CLUC, DFo

Sig. I1
  V.1.128.1 *falls.*] *falls*
Sig. I2ᵛ
  V.ii.117.1 Montezuma.] M
Sig. I3
  V.ii.132 free,] free
      134 Gold,] Gold
      134 crimes;] crimes:
      135 Climes] climes
      136 brought,] brought
      137.1 *by*] *to*
      154.1 Montezuma.] Montezu
Sig. I4ᵛ
  V.ii.218 estate] e stte

Q2, 1668

Sheet B (inner forme)
Corrected: CSmH, CtY, DFo, MiU, TxU
Uncorrected: CLUC

Sig. B1ᵛ
  I.i.23 seasons] season
      29 pour] pour,
      30 bowels,] bowels
      40 just] fit
      45 far] fair
Sig. B3ᵛ
  I.ii.110 blow:] blow.
Sig. B4
  I.ii.133 part] pa rt
      144 which] that
      163 know:] know,

Sheet B (outer forme)
Corrected: CSmH, TxU, IU, CCC
Uncorrected: CLUC

Sig. B3
  I.ii.83 I'le] 'le

Aureng-Zebe

The high design of *Aureng-Zebe*, or "The Great Mogul" as it was subtitled in the edition of 1690, surpasses that of any other drama of the Restoration in intricacy, tension, balance, contrast, and variety. It deserves admiration such as we give to a magnificent baroque reredos like the one in the chapel at Chatsworth or to Wren's brilliant west towers of St. Paul's Cathedral, which play back and forth with convex and concave lines, columns, volutes, and scroll work, leading up to a lantern and capped with an ogee. The aesthetic impulse of such work demands restless multiplication of surprises by means of sudden reversals, along with the most elevated and proper ornamentation of each little step in the story. Each reversal requires a passionate outburst and a balanced debate, determining the next sequence of choices. Moody Prior comes close to describing the design when he observes that the restraints of the unities and of decorum caused Restoration playwrights to search for other means of fulfilling the traditional English love of variety. Shakespeare could depict the full range of human differences, but Dryden had to do the most he could within stricter limits, "producing as great a multiplicity of arrangements of the pieces as was compatible with some degree of consistency in their movements and the need for arriving at a particular final arrangement of them."[1] Actually the technique is not new with Dryden or Roger Boyle, for Beaumont and Fletcher had exploited the same opportunities in *A King and No King* (acted 1611), and Ben Jonson tried it in *The Alchemist* (1610) and in *Epicoene or the Silent Woman* (1609).

The main requirement of such an artifice, as Dryden saw in his "Examen of the Silent Woman" at the end of the *Essay of Dramatic Poesy*, was a limited subject, one central concern to which everyone directs his ambition. In *Aureng-Zebe* it is the throne and the queen together. Other passages in Dryden's analysis of *Epicoene* may aptly be applied to *Aureng-Zebe*.

Many persons of various characters, driven by various desires, have "several concernments of their own, yet are all used by the poet, to the conducting of the main design to perfection." The plot is "extreme elaborate, and yet withal easy," but we cannot commend the "fabric of it, because it is altogether so full of art," that we must "unravel every scene

---

[1] *The Language of Tragedy*, p. 163.

in it to commend it" as we ought. One of the great advantages of this kind of work, according to Corneille, was to begin the representation at some greatly advanced point in time, some critical day "whereon the action of the play is to depend." The action, furthermore, must rise by degrees, making the second greater than the first, the third greater than the second, and so on. But all this while the poet must entertain us with more variety, introducing a new character, Nourmahal, in the second act, and others, Morat and Melesinda, in the third. "Thus like a skilful chessplayer, by little and little he draws out his men, and makes his pawns [Arimant, Zayda, and Dianet] of use to his greater persons."

The language of such a play, if it rises above comedy, needs to depart from ordinary speech, to be "wrought up to a higher pitch" suitable to project elevated thoughts and grand feelings. Of all his rhymed plays, Dryden has best accomplished this in *Aureng-Zebe*, for he seems to have found ways of making his line more supple and his moods more diverse. Dozens of examples can be cited of characters showing every degree of feeling: contempt, bitterness, arch disdain, indignant reproach, uncertainty, resolve, despair, violent passion, tender concern, jealousy, hatred, and indifference. Each is brilliantly depicted in an ample speech. Everyone who knows the play has his favorite passage; Dr. Johnson said the complaint of life (IV.33–44) was "celebrated" in his time; but the most spectacular of all is Nourmahal's "I burn, I more than burn; I am all fire: / See how my nostrils flame expire" (V.640–57). It is one of Dryden's most completely symbolic speeches, for the aria depicts the guilt of Nourmahal in her self-created hell after she has taken the poison that she meant to administer to her lover-stepson. "Now I'm a burning Lake, it rowls and flows; / I'll rush and pour it all upon my Foes." Her all-consuming passion is summed up in her final rage: "Fan me you Winds: what, not one breath of Air? / I burn 'em all, and yet have flames to spare." As she proudly desired to secure the throne for her son, now she sees a vision of Morat blowing with a huge bellows a new fire into her brain. And as she lusted after Aureng-Zebe, she sees him blowing all his fire into her heart. Ultimately, she must have her hell all before she dies, when she sees Aureng-Zebe and Indamora run in terror of her into each other's arms and kiss. The last scene, therefore, is capped by a union of the twisted and the beautiful, and as a consequence of Nourmahal's death Aureng-Zebe gets everything that he renounced: the mistress he so long had served and the crown his loyalty preserved. So the old, chastened emperor delivers an appropriate benediction, ending with:

Take you the Reins, while I from cares remove,
And sleep within the Chariot which I drove.

At the end of a long, effusive dedication to the Earl of Mulgrave, printed in Q1, Dryden expresses his dissatisfaction with the theater and his resolve to write a heroic poem, adding some appropriate and interesting remarks not reprinted in Watson's or Ker's editions of the essays:

In the mean time, my Lord, I take the confidence to present you with a Tragedy; the Characters of which are the nearest to those of an Heroick Poem. . . . Some things in it have pass'd your approbation, and many your amendment. You were likewise pleas'd to recommend it to the King's perusal, before the last hand was added to it, when I receiv'd the favour from him, to have the most considerable event of it modell'd by his Royal Pleasure. It may be some vanity in me to add his Testimony then, and which he graciously confirm'd afterwards, that it was the best of all my Tragedies; in which he has made Authentick my private opinion of it; at least he has given it a value by his Commendation, which it had not by my Writing.

That which was not pleasing to some of the fair ladies in the last Act of it, as I dare not vindicate, so neither can I wholly condemn, till I find more reason for their Censures. The procedure of *Indamora* and *Melesinda*, seems yet, in my judgment, natural, and not unbecoming of their Characters. If they who arraign them fail not more, the World will never blame their conduct: And I shall be glad for the honour of my Countrey, to find better Images of Virtue drawn to the life in their behaviour, than any I could feign adorn the Theatre. I confess, I have onely represented a practicable Virtue, mix'd with the frailties and imperfections of humane life. I have made my *Heroine* fearful of death, which neither *Cassandra* nor *Cleopatra* would have been; and they themselves, I doubt it not, would have outdone Romance in that particular. Yet their *Mandana* (and the *Cyrus* was written by a Lady) was not altogether so hard-hearted: for she sat down on the cold ground by the King of *Assyria*, and not onely pitti'd him, who dy'd in her defence; but allow'd him some favours, such, perhaps, as they would think, should onely be permitted to her *Cyrus*. I have made my *Melesinda*, in opposition to *Nourmahal*, a Woman passionately loving of her Husband, patient of injuries and contempt, and constant in her kindness, to the last: and in that, perhaps, I may have err'd because it is not a Virtue much in use. Those *Indian* Wives are loving Fools, and may do well to keep themselves in their own Countrey, or, at least, to keep company with the *Arria's* and *Portia's* of old *Rome*: some of our Ladies know better things. But, it may be I am too partial to my own Writings. . . . I will not be too positive. . . . As I am a Man, I must be changeable: and sometimes the gravest of us all are so, even upon ridiculous accidents. Our minds are perpetually wrought on by the temperament of our Bodies: which makes me suspect they are nearer alli'd, than either our Philosphers or School-Divines will allow them to be. I have observ'd says *Montaign*, that when the Body is out of Order, its Companion is seldom at his ease. An ill Dream, or a Cloudy day, has power to change this wretched Creature, who is so proud of a reasonable Soul, and make him think what he thought not yesterday.

Aureng-Zebe is an historical play about contemporary India, from François Bernier's *Histoire de la dernière révolution des États du Grand Mogol*, the English translation of which was published 1671. The story, according to Bernier, began when Shah-Jahan divided his provinces among his sons, for them to rule as vice kings. The third son, Aureng-Zebe ("ornament of the throne") was more serious, melancholy, and judicious than the other three: Darius (or Dara), Sultan Sujah, and Morad Bakche. Aureng-Zebe pretended to be a *Fakire* (poor) and a *Dervich* (devout), "renouncing the World, and faining not to pretend at all to the Crown, but to desire to pass his Life in Prayer and other Devotions" (p. 18). His elder brother, Dara, called him a bigot, a "great Praying man" whom Dara feared for his duplicity. Aureng-Zebe used his younger brother Morad, "the least dextrous and least judicious" (p. 20), open, mirthful, brave, and liberal, to defeat the forces of Dara. He then imprisoned the old king, arrested Morad when in a drunken stupor, and drove Sultan Sujah into exile. Dara, finally captured, was led in disgrace through the streets of Delhi and then beheaded. Bernier also mentions two sisters, one who favored Dara and one Aureng-Zebe; but the old king doted on Dara's favorite. These women may have suggested Indamora and Melesinda. Otherwise, Dryden changed several names, developed the love stories, and made the protagonist much less aggressive.

On November 17, 1675, the first known performance was

presented before royalty by the King's Company at Drury Lane, and again on November 20 of the same year and at court May 29, 1676. Entered in the Stationers' Register November 29, 1675, the first quarto (Macd 80a, W & M 391) was advertised for sale in mid-February, 1676. Frequent reprints, Q2 1685, Q3 1690, Q4 1692, Q5 1694, Q6 1699, may mean that the play was revived in those seasons.

This edition is based on the University of Chicago copy of Q1, compared with two British Museum copies (BM[1] Ashley 3136, BM[2] 841.c.31), the University of Michigan copy, and the University of Texas copy, revealing no press corrections. Later editions introduce no revisions and few corrections.

AURENG-ZEBE

A
TRAGEDY.

Acted at the

Royal Theatre.

Written by
J O H N   D R Y D E N,
Servant to his Majesty.

——*Sed, cum fregit subsellia versu,*
Esurit, intactam Paridi *nisi vendat Agaven.* **Juv.**

𝕷𝖎𝖈𝖊𝖓𝖘𝖊𝖉, *ROGER L'ESTRANGE.*

LONDON,

Printed by *T. N.* for *Henry Herringman,* at the *Anchor i*
the Lower Walk of the *New Exchange.* **1676.**

Title Page of the First Quarto, Folger Library Copy

Sed . . . Agaven] But when his verses have brought down the house, he will starve if he does n
his virgin *Agave* (an unacted pantomime) to Paris (a famous pantomimic dancer) (Juvenal, *S*
VII, 86–87, Ramsey's translation).

Persons Represented

The old Emperor.
Aureng-Zebe, his Son.
Morat, his younger Son.
Arimant, Governour of *Agra*.
Dianet.
Solyman.
Mir Baba.
Abas.   }*Indian* Lords, or *Omrahs*, of several Factions.
Asaph Chan.
Fazel Chan.

Nourmahal, the Empress.
Indamora, a Captive Queen.
Melesinda, Wife to *Morat*.
Zayda, Favourite Slave to the Empress.

Scene, *Agra*, in the Year 1660.

Persons Represented] the original cast listed in Q1: *Emperor*, Michael Mohun; *Aureng-Zebe*, Charles Hart; *Morat*, Edward Kynaston; *Arimant*, William Wintershall; *Nourmahal*, Mrs. Rebecca Marshall; *Indamora*, Mrs. Elizabeth Cox; *Melesinda*, Mrs. Mary Corbet; *Zayda*, Mrs. Susanna Uphill.

1 *old Emperor*] Shah Jahan (1592–1666) who built the Taj Mahal in Agra for his favorite wife. The Mogul Empire reached its height under him.

7–8 *Omrahs*] lords or grandees of the court of the great Mogul, under the Mohammedan conquerors of India and the succeeding Mogul emperors.

9–10 *Asaph Chan. Fazel Chan*] the spellings "Chawn" and "Chan" are variants of the modern "Khan" or prince.

12 *Indamora, a Captive Queen*] Queen of Cassimere, i.e., Kashmir.

Agra] an ancient city in northern India, on the Jumna River, 117 miles southeast of Delhi.

III

Prologue

Our Author by experience finds it true,
'Tis much more hard to please himself than you:
And out of no feign'd modesty, this day,
Damns his laborious Trifle of a Play:
Not that it's worse than what before he writ,
But he has now another taste of Wit;
And to confess a truth, (though out of time)
Grows weary of his long-lov'd Mistris, Rhyme.
Passion's too fierce to be in Fetters bound,
And Nature flies him like Enchanted Ground.
What Verse can do, he has perform'd in this,
Which he presumes the most correct of his:
But spite of all his pride a secret shame,
Invades his breast at *Shakespear's* sacred name:
Aw'd when he hears his Godlike *Romans* rage,
He, in a just despair, would quit the Stage.
And to an Age less polish'd, more unskill'd,
Does, with disdain the foremost Honours yield.
As with the greater Dead he dares not strive,
He wou'd not match his Verse with those who live:
Let him retire, betwixt two Ages cast,
The first of this, and hindmost of the last.
A losing Gamester, let him sneak away;
He bears no ready Money from the Play.
The Fate which governs Poets, thought it fit,
He shou'd not raise his Fortunes by his Wit.
The Clergy thrive, and the litigious Bar;
Dull Heroes fatten with the spoils of War:
All Southern Vices, Heav'n be prais'd, are here;
But Wit's a luxury you think too dear.
When you to cultivate the Plant are loath,
'Tis a shrewd sign 'twas never of your growth:
And Wit in Northern Climates will not blow,
Except, like *Orange-trees*, 'tis hous'd from Snow.

5

10

15

20

25

30

10 *Nature flies him like Enchanted Ground*] Dr. Johnson, *A Dictionary of the English Language*, cites Dryden's use here as an example of the meaning of "fly" in the sense of "To refuse association with"; the sense seems to be that Nature eludes him as enchanted ground does.

27 *Bar*] the whole thriving legal species, desirous of dipute.

29 *Southern Vices*] Southern Europe, notably Provence and Italy, was considered a more sensual climate than the North.

Prologue

There needs no care to put a Play-house down,   35
'Tis the most desart place of all the Town.
We and our Neighbours, to speak proudly, are
Like Monarchs, ruin'd with expensive War.
While, like wise *English*, unconcern'd, you sit,
And see us play the Tragedy of Wit.   40

    36 *desart*] deserted.
    38 *Like . . . War.*] the rivalry between the Duke's and the King's theaters.

Aureng-Zebe,

a

Tragedy

ACT I

[*Enter*] Arimant, Asaph Chawn, Fazel Chawn.

Arimant. Heav'n seems the Empire of the East to lay
On the success of this important day:
Their Arms are to the last decision bent,
And Fortune labours with the vast event:
5 She now has in her hand the greatest stake,
Which for contending Monarchs she can make.
What e'r can urge ambitious Youth to fight,
She pompously displays before their sight:
Laws, Empire, All permitted to the Sword,
10 And Fate could ne'r an ampler Scene afford.
Asaph. Four several Armies to the Field are led,
Which, high in equal hopes four Princes Head:
Indus and *Ganges*, our wide Empire's Bounds,
Swell their dy'd Currents with their Natives wounds:
15 Each purple River winding, as he runs,
His bloudy arms about his slaughter'd Sons.
Fazel. I well remember you foretold the Storm,
When first the Brothers did their Factions form:
When each, by curs'd Cabals of Women, strove
20 To draw th'indulgent King to partial Love.
Arimant. What Heav'n decrees, no prudence can prevent.
To cure their mad Ambition, they were sent
To rule a distant Province each alone.
What could a careful Father more have done?
25 He made provision against all, but Fate;
While, by his health, we held our peace of State,
The weight of seventy Winters prest him down,
He bent beneath the burthen of a Crown:
Sickness, at last, did his spent Body seize,
30 And life almost sunk under the disease:
Mortal 'twas thought, at least by them desir'd,
Who, impiously, into his years inquir'd:

As at a Signal, streight the Sons prepare
For open force, and rush to sudden War:
Meeting, like Winds broke loose upon the Main, 35
To prove, by Arms, whose Fate it was to Reign.
Asaph. Rebels and Parricides!
Arimant. Brand not their actions with so foul a name:
 Pity, at least, what we are forc'd to blame.
When Death's cold hand has clos'd the Father's eye, 40
You know the younger Sons are doom'd to die.
Less ills are chosen greater to avoid,
And Nature's Laws are by the State's destroy'd.
What courage tamely could to death consent,
And not, by striking first, the blow prevent? 45
Who falls in fight, cannot himself accuse,
And he dies greatly who a Crown pursues.

  To them, Solyman Agah.

Solyman. A new Express all *Agra* does afright:
Darah and *Aureng-Zebe* are joyn'd in Fight;
The Press of people thickens to the Court, 50
Th'impatient crowd devouring the report.
Arimant. T'each changing news they chang'd affections
  bring,
And servilely from Fate expect a King.
Solyman. The Ministers of State, who gave us Law,
In corners, with selected Friends, withdraw: 55
There, in deaf murmurs, solemnly are wise;
Whisp'ring, like Winds, ere Hurricanes arise.
The most corrupt are most obsequious grown,
And those they scorn'd, officiously they own.
Asaph. In change of Government, 60
The Rabble rule their great Oppressors Fate:
Do Sovereign Justice, and revenge the State.
Solyman. The little Courtiers, who ne'r come to know
The depth of Factions, as in Mazes go,
Where Int'rests meet and cross so oft, that they 65
With too much care are wilder'd in their way.
Arimant. What of the Emperor?
Solyman. Unmov'd, and brave, he like himself appears,
And, meriting no ill, no danger fears:
Yet mourns his former vigour lost so far, 70
To make him now spectator of a War:
Repining that he must preserve his Crown

33–36 *As . . . Reign*] See Virgil's *Aeneid*, X, 356–58 and *Georgics*, I, 318–20 (Brower).
66 *wilder'd*] having lost one's way, as of travelers.

By any help or courage but his own:
Wishes, each minute, he could unbeget
75 Those Rebel-Sons, who dare t'usurp his Seat;
To sway his Empire with unequal skill,
And mount a Throne, which none but he can fill.
Arimant. Oh! had he still that Character maintain'd,
Of Valour, which in blooming Youth he gain'd!
80 He promis'd in his East a glorious Race;
Now, sunk from his Meridian, sets apace.
But as the Sun, when he from Noon declines,
And with abated heat, less fiercely shines,
Seems to grow milder as he goes away,
85 Pleasing himself with the remains of Day:
So he who, in his Youth, for Glory strove,
Would recompence his Age with Ease and Love.
Asaph. The name of Father hateful to him grows,
Which, for one Son, produces him three Foes.
90 *Fazel. Darah*, the eldest, bears a generous mind;
But to implacable revenge inclin'd.
Too openly does Love and hatred show:
A bounteous Master, but a deadly Foe.
Solyman. From *Sujah's* valour I should much expect,
95 But he's a *Bigot* of the *Persian* Sect:
And, by a Foreign Int'rest seeks to Reign,
Hopeless by Love the Sceptre to obtain.
Asaph. Morat's too insolent, too much a Brave,
His Courage to his Envy is a Slave.
100 What he attempts, if his endeavours fail
T'effect, he is resolv'd no other shall.
Arimant. But *Aureng-Zebe*, by no strong passion sway'd,
Except his Love, more temp'rate is, and weigh'd:
This *Atlas* must our sinking State uphold;
105 In Council cool, but in Performance bold:
He sums their Virtues in himself alone,
And adds the greatest, of a Loyal Son:
His Father's Cause upon his Sword he wears,
And with his Arms, we hope, his Fortune bears.
110 *Solyman.* Two vast Rewards may well his courage move,
A Parent's Blessing, and a Mistris Love.
If he succeed, his recompence, we hear,
Must be the Captive Queen of *Cassimere*.

To them, Abas.

Abas. Mischiefs on mischiefs, greater still, and more:
115 The neighb'ring Plain with Arms is cover'd o'r:

116

The Vale an Iron-Harvest seems to yield
Of thick-sprung Lances in a waving Field.
The pollish'd Steel gleams terribly from far,
And every moment nearer shows the War.
The Horses Neighing by the Wind is blown,   120
And Castl'd-Elephants o'r-look the Town.
Arimant. If, as I fear, *Morat* these Pow'rs commands,
Our Empire on the brink of ruine stands:
Th'ambitious Empress with her Son is joyn'd,
And, in his Brother's absence, has design'd   125
The unprovided Town to take with ease,
And then, the Person of the King to seize.
Solyman. To all his former Issue she has shown
Long hate, and labour'd to advance her own.
Abas. These Troops are his.   130
    Surat he took; and thence, preventing Fame,
By quick and painful Marches hither came.
Since his approach, he to his Mother sent,
And two long hours in close debate were spent.
Arimant. I'll to my Charge, the Cittadel, repair,   135
And show my duty by my timely care.   [*Exit.*]
To them the Emperor *with a Letter in his hand: after him, an*
    Ambassador, with a Train following.

Asaph. But see, the Emperor! a fiery red
His Brows and glowing Temples does o'r-spread,
Morat has some displeasing Message sent.
Ambassador. Do not, great Sir, misconstrue his intent;   140
Nor call Rebellion what was prudent care,
To guard himself by necessary War:
While he believ'd you living, he obey'd:
His Government's but as your Vice-Roy sway'd:
But, when he thought you gone,   145
T'augment the number of the Bless'd above,
He deem'd 'em Legacies of Royal love:
Nor arm'd his Brothers Portions to invade,
But to defend the present you had made.
Emperor. By frequent Messages, and strict Commands,   150
He knew my pleasure to discharge his Bands:
Proof of my life my Royal Signet made;
Yet still he arm'd, came on, and disobey'd.
Ambassador. He thought the *Mandat* forg'd, your death
    conceal'd:

116 *The Vale . . . yield*] a literal translation of *ferrea telorum seges,*
Aeneid, III, 45–46 (Brower).
131 *preventing Fame*] acting more quickly than the news traveled.

155   And but delay'd, till truth should be reveal'd.
    Emperor. News of my death from Rumor he receiv'd;
        And what he wish'd, he easily believ'd:
        But long demurr'd, though from my hand he knew
        I liv'd, so loath he was to think it true.
160   Since he pleads ignorance to that command,
        Now let him show his duty, and disband.
    Ambassador. His Honour, Sir, will suffer in the Cause,
        He yields his Arms unjust if he withdraws:
        And begs his Loyalty may be declar'd,
165   By owning those he leads to be your guard.
    Emperor. I, in my self, have all the Guard I need;
        Bid the presumptuous Boy draw off with speed:
        If his audacious Troops one hour remain,
        My Cannon from the Fort shall scour the Plain.
170   *Ambassador*. Since you deny him entrance, he demands
        His Wife, whom cruelly you hold in Bands:
        Her, if unjustly you from him detain,
        He justly will by force of Arms regain.
    Emperor. O'r him, and his, a right from Heav'n I have;
175   Subject, and Son, he's doubly born my Slave.
        But whatsoe'r his own demerits are,
        Tell him, I shall not make on Women, War.
        And yet I'll do her Innocence the grace,
        To keep her here, as in the safer place.
180   But thou, who dar'st this bold defiance bring,
        May'st feel the rage of an offended King.
        Hence from my sight, without the least reply:
        One word, nay, one look more, and thou shalt die.
                         Exit Ambassador.

               Re-enter Arimant.

    Arimant. May Heav'n, great Monarch, still augment your
        bliss
185   With length of days, and every day like this.
        For, from the Banks of *Gemna* news is brought,
        Your Army has a bloudy Battel fought:
        Darah from Loyal *Aureng-Zebe* is fled;
        And fourty thousand of his Men lie dead.
190   To *Sujah* next your conquering Army drew;
        Him they surpris'd, and easily o'r-threw.
    Emperor. 'Tis well.
    Arimant. But well! what more could at your wish be done,
        Than two such Conquests gain'd by such a Son?
195   Your pardon, mighty Sir;

186 *Gemna*] i.e., the Jumna River that flows through Agra.

You seem not high enough your Joys to rate;
You stand indebted a vast sum to Fate:
And should large thanks for the great Blessing pay.
Emperor. My fortune owes me greater every day.
And, should my joy more high for this, appear,   200
It would have argu'd me before of fear.
How is Heav'n kind, where I have nothing won,
And Fortune onely pays me with my own?
Arimant. Great *Aureng-Zebe* did duteous care express:
And durst not push too far his good success.   205
But lest *Morat* the City should attack,
Commanded his victorious Army back;
Which, left to march as swiftly as they may,   ⎫
Himself comes first, and will be here this day, ⎬
Before a close-form'd Siege shut up his way.   ⎭   210
Emperor. Prevent his purpose, hence, hence with all thy
    speed.
Stop him; his entrance to the Town forbid.
Arimant. How, Sir? your Loyal, your Victorious Son?
Emperor. Him would I, more than all the Rebels, shun.
Arimant. Whom with your pow'r and fortune, Sir, you
    trust;   215
Now to suspect is vain, as 'tis unjust.
He comes not with a Train to move your fear,
But trusts himself, to be a pris'ner here.
You knew him brave, you know him faithful now:
He aims at Fame, but Fame from serving you.   220
'Tis said, Ambition in his breast does rage:
Who would not be the *Hero* of an Age?
All grant him prudent: prudence interest weighs,
And interest bids him seek your love and praise.
I know you grateful; When he march'd from hence,   225
You bad him hope an ample recompence:
He conquer'd in that hope; and from your hands,
His Love, the precious pledge he left, demands.
Emperor. No more; you search too deep my wounded
    mind:
And show me what I fear, and would not find.   230
My Son has all the debts of duty paid:
Our Prophet sends him to my present aid.
Such virtue to distrust were base and low:
I'm not ungrateful ——— or I was not so!
Inquire no farther, stop his coming on: 235
I will not, cannot, dare not see my Son.

201 *argu'd me before of fear*] recalling *Aeneid*, IV, 13 (Brower).

119

Arimant. 'Tis now too late his entrance to prevent:
　　Nor must I to your ruine give consent.
　　At once your People's heart and Son's you lose:
240　　And give him all, when you just things refuse.
Emperor. Thou lov'st me sure; thy faith has oft been tri'd,
　　In ten pitch'd Fields, not shrinking from my side,
　　Yet giv'st me no advice to bring me ease.
Arimant. Can you be cur'd, and tell not your disease?
　　I ask'd you, Sir.
245 *Emperor.* 　　　　Thou should'st have ask'd again:
　　There hangs a secret shame on guilty men.
　　Thou shouldst have pull'd the secret from my breast,
　　Torn out the bearded Steel to give me rest:
　　At least, thou should'st have ghess'd ——
250　　Yet thou art honest, thou could'st ne'r have ghess'd.
　　Hast thou been never base? did Love ne'r bend
　　Thy frailer Virtue, to betray thy Friend?
　　Flatter me, make thy Court, and say, It did:
　　Kings in a Crowd would have their Vices hid.
255　　We would be kept in count'nance, sav'd from shame:
　　And own'd by others who commit the same.
　　Nay, now I have confess'd. ——
　　Thou seest me naked, and without disguise:
　　I look on *Aureng-Zebe* with Rival's eyes.
260　　He has abroad my enemyes o'recome,
　　And I have sought to ruin him at home.
Arimant. This free confession showes you long did strive:
　　And virtue, though opprest, is still alive.
　　But what success did your injustice find?
265 *Emperor.* What it deserv'd, and not what I design'd.
　　Unmov'd she stood, and deaf to all my prayers,
　　As Seas and Winds to sinking Mariners.
　　But Seas grow calm, and Winds are reconcil'd:
　　Her Tyrant beauty never grows more mild.
270　　Pray'rs, promises, and threats were all in vain.
Arimant. Then cure your self by generous disdain.
Emperor. Virtue, disdain, despair, I oft have tri'd,
　　And foil'd, have with new Arms my Foe defi'd.
　　This made me with so little joy to hear
275　　The Victory, when I the Victor fear.
Arimant. Something you swiftly must resolve to do,
　　Lest *Aureng-Zebe* your secret Love should know.
　　Morat without does for your ruine wait;

---

250 ne'r] Q5; ne'er Q2–4, Q6, F; near Q1
248 *bearded*] barbed.

And would you lose the Buckler of your State?
A jealous Empress lies within your Arms,   280
Too haughty to endure neglected Charms.
Your Son is duteous, but (as Man) he's frail.
And just revenge o'r vertue may prevail.
Emperor. Go then to *Indamora,* say from me,
Two Lives depend upon her secresie.   285
Bid her conceal my passion from my Son.
Though *Aureng-Zebe* return a Conqueror,
Both he and she are still within my pow'r.
Say, I'm a Father, but a Lover too:
Much to my Son, more to my self I owe.   290
When she receives him, to her words give Law:
And even the kindness of her glances awe.
See, he appears!
           After a short whisper, Arimant *departs.*

Enter Aureng-Zebe, Dianet, *and Attendants.* Aureng-Zebe
    kneels to his Father, and kisses his hand.

Aureng-Zebe. My Vows have been successful as my Sword:
My pray'rs are heard, you have your health restor'd.   295
Once more 'tis given me to behold your face:
The best of Kings and Fathers to embrace.
Pardon my tears; 'tis joy which bids 'em flow,
A joy which never was sincere till now.
That which my Conquest gave I could not prize;   300
Or 'twas imperfect till I saw your eyes.
Emperor. Turn the discourse: I have a reason why
I would not have you speak so tenderly.
Knew you what shame your kind expressions bring,
You would in pity spare a wretched King.   305
Aureng-Zebe. A King! you rob me, Sir, of half my due:
You have a dearer name, a Father too.
Emperor. I had that name.
Aureng-Zebe.   What have I said or done,
That I no longer must be call'd your Son?
'Tis in that name, Heav'n knows, I glory more,   310
Than that of Prince, or that of Conqueror.
Emperor. Then you upbraid me; I am pleas'd to see
You're not so perfect, but can fail, like me.
I have no God to deal with.
Aureng-Zebe.   Now I find
Some slie Court-Devil has seduc'd your mind: 315
Fill'd it with black suspicions, not your own:

299 *sincere*] pure.

And all my actions through false Optics shown.
I ne'r did Crowns ambitiously regard:
Honour I sought, the generous mind's reward.

320 Long may you live! while you the Sceptre sway
I shall be still most happy to obey.

Emperor. Oh, *Aureng-Zebe*! thy virtues shine too bright, ⎫
They flash too fierce: I, like the Bird of Night, ⎬
Shut my dull eyes, and sicken at the sight. ⎭

325 Thou hast deserv'd more love than I can show:
But 'tis thy fate to give, and mine to owe.
Thou seest me much distemper'd in my mind:
Pull'd back, and then push'd forward to be kind.
Virtue, and ——— fain I would my silence break,

330 But have not yet the confidence to speak.
Leave me, and to thy needful rest repair.

Aureng-Zebe. Rest is not suiting with a Lover's care.
I have not yet my *Indamora* seen. *Is going.*

Emperor. Somewhat I had forgot; come back again:

335 So weary of a Father's company!

Aureng-Zebe. Sir, you were pleas'd your self to license me.

Emperor. You made me no relation of the Fight.
Besides, a Rebel's Army is in sight.
Advise me first: yet go ———

340 (*Aside*) He goes to *Indamora*; I should take
A kind of envious joy to keep him back.
Yet to detain him makes my love appear:
I hate his presence, and his absence fear. *Exit.*

Aureng-Zebe. To some new Clime, or to thy native Sky,

345 Oh friendless and forsaken Virtue flie.
Thy *Indian* Air is deadly to thee grown:
Deceit and canker'd malice rule thy Throne.
Why did my Arms in Battel prosp'rous prove,
To gain the barren praise of Filial love?

350 The best of Kings by Women is misled,
Charm'd by the Witchcraft of a second Bed.
Against my self I Victories have wonn,
And by my fatal absence am undone.

To him Indamora, *with* Arimant.

But here she comes!

355 In the calm Harbour of whose gentle breast,
My Tempest-beaten Soul may safely rest.

317 *false Optics*] trick lenses or odd perspectives that create an
optical illusion.
336 *license*] permit to go.

122

Oh, my heart's joy! what e'r my sorrows be,
They cease and vanish, in beholding thee!
Care shuns thy walks; as at the cheerful light,
The groaning Ghosts, and Birds obscene take flight. 360
By this one view, all my past pains are paid:
And all I have to come more easie made.
Indamora. Such sullen Planets at my Birth did shine,
They threaten every Fortune mixt with mine.
Fly the pursuit of my disastrous love, 365
And from unhappy Neighbourhood remove.
Aureng-Zebe. Bid the laborious Hind,
Whose hardned hands did long in Tillage toil,
Neglect the promis'd Harvest of the Soil.
Should I, who cultivated Love with Bloud, 370
Refuse possession of approaching good?
Indamora. Love is an aery good Opinion makes:
Which he who onely thinks he has, partakes.
Seen by a strong Imagination's Beam,
That tricks and dresses up the gaudy Dream. 375
Presented so, with rapture 'tis enjoy'd:
Rais'd by high Fancy, and by low destroy'd.
Aureng-Zebe. If Love be Vision, mine has all the fire
Which, in first Dreams, young Prophets does inspire:
I dream, in you, our promis'd Paradice: 380
An Age's tumult of continu'd bliss.
But you have still your happiness in doubt:
Or else 'tis past, and you have dream't it out.
Indamora. Perhaps not so.
Aureng-Zebe.   Can *Indamora* prove
So alter'd? Is it but, Perhaps you Love? 385
Then farewell all! I thought in you to find
A Balm, to cure my much distemper'd mind.
I came to grieve a Father's heart estrang'd;
But little thought to find a Mistris chang'd.
Nature her self is chang'd to punish me: 390
Virtue turn'd Vice, and Faith Inconstancy.
Indamora. You heard me not Inconstancy confess:
'Twas but a Friend's advice to love me less.
Who knows what adverse Fortune may befall?
Arm well your mind: hope little, and fear all. 395
Hope, with a goodly prospect, feeds your Eye:
Shows, from a rising ground, possession nigh:
Shortens the distance, or o'r-looks it quite:

---

360 *Birds obscene*] recalling *Aeneid*, III, 262 (Brower).
372 *good*] good that.

So easie 'tis to travel with the sight.

400 *Aureng-Zebe.* Then to despair you would my Love betray,
By taking hope, its last kind Friend, away.
You hold the Glass, but turn the Perspective;
And farther off the lessen'd Object drive.
· You bid me fear: in that your change I know:
405 You would prepare me for the coming blow.
But, to prevent you, take my last Adieu; ⎫
I'll sadly tell my self you are untrue, ⎬
Rather than stay to hear it told by you. ⎭ *Going.*
Indamora. Stay, *Aureng-Zebe,* I must not let you go. ⎫
410 And yet believe your self, your own worst Foe, ⎬
Think I am true, and seek no more to know. ⎭
Let in my breast the fatal Secret lie,
'Tis a sad Riddle, which, if known, we die.
Seeming to pause.
Aureng-Zebe. Fair Hypocrite, you seek to cheat in vain;
415 Your silence argues you ask time to feign,
Once more, farewel: the snare in sight is laid,
'Tis my own fault if I am now betray'd. *Going again.*
Indamora. Yet once more stay; you shall believe me true,
Though in one Fate I wrap my self and you.
Your absence ———
420 *Arimant.* Hold; you know the hard Command
I must obey: you onely can withstand
Your own mishap. I beg you on my Knee,
Be not unhappy by your own Decree.
Aureng-Zebe. Speak, Madam, by (if that be yet an Oath)
425 Your Love, I'm pleas'd we should be ruin'd both.
Both is a sound of joy.
In Death's dark Bow'rs our Bridals we will keep:
And his cold hand
Shall draw the Curtain when we go to sleep.
430 *Indamora.* Know then, that Man whom both of us did trust,
Has been to you unkind, to me unjust.
The Guardian of my Faith so false did prove,
As to sollicite me with lawless Love:
Pray'd, promis'd, threaten'd, all that Man could do,
435 Base as he's great; and need I tell you who?
Aureng-Zebe. Yes; for I'll not believe my Father meant:
Speak quickly, and my impious thoughts prevent.
Indamora. Yo've said; I wish I could some other name!
Arimant. My duty must excuse me, Sir, from blame.
A Guard there.

Enter Guards.

Aureng-Zebe.   Slave, for me?

Arimant.   My Orders are   440
  To seize this Princess, whom the Laws of War
  Long since made Prisoner.
Aureng-Zebe.   Villain.
Arimant.   Sir, I know
  Your Birth, nor durst another call me so.
Aureng-Zebe. I have redeem'd her; and as mine she's free.
Arimant. You may have right to give her liberty: 445
  But with your Father, Sir, that right dispute;
  For his commands to me were absolute;
  If she disclos'd his love, to use the right
  Of War, and to secure her from your sight.
Aureng-Zebe. I'll rescue her, or die.   *Draws.*   450
  And you, my friends, though few, are yet too brave
  To see your Gen'ral's Mistris made a Slave.   *All draw.*
Indamora. Hold, my dear Love! if so much pow'r there lies,
  As once you own'd, in *Indamora's* Eyes,
  Lose not the Honour you have early wonn;   455
  But stand the blameless pattern of a Son.
  My love your claim inviolate secures:
  'Tis writ in Fate, I can be onely yours.
  My suff'rings for you make your heart my due:
  Be worthy me, as I am worthy you.   460
Aureng-Zebe. I've thought, and bless'd be you who gave
  me time: *Putting up his sword.*
  My Virtue was surpris'd into a Crime.
  Strong Virtue, like strong Nature, struggles still:
  Exerts it self, and then throws off the ill.
  I to a Son's and Lover's praise aspire: 465
  And must fulfil the parts which both require.
  How dear the cure of jealousie has cost!
  With too much care and tenderness y'are lost.
  So the fond Youth from Hell redeem'd his Prize,
  Till looking back, she vanish'd from his eyes!   470
                              Exeunt severally.

ACT II

Betwixt the Acts, a Warlike Tune is plaid,
  shooting off Guns, and shouts of Souldiers
  are heard, as in an Assault.

[*Enter*] Aureng-Zebe, Arimant, Asaph Chawn,
      Fazel Chawn, Solyman.

Aureng-Zebe. What man could do, was by *Morat* per-
form'd:
The Fortress thrice himself in person storm'd.
Your valour bravely did th'Assault sustain;
And fill'd the Moats and Ditches with the Slain.
5   Till, mad with rage, into the Breach he fir'd:
Slew Friends and Foes, and in the Smoak retir'd.
Arimant. To us you give what praises are not due:
Morat was thrice repuls'd, but thrice by you.
High, over all, was your great conduct shown:
10   You sought our safety, but forgot your own.
Asaph. Their Standard, planted on the Battlement,
Despair and death among the Souldiers sent:
You, the bold *Omrah* tumbled from the Wall;
And shouts of Victory pursu'd his fall.
15   *Fazel.* To you, alone, we owe this prosp'rous day:
Our Wives and Children rescu'd from the prey:
Know your own int'rest Sir, where e'r you lead,
We joyntly vow to own no other Head.
Solyman. Your wrongs are known. Impose but your com-
mands;
20   This hour shall bring you twenty thousand hands.
Aureng-Zebe. Let them who truly would appear my
friends,
Employ their Swords, like mine, for noble ends.
No more: remember you have bravely done:
Shall Treason end, what Loyalty begun?
25   I own no wrongs; some grievance I confess,
But Kings, like Gods, at their own time redress.
(*Aside*) Yet, some becoming boldness I may use:
I've well deserv'd, nor will he now refuse.
I'll strike my Fortunes with him at a heat:
30   And give him not the leisure to forget.
                                Exit, attended by the Omrahs.
Arimant. Oh! *Indamora*, hide these fatal Eyes;
Too deep they wound whom they too soon surprise:
My Virtue, Prudence, Honour, Interest, all
Before this Universal Monarch fall.
35   Beauty, like Ice, our footing does betray;
Who can tread sure on the smooth slippery way?
Pleas'd with the passage, we slide swiftly on:
And see the dangers which we cannot shun.

To him, Indamora.

Indamora. I hope my liberty may reach thus far:
40   These Terras Walks within my limits are.

126

I came to seek you, and to let you know,
How much I to your generous Pity owe.
The King, when he design'd you for my Guard,
Resolv'd he would not make my Bondage hard:
If otherwise, you have deceiv'd his end;   45
And whom he meant a Guardian, made a Friend.
Arimant. A Guardian's Title I must own with shame:
But should be prouder of another Name.
Indamora. And therefore 'twas I chang'd that Name before:
I call'd you Friend, and could you wish for more?   50
Arimant. I dare not ask for what you would not grant:
But wishes, Madam, are extravagant.
They are not bounded with things possible:
I may wish more then I presume to tell:
Desire's the vast extent of humane mind,   55
It mounts above, and leaves poor hope behind.
I could wish ――――
Indamora. What?
Arimant. Why did you speak? yo've dash'd my Fancy
   quite:
Ev'n in th'approaching minute of delight.   60
I must take breath
Ere I the Rapture of my wish renew,
And tell you then, It terminates in you.
Indamora. Have you consider'd what th'event would be?
Or know you, *Arimant*, your self, or me?   65
Were I no Queen, did you my beauty weigh,
My Youth in bloom, your Age in its decay?
Arimant. I my own Judge, condemn'd my self before:
For pity aggravate my crime no more.
So weak I am, I with a frown am slain;   70
You need have us'd but half so much disdain.
Indamora. I am not cruel yet to that degree:
Have better thoughts both of your self, and me.
Beauty a Monarch is,
Which Kingly power magnificently proves,   75
By crouds of Slaves, and peopled Empire loves.
And such a Slave as you, what Queen would lose?
Above the rest, I *Arimant* would chuse:
For counsel, valour, truth, and kindness too,
All I could wish in man, I find in you.   80
Arimant. What Lover could to greater joy be rais'd!
I am, methinks, a God by you thus prais'd.
Indamora. To what may not desert, like yours, pretend?
You have all qualities ―――― that fit a Friend.
Arimant. So Mariners mistake the promis'd Coast: 85

And, with ful Sails, on the blind Rocks are lost.
Think you my aged veins so faintly beat,
They rise no higher than to Friendship's heat?
So weak your Charms, that, like a Winter's night,
90   Twinkling with Stars, they freez me while they light?
Indamora. Mistake me not, good *Arimant*, I know
My Beauty's pow'r, and what my charms can do.
You your own Talent have not learn'd so well;
But practise one, where you can ne'r excel.
95   You can at most,
To an indiff'rent Lover's praise pretend:
But you would spoil an admirable Friend.
Arimant. Never was Amity so highly priz'd;
Nor ever any Love so much despis'd.
100   Ev'n to my self ridiculous I grow;
And would be angry, if I knew but how.
Indamora. Do not. Your Anger, like your Love, is vain:
When e'r I please, you must be pleas'd again.
Knowing what pow'r I have your will to bend,
105   I'll use it; for I need just such a Friend.
You must perform, not what you think is fit:
But, to what ever I propose, submit.
Arimant. Madam, you have a strange Ascendant gain'd;
You use me like a Courser, spurr'd and rein'd:
110   If I fly out, my fierceness you command,
Then sooth, and gently stroke me with your hand.
Impose; but use your pow'r of Taxing well:
When Subjects cannot Pay, they soon Rebel.

        Enter the Emperor, *unseen by them.*

Indamora. My Rebel's punishment would easie prove:
115   You know y'are in my pow'r by making Love.
Arimant. Would I, without dispute, your will obey,
And could you, in return, my life betray?
Emperor. What danger, *Arimant*, is this you fear?
Or what Love-secret which I must not hear?
120   (*To her*) These alter'd looks some inward motion show.
His cheeks are pale, and yours with blushes glow.
Indamora. 'Tis what, with justice, may my anger move:
He has been bold, and talk'd to me of Love.
Arimant (*aside*). I am betray'd, and shall be doom'd to die!
125   *Emperor.* Did he, my Slave, presume to look so high?
That crawling Insect, who from Mud began,
Warm'd by my Beams, and kindl'd into Man?
Durst he, who does but for my pleasure live,

Intrench on Love, my great Prerogative?
Print his base Image on his Sovereign's Coin?   130
'Tis Treason if he stamp his Love with mine.
Arimant. 'Tis true, I have been bold; but if it be
    A crime ———
Indamora.   He means, 'tis onely so to me.
You, Sir, should praise, what I must disapprove:
He insolently talk'd to me of Love: 135
But, Sir, 'twas yours, he made it in your name:
You, if you please, may all he said disclaim.
Emperor. I must disclaim what e'r he can express:
His groveling sense will show my passion less.
But stay, if what he said my message be,   140
What fear, what danger could arrive from me?
He said, He fear'd you would his life betray.
Indamora. Should he presume again, perhaps I may.
Though in your hands he hazard not his life,
Remember, Sir, your fury of a Wife;   145
Who, not content to be reveng'd on you,
The Agents of your passion will pursue.
Emperor. If I but hear her nam'd, I'm sick that day;
The sound is mortal, and frights life away.
Forgive me, *Arimant,* my jealous thought: 150
Distrust in Lovers is the tender'st fault.
Leave me, and tell thy self in my excuse,
Love, and a Crown, no Rivalship can bear;
And precious things are still possess'd with fear.
                        Exit Arimant *bowing.*
This, Madam, my excuse to you may plead;   155
Love should forgive the faults which Love has made.
Indamora. From me, what pardon can you hope to have,
Robb'd of my Love, and treated as a Slave?
Emperor. Force is the last relief which Lovers find:
And 'tis the best excuse of Wooman-kind.   160
Indamora. Force never yet a generous Heart did gain:
We yield on parley, but are storm'd in vain.
Constraint, in all things, makes the pleasure less;
Sweet is the Love which comes with willingness.
Emperor. No; 'tis resistance that inflames desire: 165
Sharpens the Darts of Love, and blows his Fire.
Love is disarm'd that meets with too much ease:
He languishes, and does not care to please.
And therefore 'tis your golden Fruit you guard
With so much care, to make possession hard.   170
Indamora. Was't not enough you took my Crown away,
But cruelly you must my Love betray?

I was well pleas'd to have transferr'd my right,
And better chang'd your Claim of Lawless might,
175   By taking him, whom you esteem'd above
Your other Sons, and taught me first to love.
Emperor. My Son, by my command his course must steer:
I bad him love, I bid him now forbear.
If you have any kindness for him still,
180   Advise him not to shock a Father's will.
Indamora. Must I advise?
Then let me see him, and I'll try t'obey.
Emperor. I had forgot, and dare not trust your way.
But send him word,
185   He has not here an Army to command:
Remember he and you are in my hand.
Indamora. Yes, in a Father's hand, whom he has serv'd;
And, with the hazard of his life, preserv'd.
But piety to you, unhappy Prince,
190   Becomes a crime, and duty an offence:
Against your self, you with your Foes combine,
And seem your own destruction to design.
Emperor. You may be pleas'd your Politiques to spare:
I'm old enough, and can my self take care.
195   *Indamora.* Advice from me was, I confess, too bold:
Y'are old enough; it may be, Sir, too old.
Emperor. You please your self with your contempt of Age:
But Love, neglected, will convert to Rage.
If on your head my fury does not turn,
200   Thank that fond dotage which so much you scorn.
But, in another's person, you may prove,
There's warmth for Vengeance left, though not for Love.

Re-enter Arimant.

Arimant. The Empress has the Anti-chambers past,
And this way moves with a disorder'd haste:
205   Her brows, the stormy marks of anger bear.
Emperor. Madam, retire: she must not find you here.
Exit Indamora with Arimant.

Enter Nourmahal hastily.

Nourmahal. What have I done, that *Nourmahal* must prove
The scorn and triumph of a Rival's Love?
My eyes are still the same, each glance, each grace, ⎫
210   Keep their first lustre, and maintain their place; ⎬
Not second yet to any other face. ⎭

207 *prove*] assume the role of the object which demonstrates
or establishes the triumph of the rival.

Emperor. What rage transports you? are you well awake?
   Such Dreams distracted minds in Feavers make.
Nourmahal. Those Feavers you have giv'n, those Dreams
     have bred,
   By broken Faith, and an abandon'd Bed.   215
   Such Visions hourly pass before my sight;
   Which from my eyes their Balmy slumbers fright,
   In the severest silence of the night.
   Visions, which in this Cittadel are seen;
   Bright, glorious Visions of a Rival Queen.   220
Emperor. Have patience, my first flames can ne'r decay:
   These are but Dreams, and soon will pass away.
   Thou know'st, my Heart, my Empire, all is thine:
   In thy own Heav'n of Love serenely shine:
   Fair as the face of Nature did appear,   225
   When Flowers first peep'd, and Trees did Blossoms
     bear,
   And Winter had not yet deform'd th'inverted Year.
   Calm as the Breath which fans our Eastern Groves,
   And bright as when thy Eyes first lighted up our Loves.
   Let our eternal Peace be seal'd by this,   230
   With the first ardour of a Nuptial Kiss.
                      Offers to kiss her.
Nourmahal. Me would you have, me your faint kisses prove,
   The dregs and droppings of enervate Love?
   Must I your cold long-labouring age sustain,
   And be to empty joys provok'd in vain?   235
   Receive you sighing after other Charms,
   And take an absent Husband in my Arms?
Emperor. Even these reproaches I can bear from you:
   You doubted of my Love, believe it true.
   Nothing but Love this patience could produce;   240
   And I allow your rage that kind excuse.
Nourmahal. Call it not patience; 'tis your guilt stands mute:
   You have a cause too foul to bear dispute.
   You wrong me first, and urge my rage to rise,
   Then I must pass for mad; you, meek and wise,   245
   Good man, plead merit by your soft replies.
   Vain priviledge poor Women have of tongue:
   Men can stand silent, and resolve on wrong.

---

227 *inverted*] the "wrong side of the year," a possible pun here on
"ungreen" (see Dryden's "Song to a Fair Young Lady" and *The Hind
and the Panther*, line 1732, and Dryden's translation of the Second Epode
of Horace, line 46).
   232 *prove*] endure.
   233 *enervate*] wanting in bodily strength or physical power.

Emperor. What can I more? my friendship you refuse,
250   And even my mildness, as my crime, accuse.
Nourmahal. Your sullen silence cheats not me, false Man;
    I know you think the bloudiest things you can.
    Could you accuse me, you would raise your voice:
    Watch for my crimes, and in my guilt rejoyce.
255   But my known virtue is from scandal free,
    And leaves no shadow for your calumny.
Emperor. Such virtue is the plague of humane life:
    A virtuous Woman, but a cursed Wife.
    In vain of pompous chastity y'are proud:
260   Virtue's adultery of the Tongue, when loud.
    I, with less pain, a Prostitute could bear,
    Than the shrill sound of Virtue, virtue hear.
    In unchaste Wives
    There's yet a kind of recompensing ease:
265   Vice keeps 'em humble, gives 'em care to please:
    But against clamorous Virtue, what defence?
    It stops our mouthes, and gives your noise pretence.
Nourmahal. Since Virtue does your indignation raise,
    'Tis pity but you had that Wife you praise.
270   Your own wild appetites are prone to range;
    And then you tax our humours with your change.
Emperor. What can be sweeter than our native home!
    Thither for ease, and soft repose, we come:
    Home is the sacred refuge of our life:
275   Secur'd from all approaches, but a Wife.
    If thence we fly, the cause admits no doubt:
    None but an Inmate Foe could force us out.
    Clamours, our privacies uneasie make:
    Birds leave their Nests disturb'd, and Beasts their Haunts
        forsake.
280 *Nourmahal.* Honour's my crime that has your loathing bred:
    You take no pleasure in a virtuous Bed.
Emperor. What pleasure can their be in that estate,
    Which your unquietness has made me hate?
    I shrink far off,
285   Dissembling sleep, but wakeful with the fright.
    The day takes off the pleasure of the night.
Nourmahal. My thoughts no other joys but pow'r pursue:
    Or, if they did, they must be lost in you.
    And yet the fault's not mine ———
290   Though Youth and Beauty cannot warmth command;
    The Sun in vain shines on the barren Sand.
Emperor. 'Tis true, of Marriage-bands I'm weary grown.
    Love scorns all ties, but those that are his own.

Chains that are dragg'd, must needs uneasie prove:
For there's a God-like liberty in Love.   295
Nourmahal. What's Love to you?
  The bloom of Beauty other years demands;
  Nor will be gather'd by such wither'd hands:
  You importune it with a false desire:
  Which sparkles out, and makes no solid fire.   300
  This impudence of Age, whence can it spring?
  All you expect, and yet you nothing bring.
  Eager to ask, when you are past a grant;
  Nice in providing what you cannot want.
  Have conscience; give not her you love this pain: 305
  Sollicite not your self, and her, in vain.
  All other Debts may compensation find:
  But Love is strict, and will be paid in kind.
Emperor. Sure of all ills, Domestic are the worst;
  When most secure of blessings, we are curst.   310
  When we lay next us what we hold most dear,
  Like *Hercules*, invenom'd Shirts we wear;
  And cleaving mischiefs.
Nourmahal.   What you merit, have:
  And share, at least, the miseries you gave.
  Your days, I will alarm, I'll haunt your nights: 315
  And, worse than Age, disable your delights.
  May your sick Fame still languish, till it die: ⎫
  All Offices of Pow'r neglected lie,   ⎬
  And you grow cheap in every Subject's eye.   ⎭
  Then, as the greatest Curse that I can give;   320
  Unpiti'd, be depos'd; and after live.   *Going off.*
Emperor. Stay; and now learn,
  How criminal soe'r we Husbands are,
  'Tis not for Wives to push our crimes too far.
  Had you still Mistris of your temper been,   325
  I had been modest, and not own'd my Sin.
  Your fury hardens me: and what e'r wrong
  You suffer, you have cancell'd by your tongue.
  A Guard there; seize her: she shall know this hour,
  What is a Husband's and a Monarch's pow'r.   330
                                    Guard seizes her.

                Enter Aureng-Zebe.

Nourmahal. I see for whom your Charter you maintain: ⎫
  I must be fetter'd, and my Son be slain,   ⎬
  That *Zelyma's* ambitious Race may reign.   ⎭

333 *Zelyma*] mother of Aureng-Zebe.

Not so you promis'd, when my Beauty drew
335 All *Asia's* Vows; when *Persia* left for you,
The Realm of *Candahar* for Dow'r I brought:
That long contended Prize for which you fought.
Aureng-Zebe. The name of Step-mother, your practis'd Art,
By which you have estrang'd my Father's heart,
340 All you have done against me, or design,
Shows your aversion, but begets not mine.
Long may my Father *India's* Empire guide:
And may no breach your Nuptial Vows divide.
Emperor. Since Love obliges not, I from this hour,
345 Assume the right of Man's Despotic pow'r:
Man is by Nature form'd your Sexes head:
And is himself the Canon of his Bed.
In Bands of Iron fetter'd you shall be:
An easier yoke than what you put on me.
350 *Aureng-Zebe.* Though much I fear my int'rest is not great,
            Kneeling.
Let me your Royal Clemency intreat.
Secrets of Marriage still are Sacred held:
Their sweet and bitter by the wise conceal'd.
Errors of Wives reflect on Husbands still:
355 And, when divulg'd, proclaim you've chosen ill.
And the mysterious pow'r of Bed and Throne,
Should always be maintain'd, but rarely shown.
Emperor. To so perverse a Sex all Grace is vain:
It gives 'em courage to offend again:
360 For with feign'd tears they penitence pretend:
Again are pardon'd, and again offend.
Fathom our pity when they seem to grieve;
Onely to try how far we can forgive.
Till lanching out into a Sea of strife,
365 They scorn all pardon, and appear all Wife.
But be it as you please: for your lov'd sake,
This last and fruitless trial I will make.
In all requests, your right of merit use:
And know, There is but one I can refuse.
  He signs to the Guards, and they remove from the Empress.
Nourmahal. You've done enough, for you design'd my Chains:
370 The Grace is vanish'd, but th'Affront remains.
Nor is't a Grace, or for his merit done;

336 *Candahar*] a province in Southern Afghanistan.
347 *Canon*] lawgiver.

You durst no farther, for you fear'd my Son.
This you have gain'd by the rough course you prove;
I'm past Repentance, and you past my Love.   *Exit.*   375
Emperor. A Spirit so untam'd the world ne'r bore.
Aureng-Zebe. And yet worse usage had incens'd her more.
But since by no obligement she is ti'd,
You must betimes for your defence provide.
I cannot idle in your danger stand;   380
But beg once more I may your Arms command:
Two Battels your auspicious Cause has wonn; ⎫
My Sword can perfect what it has begun,   ⎬
And, from your Walls, dislodge that haughty Son. ⎭
Emperor. My Son, your valour has, this day, been such,   385
None can enough admire, or praise too much.
But now, with reason, your success I doubt:
Her Faction's strong within, his Arms without.
Aureng-Zebe. I left the City in a Panic fright:
Lions they are in Council, Lambs in Fight.   390
But my own Troops, by *Mirzah* led, are near:
I, by to morrow's dawn, expect 'em here.
To favour 'em, I'll Sally out ere day,
And through our slaughter'd Foes enlarge their way.
Emperor. Age has not yet   395
So shrunk my Sinews, or so chill'd my Veins,
But conscious Virtue in my breast remains.
But had I now
That strength, with which my boiling Youth was
    fraught;   ⎫
When in the Vale of *Balasor* I fought,   ⎬   400
And from *Bengale* their Captive Monarch brought; ⎭
When Elephant 'gainst Elephant did rear
His Trunck, and Castles justl'd in the Air;
My Sword thy way to Victory had shown:
And ow'd the Conquest to it self alone.   405
Aureng-Zebe. Those fair Idea's to my aid I'll call,
And emulate my great Original.
Or, if they fail, I will invoke in Arms,
The pow'r of Love, and *Indamora's* Charms.
Emperor. I doubt the happy influence of your Star: 410
T'invoke a Captive's name bodes ill in War.
Aureng-Zebe. Sir, give me leave to say, What ever now
The Omen prove, it boded well to you.
Your Royal Promise, when I went to fight,
Oblig'd me to resign a Victor's right.   415

397 *conscious Virtue*] recalling *Aeneid*, V, 455 (Brower).

135

Her liberty I fought for, and I wonn:
And claim it as your General, and your Son.

Emperor. My ears still ring with noise, I'm vext to death:
Tongue-kill'd, and have not yet recover'd breath.
420   Nor will I be prescrib'd my time by you:
First end the War, and then your Claim renew.
While to your Conduct I my Fortune trust,
To keep this pledge of duty is but just.

Aureng-Zebe. Some hidden cause your jealousie does move,
425   Or you could ne'r suspect my Loyal Love.

Emperor. What love soever by an Heir is shown,
He waits but time to step into the Throne.
You're neither justifi'd, nor yet accus'd:
Mean while, the Pris'ner with respect is us'd.

430 *Aureng-Zebe.* I know the kindness of her Guardian such,
I need not fear too little, but too much.
But how, Sir, how have you from virtue swerv'd?
Or what so ill return have I deserv'd?
You doubt not me, nor have I spent my bloud,
435   To have my faith no better understood:
Your Soul's above the baseness of distrust:
Nothing but Love could make you so unjust.

Emperor. You know your Rival then; and know 'tis fit, ⎫
The Son's should to the Father's Claim submit. ⎬
Aureng-Zebe. Sons may have right, which they can never ⎭
440   quit.
Your self first made that Title which I claim:
First bid me love, and authoris'd my flame.

Emperor. The value of my gift I did not know:
If I could give, I can resume it too.

445 *Aureng-Zebe.* Recal your gift, for I your power confess:
But first, take back my life, a gift that's less.
Long life would now but a long burthen prove:
You're grown unkind, and I have lost your love.
My grief let unbecoming speeches fall:
450   I should have di'd, and not complain'd at all.

Emperor. Witness yee Pow'rs,
How much I suffer'd, and how long I strove
Against th'assaults of this imperious Love!
I represented to my self the shame
455   Of perjur'd Faith, and violated Fame.
Your great deserts, how ill they were repay'd;
All arguments, in vain, I urg'd and weigh'd:
For mighty Love, who Prudence does despise,

420 *prescrib'd*] appointed, or fixed beforehand.

For Reason, show'd me *Indamora's* Eyes.
What would you more, my crime I sadly view,   460
Acknowledge, am asham'd, and yet pursue.
Aureng-Zebe. Since you can love, and yet your error see,
The same resistless pow'r may plead for me.
With no less ardor I my claim pursue:
I love, and cannot yield her even to you.   465
Emperor. Your elder Brothers, though o'rcome, have right:
The youngest yet in Arms prepar'd to fight.
But, yielding her, I firmly have decreed,
That you alone to Empire shall suceed.
Aureng-Zebe. To after Ages let me stand a shame,   470
When I exchange for Crowns my Love or Fame.
You might have found a mercenary Son,
To profit of the Battels he had won:
Had I been such, what hinder'd me to take
The Crown? nor had th'exchange been yours to make.   475
While you are living, I no right pretend;
Wear it, and let it where you please descend.
But from my Love, 'tis Sacrilege to part:
There, there's my Throne in *Indamora's* heart.
Emperor. 'Tis in her heart alone that you must Reign: 480
You'll find her person difficult to gain.
Give willingly what I can take by force:
And know, Obedience is your safest course.
Aureng-Zebe. I'm taught, by Honour's precepts, to obey:
Fear to Obedience is a slavish way.   485
If ought my want of duty could beget;
You take the most prevailing means, to threat.
Pardon your Bloud that boils within my veins;
It rises high, and menacing disdains,
Even death's become to me no dreadful name: 490
I've often met him, and have made him tame:
In fighting fields, where our acquaintance grew,
I saw him, and contemn'd him first for you.
Emperor. Of formal duty make no more thy boast:
Thou disobey'st where it concerns me most.   495
Fool, with both hands thus to push back a Crown:
And headlong cast thy self from Empire down.
Though *Nourmahal* I hate, her Son shall Reign:
Inglorious thou, by thy own fault remain.
Thy younger Brother I'll admit this hour: 500
So mine shall be thy Mistris, his thy Pow'r.   *Exit.*
Aureng-Zebe. How vain is Virtue which directs our ways

468 *yielding her*] if you yield her.

137

Through certain danger to uncertain praise!
Barren, and aery name! thee Fortune flies;
505   With thy lean Train, the Pious and the Wise.
Heav'n takes thee at thy word, without regard;
And lets thee poorly be thy own reward.
The World is made for the bold impious man;
Who stops at nothing, seizes all he can.
510   Justice to merit does weak aid afford;
She trusts her Ballance, and neglects her Sword.
Virtue is nice to take what's not her own;
And, while she long consults, the Prize is gone.

To him, Dianet.

Dianet. Forgive the Bearer of unhappy news:
515   Your alter'd Father openly pursues
Your ruine; and, to compass his intent,
For violent *Morat* in haste has sent.
The Gates he order'd all to be unbarr'd:
And from the Market-place to draw the Guard.
520   *Aureng-Zebe.* How look the People in this turn of State?
Dianet. They mourn your ruine as their proper Fate.
Cursing the Empress: for they think it done
By her procurement, to advance her Son.
Him too, though aw'd, they scarcely can forbear:
525   His pride they hate, his violence they fear.
All bent to rise, would you appear their Chief,
Till your own Troops come up to your relief.
Aureng-Zebe. Ill treated, and forsaken, as I am,
I'll not betray the glory of my name:
530   'Tis not for me, who have preserv'd a State,
To buy an Empire at so base a rate.
Dianet. The points of Honour Poets may produce;
Trappings of life, for Ornament, not Use:
Honour, which onely does the name advance,
535   Is the meer raving madness of Romance.
Pleas'd with a word, you may sit tamely down;
And see your younger Brother force the Crown.
Aureng-Zebe. I know my fortune in extremes does lie:
The Sons of *Indostan* must Reign, or die.
540   That desperate hazard Courage does create,

512 *nice to take*] careful about taking.
539 *Sons of Indostan*] specifically Hindustan or northern India.
But from early times, foreigners, Mohammedan and European,
have extended it to include the whole of the peninsula and this is
the general geographical use. Aureng-Zebe's reference to "Sons
of Indostan" seems a general one to the princes of India rather than
to any particular sons.

As he plays frankly, who has least Estate;
And that the World the Coward will despise,
When Life's a Blank, who pulls not for a Prize.
Dianet. Of all your knowledge, this vain fruit you have,
  To walk with eyes broad open to your Grave.   545
Aureng-Zebe. From what I've said, conclude, without reply,
  I neither would Usurp, nor tamely die.
  Th'attempt to flie, would guilt betray, or fear:
  Besides, 'twere vain; the Fort's our Prison here.
  Somewhat I have resolv'd ———   550
  Morat, perhaps, has Honour in his breast:
  And, in extremes, bold Counsels are the best.
  Like Emp'ric Remedies, they last are tri'd;
  And by th'event condemn'd, or justifi'd.
  Presence of mind and courage in distress,   555
  Are more than Armies to procure success.

                                       Exeunt.

ACT III

[*Enter*] Arimant, *with a Letter in his hand*: Indamora.

Arimant. And I the Messenger to him from you?
  Your Empire you to Tyranny pursue:
  You lay commands, both cruel and unjust,
  To serve my Rival, and betray my trust.
Indamora. You first betray'd your trust in loving me,   5
  And should not I my own advantage see?
  Serving my Love, you may my Friendship gain,
  You know the rest of your pretences vain.
  You must, my *Arimant*, you must be kind:
  'Tis in your Nature, and your Noble Mind.   10
Arimant. I'll to the King, and streight my trust resign.
Indamora. His trust you may, but you shall never mine.
  Heav'n made you love me for no other end,
  But to become my Confident and Friend:
  As such, I keep no Secret from your sight,   15
  And therefore make you judge how ill I write:
  Read it, and tell me freely then your mind:
  If 'tis indited as I meant it, kind.

541 *frankly*] unrestrictedly, without restraint.
542 *that*] i.e., as; "that" used (like French *que*) as a substitute, instead of repeating a previous conjunction or conjunctive adverb or phrase.
543 *Blank*] "Naught but a blank remain, a dead void space" (Dryden's "On the Death of a Very Young Gentleman," line 9).
543 *pulls*] draws a card from the pack, as "pull for prime."

Arimant (reading). I ask not Heav'n my freedom to restore,

20   But onely for your sake ——— I'll read no more:

And yet I must ———

(*Reading*) Less for my own, than for your sorrow, sad ———

Another line, like this, would make me mad ———

(*As reading*) Heav'n! she goes on—yet more—and yet more kind!

25   Each Sentence is a Dagger to my mind.

(*Reading*) See me this night ———

Thank Fortune, who did such a Friend provide,

For faithful *Arimant* shall be your Guide. ———

Not onely to be made an Instrument,

30   But preingag'd without my own consent!

Indamora. Unknown t'ingage you still augments my score,

And gives you scope of meriting the more.

Arimant. The best of men

Some int'rest in their actions must confess;

35   None merit but in hope they may possess.

The fatal Paper rather let me tear,

Than, like *Bellerophon*, my own Sentence bear.

Indamora. You may; but 'twill not be your best advice:

'Twill onely give me pains of writing twice.

40   You know you must obey me, soon or late:

Why should you vainly struggle with your Fate?

Arimant. I thank thee, Heav'n, thou hast been wondrous kind!

Why am I thus to slavery design'd,

And yet am cheated with a free-born mind?

45   Or make thy Orders with my reason sute,

Or let me live by Sense a glorious Brute. ———

She frowns.

You frown, and I obey with speed, before

That dreadful Sentence comes, *See me no more*:

See me no more! that sound, methinks, I hear

50   Like the last Trumpet thund'ring in my ear.

Enter Solyman.

Solyman. The Princess *Melesinda*, bath'd in tears,

And toss'd alternately with hopes and fears,

If your affairs such leisure can afford,

Would learn from you the fortunes of her Lord.

55   *Arimant.* Tell her, that I some certainty may bring;

31 *score*] the record of points in a competition.
37 *Bellerophon*] who unwittingly carried the order for his own murder.

I go this minute to attend the King.
Indamora. This lonely Turtle I desire to see:
  Grief, though not cur'd, is eas'd by Company.
Arimant (to Solyman). Say, if she please, she hither may
  repair,
  And breathe the freshness of the open Air. 60
                     Exit Solyman.
Indamora. Poor Princess! how I pity her estate,
  Wrapt in the ruines of her Husband's Fate!
  She mourn'd *Morat* should in Rebellion rise;
  Yet he offends, and she's the Sacrifice.
Arimant. Not knowing his design, at Court she staid; 65
  Till, by command, close pris'ner she was made.
  Since when,
  Her Chains with *Roman* Constancy she bore;
  But that, perhaps, an *Indian* Wife's is more.
Indamora. Go, bring her comfort; leave me here alone. 70
Arimant. My love must still be in obedience shown.
                     Exit Arimant.

Enter Melesinda, *led by* Solyman, *who retires afterwards.*

Indamora. When graceful sorrow in her pomp appears,
  Sure she is dress'd in *Melesinda's* tears.
  Your head reclin'd, (as hiding grief from view,)
  Droops, like a Rose surcharg'd with morning Dew. 75
Melesinda. Can Flow'rs but droop in absence of the Sun,
  Which wak'd their sweets? and mine, alas! is gone.
  But you the noblest Charity express:
  For they who shine in Courts still shun distress.
Indamora. Distress'd my self, like you, confin'd I live: 80
  And therefore can compassion take, and give.
  We're both Love's Captives, but with Fate so cross,
  One must be happy by the other's loss.
  Morat, or *Aureng-Zebe* must fall this day.
Melesinda. Too truly *Tamerlain's* Successors they,
  Each thinks a World too little for his sway. 85
  Could you and I the same pretences bring,
  Mankind should with more ease receive a King:
  I would to you the narrow World resign,
  And want no Empire while *Morat* was mine. 90
Indamora. Wish'd freedom I presage you soon will find;
  If Heav'n be just, and be to Virtue kind.
Melesinda. Quite otherwise my mind foretels my Fate:
  Short is my life, and that unfortunate.
  Yet should I not complain, would Heav'n afford 95
  Some little time, ere death, to see my Lord.

Indamora. These thoughts are but your melancholy's food;
   Rais'd from a lonely life, and dark abode:
   But whatsoe'r our jarring fortunes prove,
100   Though our Lords hate, me-thinks we two may love.
Melesinda. Such be our Loves as may not yield to Fate:
   I bring a heart more true than fortunate.

                        Giving their hands.

           To them Arimant.

Arimant. I come with haste surprising news to bring:
   In two hours time, since last I saw the King,
105   Th'affairs of Court have wholely chang'd their face:
   Unhappy *Aureng-Zebe* is in disgrace:
   And your *Morat*, (proclaim'd the Successor,)
   Is call'd, to awe the City with his power.
   Those Trumpets his triumphant Entry tell.
110   And now the Shouts waft near the Cittadel.
Indamora. See, Madam, see th'event by me foreshown:
   I envy not your chance, but grieve my own.
Melesinda. A change so unexpected must surprise:
   And more, because I am unus'd to joys.
115 *Indamora.* May all your wishes ever prosp'rous be,
   But I'm too much concern'd th'event to see.
   My eyes too tender are
   To view my Lord become the publick scorn.
   I came to comfort, and I go to mourn.

                        Taking her leave.

120 *Melesinda.* Stay, I'll not see my Lord,
   Before I give your sorrow some relief;
   And pay the charity you lent my grief.
   Here he shall see me first with you confin'd:
   And, if your virtue fail to move his mind,
125   I'll use my int'rest that he may be kind.
   Fear not, I never mov'd him yet in vain.
Indamora. So fair a Pleader any Cause may gain.
Melesinda. I have no taste, me-thinks, of coming joy;
   For black presages all my hopes destroy.
130   Die, something whispers, *Melesinda*, die;
   Fulfil, fulfil thy mournful Destiny.
   Mine is a gleam of bliss, too hot to last,
   Watry it shines, and will be soon o'r-cast.

---

133 *Watry*] an epithet describing heavenly bodies, portents, seasons, which are thought to bring rain, here probably associated with death.

Indamora *and* Melesinda *re-enter, as into the Chamber.*

Arimant. Fortune seems weary grown of *Aureng-Zebe,*
    While to her new-made Favourite, *Morat,*   135
    Her lavish hand is wastefully profuse:
    With Fame and flowing Honours tided in,
    Born on a swelling Current smooth beneath him.
    The King and haughty Empress, to our wonder,
    If not atton'd, yet seemingly at peace,   140
    As Fate for him that Miracle reserv'd.

    Enter in Triumph, Emperor, Morat, *and Train.*

Emperor. I have confess'd I love.
    As I interpret fairly your design,
    So look not with severer eyes on mine.
    Your Fate has call'd you to th'Imperial Seat: 145
    In duty be, as you in Arms are, great.
    For *Aureng-Zebe* a hated name is grown,
    And Love less bears a Rival than the Throne.
Morat. To me, the cries of fighting Fields are Charms:
    Keen be my Sable, and of proof my Arms.   150
    I ask no other blessing of my Stars:
    No prize but Fame, nor Mistris but the Wars.
    I scarce am pleas'd I tamely mount the Throne:
    Would *Aureng-Zebe* had all their Souls in one:
    With all my elder Brothers I would fight,   155
    And so from partial Nature force my right.
Emperor. Had we but lasting Youth, and time to spare,
    Some might be thrown away on Fame and War:
    But Youth, the perishing good, runs on too fast: ⎫
    And unenjoy'd will spend it self to waste; ⎬   160
    Few know the use of life before 'tis past. ⎭
    Had I once more thy vigour to command,
    I would not let it die upon my hand:
    No hour of pleasure should pass empty by,
    Youth should watch joys, and shoot 'em as they flie.   165
Morat. Me-thinks all pleasure is in greatness found.
    Kings, like Heav'n's Eye, should spread their beams
        around.
    Pleas'd to be seen while Glory's race they run:
    Rest is not for the Chariot of the Sun.
    Subjects are stiff-neck'd Animals, they soon   170
    Feel slacken'd Reins, and pitch their Rider down.
Emperor. To thee that drudgery of Pow'r I give:

150 *Sable*] a spelling of "Sabre."

143

Cares be thy lot: Reign thou, and let me live.
The Fort I'll keep for my security,
175   Bus'ness, and public State resign to thee.
    Morat. Luxurious Kings are to their People lost;
They live, like Drones, upon the public cost.
My Arms, from Pole to Pole, the World shall shake:
And, with my self, keep all Mankind awake.
180   *Emperor.* Believe me, Son, and needless trouble spare;
'Tis a base World, and is not worth our care.
The Vulgar, a scarce animated Clod,
Ne'r pleas'd with ought above 'em, Prince or God.
Were I a God, the drunken Globe should roul:
185   The little Emmets with the humane Soul
Care for themselves, while at my ease I sat,
And second Causes did the work of Fate.
Or, if I would take care, that care should be
For Wit that scorn'd the World, and liv'd like me.

      To them, Nourmahal, Zayda, *and Attendants.*

190   *Nourmahal.* My dear *Morat,*   *Embracing her Son.*
This day propitious to us all has been:
You're now a Monarch's Heir, and I a Queen.
Your youthful Father now may quit the State,
And find the ease he sought, indulg'd by Fate.
195   Cares shall not keep him on the Throne awake,
Nor break the golden Slumbers he would take.
    Emperor. In vain I struggl'd to the Goal of Life,   ⎫
While Rebel-Sons, and an imperious Wife   ⎬
Still dragg'd me backward into noise and strife.   ⎭
200   *Morat.* Be that remembrance lost; and be't my pride
To be your pledge of peace on either side.

      To them, Aureng-Zebe.

    Aureng-Zebe. With all th'assurance Innocence can bring,
Fearless without, because secure within,
Arm'd with my courage, unconcern'd I see
205   This pomp; a shame to you, a pride to me.
Shame is but where with wickedness 'tis joyn'd; ⎫
And, while no baseness in this breast I find,   ⎬
I have not lost the birth-right of my mind.   ⎭
    Emperor. Children (the blind effect of Love and Chance,
210   Form'd by their sportive Parents ignorance)

183 above 'em,] above 'em Q3; 'em, above Q1–2, Q4–6, F
194 find] Q3; finds Q1–2, Q4–6, F

187 *second Causes*] natural causes, those distinguished from the
First Cause, God.
193 *youthful*] ironically spoken.

Bear from their birth th'impressions of a Slave:
Whom Heav'n for play-games first, and then for service
   gave.
One then may be displac'd, and one may Reign:
And want of Merit, render Birth-right vain.
Morat. Comes he t'upbraid us with his innocence?   215
Seize him, and take the preaching *Brachman* hence.
Aureng-Zebe (to his Father). Stay, Sir; I, from my years, no
   merit plead:
All my designs and acts to duty lead.
Your Life and Glory are my onely end;
And for that Prize I with *Morat* contend.   220
Morat. Not him alone; I all Mankind defie.
Who dares adventure more for both than I?
Aureng-Zebe. I know you brave, and take you at your
   word:
That present service which you vaunt, afford.
Our two Rebellious Brothers are not dead: 225
Though vanquish'd, yet again they gather head.
I dare you, as your Rival in renown,
March out your Army from th'Imperial Town:
Chuse whom you please, the other leave to me:
And set our Father absolutely free.   230
This, if you do, to end all future strife,
I am content to lead a private life:
Disband my Army to secure the State,
Nor aim at more, but leave the rest to Fate.
Morat. I'll do't. Draw out my Army on the Plain: 235
War is to me a pastime, Peace a pain.
Emperor (to Morat). Think better first.
(*To Aureng-Zebe*) You see your self inclos'd beyond
   escape,
And therefore, *Proteus*-like, you change your shape.
Of promise prodigal, while pow'r you want,   240
And preaching in the Self-denying Cant.
Morat. Plot better; for these Arts too obvious are,
Of gaining time, the Masterpiece of War:
Is *Aureng-Zebe* so known?
Aureng-Zebe.   If Acts like mine,
So far from int'rest, profit, or design,   245
Can show my heart, by those I would be known:
I wish you could as well defend your own.
My absent Army for my Father fought:

216 *Brachman*] Brahmin, a derogatory name since the characters
in the play are Moslems.

145

Yours, in these Walls, is to inslave him brought.
250 If I come singly, you an armed guest,
The World with ease may judge whose Cause is best.
Morat. My Father saw you ill designs pursue:
And my admission show'd his fear of you.
Aureng-Zebe. Himself best knows why he his Love with-
draws:
255 I owe him more than to declare the cause.
But still I press our duty may be shown
By Arms.
Morat. I'll vanquish all his foes alone.
Aureng-Zebe. You speak as if you could the Fates com-
mand,
And had no need of any other hand.
260 But, since my Honour you so far suspect,
'Tis just I should on your designs reflect.
To prove your self a Loyal Son, declare
You'll lay down Arms when you conclude the War.
Morat. No present answer your demand requires;
265 The War once done, I'll do what Heav'n inspires.
And while the Sword this Monarchy secures,
'Tis manag'd by an abler Arm than yours.
Emperor (apart). *Morat's* design a doubtful meaning bears:
In *Aureng-Zebe* true Loyalty appears.
270 He, for my safety, does his own despise;
Still, with his wrongs, I find his duty rise.
I feel my Virtue strugling in my Soul,
But stronger Passion does its pow'r controul.
(To Aureng-Zebe apart) Yet be advis'd your ruine to
prevent.
275 You might be safe, if you would give consent.
Aureng-Zebe. So to your welfare I of use may be,
My life or death are equal both to me.
Emperor. The People's hearts are yours; the Fort yet mine:
Be wise, and *Indamora's* love resign.
280 I am observ'd: remember that I give
This my last proof of kindness, die, or live.
Aureng-Zebe. Life, with my *Indamora*, I would chuse;
But, losing her, the end of living lose.
I had consider'd all I ought before;
285 And fear of death can make me change no more.
The People's love so little I esteem,
Condemn'd by you, I would not live by them.
May he who must your favour now possess,
Much better serve you, and not love you less.
290 *Emperor (aloud).* I've heard you; and, to finish the debate,

Commit that Rebel pris'ner to the State.
Morat. The deadly draught he shall begin this day:
And languish with insensible decay.
Aureng-Zebe. I hate the lingring summons to attend,
Death all at once would be the nobler end.   295
Fate is unkind! me-thinks a General
Should warm, and at the head of Armies fall.
(*To his Father*) And my ambition did that hope pursue,
That so I might have di'd in fight for you.
Morat. Would I had been disposer of thy Stars;   300
Thou shouldst have had thy wish, and di'd in Wars.
'Tis I, not thou, have reason to repine,
That thou shouldst fall by any hand, but mine.
Aureng-Zebe. When thou wert form'd, Heav'n did a Man
    begin;
But the brute Soul, by chance, was shuffl'd in.   305
In Woods and Wilds thy Monarchy maintain:
Where valiant Beasts, by force and rapine, reign.
In Life's next Scene, if Transmigration be,
Some Bear or Lion is reserv'd for thee.
Morat. Take heed thou com'st not in that Lion's way: ⎫   310
I prophecy thou wilt thy Soul convey   ⎬
Into a Lamb, and be again my Prey.   ⎭
Hence with that dreaming Priest.
Nourmahal.   Let me prepare
The pois'nous draught: his death shall be my care.
Near my Apartment let him pris'ner be: 315
That I his hourly ebbs of life may see.
Aureng-Zebe. My life I would not ransome with a pray'r.
'Tis vile, since 'tis not worth my Father's care.
I go not, Sir, indebted to my grave:
You pai'd your self, and took the life you gave.   *Exit.*   320
Emperor (*aside*). O that I had more sense of vertue left,
Or were of that, which yet remains, bereft.
I've just enough to know how I offend,
And, to my shame, have not enough to mend.
Lead to the Mosque. ——   325
Morat. Love's pleasures why should dull devotion stay?
Heav'n to my *Melesinda*'s but the way.
                    Exeunt Emperor, Morat, *and Train.*
Zayda. Sure *Aureng-Zebe* has somewhat of Divine,
Whose virtue through so dark a clowd can shine.
Fortune has from *Morat* this day remov'd   330

325 *Mosque*] the Pearl Mosque built by Shah Jahan in the fort at
Agra.

147

The greatest Rival, and the best belov'd.
Nourmahal. He is not yet remov'd.
Zayda.   He lives, 'tis true;
But soon must die, and, what I mourn, by you.
Nourmahal. My *Zayda*, may thy words prophetic be:
                                Embracing her eagerly.
335   I take the Omen, let him die by me.
He stifl'd in my arms shall lose his breath:
And Life it self shall envious be of Death.
Zayda. Bless me, you Pow'rs above!
Nourmahal.   Why dost thou start?
Is Love so strange? or have not I a heart?
340   Could *Aureng-Zebe* so lovely seem to thee,
And I want eyes that noble worth to see?
Thy little Soul was but to wonder mov'd:
My sense of it was higher, and I lov'd.
That Man, that God-like Man, so brave, so great;
345   But these are thy small praises I repeat.
I'm carri'd by a Tide of Love away:
He's somewhat more than I my self can say.
Zayda. Though all th'Idea's you can form be true,
He must not, cannot be possess'd by you.
350   If contradicting int'rests could be mixt,
Nature her self has cast a bar betwixt.
And, ere you reach to this incestuous Love,
You must Divine and Humane Rights remove.
Nourmahal. Count this among the Wonders Love has done:
355   I had forgot he was my Husband's Sone!
Zayda. Nay, more; you have forgot who is your own:
For whom your care so long design'd the Throne.
Morat must fall, if *Aureng-Zebe* should rise.
Nourmahal. 'Tis true; but who was ere in love, and wise?
360   Why was that fatal knot of Marriage ti'd,
Which did, by making us too near, divide?
Divides me from my Sex! for Heav'n, I find,
Excludes but me alone of Woman-kind.
I stand with guilt confounded, lost with shame,
365   And yet made wretched onely by a name.
If names have such command on humane Life,
Love sure's a name that's more Divine than Wife.
That Sovereign power all guilt from action takes,
At least the stains are beautiful it makes.
370   *Zayda.* Th'incroaching ill you early should oppose:
Flatter'd 'tis worse, and by indulgence grows.

351 has] S-S; hast Q1; hath Q2-6, F

Nourmahal. Alas! and what have I not said or done?
I fought it to the last: and Love has wonn.
A bloudy Conquest; which destruction brought,
And ruin'd all the Countrey where he fought.   375
Whether this Passion from above was sent
The Fate of him Heav'n favours to prevent,
Or as the curse of Fortune in excess;
That, stretching, would beyond its reach possess:
And, with a taste which plenty does deprave,   380
Loaths lawful good, and lawless ill does crave?
Zayda. But yet consider ———
Nourmahal.   No, 'tis loss of time:
Think how to farther, not divert my crime.
My artful Engines instantly I'll move:
And chuse the soft and gentlest hour of Love.   385
The Under-Provost of the Fort is mine.
But see, *Morat!* I'll whisper my design.

   Enter Morat *with* Arimant, *as talking: Attendants.*

Arimant. And for that cause was not in public seen:
But stays in Prison with the captive Queen.
Morat. Let my Attendants wait; I'll be alone: 390
Where least of State, there most of Love is shown.
                  [*Exit* Arimant, *and Attendants.*]
Nourmahal (*to* Morat). My Son, your bus'ness is not hard to
   ghess;
Long absence makes you eager to possess:
I will not importune you by my stay;
She merits all the Love which you can pay.   395
                  Exit with Zayda.

   Re-enter Arimant, *with* Melesinda; *then Exit.* Morat
     runs to Melesinda, *and embraces her.*

Morat. Should I not chide you, that you chose to stay
In gloomy shades, and lost a glorious day?
Lost the first fruits of joy you should possess
In my return, and made my Triumph less?
Melesinda. Should I not chide, that you could stay and see   400
Those joys, preferring public Pomp to me?
Through my dark Cell your shouts of Triumph rung:
I heard with pleasure; but I thought 'em long.
Morat. The Public will in Triumphs rudely share:
And Kings the rudeness of their joys must bear.   405
But I made haste to set my Captive free:
And thought that work was onely worthy me.
The Fame of antient Matrons you pursue;

And stand a blameless pattern to the new.
410   I have not words to praise such Acts as these:
    But take my Heart, and mold it as you please.
Melesinda. A trial of your kindness I must make,
    Though not for mine so much as Virtue's sake.
    The Queen of *Cassimeer* ———
Morat.   No more, my love;
415   That onely suit I beg you not to move.
    That she's in Bonds for *Aureng-Zebe* I know,
    And should, by my consent, continue so.
    The good old man, I fear, will pity show.
    My Father dotes, and let him still dote on;
420   He buys his Mistris dearly with his Throne.
Melesinda. See her; and then be cruel if you can.
Morat. 'Tis not with me as with a private Man.
    Such may be sway'd by Honour, or by Love;
    But Monarchs, onely by their int'rest move.
425   *Melesinda.* Heav'n does a Tribute for your pow'r demand:
    He leaves th'opprest and poor upon your hand.
    And those who Stuards of his pity prove,
    He blesses, in return, with public Love.
    In his distress, some Miracle is shown:
430   If exil'd, Heav'n restores him to his Throne.
    He needs no Guard while any Subject's near:
    Nor, like his Tyrant Neighbours, lives in fear:
    No Plots th'Alarm to his retirements give:
    'Tis all Mankind's concern that he should live.
435   *Morat.* You promis'd friendship in your low estate;
    And should forget it in your better Fate;
    Such Maxims are more plausible than true;
    But somewhat must be given to Love and you.
    I'll view this Captive Queen; to let her see,
440   Pray'rs and complaints are lost on such as me.
Melesinda. I'll bear the news: Heav'n knows how much I'm
        pleas'd,
    That, by my care, th'afflicted may be eas'd.

As she is going off, Enter Indamora.

Indamora. I'll spare your pains, and venture out alone,
    Since you, fair Princess, my protection own.
                    To Morat *kneeling, who takes her up.*
445   But you, brave Prince, a harder task must find;
    In saving me, you would but half be kind.
    An humble Supplaint at your feet I lie;

414 *Cassimeer*] Kashmir.

You have condemn'd my better part to die.
Without my *Aureng-Zebe* I cannot live;
Revoke his Doom, or else my Sentence give. 450
Melesinda. If *Melesinda* in your love have part,
  Which, to suspect, would break my tender heart:
  If Love, like mine, may for a Lover plead,
  By the chaste pleasures of our Nuptial Bed,
  By all the int'rest my past suff'rings make, 455
  And all I yet would suffer for your sake;
  By you your self, the last and dearest tie ———
Morat. You move in vain; for *Aureng-Zebe* must die.
Indamora. Could that Decree from any Brother come?
  Nature her self is sentenc'd in your doom. 460
  Piety is no more, she sees her place
  Usurp'd by Monsters, and a savage Race.
  From her soft Eastern Climes you drive her forth,
  To the cold Mansions of the utmost North.
  How can our Prophet suffer you to Reign, 465
  When he looks down, and sees your Brother slain?
  Avenging Furies will your life pursue:
  Think there's a Heav'n, *Morat*, though not for you.
Melesinda. Her words imprint a terror on my mind.
  What if this death, which is for him design'd, 470
  Had been your Doom, (far be that Augury!)
  And you, not *Aureng-Zebe*, condemn'd to die?
  Weigh well the various turns of Humane Fate,
  And seek, by Mercy, to secure your State.
Indamora. Had Heav'n the Crown for *Aureng-Zebe*
    design'd,
  Pity, for you, had pierc'd his generous mind. 475
  Pity does with a Noble Nature suit:
  A Brother's life had suffer'd no dispute.
  All things have right in life, our Prophet's care
  Commands the beings eve'n of Brutes to spare. 480
  Though int'rest his restraint has justifi'd,
  Can life, and to a Brother, be deni'd?
Morat. All Reasons for his safety urg'd, are weak:
  And yet, me-thinks, 'tis Heav'n to hear you speak.
Melesinda. 'Tis part of your own being to invade ——— 485
Morat. Nay, if she fail to move, would you perswade?
  (*Turning to Indamora*) My Brother does a glorious Fate
    pursue.
  I envy him, that he must fall for you.
  He had been base had he releas'd his right:

465 *Prophet*] Mohammed.

490   For such an Empire none but Kings should fight.
     If with a Father, he disputes this prize,
     My wonder ceases when I see these Eyes.
     Melesinda. And can you then deny those Eyes you praise?
     Can Beauty wonder, and not pity raise?
495   *Morat.* Your intercession now is needless grown:
     Retire, and let me speak with her alone.
         Melesinda *retires, weeping, to the side of the Theatre.*
     Queen, that you may not fruitless tears employ,
         Taking Indamora's *hand.*
     I bring you news to fill your heart with joy:
     Your Lover King of all the East shall Reign:
500   For *Aureng-Zebe* to morrow shall be slain.
     Indamora. The hopes you rais'd y'ave blasted with a
         breath: *Starting back.*
     With Triumphs you began, but end with Death.
     Did you not say, my Lover should be King?
     Morat. I, in *Morat,* the best of Lovers bring!
505   For one forsaken both of Earth and Heav'n,
     Your kinder Stars a nobler choice have given:
     My Father, while I please, a King appears;
     His Pow'r is more declining than his Years.
     An Emperor and Lover, but in show:
510   But you, in me, have Youth and Fortune too.
     As Heav'n did to your eyes and form Divine,
     Submit the Fate of all th'Imperial Line;
     So was it order'd by its wise Decree,
     That you should find 'em all compris'd in me.
515   *Indamora.* If, Sir, I seem not discompos'd with rage,
     Feed not your fancy with a false presage.
     Farther to press your Courtship is but vain:
     A cold refusal carries more disdain.
     Unsetled Virtue stormy may appear;
520   Honour, like mine, serenely is severe.
     To scorn your person, and reject your Crown,
     Disorder not my face into a frown.   *Turns from him.*
     Morat. Your Fortune you should rev'rently have us'd:
     Such offers are not twice to be refus'd.
525   I go to *Aureng-Zebe,* and am in haste:
     For your Commands, they're like to be the last.
     Indamora. Tell him,
     With my own death I would his life redeem;
     But, less than Honour, both our Lives esteem.
     Morat. Have you no more?
530   *Indamora* (*aside*).   What shall I do or say?
     He must not in this fury go away.

[*To him*] Tell him, I did in vain his Brother move;
And yet he falsly said, he was in love.
Falsly; for had he truly lov'd, at least,
He would have giv'n one day to my request.   535
Morat [*aside*]. A little yielding may my love advance:
She darted from her eyes a sidelong glance,
Just as she spoke; and, like her words, it flew:
Seem'd not to beg, what yet she bid me do.
(*To her*) A Brother, Madam, cannot give a day;   540
A Servant, and who hopes to merit, may.
Melesinda. If, Sir ———   *Coming to him.*
Morat. No more ——— set speeches, and a formal tale,
With none but States-men and grave Fools prevail.
Dry up your tears, and practise every Grace,   545
That fits the Pageant of your Royal place.   *Exit.*
Melesinda (*to Indamora*). Madam, the strange reverse of
Fate you see:
I piti'd you, now you may pity me.   *Exit after him.*
Indamora. Poor Princess! thy hard Fate I could bemoan,
Had I not nearer sorrows of my own.   550
Beauty is seldom fortunate, when great:
A vast Estate, but overcharg'd with Debt.
Like those whom want to baseness does betray:
I'm forc'd to flatter him I cannot pay.
O would he be content to seize the Throne: 555
I beg the life of *Aureng-Zebe* alone.
Whom Heav'n would bless, from Pomp it will remove,
And make their wealth in privacy and Love.
          Exit.

ACT IV

[*Enter*] Aureng-Zebe *solus.*

Aureng-Zebe. Distrust, and darkness, of a future state,
Make poor Mankind so fearful of their Fate.
Death, in it self, is nothing; but we fear
To be we know not what, we know not where.
          Soft Music.
This is the Ceremony of my Fate: 5
A parting Treat; and I'm to die in State.
They lodge me, as I were the *Persian* King:
And with luxurious Pomp my death they bring.

          To him Nourmahal.

Nourmahal. I thought, before you drew your latest breath,
To smooth your passage, and to soften death;   10

153

For I would have you, when you upward move,
Speak kindly of me, to our Friends above:
Nor name me there th'occasion of your Fate;
Or what my Interest does, impute to Hate.

15 *Aureng-Zebe.* I ask not for what end your Pomp's design'd;
Whether t'insult, or to compose my mind:
I mark'd it not;
But, knowing Death would soon th'Assault begin,
Stood firm collected in my Strength within:
20 To guard that breach did all my Forces guide,
And left unmann'd the quiet Senses side.

Nourmahal. Because *Morat* from me his being took,
All I can say will much suspected look:
'Tis little to confess your Fate I grieve;
25 Yet more than you would easily believe.

Aureng-Zebe. Since my inevitable death you know,
You safely unavailing pity show:
'Tis Popular to mourn a dying Foe.

Nourmahal. You made my Liberty your late request:
30 Is no return due from a grateful breast?
I grow impatient, till I find some way
Great Offices, with greater, to repay.

Aureng-Zebe. When I consider Life, 'tis all a cheat;
Yet, fool'd with hope, men favour the deceit;
35 Trust on, and think to morrow will repay:
To morrow's falser than the former day;
Lies worse; and while it says, We shall be blest
With some new joys, cuts off what we possest.
Strange couzenage! none would live past years again,
40 Yet all hope pleasure in what yet remain;
And, from the dregs of Life, think to receive
What the first sprightly running could not give.
I'm tir'd with waiting for this Chymic Gold,
Which fools us young, and beggars us when old.

45 *Nourmahal.* 'Tis not for nothing that we life pursue;
It pays our hopes with something still that's new:
Each day's a Mistris, unenjoy'd before;
Like Travellers, we're pleas'd with seeing more.
Did you but know what joys your way attend,
50 You would not hurry to your journey's end.

Aureng-Zebe. I need not haste the end of Life to meet;
The precipice is just beneath my feet.

Nourmahal. Think not my sense of Virtue is so small:
I'll rather leap down first, and break your fall.

43 *Chymic*] chemic, alchemy metal, i.e., counterfeit gold.

My *Aureng-Zebe*, (may I not call you so?)   55
                    Taking him by the hand.
Behold me now no longer as your Foe;
I am not, cannot be your Enemy:
Look, is there any malice in my eye?
Pray sit. ——   *Both sit.*
That distance shows too much respect, or fear: 60
You'll find no danger in approaching near.
Aureng-Zebe. Forgive th'amazement of my doubtful state:
This kindness from the Mother of *Morat*!
Or is't some Angel, pitying what I bore,
Who takes that shape, to make my wonder more?   65
Nourmahal. Think me your better *Genius* in disguise;
Or any thing that more may charm your eyes.
Your Guardian Angel never could excel
In care, nor could he love his charge so well.
Aureng-Zebe. Whence can proceed so wonderful a change?   70
Nourmahal. Can kindness to desert, like yours, be strange?
Kindness by secret Sympathy is ty'd;
For Noble Souls in Nature are alli'd.
I saw with what a brow you brav'd your Fate;
Yet with what mildness bore your Father's hate.   75
My Virtue, like a String wound up by Art, ⎫
To the same sound, when yours was touch'd, took ⎬
    part,   ⎪
At distance shook, and trembled at my heart. ⎭
Aureng-Zebe. I'll not complain my Father is unkind,
Since so much pity from a Foe I find.
Just Heav'n reward this act.   80
Nourmahal. 'Tis well the debt no payment does demand,
You turn me over to another hand.
But happy, happy she,
And with the Bless'd above to be compar'd,   85
Whom you your self would, with your self, reward:
The greatest, nay, the fairest of her kind,
Would envy her that Bliss which you design'd.
Aureng-Zebe. Great Princes thus, when Favourites they
    raise,
To justifie their Grace, their Creatures praise.   90
Nourmahal. As Love the Noblest Passion we account,
So to the highest Object it should mount.
It shows you brave when mean desires you shun.
An Eagle onely can behold the Sun:
And so must you; if yet, presage Divine   95
There be in Dreams, or was't a Vision mine?
Aureng-Zebe. Of me?

Nourmahal.   And who could else employ my
          thought?
I dream'd, your Love was by Love's Goddess sought;
Officious Cupids, hov'ring o'r your head,
100   Held Myrtle wreaths: beneath your feet were spread
What Sweets soe'r *Sabean* Springs disclose,
Our *Indian* Jasmine, or the *Syrian* Rose:
The wanton Ministers arround you strove
For service, and inspir'd their Mother's Love:
105   Close by your side, and languishing, she lies,
With blushing cheeks, short breath, and wishing eyes;
Upon your breast supinely lay her head,
While, on your face, her famish'd sight she fed.
Then, with a sigh, into these words she broke,
110   (And gather'd humid kisses as she spoke.)
Dull, and ingrateful! must I offer love?
Desir'd of Gods, and envi'd ev'n by *Jove*:
And dost thou ignorance or fear pretend?
Mean Soul! and dar'st not gloriously offend?
Then, pressing thus his hand ———
115   *Aureng-Zebe (rising up).*   I'll hear no more.
'Twas impious to have understood before;
And I, till now, endeavour'd to mistake
Th'incestuous meaning which too plain you make.
Nourmahal. And why this niceness to that pleasure shown,
120   Where Nature sums up all her joys in one;
Gives all she can, and labouring still to give,
Makes it so great, we can but taste and live:
So fills the Senses, that the Soul seems fled,
And thought it self does, for the time, lie dead;
125   Till, like a String scru'd up with eager haste,
It breaks, and is too exquisite to last?
Aureng-Zebe. Heav'ns! can you this, without just ven-
          geance, hear?
When will you thunder, if it now be clear?
Yet her alone let not your Thunder seize:
130   I, too, deserve to die, because I please.
Nourmahal. Custom our Native Royalty does awe;

98–115 *I dream'd . . . hand*] a favorite subject for baroque painters,
of the indifferent young Adonis and the aggressive, older Venus.
Nicholas Poussin's "Venus and Adonis" (*ca.* 1624), in the Providence, R.I., Museum of Art, corresponds fairly closely to this
passage, although both lovers are asleep and his head is on her breast
in the painting, but Titian's well-known painting fits as well.
119 *niceness*] fastidiousness.
125 *like a String scru'd up*] the winding string on a watch, which
if wound too fast forced the stop and broke the string.

Promiscuous Love is Nature's general Law:
For whosoever the first Lovers were,
Brother and Sister made the second Pair,
And doubled, by their love, their piety.   135
Aureng-Zebe. Hence, hence, and to some barbarous
   Climate fly,
Which onely Brutes in humane form does yield,
And Man grows wild in Nature's common Field.
Who eat their Parents, piety pretend;
Yet there no Sons their Sacred Bed ascend.   140
To vail great Sins, a greater Crime you chuse;
And, in your Incest, your Adult'ry lose.
Nourmahal. In vain this haughty fury you have shown.
How I adore a Soul so like my own!
You must be mine, that you may learn to live: 145
Know joys, which onely she who loves can give.
Nor think that action you upbraid, so ill:
I am not chang'd; I love my Husband still;
But love him as he was, when youthful grace,
And the first down began to shade his face: 150
That Image does my Virgin-flames renew,
And all your Father shines more bright in you.
Aureng-Zebe. In me a horrour of my self you raise;
Curs'd by your love, and blasted by your praise.
You find new ways to prosecute my Fate;   155
And your least-guilty passion was your Hate.
Nourmahal. I beg my death, if you can Love deny.
                      Offering him a Dagger.
Aureng-Zebe. I'll grant you nothing; no, not ev'n to die.
Nourmahal. Know then, you are not half so kind as I.
                      Stamps with her foot.

Enter Mutes, some with Swords drawn, one with a Cup.

You've chosen, and may now repent too late.   160
Behold th'effect of what you wish'd, my Hate.
This Cup, a cure for both our ills has brought:
You need not fear a Philtre in the Draught.
             Taking the Cup to present him.
Aureng-Zebe. All must be poison which can come from
   thee;   *Receiving it from her.*
But this the least. T'immortal Liberty   165
This first I pour ——— like dying *Socrates*;
               Spilling a little of it.

139–40 *Who . . . ascend*] See Sir James Frazer, *The Golden Bough*
(1911–15), IV, 14–15; and Montaigne, *Essays*, II, 12.

Grim though he be, Death pleases when he frees.

As he is going to drink, Enter Morat *attended.*

Morat. Make not such haste, you must my leisure stay:
Your Fate's deferr'd, you shall not die to day.
Taking the Cup from him.

170 *Nourmahal.* What foolish pity has possess'd your mind,
To alter what your prudence once design'd?
Morat. What if I please to lengthen out his date
A day, and take a pride to cozen Fate?
Nourmahal. 'Twill not be safe to let him live an hour.
175 *Morat.* I'll do't, to show my Arbitrary pow'r.
Nourmahal. Fortune may take him from your hands again,
And you repent th'occasion lost in vain.
Morat. I smile at what your Female fear foresees:
I'm in Fate's place, and dictate her Decrees.
180 Let *Arimant* be call'd. *Exit one of his Attendants.*
Aureng-Zebe. Give me the poison, and I'll end your strife:
I hate to keep a poor precarious life.
Would I my safety on base terms receive,
Know, Sir, I could have liv'd without your leave.
185 But those I could accuse, I can forgive:
By my disdainful silence, let 'em live.
Nourmahal (to Morat). What am I, that you dare to bind my
hand?
So low, I've not a Murder at command!
Can you not one poor Life to her afford,
190 Her who gave up whole Nations to your Sword?
And from th'abundance of whose Soul and Heat,
Th'o'rflowing serv'd to make your mind so great.
Morat. What did that greatness in a Woman's mind?
Ill lodg'd, and weak to act what it design'd.
195 Pleasure's your portion, and your slothful ease:
When Man's at leisure, study how to please.
Soften his angry hours with servile care,
And when he calls, the ready Feast prepare.
From Wars, and from affairs of State abstain:
200 Women Emasculate a Monarch's Reign;
And murmuring Crouds, who see 'em shine with Gold,
That pomp, as their own ravish'd Spoils behold.
Nourmahal (aside). Rage choaks my words: 'tis Womanly to
weep:
In my swoll'n breast my close revenge I'll keep;
205 I'll watch his tender'st part, and there strike deep. *Exit.*
Aureng-Zebe. Your strange proceeding does my wonder
move;

Yet seems not to express a Brother's love.
Say to what Cause my rescu'd life I owe.
Morat. If what you ask would please, you should not
    know.
But since that knowledge, more than Death, will grieve,   210
Know, *Indamora* gain'd you this Reprieve.
Aureng-Zebe. And whence had she the pow'r to work your
    change?
Morat. The pow'r of Beauty is not new or strange.
Should she command me more, I could obey;
But her request was bounded with a day.   215
Take that; and, if you'll spare my farther crime,
Be kind, and grieve to death against your time.

    Enter Arimant.

Remove this Pris'ner to some safer place:
He has, for *Indamora's* sake, found grace:
And, from my Mother's rage must guarded be,   220
Till you receive a new Command from me.
Arimant (aside). Thus Love, and Fortune, persecute me still,
And make me Slave to every Rival's will.
Aureng-Zebe. How I disdain a Life, which I must buy
With your contempt, and her inconstancy!   225
For a few hours, my whole content I pay:
You shall not force on me another day.
    Exit with Arimant.

    Enter Melesinda.

Melesinda. I have been seeking you this hour's long space,
And fear'd to find you in another place;
But, since you're here, my jealousie grows less: 230
You will be kind to my unworthiness.
What shall I say? I love to that degree,
Each glance another way is robb'd from me.
Absence, and Prisons, I could bear again;
But sink, and die, beneath your least disdain.   235
Morat. Why do you give your mind this needless care,
And, for your self, and me, new pains prepare?
I ne'r approv'd this passion in excess:
If you would show your love, distrust me less.
I hate to be pursu'd from place to place: 240
Meet, at each turn, a stale domestic face.
Th'approach of jealousie Love cannot bear,

---

216 *spare my farther crime*] prevent my committing a crime later
(Saintsbury).

159

He's wild, and soon on wing, if watchful eyes come
near.
Melesinda. From your lov'd presence, how can I depart?
245   My eyes pursue the object of my heart.
Morat. You talk as if it were our Bridal night:
Fondness is still th'effect of new delight;
And Marriage but the pleasure of a day:
The Metall's base, the Gilding worn away.
250   *Melesinda.* I fear I'm guilty of some great offence,
And that has bred this cold indifference.
Morat. The greatest in the world to flesh and bloud:
You fondly love much longer than you shou'd.
Melesinda. If that be all which makes your discontent,
255   Of such a crime I never can repent.
Morat. Would you force Love upon me, which I shun?
And bring course fare, when appetite is gone?
Melesinda. Why did I not, in Prison, die before
My fatal freedom made me suffer more?
260   I had been pleas'd to think I dy'd for you,
And doubly pleas'd, because you then were true:
Then I had hope; but now, alas, have none.
Morat. You say you love me; let that love be shown.
'Tis in your power to make my happiness.
265   *Melesinda.* Speak quickly: to command me is to bless.
Morat. To *Indamora* you my Suit must move:
You'll sure speak kindly of the man you love.
Melesinda. Oh! rather let me perish by your hand,
Than break my heart, by this unkind command:
270   Think 'tis the onely one I could deny;
And that 'tis harder to refuse than die.
Try, if you please, my Rival's heart to win:
I'll bear the pain, but not promote the sin.
You own what e'r perfections man can boast,
275   And if she view you with my eyes, she's lost.
Morat. Here I renounce all love, all Nuptial ties:
Henceforward live a stranger to my eyes:
When I appear, see you avoid the place,
And haunt me not with that unlucky face.
280   *Melesinda.* Hard, as it is, I this command obey,
And haste, while I have life, to go away:
In pity stay some hours, till I am dead,
That blameless you may court my Rival's Bed.
My hated face I'll not presume to show;
285   Yet I may watch your steps where e'r you go.
Unseen, I'll gaze; and with my latest breath,
Bless, while I die, the Author of my death.   *Weeping.*

Enter Emperor.

Emperor. When your Triumphant Fortune high appears,
  What cause can draw these unbecoming tears?
  Let cheerfulness on happy Fortune wait,   290
  And give not thus the Counter-time to Fate.
Melesinda. Fortune long frown'd, and has but lately smil'd:
  I doubt a Foe so newly reconcil'd.
  You saw but sorrow in its waning form,
  A working Sea remaining from a Storm;   295
  When the now weary Waves roul o'r the Deep,
  And faintly murmur ere they fall asleep.
Emperor. Your inward griefs you smother in your mind;
  But Fame's loud voice proclaims your Lord unkind.
Morat. Let Fame be busie where she has to do: 300
  Tell of fought Fields, and every pompous Show.
  Those Tales are fit to fill the People's ears;
  Monarchs, unquestion'd, move in higher Spheres.
Melesinda. Believe not Rumor, but your self; and see
  The kindness 'twixt my plighted Lord and me.   305
                     Kissing Morat.
  This is our State; thus happily we live;
  These are the quarrels which we take and give.
  (*Aside to Morat*) I had no other way to force a Kiss.
  Forgive my last Farewel to you, and Bliss.   *Exit.*
Emperor. Your haughty carriage shows too much of scorn,   310
  And love, like hers, deserves not that return.
Morat. You'll please to leave me judge of what I do,
  And not examine by the outward show.
  Your usage of my Mother might be good:
  I judg'd it not.
Emperor.   Nor was it fit you shou'd.   315
Morat. Then, in as equal Ballance weigh my deeds.
Emperor. My Right, and my Authority, exceeds.
  Suppose (what I'll not grant) Injustice done;
  Is judging me the duty of a Son?
Morat. Not of a Son, but of an Emperor: 320
  You cancell'd Duty when you gave me pow'r.
  If your own Actions on your Will you ground,
  Mine shall hereafter know no other bound.
  What meant you when you call'd me to a Throne?
  Was it to please me with a Name alone?   325
Emperor. 'Twas that I thought your gratitude would know
  What to my partial kindness you did owe:
  That what your Birth did to your Claim deny,
  Your merit of Obedience might supply.

330

335

340

345

350

355

360

365

Morat. To your own thoughts such hopes you might
    propose;
But I took Empire not on terms like those.
Of business you complain'd; now take your ease:
Enjoy what e're decrepid Age can please:
Eat, Sleep, and tell long Tales of what you were
In flow'r of Youth, if any one will hear.
Emperor. Pow'r like new Wine, does your weak Brain
    surprise,
And its mad fumes, in hot discourses, rise;
But time these giddy vapours will remove;
Mean while I'll taste the sober joys of Love.
Morat. You cannot Love, nor pleasures take, or give;
But life begin, when 'tis too late to live.
On a tir'd Courser you pursue delight,
Let slip your morning and set out at night.
If you have liv'd, take thankfully the past:
Make, as you can, the sweet remembrance last.
If you have not enjoy'd what Youth could give,
But life sunk through you like a leaky Sieve,
Accuse your self you liv'd not while you might;
But, in the Captive Queen resign your right.
I've now resolv'd to fill your useless place;
I'll take that Post to cover your disgrace,
And love her, for the honour of my Race.
Emperor. Thou dost but try how far I can forbear,
Nor art that Monster which thou wouldst appear:
But do not wantonly my passion move;
I pardon nothing that relates to Love.
My fury does, like jealous Forts, pursue
With death, ev'n Strangers who but come to view.
Morat. I did not onely view, but will invade:
Could you shed venom from your reverend shade,
Like Trees, beneath whose arms 'tis death to sleep;
Did rouling Thunder your fenc'd Fortress keep,
Thence would I snatch my *Semele*, like *Jove*,
And midst the dreadful Rack enjoy my Love.
Emperor. Have I for this, ungrateful as thou art,
When Right, when Nature, struggl'd in my heart;

357 *jealous*] zealous, vigilant, or careful in guarding.
361 *Like Trees . . . sleep*] perhaps this refers to yew trees, whose
leaves were thought poisonous and which traditionally grew over
graves. Tales concerning the poison upas tree do not mention sleeping beneath the upas.
364 *Rack*] wrack, destruction, as when Jupiter appeared to
Semele in his full glory (Ovid, *Metamorphoses*, III, 260).

When Heav'n call'd on me for thy Brother's claim,
Broke all, and sulli'd my unspotted Fame?
Wert thou to Empire, by my baseness, brought,
And wouldst thou ravish what so dear I bought?   370
Dear! for my Conscience and its peace I gave:
Why was my Reason made my passion's slave?
I see Heav'n's Justice; thus the Pow'rs Divine,
Pay Crimes with Crimes and punish mine by thine.
Morat. Crimes let them pay, and punish as they please: 375
What Pow'r makes mine, by Pow'r I mean to seize.
Since 'tis to that they their own greatness owe
Above, why should they question mine below?   *Exit.*
Emperor. Prudence, thou vainly in our Youth art sought,
And with Age purchas'd art too dearly bought: 380
We're past the use of Wit, for which we toil;
Late Fruit, and planted in too cold a Soil.
My Stock of Fame is lavish'd and decay'd;
No profit of the vast profusion made.
Too late my folly I repent; I know   385
My *Aureng-Zebe* would ne'r have us'd me so.
But, by his ruine I prepar'd my own;
And, like a naked Tree, my shelter gone,
To Winds and Winter-storms must stand expos'd
    alone.
                                              Exit.

    [*Enter*] Aureng-Zebe, Arimant.

Arimant. Give me not thanks, which I will ne'r deserve;   390
But know, 'tis for a Nobler Price I serve.
By *Indamora's* will you're hither brought:
All my reward, in her command I sought.
The rest your Letter tells you. —— See, like Light,
She comes; and I must vanish, like the Night.   *Exit.*   395

    Enter Indamora.

Indamora. 'Tis now that I begin to live again:
Heav'ns, I forgive you all my fear and pain:
Since I behold my *Aureng-Zebe* appear,
I could not buy him at a Price too dear.
His name alone afforded me relief,   400
Repeated as a charm to cure my grief.
I that lov'd name did, as some God, invoke,
And printed kisses on it while I spoke.
Aureng-Zebe. Short ease; but long, long pains from you I
    find:
Health, to my eyes; but poison, to my mind.   405

Why are you made so excellently fair?
So much above what other Beauties are,
That, ev'n in cursing, you new form my breath;
And make me bless those Eyes which give me death?

410   *Indamora.* What reason for your curses can you find? ⎫
    My Eyes your conquest, not your death, design'd. ⎬
    If they offend, 'tis that they are too kind. ⎭

  Aureng-Zebe. The ruines they have wrought, you will not
    see:
    Too kind they are, indeed, but not to me.

  Indamora. Think you base Interest Souls, like mine, can
415   sway?
    Or that, for Greatness, I can Love betray?
    No, *Aureng-Zebe*, you merit all my heart,
    And I'm too Noble but to give a part.

    Your Father, and an Empire! am I known ⎫
420   No more? or have so weak a judgment shown, ⎬
    In chusing you, to change you for a Throne? ⎭

  Aureng-Zebe. How, with a Truth, you would a Falshood ⎫
    blind! ⎬
    'Tis not my Father's love you have design'd; ⎬
    Your choice is fix'd where Youth and Pow'r are ⎬
    joyn'd. ⎭

  Indamora. Where Youth and Pow'r are joyn'd! has he a
425   name?

  Aureng-Zebe. You would be told; you glory in your
    shame:
    There's Music in the Sound; and, to provoke
    Your pleasure more, by me it must be spoke.
    Then, then it ravishes, when your pleas'd ear
430   The sound does from a wretched Rival hear.
    Morat's the name your heart leaps up to meet,
    While *Aureng-Zebe* lies dying at your feet.

  Indamora. Who told you this?
  Aureng-Zebe.   Are you so lost to shame?
    Morat, Morat, Morat: You love the name
435   So well, your ev'ry question ends in that;
    You force me still to answer you, *Morat*.
    Morat, who best could tell what you reveal'd;
    Morat, too proud to keep his joy conceal'd.

  Indamora. Howe'r unjust your jealousie appear,
440   It shows the loss, of what you love, you fear;
    And does my pity, not my anger move:
    I'll fond it, as the froward Child of Love.

442 *fond*] show fondness for, caress, fondle. "The *Tyrian* hugs, and
fonds thee on her breast." (*Aeneid*, I, 962, Dryden's translation).

To show the truth of my unalter'd breast,
Know, that your life was given at my request:
At least Repriev'd. When Heav'n deni'd you aid,   445
She brought it; she, whose falshood you upbraid.
Aureng-Zebe. And 'tis by that you would your falshood
   hide;
Had you not ask'd, how happy had I dy'd!
Accurst Reprieve! not to prolong my breath,
It brought a ling'ring, and more painful death.   450
I have not liv'd since first I heard the news;
The gift the guilty giver does accuse.
You knew the price, and the request did move,
That you might pay the Ransome with your love.
Indamora. Your accusation must, I see, take place;   455
And I am guilty, infamous, and base!
Aureng-Zebe. If you are false, those Epithets are small;
You're then the things, the abstract of 'em all.
And you are false: you promis'd him your love.
No other price a heart so hard could move.   460
Do not I know him? could his Brutal mind
Be wrought upon? could he be just, or kind?
Insultingly, he made your love his boast;
Gave me my life, and told me what it cost.
Speak; answer. I would fain yet think you true: 465
Lie; and I'll not believe my self, but you.
Tell me you love; I'll pardon the deceit,
And, to be fool'd, my self assist the cheat.
Indamora. No; 'tis too late: I have no more to say.
If you'll believe I have been false, you may.   470
Aureng-Zebe. I would not; but your crimes too plain
   appear:
Nay, even that I should think you true, you fear.
Did I not tell you, I would be deceiv'd?
Indamora. I'm not concern'd to have my truth believ'd.
You would be cozin'd! would assist the cheat!   475
But I'm too plain to joyn in the deceit:
I'm pleas'd you think me false ———
And, whatsoe'r my Letter did pretend,
I made this meeting for no other end.
Aureng-Zebe. Kill me not quite, with this indifference: 480
When you are guiltless, boast not an offence.
I know you better than your self you know:
Your heart was true, but did some frailty show:
You promis'd him your Love, that I might live;
But promis'd what you never meant to give.   485
Speak, was't not so? confess; I can forgive.

165

Indamora. Forgive! what dull excuses you prepare!
    As if your thoughts of me were worth my care.
Aureng-Zebe. Ah Traitress! Ah ingrate! Ah faithless
    mind!

490   Ah Sex, invented first to damn Mankind!
    Nature took care to dress you up for sin:
    Adorn'd, without; unfinish'd left, within.
    Hence, by no judgment you your loves direct;
    Talk much, ne'r think, and still the wrong affect.

495   So much self-love in your composure's mix'd,
    That love to others still remains unfix'd:
    Greatness, and Noise, and Show, are your delight;
    Yet wise men love you, in their own despight:
    And, finding in their native Wit no ease,

500   Are forc'd to put your folly on to please.
Indamora. Now you shall know what cause you have to
    rage;
    But to increase your fury, not asswage:
    I found the way your Brother's heart to move,
    Yet promis'd not the least return of Love.

505   His Pride, and Brutal fierceness I abhor;
    But scorn your mean suspitions of me more.
    I ow'd my Honour and my Fame this care:
    Know what your folly lost you, and despair.
                              Turning from him.
Aureng-Zebe. Too cruelly your innocence you tell

510   Show Heav'n, and damn me to the pit of Hell.
    Now I believe you; tis not yet too late:
    You may forgive, and put a stop to Fate:
    Save me, just sinking, and no more to rise.
                                  She frowns.

    How can you look with such relentless eyes?

515   Or let your mind by penitence be mov'd,
    Or I'm resolv'd to think you never lov'd.
    You are not clear'd, unless you mercy speak:
    I'll think you took th'occasion thus to break.
Indamora. Small jealousies, 'tis true, inflame desire;

520   Too great, not Fan, but quite blow out the Fire:
    Yet I did love you, till such pains I bore,
    That I dare trust my self and you no more.
    Let me not love you; but here end my pain:
    Distrust may make me wretched once again.

525   Now, with full Sails, into the Port I move,
    And safely can unlade my breast of Love;
    Quiet, and calm: why should I then go back,
    To tempt the second hazard of a Wrack?

Aureng-Zebe. Behold these dying eyes, see their submissive
    awe;
    These tears, which fear of death could never draw: 530
    Heard you that sigh? from my heav'd heart it past,
    And said, If you forgive not, 'tis my last.
    Love mounts, and rowls about my stormy mind,
    Like Fire, that's born by a tempestuous Wind.
    Oh, I could stifle you, with eager haste!   535
    Devour your kisses with my hungry taste!
    Rush on you! eat you! wander o'r each part,
    Raving with pleasure, snatch you to my heart!
    Then hold you off, and gaze! then, with new rage,
    Invade you, till my conscious Limbs presage   540
    Torrents of joy, which all their banks o'rflow!
    So lost, so blest, as I but then could know!
Indamora. Be no more jealous.   *Giving him her hand.*
Aureng-Zebe.   Give me cause no more:
    The danger's greater after, than before.
    If I relapse; to cure my jealousie   545
    Let me (for that's the easiest parting) die.
Indamora. My life!
Aureng-Zebe.   My Soul!
Indamora.   My all that Heav'n can give!
    Death's life with you; without you, death to live.

        To them Arimant *hastily.*

Arimant. Oh, we are lost, beyond all humane aid!
    The Citadel is to *Morat* betraid.   550
    The Traitor, and the Treason, known too late;   ⎫
    The false *Abas* deliver'd up the Gate.   ⎬
    Ev'n, while I speak, we're compass'd round with Fate. ⎭
    The Valiant cannot fight, or Coward flie;
    But both in undistinguish'd Crouds must die.   555
Aureng-Zebe. Then my Prophetic fears are come to pass:
    Morat was always bloudy; now, he's base:
    And has so far in Usurpation gone,
    He will by Paricide secure the Throne.

        To them the Emperor.

Emperor. Am I forsaken, and betray'd, by all?   560
    Not one brave man dare, with a Monarch, fall?
    Then, welcome death, to cover my disgrace;
    I would not live to Reign o'r such a Race.
    My *Aureng-Zebe*!   *Seeing* Aureng-Zebe.

548.1 *To*] Q1 *text; Enter* Q1 *catchword*

565　　　　　But thou no more art mine; my cruelty
　　　　　　Has quite destroy'd the right I had in thee.
　　　　　　I have been base,
　　　　　　Base ev'n to him from whom I did receive
　　　　　　All that a Son could to a Parent give:
570　　　　　Behold me punish'd in the self-same kind,
　　　　　　Th'ungrateful does a more ungrateful find.
　　　Aureng-Zebe. Accuse your self no more; you could not be
　　　　　　Ungrateful: could commit no crime to me:
　　　　　　I onely mourn my yet uncancell'd score:
575　　　　　You put me past the pow'r of paying more:
　　　　　　That, that's my grief, that I can onely grieve,
　　　　　　And bring but pity, where I would relieve;
　　　　　　For had I yet ten thousand lives to pay,
　　　　　　The mighty sum should go no other way.
580　　　*Emperor.* Can you forgive me? 'tis not fit you shou'd.
　　　　　　Why will you be so excellently good?
　　　　　　'Twill stick too black a brand upon my name:
　　　　　　The Sword is needless; I shall die with shame.
　　　　　　What had my age to do with Love's delight,
585　　　　　Shut out from all enjoyments but the sight?
　　　Arimant. Sir, you forget the danger's imminent: ⎫
　　　　　　This minute is not for excuses lent.　　　　 ⎪
　　　Emperor. Disturb me not ——　　　　　　　　 ⎬
　　　　　　How can my latest hour be better spent?　　⎭
590　　　　　To reconcile my self to him is more,
　　　　　　Than to regain all I possess'd before.
　　　　　　Empire, and Life are now not worth a pray'r:
　　　　　　His love, alone, deserves my dying care.
　　　Aureng-Zebe. Fighting for you, my death will glorious be.
595　　　*Indamora.* Seek to preserve your self, and live for me.
　　　Arimant. Lose then no farther time.
　　　　　　Heav'n has inspir'd me with a sudden thought,　⎫
　　　　　　Whence your unhop'd for safety may be wrought, ⎬
　　　　　　Though with the hazard of my bloud 'tis bought. ⎭
600　　　　　But, since my life can ne'r be fortunate,
　　　　　　'Tis so much sorrow well redeem'd from Fate.
　　　　　　You, Madam, must retire;
　　　　　　Your Beauty is its own security,
　　　　　　And leave the conduct of the rest to me.
605　　　　　(*Aside*) Glory will crown my life, if I succeed;
　　　　　　If not, she may afford to love me dead.
　　　Aureng-Zebe. My Father's kind; and, Madam, you forgive:
　　　　　　Were Heav'n so pleas'd, I now could wish to live.
　　　　　　And, I shall live.
610　　　　　With Glory, and with Love, at once I burn:

I feel th'inspiring heat, and absent God return.

Exeunt.

ACT V.

[*Enter*] Indamora *alone.*

Indamora. The night seems doubled with the fear she
brings,
And, o'r the Cittadel, new spreads her wings.
The Morning, as mistaken, turns about,
And all her early fires again go out.
Shouts, cries, and groans, first pierce my ears, and then 〕   5
A flash of Lightning draws the guilty Scene, 　　　　　　 〕
And shows me Arms, and Wounds, and Dying men. 〕
Ah, should my *Aureng-Zebe* be fighting there, 　　　　 〕
And envious Winds distinguish'd to my ear, 　　　　　　 〕
His dying groans, and his last accents bear! 　　　　　 〕   10

To her Morat, *attended.*

Morat. The bloudy bus'ness of the Night is done,
And, in the Cittadel, an Empire wonn.
Our Swords so wholly did the Fates employ,
That they, at length, grew weary to destroy:
Refus'd the work we brought; and, out of breath,   15
Made Sorrow and Despair attend for Death.
But what of all my Conquest can I boast?
My haughty pride, before your eyes, is lost:
And Victory but gains me to present
That Homage, which our Eastern World has sent.   20
Indamora. Your Victory, alas, begets my fears:
Can you not then triumph without my tears?
Resolve me; (for you know my Destiny
In *Aureng-Zebe's*) say, do I live, or die?
Morat. Urg'd by my Love, by hope of Empire fir'd;   25
'Tis true, I have perform'd what both requir'd:
What Fate decreed; for when great Souls are giv'n,
They bear the marks of Sov'reignty from Heav'n.
My Elder Brothers my fore-runners came;
Rough-draughts of Nature, ill design'd, and lame: 30
Blown off, like Blossoms, never made to bear;
Till I came, finish'd; her last labour'd care.
Indamora. This Prologue leads to your succeeding sin:
Bloud ended what Ambition did begin.
Morat. 'Twas rumor'd, but by whom I cannot tell,   35

23 *Resolve*] satisfy, answer.

My Father scap'd from out the Cittadel:
My Brother too may live.

Indamora.   He may?

Morat.   He must:
I kill'd him not: and a less Fate's unjust.
Heav'n owes it me, that I may fill his room;
40   A Phœnix-Lover, rising from his Tomb.
In whom you'll lose your sorrows for the dead;
More warm, more fierce, and fitter for your Bed.

Indamora. Should I from *Aureng-Zebe* my heart divide, ⎫
To love a Monster, and a Paricide?   ⎬
45   These names your swelling Titles cannot hide.   ⎭
Severe Decrees may keep our Tongues in awe;
But to our thoughts, what Edict can give Law?
Ev'n you your self, to your own breast, shall tell
Your crimes; and your own Conscience be your Hell.

50   *Morat.* What bus'ness has my Conscience with a Crown?
She sinks in Pleasures, and in Bowls will drown.
If mirth should fail, I'll busie her with cares;
Silence her clamorous voice with louder Wars:
Trumpets and Drums shall fright her from the Throne,
55   As sounding Cymbals aid the lab'ring Moon.

Indamora. Repell'd by these, more eager she will grow;
Spring back more strongly than a *Scythian* Bowe:
Amidst your Train, this unseen Judge will wait;
Examine how you came by all your State;
60   Upbraid your impious Pomp; and, in your ear,
Will hallow, *Rebel*, *Tyrant*, *Murderer*.
Your ill-got Pow'r, wan looks and care shall bring:
Known but by discontent to be a King.
Of Crouds afraid, yet anxious when alone;
65   You'l sit and brood your sorrows on a Throne.

Morat. Birthright's a vulgar road to Kingly sway;
'Tis ev'ry dull-got Elder Brother's way.
Dropt from above, he lights into a Throne;   ⎫
Grows of a piece with that he sits upon,   ⎬
70   Heav'n's choice, a low, inglorious, rightful Drone. ⎭
But who by force a Scepter does obtain,
Shows he can govern that which he could gain.
Right comes of course, what e'r he was before;
Murder and Usurpation are no more.

75   *Indamora.* By your own Laws you such Dominion make,
As ev'ry stronger Pow'r has right to take:
And Paricide will so deform your name,

61 *hallow*] halloo, shout aloud.

170

That dispossessing you will give a claim.
Who next Usurps, will a just Prince appear;
So much your ruine will his Reign endear.   80
Morat. I without guilt, would mount the Royal Seat;
But yet 'tis necessary to be great.
Indamora. All Greatness is in Virtue understood:
'Tis onely necessary to be good.
Tell me, what is't at which great Spirits aim,   85
What most your self desire?
Morat.   Renown, and Fame,
And Pow'r, as uncontrol'd as is my will.
Indamora. How you confound desires of good and ill!
For true renown is still with Virtue joyn'd;
But lust of Pow'r lets loose th'unbridl'd mind.   90
Yours is a Soul irregularly great,   ⎫
Which wanting temper, yet abounds with heat: ⎬
So strong, yet so unequal pulses beat.   ⎭
A Sun which does, through vapours dimnly shine:
What pity 'tis you are not all Divine!   95
New molded, thorow lighten'd, and a breast
So pure, to bear the last severest test;
Fit to command, an Empire you should gain
By Virtue, and without a blush to Reign.
Morat. You show me somewhat I ne'r learnt before;   100
But 'tis the distant prospect of a Shore,
Doubtful in mists; which, like inchanted ground,
Flies from my sight, before 'tis fully found.
Indamora. Dare to be great, without a guilty Crown;
View it, and lay the bright temptation down: 105
'Tis base to seize on all, because you may;
That's Empire, that which I can give away:
There's joy when to wild Will you Laws prescribe,
When you bid Fortune carry back her Bribe:
A joy, which none but greatest minds can taste;   110
A Fame, which will to endless Ages last.
Morat. Renown, and Fame, in vain, I courted long;
And still pursu'd 'em, though directed wrong.
In hazard, and in toils, I heard they lay;
Sail'd farther than the Coast, but miss'd my way: 115
Now you have giv'n me Virtue for my guide;
And, with true Honour, ballasted my Pride.
Unjust Dominion I no more pursue;
I quit all other claims but those to you.
Indamora. Oh be not just to halves! pay all you owe: 120

96 *thorow lighten'd*] thoroughly enlightened.

171

Think there's a debt to *Melesinda* too.
To leave no blemish on your after life;
Reward the virtue of a Suff'ring Wife.
Morat. To love once past, I cannot backward move;

125   Call yesterday again, and I may love.
'Twas not for nothing I the Crown resign'd;
I still must own a Mercenary mind:
I, in this venture, double gains pursue,
And laid out all my Stock to purchase you.

To them Asaph Chan.

130   Now, what success? does *Aureng-Zebe* yet live?
Asaph. Fortune has giv'n you all that she can give,
Your Brother ———
Morat.   Hold; thou show'st an impious joy,
And think'st I still take pleasure to destroy:
Know, I am chang'd, and would not have him slain.

135   *Asaph.* 'Tis past; and you desire his life in vain.
He prodigal of Soul, rush'd on the stroke
Of lifted Weapons, and did wounds provoke:
In scorn of Night, he would not be conceal'd;
His Souldiers, where he fought, his name reveal'd:

140   In thickest crouds, still *Aureng-Zebe* did sound: ⎫
The vaulted Roofs did *Aureng-Zebe* rebound,   ⎬
Till late, and in his fall, the name was drown'd. ⎭
Indamora. Wither that hand which brought him to his fate,
And blasted be the tongue which did relate.
Asaph. His Body ———

145   *Morat.*   Cease to inhanse her misery:
Pity the Queen, and show respect to me.
'Tis ev'ry Painter's Art to hide from sight,
And cast in shades, what seen would not delight.
(*To her*) Your grief, in me such sympathy has bred,

150   I mourn; and wish I could recall the dead.
Love softens me; and blows up fires, which pass
Through my tough heart, and melt the stubborn Mass.
Indamora. Break, heart; or choak, with sobs, my hated breath;
Do thy own work: admit no forreign death.

155   Alas! why do I make this useless moan?
I'm dead already, for my Soul is gone.

To them, Mir Baba.

Mir Baba. What tongue the terror of this night can tell,
Within, without, and round the Citadel!
A new-form'd Faction does your pow'r oppose;

The Fight's confus'd, and all who meet are foes: 160
A second clamour, from the Town, we hear;
And the far noise so loud, it drowns the near.
Abas, who seem'd our Friend, is either fled;
Or, what we fear, our Enemies does head:
Your frighted Soldiers scarce their ground maintain. 165
Morat. I thank their fury; we shall fight again:
They rouse my rage; I'm eager to subdue:
'Tis fatal to with-hold my eyes from you.
                    Exit with the two Omrahs.

            Enter Melesinda.

Melesinda. Can misery no place of safety know?
The noise pursues me wheresoe'r I go, 170
As Fate sought onely me, and where I fled,
Aim'd all its Darts at my devoted head.
And let it; I am now past care of life;
The last of Women; an abandon'd Wife.
Indamora. Whether Design or Chance has brought you
    here,
I stand oblig'd to Fortune, or to Fear: 175
Weak Women should, in danger, herd like Deer.
But say, from whence this new combustion springs?
Are there yet more *Morats*? more fighting Kings?
Melesinda. Him from his Mother's love your eyes divide, 180
And now her Arms the cruel strife decide.
Indamora. What strange misfortunes my vext life attend?
Death will be kind, and all my sorrows end.
If *Nourmahal* prevail, I know my fate.
Melesinda. I pity, as my own, your hard estate; 185
But what can my weak charity afford?
I have no longer int'rest in my Lord:
Nor in his Mother, He: she owns her hate
Aloud, and would her self Usurp the State.
Indamora. I'm stupifi'd with sorrow, past relief 190
Of tears; parch'd up, and wither'd with my grief.
Melesinda. Dry mourning will decays more deadly bring,
As a North Wind burns a too forward Spring.
Give sorrow vent, and let the sluces go.
Indamora. My tears are all congeal'd, and will not flow. 195
Melesinda. Have comfort; yield not to the blows of Fate.
Indamora. Comfort, like Cordials after death, comes late.
Name not so vain a word; my hopes are fled:
Think your *Morat* were kind, and think him dead.
Melesinda. I can no more ———— 200
Can no more arguments, for comfort, find:

Your boding words have quite o'r-whelm'd my mind.
Clattering of weapons within.
Indamora. The noise increases, as the Billows rore,
When rowling from afar they threat the Shore.

205 She comes; and feeble Nature now I find
Shrinks back in danger, and forsakes my mind.
I wish to die, yet dare not death endure;
Detest the Med'cine, yet desire the Cure.
I would have death; but mild, and at command:

210 I dare not trust him in another's hand.
In *Nourmahal's*, he would not mine appear;
But arm'd with terror, and disguis'd with fear.
Melesinda. Beyond this place you can have no retreat:
Stay here, and I the danger will repeat.

215 I fear not death, because my life I hate:
And envious death will shun th'unfortunate.
Indamora. You must not venture.
Melesinda.   Let me: I may do
My self a kindness, in obliging you.
In your lov'd name, I'll seek my angry Lord;

220 And beg your safety from his conqu'ring Sword:
So his protection all your fears will ease,
And I shall see him once, and not displease.   *Exit.*
Indamora. Oh wretched Queen! what pow'r thy life can
save?
A stranger, and unfriended, and a slave!

225 Alas, she's here!

Enter Nourmahal, Zayda, and Abas, with Souldiers.

Indamora *withdraws to the inner part of the Scene.*
Nourmahal. Heartless they fought, and quitted soon their
ground,
While ours with easie victory were crown'd.
To you, *Abas*, my Life and Empire too,
And, what's yet dearer, my Revenge, I owe.

230 Abas. The vain *Morat*, by his own rashness wrought,
Too soon discover'd his ambitious thought;
Believ'd me his, because I spoke him fair,
And pitch'd his head into the ready snare:
Hence 'twas I did his Troops at first admit;

235 But such, whose numbers could no fears beget;
By them th'Emperor's Party first I slew,
Then turn'd my Arms the Victors to subdue.
Nourmahal. Now let the head-strong Boy my will con-
troul:
Virtue's no slave of Man; no Sex confines the Soul:

I, for my self, th'Imperial Seat will gain,   240
And he shall wait my leisure for his Reign.
But *Aureng-Zebe* is no where to be found.
And now perhaps in Death's cold arms he lies:
I fought, and conquer'd, yet have lost the prize.
Zayda. The chance of War determin'd well the strife,   245
That rack'd you, 'twixt the Lover and the Wife.
He's dead, whose love had sulli'd all your Reign,
And made you Empress of the World in vain.
Nourmahal. No; I my pow'r and pleasure would divide:
The Drudge had quench'd my flames, and then had di'd.   250
I rage, to think without that Bliss I live;
That I could wish what Fortune would not give:
But, what Love cannot, Vengeance must supply;
She, who bereav'd me of his heart, shall die.
Zayda. I'll search: far distant hence she cannot be.   255
                                                    Goes in.
Nourmahal. This wondrous Master-piece I fain would see;
This fatal *Helen*, who can Wars inspire,
Make Kings her Slaves, and set the World on fire.
My Husband lock'd his Jewel from my view;
Or durst not set the false one by the true.   260

        Re-enter Zayda, *leading* Indamora.

Zayda. Your frighted Captive, ere she dies, receive;
Her Soul's just going else, without your leave.
Nourmahal. A fairer Creature did my eyes ne'r see!
Sure she was form'd by Heav'n in spite to me!
Some Angel copi'd, while I slept, each grace,   265
And molded ev'ry feature from my face.
Such Majesty does from her forehead rise,
Her cheeks such blushes cast, such rays her eyes,
Nor I, nor Envy, can a blemish find;
The Palace is, without, too well design'd: 270
Conduct me in, for I will view thy mind.
(*To her*) Speak, if thou hast a Soul, that I may see,
If Heav'n can make throughout another Me.
Indamora (kneeling). My tears and miseries must plead my
     cause;
My words, the terror of your presence awes;   275
Mortals, in sight of Angels, mute become;
The Nobler Nature strikes th'Inferiour dumb.
Nourmahal. The Palm is, by the Foe's confession, mine;
But I disdain what basely you resign.

246 *rack'd*] kept on a rack, pulled.

175

280 Heav'n did, by me, the outward model build:
Its inward work, the Soul, with rubbish fill'd.
Yet, Oh! th'imperfect Piece moves more delight;
'Tis gilded o'r with Youth, to catch the sight.
The Gods have poorly robb'd my Virgin bloom,
285 And what I am, by what I was, o'rcome.
Traitress, restore my Beauty and my Charms,
Nor steal my Conquests with my proper Arms.
Indamora. What have I done, thus to inflame your hate?
I am not guilty, but unfortunate.
290 *Nourmahal.* Not guilty, when thy looks my pow'r betray, ⎫
Seduce Mankind, my Subject, from my Sway, ⎬
Take all my Hearts, and all my Eyes away? ⎭
My Husband first; but that I could forgive:
He onely mov'd, and talk'd, but did not live.
295 My *Aureng-Zebe*, for I dare own the name,
The glorious sin, and the more glorious flame;
Him, from my beauty, have thy eyes misled, ⎫
And starv'd the joys of my expected Bed. ⎬
Indamora. His love, so sought, he's happy that he's dead. ⎭
300 O had I courage but to meet my Fate;
That short dark passage to a future state;
That melancholly Riddle of a breath.
Nourmahal. That something, or that nothing, after death:
Take this,   *Giving a Dagger.*
And teach thy self.
Indamora.   Alas!
305 *Nourmahal.*   Why dost thou shake?
Dishonour not the vengeance I design'd:
A Queen, and own a base Plebeian mind!
Let it drink deep in thy most vital part:
Strike home, and do me reason in thy heart.
Indamora. I dare not.
310 *Nourmahal.*   Do't, while I stand by and see,
At my full gust, without the drudgery.
I love a Foe, who dares my stroke prevent,
Who gives me the full Scene of my content,
Shows me the flying Soul's convulsive strife,
315 And all the anguish of departing life:
Disdain my mercy, and my rage defie; ⎫
Curse me with thy last breath; and make me see ⎬
A Spirit worthy to have Rival'd me. ⎭
Indamora. Oh, I desire to die; but dare not yet:

309 *do me reason*] drink to me, a common phrase for pledging
a health; also meaning do justice.
311 *gust*] keen relish, gusto.

Give me some respite, I'll discharge the debt.   320
Without my *Aureng-Zebe* I would not live.
Nourmahal. Thine, Traitress! thine! that word has wing'd
    thy fate,
And put me past the tedious forms of hate.
I'll kill thee with such eagerness and haste,
As Fiends, let loose, would lay all Nature waste.   325
    Indamora *runs back: as* Nourmahal *is running to her.*
            Clashing of Swords is heard within.
Soldiers (within). Yield, y'are o'rpow'r'd: resistance is in
    vain.
Morat (within). Then death's my choice: submission I
    disdain.
Nourmahal. Retire, you Slaves: (*at the door*) Ah whether
    does he run
On pointed Swords? Disarm, but save my Son.

    Enter Morat *staggering, and upheld by Souldiers.*

Morat. She lives! and I shall see her once again!   330
I have not thrown away my life in vain.
    Catches hold of Indamora's *Gown, and falls by her:*
                                              she sits.
I can no more; yet, ev'n in death, I find
My fainting body byass'd by my mind:
I fall toward you; still my contending Soul
Points to your breast, and trembles to its Pole.   335

    To them Melesinda, *hastily, casting her self on the other*
            side of Morat.

Melesinda. Ah wo, wo, wo! the worst of woes I find!
Live still: Oh live; live ev'n to be unkind.
With half-shut eyes he seeks the doubtful day;
But, Ah! he bends his sight another way.
He faints! and in that sigh his Soul is gone;   340
Yet Heaven's unmov'd, yet Heav'n looks careless on.
Nourmahal. Where are those Pow'rs which Monarchs
    should defend?
Or do they vain Authority pretend,
O'r humane Fates, and their weak Empire show,
Which cannot guard their Images below?   345
If, as their Image, he was not Divine,
They ought to have respected him as mine.

328 *whether*] i.e., whither.
333 *byass'd*] a metaphor from bowling, with a biased ball that in-
clines in one direction.

I'll waken them with my revenge; and she
Their *Indamora* shall my Victim be,
350   And Helpless Heav'n shall mourn in vain, like me.

As she is going to stab Indamora, Morat *raises himself,*
and holds her hand.

Morat. Ah, what are we,
   Who dare maintain with Heav'n this wretched strife,
   Puft with the pride of Heav'n's own gift, frail life?
   That blast which my ambitious Spirit swell'd,
355   See by how weak a Tenure it was held!
   I onely stay to save the Innocent:
   Oh envy not my Soul its last content.
Indamora. No, let me die; I'm doubly summon'd now;
   First, by my *Aureng-Zebe*; and, since, by you.
360   My Soul grows hardy, and can death endure:
   Your Convoy makes the dang'rous way secure.
Melesinda. Let me, at least, a Funeral Marriage crave:
   Nor grudge my cold embraces in the Grave.
   I have too just a Title in the strife:
365   By me, unhappy me, he lost his life:
   I call'd him hither; 'twas my fatal breath;
   And I the Screech-Owl that proclaim'd his death.

Shout within.

Abas. What new Alarms are these? I'll haste and see.

Exit.

Nourmahal. Look up, and live: an Empire shall be thine.
370   *Morat.* That I contemn'd, ev'n when I thought it mine.
   (*To* Indamora) Oh, I must yield to my hard Destinies,
   And must for ever cease to see your eyes.
Melesinda. Ah turn your sight to me, my dearest Lord!
   Can you not one, one parting look afford?
375   Ev'n so unkind in death? but 'tis in vain;
   I lose my breath, and to the Winds complain:
   Yet 'tis as much in vain your cruel scorn;
   Still I can love, without this last return.
   Nor Fate, nor You, can my vow'd faith controul;
380   Dying, I'll follow your disdainful Soul:
   A Ghost, I'll haunt your Ghost; and, where you go,
   With mournful murmurs fill the Plains below.
Morat. Be happy, *Melesinda*, cease to grieve,
   And, for a more deserving Husband, live:
   Can you forgive me?
385   *Melesinda.*   Can I! Oh my heart!
   Have I heard one kind word before I part?
   I can, I can forgive: is that a task
   To love, like mine? Are you so good to ask?

One kiss ——— Oh 'tis too great a blessing this;
I would not live to violate the bliss.   *Kisses him.*   390

                    Re-enter Abas.

Abas. Some envious Devil has ruin'd us yet more:
The Fort's revolted to the Emperor;
The Gates are open'd, the Portcullis drawn;
And deluges of Armies, from the Town,
Come pow'ring in: I heard the mighty flaw,   395
When first it broke; the crowding Ensigns saw,
Which choak'd the passage; and, (what least I fear'd,)
The waving Arms of *Aureng-Zebe* appear'd,
Display'd with your *Morat's*:
In either's Flag the golden Serpents bear,   ⎫   400
Erected Crests alike, like Volumes rear,   ⎬
And mingle friendly hissings in the Air.   ⎭
Their Troops are joyn'd, and our destruction nigh.
Nourmahal. 'Tis vain to fight, and I disdain to flie.
I'll mock the Triumphs which our Foes intend;   405
And, spite of Fortune, make a glorious end.
In pois'nous draughts my liberty I'll find:
And from the nauseous World set free my mind.
                                        Exit.

At the other end of the Stage, Enter Aureng-Zebe, Dianet, *and
Attendants.* Aureng-Zebe *turns back, and speaks, entring.*

Aureng-Zebe. The lives of all, who cease from combat,
          spare;
My Brother's be your most peculiar care: 410
Our impious use no longer shall obtain;
Brothers no more, by Brothers, shall be slain.
                    Seeing Indamora *and* Morat.
Ha! do I dream? is this my hop'd success?
I grow a Statue, stiff, and motionless.
Look, *Dianet*; for I dare not trust these eyes;   415
They dance in mists, and dazle with surprise.
Dianet. Sir, 'tis *Morat*; dying he seems, or dead:
And *Indamora's* hand ———
Aureng-Zebe (sighing).   Supports his head.
Thou shalt not break yet heart, nor shall she know
My inward torments, by my outward show;   420
To let her see my weakness were too base:
Dissembled Quiet sit upon my face:

---

395 *flaw*] a sudden uproar or tumult.
400–402 *In . . . Air*] recalling *Aeneid,* II, 203–27 (Brower).

                    179

My sorrow to my eyes no passage find,
But let it inward sink, and drown my mind.
425   Falshood shall want its Triumph: I begin
To stagger; but I'll prop my self within.
The specious Tow'r no ruine shall disclose,
Till down, at once, the mighty Fabrick goes.
Morat (to Indamora). In sign that I die yours, reward my love,
430   And seal my Pasport to the Bless'd above.
                      Kissing her hand.
Indamora. Oh stay; or take me with you when you go:
There's nothing now worth living for below.
Morat. I leave you not; for my expanded mind
Grows up to Heav'n, while it to you is joyn'd:
435   Not quitting, but enlarg'd! A blazing Fire,
Fed from the Brand.   *Dies.*
Melesinda. Ah me! he's gone! I die!   *Swoons.*
Indamora.   Oh dismal day!
Fate, thou hast ravish'd my last hope away.
     She turns, and sees Aureng-Zebe *standing by her, and*
                         starts.
O Heav'n! my *Aureng-Zebe* ——— What strange
surprise!
440   Or does my willing mind delude my eyes,
And shows the Figure always present there?
Or liv'st thou? am I bless'd, and see thee here?
Aureng-Zebe. My Brother's body see convey'd with care,
       Turning from her, to his Attendants.
Where we may Royal Sepulture prepare.
445   With speed to *Melesinda* bring relief;
Recal her spirits, and moderate her grief.—
           Half turning to Indamora.
I go, to take for ever from your view
Both the lov'd Object, and the hated too.
      Going away after the Bodies, which are carried off.
Indamora. Hear me; yet think not that I beg your stay:
             Laying hold of him.
450   I will be heard, and after take your way.
          He struggles still: She lets him go.
Go; but your late repentance shall be vain:
I'll never, never see your face again.   *Turning away*.
Aureng-Zebe. Madam, I know what ever you can say:
You might be pleas'd not to command my stay.
455   All things are yet disorder'd in the Fort;
I must crave leave your audience may be short.
Indamora. You need not fear I shall detain you long;
Yet you may tell me your pretended wrong.

Aureng-Zebe. Is that the bus'ness? then my stay is vain.
Indamora. How are you injur'd?
Aureng-Zebe.   When did I complain?   460
Indamora. Leave off your forc'd respect
   And show your rage in its most furious form:
   I'm arm'd with innocence to brave the Storm.
   You heard, perhaps, your Brother's last desire;
   And after saw him in my arms expire: 465
   Saw me, with tears, so great a loss bemoan:
   Heard me complaining my last hopes were gone.
Aureng-Zebe. Oh stay, and take me with you when you go.
   There's nothing now worth living for below.
   Unhappy Sex! whose Beauty is your snare;   470
   Expos'd to trials; made too frail to bear.
   I grow a fool, and show my rage again:
   'Tis Nature's fault; and why should I complain?
Indamora. Will you yet hear me?
Aureng-Zebe.   Yes, till you relate
   What pow'rful Motives did your change create.   475
   You thought me dead, and prudently did weigh
   Tears were but vain, and brought but Youth's decay.
   Then, in *Morat*, your hopes a Crown design'd;
   And all the Woman work'd within your mind.
   I rave again, and to my rage return,   480
   To be again subjected to your scorn.
Indamora. I wait till this long storm be over-blown.
Aureng-Zebe. I'm conscious of my folly: I have done.
   I cannot rail; but silently I'll grieve.
   How did I trust! and how did you deceive!   485
   Oh, *Arimant*, would I had di'd for thee!
   I dearly buy thy generosity.   ⎫
Indamora. Alas, is he then dead?   ⎬
Aureng-Zebe.   Unknown to me,   ⎭
   He took my Arms; and while I forc'd my way,
   Through Troops of Foes, which did our passage stay,   490
   My Buckler o'r my aged Father cast,
   Still fighting, still defending as I past,
   The noble *Arimant* usurp'd my name;
   Fought, and took from me, while he gave me, fame.
   To *Aureng-Zebe*, he made his Souldiers cry,   ⎫   495
   And seeing not, where he heard danger nigh,   ⎬
   Shot, like a Star, through the benighted Sky.   ⎭
   A short, but mighty aid: at length he fell.
   My own adventures 'twere lost time to tell;
   Or how my Army, entring in the night,   500
   Surpris'd our Foes: the dark disorder'd fight:

How my appearance, and my Father shown,
Made peace; and all the rightful Monarch own.
I've summ'd it briefly, since it did relate
505   Th'unwelcome safety of the man you hate.
Indamora. As briefly will I clear my innocence:
Your alter'd Brother di'd in my defence.
Those tears you saw, that tenderness I show'd,
Were just effects of grief and gratitude.
He di'd my Convert.
510   *Aureng-Zebe.*   But your Lover too:
I heard his words, and did your actions view;
You seem'd to mourn another Lover dead:
My sighs you gave him, and my tears you shed.
But worst of all,
515   Your gratitude for his defence was shown:
It prov'd you valu'd life when I was gone.
Indamora. Not that I valu'd life; but fear'd to die:
Think that my weakness, not inconstancy.
Aureng-Zebe. Fear show'd you doubted of your own
     intent:
520   And she who doubts becomes less innocent.
Tell me not you could fear;
Fear's a large promiser, who subject live
To that base passion, know not what they give.
No circumstance of grief you did deny;
525   And what could she give more who durst not die?
Indamora. My love, my faith.
Aureng-Zebe.   Both so adult'rate grown,
When mix'd with fear, they never could be known.
I wish no ill might her I love befall;
But she ne'r lov'd who durst not venture all.
530   Her life and fame should my concernment be;
But she should onely be afraid for me.
Indamora. My heart was yours; but, Oh! you left it here,
Abandon'd to those Tyrants, Hope and Fear:
If they forc'd from me one kind look or word,
535   Could you not that, not that small part afford?
Aureng-Zebe. If you had lov'd, you nothing yours could
     call:
Giving the least of mine, you gave him all.
True love's a Miser; so tenacious grown:
He weighs to the least grain of what's his own.
540   More delicate than Honour's nicest sense:
Neither to give not take the least offence.
With, or without you, I can have no rest:
What shall I do? y'are lodg'd within my breast:

Your Image never will be thence displac'd;
But there it lies, stabb'd, mangled, and defac'd.   545
Indamora. Yet, to restore the quiet of your heart,
There's one way left.
Aureng-Zebe.   Oh name it.
Indamora.   'Tis to part.
Since perfect bliss with me you cannot prove,
I scorn to bless by halves the man I love.
Aureng-Zebe. Now you distract me more: shall then the
    day,   550
Which views my Triumph, see our love's decay?
Must I new bars to my own joy create?
Refuse, my self, what I had forc'd from Fate?
What though I am not lov'd?
Reason's nice taste does our delights destroy: 555
Brutes are more bless'd, who grosly feed on joy.
Indamora. Such endless jealousies your love pursue,
I can no more be fully bless'd than you.
I therefore go, to free us both from pain:
I pris'd your Person, but your Crown disdain.   560
Nay, ev'n my own ———
I give it you; for since I cannot call
Your heart my Subject, I'll not Reign at all.   *Exit.*
Aureng-Zebe. Go: though thou leav'st me tortur'd on the
    Rack,
'Twixt Shame and Pride, I cannot call thee back.   565
She's guiltless, and I should submit; but Oh!   ⎫
When she exacts it, can I stoop so low?   ⎬
Yes; for she's guiltless;—but she's haughty too.   ⎭
Great Souls long struggle ere they own a crime:
She's gone; and leaves me no repenting time.   570
I'll call her now; sure, if she loves, she'll stay;
Linger at least, or not go far away,
                    Looks to the door, and returns.
For ever lost, and I repent too late.   ⎫
My foolish pride, would set my whole Estate,   ⎬
Till, at one throw, I lost all back to Fate.   ⎭   575

To him the Emperor, *drawing in* Indamora: *Attendants.*

Emperor. It must not be, that he, by whom we live,
Should no advantage of his gift receive.
Should he be wholly wretched? he alone,
In this bless'd day, a day so much his own?
(*To* Indamora) I have not quitted yet a Victor's right: 580
I'll make you happy in your own despight.
I love you still; and if I struggle hard

183

To give, it shows the worth of the reward.
Indamora. Suppose he has o'rcome; must I find place
585   Among his conquer'd Foes, and sue for grace?
Be pardon'd, and confess I lov'd not well?
What though none live my innocence to tell?
I know it: Truth may own a gen'rous pride:
I clear my self, and care for none beside.
590 *Aureng-Zebe.* Oh, *Indamora*, you would break my heart!
Could you resolve, on any terms, to part?
I thought your love eternal: was it ti'd
So loosly, that a quarrel could divide?
I grant that my suspitions were unjust;
595   But would you leave me for a small distrust?
Forgive those foolish words ———— *Kneeling to her.*
They were the froth my raging folly mov'd,
When it boil'd up: I knew not then I lov'd;
Yet then lov'd most.
Indamora. You would but half be blest!
               To Aureng-Zebe. *Giving her hand, smiling.*
600 *Aureng-Zebe.*   Oh do but try
My eager love: I'll give my self the lie.
The very hope is a full happiness;
Yet scantly measures what I shall possess.
Fancy it self, ev'n in enjoyment, is
605   But a dumb Judge, and cannot tell its bliss.
Emperor. Her eyes a secret yielding do confess,
And promise to partake your happiness.
May all the joys I did my self pursue,
Be rais'd by her, and multipli'd on you.

     A Procession of Priests, Slaves following, and last
            Melesinda *in white.*

610 *Indamora.* Alas! what means this Pomp?
Aureng-Zebe. 'Tis the Procession of a Funeral Vow,
Which cruel Laws to *Indian* Wives allow,
When fatally their Virtue they approve;
Chearful in flames, and Martyrs of their Love.
615 *Indamora.* Oh my foreboding heart! th'event I fear;
And see! sad *Melesinda* does appear.
Melesinda. You wrong my love; what grief do I betray?
This is the Triumph of my Nuptial day.
My better Nuptials; which, in spight of Fate,
620   For ever joyn me to my dear *Morat*.
Now I am pleas'd; my jealousies are o'r:

613 *approve*] prove.

He's mine; and I can lose him now no more.
Emperor. Let no false show of Fame your reason blind.
Indamora. You have no right to die; he was not kind.
Melesinda. Had he been kind, I could no love have shown: 625
    Each vulgar Virtue would as much have done.
    My love was such, it needed no return;
    But could, though he suppli'd no fuel, burn.
    Rich in it self, like Elemental fire,
    Whose pureness does no Aliment require.   630
    In vain you would bereave me of my Lord:
    For I will die: die is too base a word;
    I'll seek his breast, and kindling by his side,
    Adorn'd with flames, I'll mount a glorious Bride.

                                      Exit.

       Enter Nourmahal *distracted, with* Zayda.

Zayda. She's lost, she's lost! but why do I complain   635
    For her, who generously did life disdain!
    Poison'd, she raves ———
    Th'invenom'd Body does the Soul attack;
    Th'invenom'd Soul works its own poison back.
Nourmahal. I burn, I more than burn; I am all fire: 640
    See how my mouth and nostrils flame expire.
    I'll not come near my self ———
    Now I'm a burning Lake, it rowls and flows;
    I'll rush, and pour it all upon my Foes.
    Pull, pull that reverend piece of Timber near: 645
    Throw't on ——— 'tis dry ——— 'twill burn ———
    Ha, ha! how my old Husband crackles there!
    Keep him down, keep him down, turn him about:
    I know him; he'll but whiz, and strait go out.
    Fan me, you Winds: what, not one breath of Air?   650
    I burn 'em all, and yet have flames to spare.
    Quench me: pour on whole Rivers. 'Tis in vain:
    Morat stands there to drive 'em back again:
    With those huge Bellows in his hands, he blows
    New fire into my head: my Brain-pan glows.   655
    See, see! there's *Aureng-Zebe* too takes his part:
    But he blows all his fire into my heart.
Aureng-Zebe. Alas, what fury's this?
Nourmahal.   That's he, that's he!
    I know the dear man's voice:
               Staring upon him, and catching at him.
    And this my Rival, this the cursed she.   660

649 *whiz*] hiss, sizzle.

185

They kiss; into each other's arms they run:
Close, close, close! must I see, and must have none?
Thou art not hers: give me that eager kiss.
Ingrateful! have I lost *Morat* for this?
665   Will you?—before my face?—poor helpless I
See all; and have my Hell before I die!   *Sinks down.*
Emperor. With thy last breath thou hast thy crimes confest:
Farewel; and take, what thou ne'r gav'st me, rest.
But you, my Son, receive it better here:
                    Giving him Indamora's *hand.*
670   The just rewards of Love and Honour wear.
Receive the Mistris you so long have serv'd;
Receive the Crown your Loialty preserv'd.
Take you the Reins, while I from cares remove,
And sleep within the Chariot which I drove.
                         [Exeunt.]

Epilogue

A pretty task! and so I told the Fool,
Who needs would undertake to please by Rule:
He thought that, if his Characters were good,
The Scenes entire, and freed from noise and bloud;
The Action great, yet circumscrib'd by Time,   5
The Words not forc'd, but sliding into Rhime,
The Passions rais'd and calm'd by just Degrees,
As Tides are swell'd, and then retire to Seas;
He thought, in hitting these, his bus'ness done,
Though he, perhaps, has fail'd in ev'ry one: 10
But, after all, a Poet must confess,
His Art's like Physick, but a happy ghess.
Your Pleasure on your Fancy must depend:
The Lady's pleas'd, just as she likes her Friend.
No Song! no Dance! no Show! he fears you'l say,   15
You love all naked Beauties, but a Play.
He much mistakes your methods to delight;
And, like the *French*, abhors our Target-fight:
But those damn'd Dogs can never be i'th' right.
True *English* hate your *Monsieur's* paltry Arts;   20
For you are all Silk-weavers, in your hearts.
Bold *Brittons*, at a brave Bear-garden Fray,
Are rouz'd: and, clatt'ring Sticks, cry, *Play, play, play.*
Mean time, your filthy Forreigner will stare,
And mutter to himself, *Ha gens Barbare!*   25
And, Gad, 'tis well he mutters; well for him;
Our Butchers else would tear him limb from limb.
'Tis true, the time may come, your Sons may be
Infected with this *French* civility;
But this in After-ages will be done: 30
Our Poet writes a hundred years too soon.
This Age comes on too slow, or he too fast:
And early Springs are subject to a blast!
Who would excel, when few can make a Test
Betwixt indiff'rent Writing and the best?   35
For Favours cheap and common, who wou'd strive,
Which, like abandon'd Prostitutes, you give?
Yet scatter'd here and there I some behold,

---

21 *Silk-weavers*] "Enemies, like the English silk-weavers, to the
manufacturers of France" (Scott).

25 *gens Barbare*] savages. As Saintsbury noted, it ought to be *gent
Barbare* or *gens Barbares*, if the rhyme would fit.

Who can discern the Tinsel from the Gold:
40 To these he writes; and, if by them allow'd,
'Tis their Prerogative to rule the Crowd.
For he more fears (like a presuming Man)
Their Votes who cannot judge, than theirs who can.

I.26 State,] ~.   43 State's] States   75 Seat;] ~ :
II.142 fear'd] feard   196 enough;] ~ ‸   260 loud.] ~ ,   284 off,]
~ —   335 you,] ~ ‸   353 Their] There   540 create,] ~ ;   541
Estate;] ~ ,   556.1 *Exeunt.*] *Exit.*
III.28 Guide.—] ~ . ‸   103 surprising] suprising   107 Successor,]
~ ‸   140 peace,] ~ .   306 Monarchy] Monarehy   362 find,]
~ ‸   395.2 Arimant] Arimaut   395.3 Melesinda] Melecinda
404 share:] ~ .   405 bear.] ~ :   504 bring!] ~ ?   518 disdain.]
~ ,

IV.249 base,] ~ ‸   435 ev'ry] e'ry   487 Forgive!] ~ ‸   499
ease,] ~ .   511 you:...late;] ~ ;...~ :   544 before.] ~ ,
V.37 may?] ~ .   53 Silence‸] ~ ,   62 Pow'r,] ~ ‸   98 Command,]
~ ‸   304–305 *one line in* Q   551 love's] loves   568 too.] ~ ‸

All for Love

When Dryden announced that he wrote *All for Love* "in Imitation of Shakespeare's Stile" he did not mean that he tried to return to the techniques of Elizabethan drama nor that he hoped to reproduce Shakespeare's language and characterization. So we should not, like many good critics, solemnly conclude that Dryden "misunderstood" Shakespeare. It is we who misunderstand Dryden, for he meant something very different in the context of the humanist tradition of imitation. Speaking of three kinds of translation—metaphrase, paraphrase, and imitation—he defines imitation of an author as "an endeavour of a later poet to write like one who has written before him on the same subject; that is, not to translate his words, or to be confined to his sense, but only to set him as a pattern, and to write, as he supposes that author would have done, had he lived in our age, and in our country." This method, he says, is particularly suitable for translating writers like Pindar who are "dark" and who "want connection" or "who soar out of sight, and leave his reader at a gaze." (*Essays*, I, 270–71). Imitation as Dryden defines it requires an act of imaginative transposition: the recognition of what in an author is different, what has changed in the history of the art and in the "refining" of the language. In short, it is a conscious recreation, a witty attempt to adapt a classic so that the audience may very well see the differences between the original and the imitation, like Pope's imitations of Horace or Rochester's "Allusion to Horace." In this sense, *All for Love* was to be consciously different from *Antony and Cleopatra*, at least in so far as it reflected the differences between the best of Restoration and Elizabethan taste.[1]

The "pattern" of the original must still be followed, however. Dryden clarifies this term in his preface to *Troilus and Cressida* (1679), in which he explains how he modeled the scene between Troilus and Hector[2] on the debate between Brutus and Cassius in *Julius Caesar*. He goes on to paraphrase Longinus, concerning Plato's imitation of Homer.

We ought not to regard a good imitation as a theft, but as a beautiful idea of him who undertakes to imitate, by

---

[1] For a discussion of the other sources Dryden used, see H. Neville Davies, "Dryden's 'All for Love' and Thomas May's 'The Tragedie of Cleopatra,'" *Notes and Queries*, XII (1965), 139–44.

[2] See the General Introduction for comment on this scene, pp. 1–3.

forming himself on the invention and the work of another man; for he enters into the lists like a new wrestler, to dispute the prize with the former champion. This sort of emulation, says Hesiod, is honourable ... when we combat for victory with a hero, and are not without glory even in our overthrow. Those great men whom we propose to ourselves as patterns of our imitation serve us as a torch, which is lifted up before us to enlighten our passage; and often elevate our thoughts as high as the conception we have of our author's genius.

[*Essays*, I, 242–43.]

Like the theory of admiration, outlined in the general introduction, Dryden thinks of imitation as a process inspired by great models, but the "pattern" one follows is an ideal construct, drawn from the imitator's conception of the author's genius—that is, his inclinations, his spirit—abstracted from the peculiar conventions and language of his time.

Dryden always thought that Shakespeare's genius lay in his ability to make excellent scenes of passion, because he was a "natural" poet who looked not in books but into his mind. What Shakespeare describes we not only see but feel. Unfortunately, he had few occasions on which to display his genius, but on a great occasion he was always great. (*Essays*, I, 41, 66–68 and 157). These occasions were apparently like the scene between Brutus and Cassius, two of the heroes of their age (*Essays*, I, 241), which occasion permits Shakespeare to paint the passions vividly. Therefore it is not surprising that Dryden's transposition of *Antony and Cleopatra* into the Restoration should take the form of a series of striking confrontation scenes fitted with suitable bravura passages. Strongly felt descriptions are taken over from the original but are tidied up with more "refined" language. The inner workings of the play are essentially Dryden's own conception, however, and we are invited to recognize the different way that he has managed the spiritual development of the characters.

Cleopatra has been transformed from a fascinating temptress into a sentimentalized and virtuous mistress, whose highest purpose is to be a loving wife. The role of Alexas must therefore be expanded into a cold and calculating yet fearful and almost sympathetic villain, because guilt must be transferred to him from Cleopatra. Ventidius, a minor character in Shakespeare, becomes the valorous confidant of Antony, the foil to Dollabella and Alexas. Octavia is brought on in Act III to show the high-minded claims of family duty.

191

That the subordinate figures may not seem too highly simplified, Dryden gives each a modifying quality to mitigate the
idealized pattern. Thus Ventidius once confesses that he could
easily love Cleopatra himself (IV.i.241–43), Octavia shows
feminine jealousy (IV.i.405–12), and Alexas betrays gentle
human feelings (III.i.379–92). The main character's soul remains large and intensely agitated through the whole play.
Deep down he is always devastatingly and helplessly in love
with Cleopatra, but on the surface he temporarily responds to
other valid claims to his loyalty. This two-leveled nature of
Antony stays before the audience in every scene, for no matter what his mood, Antony always qualifies it by reference to
his love; no matter what his resolve, he sees that he must be
"kind" to Cleopatra. Without such a carefully wrought
psychology, the hero would fly apart or merely be a sequence
of emotional states. This, it seems to me, is Dryden's most
important accomplishment in the play: maintaining a con-
tinuity of Antony's mind, creating an inner force, so that
Antony willingly and knowingly embraces his destruction,
which becomes at the same time his triumph of love.

On December 12, 1677, the King's Company performed
the play at the Theatre Royal in Drury Lane, but the attendance of only 249 people seems too small for this performance
to have been a first night.[3] Dryden was granted a benefit on
the third day, even though as a shareholder in the company
he was said to have received three or four hundred pounds
yearly by contract to write three plays. Other performances
were recorded for the winter of 1684, on January 20, 1686,
May 9, 1694, and possibly in the seasons of 1692 and 1696.
Apparently not an early success, "from its first Run . . . to the
beginning of last Winter [1718], it . . . never brought four
Audiences together."[4] By the late eighteenth century, however, it was "by universal consent accounted the work in
which [Dryden had] admitted the fewest improprieties of
style of character,"[5] and it was more frequently acted. A
revival at the Mark Hellinger Theater in New York, January,
1949, ran for 121 performances.

In the late summer or the fall of 1677 Rymer's *Tragedies
of the Last Age* came into Dryden's hands, after he had written
All for Love, and he prepared some highly interesting notes or
"Heads of an Answer to Rymer." Having read Rapin and Le
Bossu at about the same time, he found a similar moralistic

---

[3] *The Theatrical Inquisitor and Monthly Mirror*, July, 1816, p. 25;
cited in *The London Stage*, ed. Van Lennep, I, 265.

[4] John Dennis, *Works*, II, 164–65.

[5] Johnson, *Lives of the Poets*, ed. G. B. Hill (1905), I, 361.

bias without Rymer's "ill nature." As a consequence, at least
the first paragraph of the Preface to *All for Love*, published in
March 1678,[6] bears the stamp of his recent thinking. He chose
his subject because of the "excellency of the moral," for the
lovers are "patterns of unlawful love; and their end accordingly was unfortunate," whereas for most of us the play makes
little of "unlawful love" and the overwhelming impression is
that for such a love we would indeed lose the whole world.
Our sympathy and pity for the distresses of heroic love far
outweigh any sense of poetic justice in the action. Hence I
think Mr. Bruce King is generally right to point out this in-
congruity between the preface and the play,[7] like similar
disjunctions that may be found between *An Evening's Love* and
its preface. Otto Reinert has objected, however, that although
the lovers "have our sympathy at the end, there is no question
of *endorsement* of their conduct as a virtuous, prudent, or
admirable general way of life."[8] Dr. Johnson seemed to find
some question, for he thought the play had "one fault equal
to many, though rather moral than critical, that by admitting
the romantic omnipotence of Love, [Dryden] has recom-
mended as laudable and worthy of imitation that Conduct
which, through all ages, the good have censured as vicious, and
the bad despised as foolish" (*Lives*, I, 266). Without sharing
Johnson's moral disapprobation, most of us find him closer
to the mark.

The first quarto, 1678 (Macd. 82a, W & M 379), Univer-
sity of Chicago copy, served as the copy-text of this edition.
It has been compared with copies in the Bodleian Library
(Mal. B. 288[1]), the Morgan Library, and the British Museum

(BM¹ 644.g.68 and BM² T 1945 [4]), revealing press correction in four formes.[9] Q2 1692, Q3 1696, and F1 1701 introduce some small and obvious corrections.

[9] The single variant in inner B was pointed out by Peter Caracciolo, "Some Unrecorded Variants in the First Edition of Dryden's *All for Love*, 1678," *The Book Collector*, XIII (1964), 498–500.

John Dryden as an old man, James Maubert.
Courtesy of the National Portrait Gallery

ALL FOR LOVE:

OR, THE

World well Loſt.

A

TRAGEDY,

As it is Acted at the

THEATRE-ROYAL;

And Written in Imitation of *Shakeſpeare's* Stile.

By *John Dryden*, Servant to His Majeſty.

Facile eſt verbum aliquod ardens (ut ita dicam) notare : idque re-
ſtinctis animorum incendiis irridere. Cicero.

In the SAVOY:

Printed by *Tho. Newcomb*, for *Henry Herringman*, at the Blew Anchor in the Lower Walk of the *New-Exchange.* 1 6 7 8.

The Title Page of the First Quarto, University of Chicago Copy

Facile . . . irridere] It is easy to cite some passionate word, if I may say
so, and to laugh at it when the fires of the mind are cooled (Cicero,
Orator ad M. Brutum, xxvii. The received text reads *enim verbum* and
iam animorum).

Preface

The death of *Anthony* and *Cleopatra*, is a Subject which has been treated by the greatest Wits of our Nation, after *Shakespeare*; and by all so variously, that their example has given me the confidence to try my self in this Bowe of *Ulysses* amongst the Crowd of Sutors; and, withal, to take my own measures, in aiming at the Mark. I doubt not but the same Motive has prevailed with all of us in this attempt; I mean the excellency of the Moral: for the chief persons represented, were famous patterns of unlawful love; and their end accordingly was unfortunate. All reasonable men have long since concluded, That the Heroe of the Poem, ought not to be a character of perfect Virtue, for, then, he could not, without injustice, be made unhappy; nor yet altogether wicked, because he could not then be pitied: I have therefore steer'd the middle course; and have drawn the character of *Anthony* as favourably as *Plutarch*, *Appian*, and *Dion Cassius* wou'd give me leave: the like I have observ'd in *Cleopatra*. That which is wanting to work up the pity to a greater heighth, was not afforded me by the story: for the crimes of love which they both committed, were not occasion'd by any necessity, or fatal ignorance, but were wholly voluntary; since our passions are, or ought to be, within our power. The Fabrick of the Play is regular enough, as to the inferior parts of it; and the Unities of Time, Place and Action, more exactly observ'd, than, perhaps, the English Theater requires. Particularly, the Action is so much one, that it is the only of the kind without Episode, or Underplot; every Scene in the Tragedy conducing to the main design, and every Act concluding with a turn of it. The greatest errour in the contrivance seems to be in the person of *Octavia*: For, though I might use the priviledge of a Poet, to introduce her into *Alexandria*, yet I had not enough consider'd, that the compassion she mov'd to her self and children, was destructive to that which I reserv'd for *Anthony* and *Cleopatra*; whose mutual love being founded upon vice, must lessen the favour of the Audience to them, when Virtue and Innocence were

---

2 *Wits*] Sir Charles Sedley's *Antony and Cleopatra* (1671) was the most recent, performed by the Duke's Company. Earlier treatments were Fletcher's *The False One* (ca. 1620), Thomas May's *The Tragedie of Cleopatra* (acted 1626), and Samuel Daniel's *The Tragedy of Cleopatra* (ca. 1593).
29 *turn*] a change in affairs, a change for the better or worse at a crisis.

oppress'd by it. And, though I justified *Anthony* in some measure, by making *Octavia's* departure, to proceed wholly from her self; yet the force of the first Machine still remain'd; and the dividing of pity, like the cutting of a River into many Channels, abated the strength of the natural stream. But this is an Objection which none of my Critiques have urg'd against me; and therefore I might have let it pass, if I could have resolv'd to have been partial to my self. The faults my Enemies have found, are rather cavils concerning little, and not essential Decencies; which a Master of the Ceremonies may decide betwixt us. The *French* Poets, I confess, are strict Observers of these Punctilio's: They would not, for example, have suffer'd *Cleopatra* and *Octavia* to have met; or if they had met, there must only have pass'd betwixt them some cold civilities, but no eagerness of repartée, for fear of offending against the greatness of their Characters, and the modesty of their Sex. This Objection I foresaw, and at the same time contemn'd: for I judg'd it both natural and probable, that *Octavia*, proud of her new-gain'd Conquest, would search out *Cleopatra* to triumph over her; and that *Cleopatra*, thus attacqu'd, was not of a spirit to shun the encounter: and 'tis not unlikely, that two exasperated Rivals should use such Satyre as I have put into their mouths; for after all, though the one were a *Roman*, and the other a Queen, they were both Women. 'Tis true, some actions, though natural, are not fit to be represented; and broad obscenities in words, ought in good manners to be avoided: expressions therefore are a modest cloathing of our thoughts, as Breeches and Petticoats are of our bodies. If I have kept my self within the bounds of modesty, all beyond it is but nicety and affectation; which is no more but modesty deprav'd into a vice: they betray themselves who are too quick of apprehension in such cases, and leave all reasonable men to imagine worse of them, than of the Poet.

Honest *Montaigne* goes yet farther: *Nous ne sommes que ceremonie; la ceremonie nous emporte, et laissons la substance des*

39 *Machine*] device or artistic contrivance.
71–80 *Nous . . . croid*] We are nought but ceremonie; ceremonie doth transport us, and wee leave the substance of things; wee hold-fast by the boughs, and leave the trunke or body. Wee have taught Ladies to blush, onely by hearing named, which they nothing feare to doe. Wee dare not call our members by their proper names, feare not to employ them in all kind dissoluteness. Ceremonie forbids us by words to expresse lawfull and naturall things; and we beleeve it. Reason willeth us to doe no bad or unlawfull things, and no man giveth credit unto it (*The Essays of Michael, Lord of Montaigne*, Book II, chap xvii, "Of Presumption," Florio's translation, 1928 edition).

choses: *Nous nous tenons aux branches, et abandonnons le tronc et
le corps. Nous avons appris aux Dames de rougir, oyans seulement*
75   *nommer ce qu'elles ne craignent aucunement a faire: Nous n'asons
appeller a droict nos membres, et ne craignons pas de les employer
a toute sorte de debauche. La ceremonie nous defend d'exprimer par
paroles les choses licites et naturelles, et nous l'en croyons; la raison
nous defend de n'en faire point d'illicites et mauvaises, et personne*
80   *ne le'n croid.* My comfort is, that by this opinion my Enemies
are but sucking Critiques, who wou'd fain be nibbling ere
their teeth are come.

Yet, in this nicety of manners does the excellency of *French*
Poetry consist: their Heroes are the most civil people breath-
85   ing; but their good breeding seldom extends to a word of
sense: All their Wit is in their Ceremony; they want the
Genius which animates our Stage; and therefore 'tis but
necessary when they cannot please, that they should take care
not to offend. But, as the civilest man in the company is
90   commonly the dullest, so these Authors, while they are
afraid to make you laugh or cry, out of pure good manners,
make you sleep. They are so careful not to exasperate a
Critique, that they never leave him any work; so busie with
the Broom, and make so clean a riddance, that there is little
95   left either for censure or for praise: for no part of a Poem is
worth our discommending, where the whole is insipid; as
when we have once tasted of pall'd Wine, we stay not to
examine it Glass by Glass. But while they affect to shine in
trifles, they are often careless in essentials. Thus their *Hippo-*
100   *litus* is so scrupulous in point of decency, that he will rather
expose himself to death, than accuse his Stepmother to his
Father; and my Critiques I am sure will commend him for it:
but we of grosser apprehensions, are apt to think that this
excess of generosity, is not practicable but with Fools and
105   Madmen. This was good manners with a vengeance; and
the Audience is like to be much concern'd at the misfortunes
of this admirable Heroe: but take *Hippolitus* out of his
Poetique Fit, and I suppose he would think it a wiser part, to
set the Saddle on the right Horse, and chuse rather to live with
110   the reputation of a plain-spoken honest man, than to die with
the infamy of an incestuous Villain. In the mean time we may
take notice, that where the Poet ought to have preserv'd the
character as it was deliver'd to us by Antiquity, when he
should have given us the picture of a rough young man, of

80 *Enemies*] The Earl of Rochester in "An Allusion to Horace"
(*ca.* 1675) had scored Dryden's use of the "dry Bawdy bob."
97 *pall'd*] stale.
99–100 *Hippolitus*] in Racine's *Phèdre* (1677).

the *Amazonian* strain, a jolly Huntsman, and both by his 115
profession and his early rising a Mortal Enemy to love, he
has chosen to give him the turn of Gallantry, sent him to
travel from *Athens* to *Paris*, taught him to make love, and
transform'd the *Hippolitus* of *Euripides* into Monsieur *Hippo-*
lite. I should not have troubled my self thus far with French 120
Poets, but that I find our *Chedreux* Critiques wholly form
their judgments by them. But for my part, I desire to be
try'd by the Laws of my own Country; for it seems unjust
to me, that the French should prescribe here, till they have
conquer'd. Our little Sonnettiers who follow them, have too 125
narrow Souls to judge of Poetry. Poets themselves are the
most proper, though I conclude not the only Critiques. But
till some Genius as Universal, as *Aristotle*, shall arise, one who
can penetrate into all Arts and Sciences, without the practice
of them, I shall think it reasonable, that the Judgment of an 130
Artificer in his own Art should be preferable to the opinion
of another man; at least where he is not brib'd by interest, or
prejudic'd by malice: and this, I suppose, is manifest by plain
induction: For, first, the Crowd cannot be presum'd to have
more than a gross instinct, of what pleases or displeases them: 135
every man will grant me this; but then, by a particular kindness to himself, he draws his own stake first, and will be
distinguish'd from the multitude, of which other men may
think him one. But, if I come closer to those who are allow'd
for witty men, either by the advantage of their quality, or by 140
common fame, and affirm that neither are they qualified to
decide Sovereignly, concerning Poetry, I shall yet have a
strong party of my opinion; for most of them severally will
exclude the rest, either from the number of witty men, or at
least of able Judges. But here again they are all indulgent to 145
themselves: and every one who believes himself a Wit, that
is, every man, will pretend at the same time to a right of
judging. But to press it yet farther, there are many witty
men, but few Poets; neither have all Poets a taste of Tragedy.
And this is the Rock on which they are daily splitting. 150
Poetry, which is a Picture of Nature, must generally please:
but 'tis not to be understood that all parts of it must please
every man; therefore is not Tragedy to be judg'd by a witty
man, whose taste is only confin'd to Comedy. Nor is every
man who loves Tragedy a sufficient Judge of it: he must 155
understand the excellencies of it too, or he will only prove a
blind Admirer, not a Critique. From hence it comes that so

121 *Chedreux*] fashionable.
137 *draws his own stake first*] as when a gambler withdraws his bet.
140 *witty men*] such as Rochester.

160

many Satyrs on Poets, and censures of their Writings, fly
abroad. Men of pleasant Conversation, (at least esteem'd so)
and indu'd with a triffling kind of Fancy, perhaps help'd out
with some smattering of Latine, are ambitious to distinguish
themselves from the Herd of Gentlemen, by their Poetry;

> *Rarus enim fermè sensus communis in illâ*
> *Fortunâ.*

165

170

175

180

185

190

And is not this a wretched affectation, not to be contented
with what Fortune has done for them, and sit down quietly
with their Estates, but they must call their Wits in question,
and needlessly expose their nakedness to publick view? Not
considering that they are not to expect the same approbation
from sober men, which they have found from their flatterers
after the third Bottle? If a little glittering in discourse has
pass'd them on us for witty men, where was the necessity
of undeceiving the World? Would a man who has an ill
Title to an Estate, but yet is in possession of it, would he
bring it of his own accord, to be try'd at *Westminster*? We
who write, if we want the Talent, yet have the excuse that
we do it for a poor subsistence; but what can be urg'd in
their defence, who not having the Vocation of Poverty to
scribble, out of meer wantonness take pains to make themselves ridiculous? *Horace* was certainly in the right, where he
said, That *no man is satisfied with his own condition.* A Poet is
not pleas'd because he is not rich; and the Rich are discontented, because the Poets will not admit them of their
number. Thus the case is hard with Writers: if they succeed
not, they must starve; and if they do, some malicious Satyr
is prepar'd to level them for daring to please without their
leave. But while they are so eager to destroy the fame of
others, their ambition is manifest in their concernment:
some Poem of their own is to be produc'd, and the Slaves
are to be laid flat with their faces on the ground, that the
Monarch may appear in the greater Majesty.
    Dionysius and *Nero* had the same longings, but with all
their power they cou'd never bring their business well about.
'Tis true, they proclaim'd themselves Poets by sound of

163–64 *Rarus . . . Fortuna*] "For common sense is rare in that sta-
tion of life" (apparently Dryden's meaning); Juvenal, *Satire VIII*,
73–74, where the context requires that *sensus communis* mean "regard
for others."
180 *Horace*] *Satires*, I.i.1–3.
192 *Dionysius*] the tyrant of Syracuse who wrote plays.

Trumpet; and Poets they were upon pain of death to any 195
man who durst call them otherwise. The Audience had a
fine time on't, you may imagine; they sate in a bodily fear,
and look'd as demurely as they could: for 'twas a hanging
matter to laugh unseasonably; and the Tyrants were suspicious, as they had reason, that their Subjects had 'em in the 200
wind: so, every man in his own defence set as good a face
upon the business as he could: 'Twas known beforehand
that the Monarchs were to be Crown'd Laureats; but when
the shew was over, and an honest man was suffer'd to depart
quietly, he took out his laughter which he had stiffled; with a 205
firm resolution never more to see an Emperor's Play, though
he had been ten years a making it. In the mean time the true
Poets were they who made the best Markets, for they had
Wit enough to yield the Prize with a good grace, and not
contend with him who had thirty Legions: They were sure 210
to be rewarded if they confess'd themselves bad Writers,
and that was somewhat better than to be Martyrs for their
reputation. *Lucan's* example was enough to teach them
manners; and after he was put to death, for overcoming
Nero, the Emperor carried it without dispute for the best 215
Poet in his Dominions: No man was ambitious of that
grinning honour; for if he heard the malicious Trumpetter
proclaiming his name before his betters, he knew there was
but one way with him. *Mecenas* took another course, and we
know he was more than a great man, for he was witty too: 220
but finding himself far gone in Poetry, which *Seneca* assures
us was not his Talent, he thought it his best way to be well
with *Virgil* and with *Horace*; that at least he might be a Poet
at the second hand; and we see how happily it has succeeded
with him; for his own bad Poetry is forgotten, and their 225
Panegyricks of him still remain. But they who should be our
Patrons, are for no such expensive ways to fame: they have
much of the Poetry of *Mecenas,* but little of his liberality.
They are for persecuting *Horace* and *Virgil,* in the persons of
their Successors, (for such is every man, who has any part of 230
their Soul and Fire, though in a lesse degree.) Some of their
little *Zanies* yet go farther; for they are Persecutors even of

210 *who had thirty Legions*] A philosopher, when reproached for
disputing but weakly with the Emperor Hadrian, answered "Why,
would you have me contend with him that commands thirty legions?"
217 *grinning honour*] death; an allusion to Falstaff's remarks, *I Henry
IV,* V.iii.62, on the death of Sir Walter Blount, wittily associated below
with the death of Falstaff.
221–22 *Seneca*] *Epistulae Morales,* 114.4–6.
232 *Zanies*] a glance at Rochester who once disguised as an astrologer.

235

240

Horace himself, as far as they are able, by their ignorant and vile imitations of him; by making an unjust use of his Authority, and turning his Artillery against his Friends. But how would he disdain to be Copyed by such hands! I dare answer for him, he would be more uneasie in their company, than he was with *Crispinus* their Forefather in the *Holy Way*; and would no more have allow'd them a place amongst the Critiques, than he would *Demetrius* the Mimique, and *Tigellius* the Buffoon;

———— *Demetri, teque Tigelli,*
Discipulorum inter jubeo plorare Cathedras.

245

With what scorn would he look down on such miserable Translators, who make Doggrel of his Latine, mistake his meaning, misapply his censures, and often contradict their own? He is fix'd as a Land-Mark to set out the bounds of Poetry,

———— *Saxum, antiquum ingens*
Limes agro positus litem ut discerneret arvis.

250

But other Arms than theirs, and other Sinews are requir'd, to raise the weight of such an Author; and when they would toss him against their Enemies,

255

Genua labant, gelidus concrevit frigore sanguis,
Tum lapis ipse, viri vacuum per inane volutus
Nec spatium evasit totum, nec pertulit ictum.

260

For my part, I would wish no other revenge, either for my self or the rest of the Poets, from this Rhyming Judge of the Twelve-penny Gallery, this Legitimate Son of *Sternhold*, than that he would subscribe his Name to his censure, or (not to

233 *Horace himself*] Rochester's "An Allusion to Horace The 10th Satyr of the 1st Book."

238 *Holy Way*] the Via Sacra in Rome where Horace met a bore, commonly identified as Crispinus (*Satires*, I.i.120).

242–43 *Demetri . . . Cathedras*] Demetrius and you, Tigelius, go and whine in the seats of your pupils. (Dryden points his retort by quoting Horace's Tenth Satire, ll. 90–91, changing *discipularum* to the masculine.)

249–50 *Saxum . . . arvis*] An Antique Stone he saw: the Common Bound / Of Neighb'ring Fields; and Barrier of the Ground (*Aeneid*, XII, 897–98; 1300–1301 of Dryden's translation).

254–56 *Genua . . . ictum*] His knocking Knees are bent beneath the Load: / And shiv'ring Cold congeals his vital Blood. / The Stone drops from his arms: and falling short, / For want of Vigor, mocks his vain Effort (*Aeneid*, XII, 905–07; 1308–11 of Dryden's translation).

259 *Sternhold*] Thomas Sternhold, who made a popular metrical version of the *Psalms*; the prototype of a bad poet.

tax him beyond his learning) set his Mark: for shou'd he own
himself publickly, and come from behind the Lyon's Skin,
they whom he condemns wou'd be thankful to him, they
whom he praises wou'd chuse to be condemned; and the
Magistrates whom he has elected, wou'd modestly withdraw   265
from their employment, to avoid the scandal of his nomina-
tion. The sharpness of his Satyr, next to himself, falls most
heavily on his Friends, and they ought never to forgive him
for commending them perpetually the wrong way, and sometimes by contraries. If he have a Friend whose hastiness in   270
writing is his greatest fault, *Horace* wou'd have taught him to
have minc'd the matter, and to have call'd it readiness of
thought, and a flowing fancy; for friendship will allow a man
to Christen an imperfection by the name of some neighbour
virtue: 275

> *Vellem in amicitiâ sic erraremus; et isti*
> *Errori, nomen virtus posuisset honestum.*

But he would never have allow'd him to have call'd a slow
man hasty, or a hasty Writer a slow Drudge, as *Juvenal*
explains it: 280

> ———— *Canibus pigris, scabieque vetustâ*
> *Levibus, et siccæ lambentibus ora lucernæ*
> *Nomen erit, Pardus, Tygris, Leo; si quid adhuc est*
> *Quod fremit in terris violentius.*

Yet *Lucretius* laughs at a foolish Lover, even for excusing   285
the Imperfections of his Mistress:

> *Nigra* μελίροος *est, immunda et fœtida* ἄκοσμος
> *Balba loqui non quit,* τραυλίζει; *muta pudens est, &c.*

262 *Lyon's Skin*] The ass disguised as a lion was detected by its bray.
265 *Magistrates whom he has elected*] the names of critics approved by
Rochester in his "Allusion to Horace."
276–77 *Vellem . . . honestum*] I wish that we might blunder thus in
friendship, and that good sense had put an honorable name on errors
such as these.
278–79 *call'd a slow man hasty, or a hasty Writer a slow Drudge*]
Rochester spoke of "hasty Shadwell and slow Wycherley."
281–84 *Canibus . . . violentius*] Lazy dogs, bare from long standing
mange, who lick the edges of a dry lamp [for oil], will be called "Panther," "Tiger," "Lion," or whatever fiercer beast roars in the world
(*Satires*, vii, 34–37).
287–88 *Nigra . . . est, &c.*] The Sallow Skin is for the Swarthy put, /
And love can make a Slattern of a Slut . . . / She stammers, Oh what
grace in lisping lies, / If she sayes nothing, to be sure she's wise (*De
Rerum Natura*, IV, 1160, 1164; 145–46, 151–52 of Dryden's translation).

But to drive it, *ad Æthiopem Cygnum*, is not to be indur'd.
290 I leave him to interpret this by the benefit of his French
Version on the other side, and without farther considering
him, than I have the rest of my illiterate Censors, whom I
have disdain'd to answer, because they are not qualified for
Judges. It remains that I acquaint the Reader, that I have
295 endeavoured in this Play to follow the practise of the Ancients,
who, as Mr. *Rymer* has judiciously observ'd, are and ought to
be our Masters. *Horace* likewise gives it for a Rule in his Art
of Poetry,

——— *Vos exemplaria Græca*
300 *Nocturnâ versate manu, versate diurnâ.*

Yet, though their Models are regular, they are too little for
English Tragedy; which requires to be built in a larger compass. I could give an instance in the *Oedipus Tyrannus*, which
was the Masterpiece of *Sophocles*; but I reserve it for a more
305 fit occasion, which I hope to have hereafter. In my Stile I
have profess'd to imitate the Divine *Shakespeare*; which that
I might perform more freely, I have dis-incumber'd my self
from Rhyme. Not that I condemn my former way, but that
this is more proper to my present purpose. I hope I need not
310 to explain my self, that I have not Copy'd my Author
servilely: Words and Phrases must of necessity receive a
change in succeeding Ages: but 'tis almost a Miracle that
much of his Language remains so pure; and that he who
began Dramatique Poetry amongst us, untaught by any, and,
315 as *Ben Johnson* tells us, without Learning, should by the force
of his own Genius perform so much, that in a manner he has
left no praise for any who come after him. The occasion is
fair, and the subject would be pleasant, to handle the difference of Stiles betwixt him and *Fletcher*, and wherein, and how
320 far they are both to be imitated. But since I must not be over-
confident of my own performance after him, it will be

289 *ad Æthiopem Cygnum*] an allusion to Juvenal, *Satires*, VIII.33,
"to the point of calling an Ethiopian a swan," attacking Rochester for
being an ignoble nobleman. Rochester's masquerade as Alexander
Bendo occurred next door to the Black Swan Tavern on Tower Hill
(F. L. Huntley, "Dryden, Rochester, and The Eighth Satire of Juvenal,"
PQ, XVIII (1939), 281–82).
296 *Rymer*] See the introduction to *All for Love* for the discussion
of Thomas Rymer's influence on this preface.
299–300 *Vos . . . diurnâ*] Study your Greek models night and day
(*Ars Poetica*, 268–69).
305 *have hereafter*] his *Oedipus* was written with Nathaniel Lee in
1678.

prudence in me to be silent. Yet I hope I may affirm, and without vanity, that by imitating him, I have excell'd my self throughout the Play; and particularly, that I prefer the Scene betwixt *Anthony* and *Ventidius* in the first Act, to any thing which I have written in this kind.   325

Persons Represented

Marc Anthony.
Ventidius, his General.
Dollabella, his Friend.
Alexas, the Queen's Eunuch.
Serapion, Priest of *Isis.*
[*Myris,*] Another Priest.
Servants to *Anthony.*

Cleopatra, Queen of *Egypt.*
Octavia, Anthony's Wife.
Charmion, ⎫
Iras,   ⎬ *Cleopatra's* Maids.
Anthony's two little Daughters.

Scene *Alexandria.*

Persons Represented] the cast as listed in Q1: *Antony,* Charles Hart; *Ventidius,* Michael Mohun; *Dollabella,* Thomas Clarke; *Alexas,* Cardell Goodman; *Serapion,* Philip Griffin; *Myris,* John (?) Coysh; *Cleopatra,* Mrs. Elizabeth Boutell; *Octavia,* Mrs. Katherine Corey.

Prologue

to

Anthony and *Cleopatra*

What Flocks of Critiques hover here to day, ⎫
As Vultures wait on Armies for their Prey, ⎬
All gaping for the Carcass of a Play! ⎭
With Croaking Notes they bode some dire event;
And follow dying Poets by the scent.   5
Ours gives himself for gone; y'have watch'd your time!
He fights this day unarm'd; without his Rhyme.
And brings a Tale which often has been told;
As sad as *Dido's*; and almost as old.
His Heroe, whom you Wits his Bully call,   10
Bates of his mettle; and scarce rants at all:
He's somewhat lewd; but a well-meaning mind;
Weeps much; fights little; but is wond'rous kind.
In short, a Pattern, and Companion fit,
For all the keeping Tonyes of the Pit.   15
I cou'd name more; A Wife, and Mistress too; ⎫
Both (to be plain) too good for most of you: ⎬
The Wife well-natur'd, and the Mistress true. ⎭
    Now, Poets, if your fame has been his care;
Allow him all the candour you can spare.   20
A brave Man scorns to quarrel once a day;
Like Hectors, in at every petty fray.
Let those find fault whose Wit's so very small,
They've need to show that they can think at all:
Errours like Straws upon the surface flow;   25
He who would search for Pearls must dive below.
Fops may have leave to level all they can;
As Pigmies wou'd be glad to lopp a Man.
Half-Wits are Fleas; so little and so light;
We scarce cou'd know they live, but that they bite.   30
But, as the Rich, when tir'd with daily Feasts,
For change, become their next poor Tenant's Ghests;
Drink hearty Draughts of Ale, from plain brown Bowls,

0.1 *Anthony and Cleopatra*] possibly Dryden's own title. In his
preface to *A Parallel to Poetry and Painting* he said, "I never writ anything for myself but *Anthony and Cleopatra*" (*Essays*, II, 207).
   11 *Bates of his mettle*] abates the bombast of heroic drama.
   15 *Tonyes*] simpletons; a pun on Antony.
   22 *Hectors*] street brawlers.

35

And snatch the homely Rasher from the Coals:
So you, retiring from much better Cheer,
For once, may venture to do penance here.
And since that plenteous Autumn now is past,
Whose Grapes and Peaches have Indulg'd your taste,
Take in good part from our poor Poet's boord,

40

Such rivell'd Fruits as Winter can afford.

40 *rivell'd*] shrivelled.

All for Love;
or, the
World well Lost

ACT I. SCENE, *The Temple of Isis*

Enter Serapion, Myris, *Priests of* Isis.

Serapion. Portents, and Prodigies, are grown so frequent,
That they have lost their Name. Our fruitful *Nile*
Flow'd ere the wonted Season, with a Torrent
So unexpected, and so wondrous fierce,
That the wild Deluge overtook the haste   5
Ev'n of the Hinds that watch'd it: Men and Beasts
Were born above the tops of Trees, that grew
On th'utmost Margin of the Water-mark.
Then, with so swift an Ebb, the Floud drove backward
It slipt from underneath the Scaly Herd: 10
Here monstrous *Phocæ* panted on the Shore;
Forsaken *Dolphins* there, with their broad tails,
Lay lashing the departing Waves: Hard by 'em,
Sea-Horses floundring in the slimy mud,
Toss'd up their heads, and dash'd the ooze about 'em.   15

Enter Alexas *behind them.*

Myris. Avert these Omens, Heav'n.
Serapion. Last night, between the hours of Twelve and One,
In a lone Isle o'th' Temple while I walk'd,
A Whirl-wind rose, that, with a violent blast,
Shook all the *Dome*: the Doors around me clapt;   20
The Iron Wicket, that defends the Vault,
Where the long Race of *Ptolomies* is lay'd,
Burst open, and disclos'd the mighty dead.
From out each Monument, in order plac'd,
An Armed Ghost start up: the Boy-King last   25
Rear'd his inglorious head. A peal of groans
Then follow'd, and a lamentable voice
Cry'd, *Ægypt* is no more. My blood ran back,
My shaking knees against each other knock'd;

11 *Phocae*] sea calves, seals.
14 *Sea-Horses*] hippopotami.
25 *Boy-King*] Ptolemy, Cleopatra's brother, whom she had killed.

30 On the cold pavement down I fell intranc'd,
    And so unfinish'd left the horrid Scene.
Alexas (*showing himself*). And, Dream'd you this? or, Did
    invent the Story?
    To frighten our *Ægyptian* Boys withal,
    And train 'em up betimes in fear of Priesthood?
35 *Serapion.* My Lord, I saw you not,
    Nor meant my words should reach your ears; but what
    I utter'd was most true.
Alexas.   A foolish Dream,
    Bred from the fumes of indigested Feasts,
    And holy Luxury.
Serapion.   I know my duty:
    This goes no farther.
40 *Alexas.*   'Tis not fit it should.
    Nor would the times now bear it, were it true.
    All Southern, from yon hills, the *Roman* Camp
    Hangs o'er us black and threatning, like a Storm
    Just breaking on our heads.
45 *Serapion.* Our faint *Ægyptians* pray for *Antony*;
    But in their Servile hearts they own *Octavius*.
Myris. Why then does *Antony* dream out his hours,
    And tempts not Fortune for a noble Day,
    Which might redeem, what *Actium* lost?
Alexas. He thinks 'tis past recovery.
50 *Serapion.*   Yet the Foe
    Seems not to press the Siege.
Alexas.   O, there's the wonder.
    Mæcenas and *Agrippa*, who can most
    With *Cæsar*, are his Foes. His Wife *Octavia*,
    Driv'n from his House, solicits her revenge;
55 And *Dolabella*, who was once his Friend,
    Upon some private grudge, now seeks his ruine:
    Yet still War seems on either side to sleep.
Serapion. 'Tis strange that *Antony*, for some dayes past,
    Has not beheld the face of *Cleopatra*;
60 But here, in *Isis* Temple, lives retir'd,
    And makes his heart a prey to black despair.
Alexas. 'Tis true; and we much fear he hopes by absence
    To cure his mind of Love.
Serapion.   If he be vanquish'd,
    Or make his peace, *Ægypt* is doom'd to be
65 A *Roman* Province; and our plenteous Harvests

49 *Actium*] the scene of Antony's defeat by Octavius, 31 B.C.,
when the Egyptian fleet withdrew, led by Cleopatra.
52 *can*] can do.

Must then redeem the scarceness of their Soil.
While *Antony* stood firm, our *Alexandria*
Rival'd proud *Rome* (Dominion's other Seat)
And Fortune striding, like a vast *Colossus*,
Cou'd fix an equal foot of Empire here.   70
Alexas. Had I my wish, these Tyrants of all Nature
Who Lord it o'er Mankind, should perish, perish,
Each by the other's Sword; but, since our will
Is lamely follow'd by our pow'r, we must
Depend on one; with him to rise or fall.   75
Serapion. How stands the Queen affected?
Alexas.   O, she dotes,
She dotes, *Serapion*, on this vanquish'd Man,
And winds her self about his mighty ruins,
Whom would she yet forsake, yet yield him up,
This hunted prey, to his pursuer's hands,   80
She might preserve us all; but 'tis in vain ———
This changes my designs, this blasts my Counsels,
And makes me use all means to keep him here,
Whom I could wish divided from her Arms
Far as the Earth's deep Center. Well, you know   85
The state of things; no more of your ill Omens,
And black Prognosticks; labour to confirm
The people's hearts.

      Enter Ventidius, *talking aside with a Gentleman of*
                Antony's.

Serapion.   These *Romans* will o'rehear us.
But, Who's that Stranger? By his Warlike port,
His fierce demeanor, and erected look,   90
He's of no vulgar note.
Alexas.   O 'tis *Ventidius*,
Our Emp'ror's great Lieutenant in the East,
Who first show'd *Rome* that *Parthia* could be conquer'd.
When *Antony* return'd from *Syria* last,
He left this Man to guard the *Roman* Frontiers.   95
Serapion. You seem to know him well.
Alexas. Too well. I saw him in *Cilicia* first,
When *Cleopatra* there met *Antony*:
A mortal foe he was to us, and *Ægypt*.
But, let me witness to the worth I hate,   100
A braver Roman never drew a Sword.
Firm to his Prince; but, as a friend, not slave.
He ne'r was of his pleasures; but presides
O're all his cooler hours and morning counsels:

211

105   In short, the plainness, fierceness, rugged virtue
        Of an old true-stampt Roman lives in him.
        His coming bodes I know not what of ill
        To our affairs. Withdraw, to mark him better;
        And I'll acquaint you why I sought you here,
        And what's our present work.
                They withdraw to a corner of the Stage; and Ventidius,
                        with the other, comes forwards to the front.
110   *Ventidius.*   Not see him, say you?
        I say, I must, and will.
        1. Gentleman.   He has commanded,
        On pain of death, none should approach his presence.
        Ventidius. I bring him news will raise his drooping Spirits,
        Give him new life.
        1. Gentleman.   He sees not *Cleopatra.*
115   *Ventidius.* Would he had never seen her.
        1. Gentleman. He eats not, drinks not, sleeps not, has no use
        Of any thing, but thought; or, if he talks,
        'Tis to himself, and then 'tis perfect raving:
        Then he defies the World, and bids it pass;
120   Sometimes he gnawes his Lip, and Curses loud
        The Boy *Octavius*; then he draws his mouth
        Into a scornful smile, and cries, Take all,
        The World's not worth my care.
        Ventidius.   Just, just his nature.
        Virtue's his path; but sometimes 'tis too narrow
125   For his vast Soul; and then he starts out wide,
        And bounds into a Vice that bears him far
        From his first course, and plunges him in ills:
        But, when his danger makes him find his fault,
        Quick to observe, and full of sharp remorse,
130   He censures eagerly his own misdeeds,
        Judging himself with malice to himself,
        And not forgiving what as Man he did,
        Because his other parts are more than Man.
        He must not thus be lost.
                        Alexas *and the* Priests *come forward.*
135   *Alexas.* You have your full Instructions, now advance;
        Proclaim your Orders loudly.
        Serapion. Romans, Ægyptians, hear the Queen's Command.
        Thus *Cleopatra* bids, Let Labor cease,
        To Pomp and Triumphs give this happy day,
140   That gave the World a Lord: 'tis *Antony's.*
        Live, *Antony*; and *Cleopatra* live.

        121 *Boy Octavius*] who was twenty years younger than Antony.

Be this the general voice sent up to Heav'n,
And every publick place repeat this eccho.
Ventidius (aside). Fine Pageantry!
Serapion.   Set out before your doors
    The Images of all your sleeping Fathers,   145
    With Laurels crown'd; with Laurels wreath your posts,
    And strow with Flow'rs the Pavement; Let the Priests
    Do present Sacrifice; pour out the Wine,
    And call the Gods to joyn with you in gladness.
Ventidius. Curse on the tongue that bids this general joy.   150
    Can they be friends of *Antony,* who Revel
    When *Antony*'s in danger? Hide, for shame,
    You *Romans,* your Great grandsires Images,
    For fear their Souls should animate their Marbles,
    To blush at their degenerate Progeny.   155
Alexas. A love which knows no bounds to *Antony,*
    Would mark the Day with honors; when all Heaven
    Labor'd for him, when each propitious Star
    Stood wakeful in his Orb, to watch that hour,
    And shed his better influence. Her own Birth-day   160
    Our Queen neglected, like a vulgar Fate,
    That pass'd obscurely by.
Ventidius.   Would it had slept,
    Divided far from his; till some remote
    And future Age had call'd it out, to ruin
    Some other Prince, not him.
Alexas.   Your Emperor,   165
    Tho grown unkind, would be more gentle, than
    T'upbraid my Queen, for loving him too well.
Ventidius. Does the mute Sacrifice upbraid the Priest?
    He knows him not his Executioner.
    O, she has deck'd his ruin with her love,   170
    Led him in golden bands to gaudy slaughter,
    And made perdition pleasing: She has left him
    The blank of what he was;
    I tell thee, Eunuch, she has quite unman'd him:
    Can any *Roman* see, and know him now,   175
    Thus alter'd from the Lord of half Mankind,
    Unbent, unsinew'd, made a Woman's Toy,
    Shrunk from the vast extent of all his honors,
    And crampt within a corner of the World?
    O, *Antony!*   180
    Thou bravest Soldier, and thou best of Friends!
    Bounteous as Nature; next to Nature's God!

148 *present*] immediate.

213

Could'st thou but make new Worlds, so wouldst thou
        give 'em,
    As bounty were thy being. Rough in Battel,
185   As the first *Romans*, when they went to War;
    Yet, after Victory, more pitiful,
    Than all their Praying Virgins left at home!
Alexas. Would you could add to those more shining
        Virtues,
    His truth to her who loves him.
Ventidius.   Would I could not.
190   But, Wherefore waste I precious hours with thee?
    Thou art her darling mischief, her chief Engin,
    Antony's other Fate. Go, tell thy Queen,
    Ventidius is arriv'd, to end her Charms.
    Let your *Ægyptian* Timbrels play alone;
195   Nor mix Effeminate Sounds with *Roman* Trumpets.
    You dare not fight for *Antony*; go Pray,
    And keep your Cowards-Holy-day in Temples.
                        Exeunt Alexas, Serapion.

        Enter another Gentleman of Marc Antony.

2. Gentleman. The Emperor approaches, and commands,
    On pain of Death, that none presume to stay.
1. Gentleman. I dare not disobey him.
                    Going out with the other.
200   *Ventidius.*   Well, I dare.
    But, I'll observe him first unseen, and find
    Which way his humour drives: the rest I'll venture.
                            Withdraws.

        Enter Antony, *walking with a disturb'd Motion,*
                before he speaks.

Antony. They tell me, 'tis my Birth-day, and I'll keep it
    With double pomp of sadness.
205   'Tis what the day deserves, which gave me breath.
    Why was I rais'd the Meteor of the World,
    Hung in the Skies, and blazing as I travel'd,
    Till all my fires were spent; and then cast downward
    To be trod out by *Cæsar*?
Ventidius (*aside*).   On my Soul,
    'Tis mournful, wondrous mournful!
210   *Antony.*   Count thy gains.
    Now, *Antony*, Wouldst thou be born for this?
    Glutton of Fortune, thy devouring youth

        197.1 *Enter another*] Noyes; *Re-enter the* Qq F.

214

Has starv'd thy wanting Age.
Ventidius (aside).   How sorrow shakes him!
  So, now the Tempest tears him up by th' Roots,
  And on the ground extends the noble ruin.   215
             Antony *having thrown himself down.*
Antony. Lye there, thou shadow of an Emperor;
  The place thou pressest on thy Mother Earth
  Is all thy Empire now: now it contains thee;
  Some few dayes hence, and then twill be too large,
  When thou'rt contracted in thy narrow Urn,   220
  Shrunk to a few cold Ashes; then *Octavia*,
  (For *Cleopatra* will not live to see it)
  Octavia then will have thee all her own,
  And bear thee in her Widow'd hand to *Cæsar*;
  Cæsar will weep, the Crocodile will weep,   225
  To see his Rival of the Universe
  Lye still and peaceful there. I'll think no more on't.
  Give me some Musick; look that it be sad:
  I'll sooth my Melancholy, till I swell,
  And burst my self with sighing. ———   *Soft Musick.*   230
  'Tis somewhat to my humor. Stay, I fancy
  I'm now turn'd wild, a Commoner of Nature;
  Of all forsaken, and forsaking all;
  Live in a shady Forrest's *Sylvan* Scene,
  Stretch'd at my length beneath some blasted Oke;   235
  I lean my head upon the Mossy Bark,
  And look just of a piece, as I grew from it:
  My uncomb'd Locks, matted like *Misleto*,
  Hang o're my hoary Face; a murm'ring Brook
  Runs at my foot.
Ventidius.   Methinks I fancy   240
  My self there too.
Antony.   The Herd come jumping by me,
  And fearless, quench their thirst, while I look on,
  And take me for their fellow-Citizen.
  More of this Image, more; it lulls my thoughts.
               Soft Musick again.
Ventidius. I must disturb him; I can hold no longer.   245
             Stands before him.
Antony (starting up). Art thou *Ventidius*?
Ventidius.   Are you *Antony*?

229 *sooth*] encourage.
232 *turn'd wild*] in self-indulgent melancholy like Jacques in *As You Like It*, II.i.25–63.
232 *Commoner*] one who lives by his common right in nature like an animal.

I'm liker what I was, than you to him
I left you last.
Antony.   I'm angry.
Ventidius.   So am I.
Antony. I would be private: leave me.
Ventidius.   Sir, I love you,
And therefore will not leave you.

250 *Antony.*   Will not leave me?
Where have you learnt that Answer? Who am I?
Ventidius. My Emperor; the Man I love next Heaven:
If I said more, I think 'twere scarce a Sin;
Y'are all that's good, and god-like.
Antony.   All that's wretched.
You will not leave me then?

255 *Ventidius.*   'Twas too presuming
To say I would not; but I dare not leave you:
And, 'tis unkind in you to chide me hence
So soon, when I so far have come to see you.
Antony. Now thou hast seen me, art thou satisfy'd?

260 For, if a Friend, thou hast beheld enough;
And, if a Foe, too much.
Ventidius (weeping). Look, Emperor, this is no common
Deaw,
I have not wept this Forty year; but now
My Mother comes afresh into my eyes;

265 I cannot help her softness.
Antony. By Heav'n, he weeps, poor good old Man, he
weeps!
The big round drops course one another down
The furrows of his cheeks. Stop 'em, *Ventidius,*
Or I shall blush to death: they set my shame,
That caus'd 'em, full before me.

270 *Ventidius.*   I'll do my best.
Antony. Sure there's contagion in the tears of Friends:
See, I have caught it too. Believe me, 'tis not
For my own griefs, but thine. —— Nay, Father.
Ventidius.   Emperor.
Antony. Emperor! Why, that's the stile of Victory.

275 The Conqu'ring Soldier, red with unfelt wounds,
Salutes his General so: but never more
Shall that sound reach my ears.
Ventidius.   I warrant you.
Antony. Actium, Actium! Oh ——
Ventidius.   It sits too near you.

254 god-like] Congreve; good-like Qq F

Antony. Here, here it lies; a lump of Lead by day,
And, in my short distracted nightly slumbers,   280
The Hag that rides my Dreams. ———
Ventidius. Out with it; give it vent.
Antony.   Urge not my shame.
I lost a Battel.
Ventidius.   So has *Julius* done.
Antony. Thou favour'st me, and speak'st not half thou
think'st;
For *Julius* fought it out, and lost it fairly: 285
But *Antony* ———
Ventidius.   Nay, stop not.
Antony.   *Antony*,
(Well, thou wilt have it) like a coward, fled,
Fled while his Soldiers fought; fled first, *Ventidius*.
Thou long'st to curse me, and I give thee leave.
I know thou cam'st prepar'd to rail.
Ventidius.   I did.   290
Antony. I'll help thee. ——— I have been a Man, *Venti-*
dius ———
Ventidius. Yes, and a brave one; but ———
Antony.   I know thy meaning.
But, I have lost my Reason, have disgrac'd
The name of Soldier, with inglorious ease.
In the full Vintage of my flowing honors,   295
Sate still, and saw it prest by other hands.
Fortune came smiling to my youth, and woo'd it,
And purple greatness met my ripen'd years.
When first I came to Empire, I was born
On Tides of People, crouding to my Triumphs;   300
The wish of Nations; and the willing World
Receiv'd me as its pledge of future peace;
I was so great, so happy, so belov'd,
Fate could not ruine me; till I took pains
And work'd against my Fortune, chid her from me,   305
And turn'd her loose; yet still she came again.
My careless dayes, and my luxurious nights,
At length have weary'd her, and now she's gone,
Gone, gone, divorc'd for ever. Help me, Soldier,
To curse this Mad-man, this industrious Fool,   310
Who labour'd to be wretched: pr'ythee curse me.
Ventidius. No.
Antony.   Why?
Ventidius.   You are too sensible already
Of what y'have done, too conscious of your failings,
And like a Scorpion, whipt by others first

315   To fury, sting your self in mad revenge.
             I would bring Balm, and pour it in your wounds,
             Cure your distemper'd mind, and heal your fortunes.
Antony. I know thou would'st.
Ventidius.   I will.
Antony.   Ha, ha, ha, ha.
Ventidius. You laugh.
Antony.   I do, to see officious love
             Give Cordials to the dead.

320 *Ventidius.*   You would be lost then?
Antony. I am.
Ventidius.   I say, you are not. Try your fortune.
Antony. I have, to th'utmost. Dost thou think me desperate
             Without just cause? No, when I found all lost
             Beyond repair, I hid me from the World,
325   And learnt to scorn it here; which now I do
             So heartily, I think it is not worth
             The cost of keeping.
Ventidius.   *Cæsar* thinks not so:
             He'l thank you for the gift he could not take.
             You would be kill'd, like *Tully*, would you? do,
330   Hold out your Throat to *Cæsar*, and dye tamely.
Antony. No, I can kill my self; and so resolve.
Ventidius. I can dy with you too, when time shall serve;
             But Fortune calls upon us now to live,
             To fight, to Conquer.
Antony.   Sure thou Dream'st, *Ventidius.*
335 *Ventidius.* No; 'tis you Dream; you sleep away your hours
             In desperate sloth, miscall'd *Phylosophy.*
             Up, up, for Honor's sake; twelve Legions wait you,
             And long to call you Chief: by painful journeys,
             I led 'em, patient, both of heat and hunger,
340   Down from the *Parthian* Marches, to the *Nile.*
             'Twill do you good to see their Sun-burnt faces,
             Their skar'd cheeks, and chopt hands; there's virtue in
              'em,
             They'l sell those mangled limbs at dearer rates
             Than yon trim Bands can buy.
Antony.   Where left you them?
Ventidius. I said, in lower *Syria.*

319 *officious*] fond.
329 *Tully*] When Cicero, ordered killed by Antony, was over-taken in flight, he thrust his head out of the litter, offering his neck to the executioners.
340 *Marches*] boundaries.
342 *chopt*] chapped.

Antony.   Bring 'em hither;   345
  There may be life in these.
Ventidius.   They will not come.
Antony. Why did'st thou mock my hopes with promis'd aids
  To double my despair? They'r mutinous.
Ventidius. Most firm and loyal.
Antony.   Yet they will not march
  To succor me. Oh trifler!
Ventidius.   They petition   350
  You would make hast to head 'em.
Antony.   I'm besieg'd.
Ventidius. There's but one way shut up: How came I
  hither?
Antony. I will not stir.
Ventidius.   They would perhaps desire
  A better reason.
Antony.   I have never us'd
  My Soldiers to demand a reason of   355
  My actions. Why did they refuse to March?
Ventidius. They said they would not fight for *Cleopatra*.
Antony. What was't they said?
Ventidius. They said, they would not fight for *Cleopatra*.
  Why should they fight indeed, to make her Conquer,   360
  And make you more a Slave? to gain you Kingdoms,
  Which, for a kiss, at your next midnight Feast,
  You'l sell to her? then she new names her Jewels,
  And calls this Diamond such or such a Tax,
  Each Pendant in her ear shall be a Province.   365
Antony. Ventidius, I allow your Tongue free licence
  On all my other faults; but, on your life,
  No word of *Cleopatra*: She deserves
  More World's than I can lose.
Ventidius.   Behold, you Pow'rs,
  To whom you have intrusted Humankind;   370
  See *Europe, Africk, Asia* put in ballance,
  And all weigh'd down by one light worthless Woman!
  I think the gods are *Antony's*, and give
  Like Prodigals, this neather World away,
  To none but wastful hands.
Antony.   You grow presumptuous.   375
Ventidius. I take the priviledge of plain love to speak.
Antony. Plain love! plain arrogance, plain insolence:
  Thy Men are Cowards; thou, an envious Traitor;
  Who, under seeming honesty, hast vented

354 *us'd*] accustomed.
373 *Antony's*] i.e., Antonies (cf. l. 369).

380

The burden of thy rank o'reflowing Gall.
O that thou wert my equal, great in Arms
As the first *Cæsar* was, that I might kill thee
Without a Stain to Honor!

Ventidius.   You may kill me;
You have done more already, call'd me Traitor.

Antony. Art thou not one?

385

Ventidius.   For showing you your self,
Which none else durst have done; but had I been
That name, which I disdain to speak again,
I needed not have sought your abject fortunes,
Come to partake your fate, to dye with you.

390

What hindred me t'have led my Conqu'ring Eagles
To fill *Octavius's* Bands? I could have been
A Traitor then, a glorious happy Traitor,
And not have been so call'd.

Antony.   Forgive me, Soldier:
I've been too passionate.

Ventidius.   You thought me false;

395

Thought my old age betray'd you: kill me, Sir;
Pray kill me; yet you need not, your unkindness
Has left your Sword no work.

Antony.   I did not think so;
I said it in my rage: pr'ythee forgive me:
Why did'st thou tempt my anger, by discovery
Of what I would not hear?

400

Ventidius.   No Prince but you,
Could merit that sincerity I us'd,
Nor durst another Man have ventur'd it;
But you, ere Love misled your wandring eyes,
Were sure the chief and best of Human Race,

405

Fram'd in the very pride and boast of Nature,
So perfect, that the gods who form'd you wonder'd
At their own skill, and cry'd, A lucky hit
Has mended our design. Their envy hindred,
Else you had been immortal, and a pattern,

410

When Heav'n would work for ostentation sake,
To copy out again.

Antony.   But *Cleopatra* ——
Go on; for I can bear it now.

Ventidius.   No more.

Antony. Thou dar'st not trust my Passion; but thou may'st;
Thou only lov'st; the rest have flatter'd me.

Ventidius. Heav'n's blessing on your heart, for that kind

415

word.
May I believe you love me? speak again.

Antony. Indeed I do. Speak this, and this, and this.
Hugging him.
Thy praises were unjust; but, I'll deserve 'em,
And yet mend all. Do with me what thou wilt;
Lead me to victory, thou know'st the way.　　　　　420
Ventidius. And, Will you leave this ──────
Antony. 　　　　　　　　Pr'ythee do not curse her,
And I will leave her; though, Heav'n knows, I love
Beyond Life, Conquest, Empires; all, but Honor:
But I will leave her.
Ventidius. 　　　　　　That's my Royal Master.
And, Shall we fight?
Antony. 　　　　　　I warrant thee, old Soldier,　　425
Thou shalt behold me once again in Iron,
And at the head of our old Troops, that beat
The *Parthians*, cry alloud, Come follow me.
Ventidius. O now I hear my Emperor! in that word
Octavius fell. Gods, let me see that day,　　　　　430
And, if I have ten years behind, take all;
I'll thank you for th'exchange.
Antony. 　　　　　　　　Oh *Cleopatra!*
Ventidius. Again?
Antony. 　　　　I've done: in that last sigh, she went.
Cæsar shall know what 'tis to force a Lover,
From all he holds most dear.
Ventidius. 　　　　　　　　Methinks you breath　　435
Another Soul: Your looks are more Divine;
You speak a Heroe, and you move a God.
Antony. O, thou hast fir'd me; my Soul's up in Arms,
And Mans each part about me: once again,
That noble eagerness of fight has seiz'd me;　　　440
That eagerness, with which I darted upward
To *Cassius's* Camp: In vain the steepy Hill,
Oppos'd my way; in vain a War of Speares
Sung round my head; and planted all my shield:
I won the Trenches, while my formost Men　　　445
Lag'd on the Plain below.
Ventidius. 　　　　　　　Ye Gods, ye Gods,
For such another hour.
Antony. 　　　　　　Come on, My Soldier!
Our hearts and armes are still the same: I long
Once more to meet our foes; that Thou and I,
Like Time and Death, marching before our Troops,　　450
May taste fate to e'm; Mowe e'm out a passage,

451 *May taste fate to e'm*] certify to our good fortune in battle, as a royal taster tests food before it reaches a king's mouth.

And, entring where the foremost Squadrons yield,
Begin the noble Harvest of the Field.

Exeunt.

ACT II

[*Enter*] Cleopatra, Iras, *and* Alexas.

Cleopatra. What shall I do, or whither shall I turn?
Ventidius has o'rcome, and he will go.
Alexas. He goes to fight for you.
Cleopatra. Then he wou'd see me, ere he went to fight:
5   Flatter me not: if once he goes, he's lost:
And all my hopes destroy'd.
Alexas.   Does this weak passion
Become a Mighty Queen?
Cleopatra.   I am no Queen;
Is this to be a Queen, to be besieg'd
By yon insulting *Roman*; and to wait
10   Each hour the Victor's Chain? These ills are small;
For *Antony* is lost, and I can mourn
For nothing else but him. Now come, *Octavius*,
I have no more to lose; prepare thy Bands;
I'm fit to be a Captive: *Antony*
15   Has taught my mind the fortune of a Slave.
Iras. Call Reason to assist you.
Cleopatra.   I have none.
And none would have: my Love's a noble madness,
Which shows the cause deserv'd it. Moderate sorrow
Fits vulgar Love; and for a vulgar Man:
20   But I have lov'd with such transcendent passion,
I soar'd, at first, quite out of Reason's view,
And now am lost above it. —— No, I'm proud
'Tis thus: would *Antony* could see me now;
Think you he would not sigh? though he must leave me,
25   Sure he would sigh; for he is noble-natur'd,
And bears a tender heart: I know him well.
Ah, no, I know him not; I knew him once,
But now 'tis past.
Iras.   Let it be past with you:
Forget him, Madam.
Cleopatra.   Never, never, *Iras.*
30   He once was mine; and once, though now 'tis gone,
Leaves a faint Image of possession still.
Alexas. Think him unconstant, cruel, and ungrateful.
Cleopatra. I cannot: if I could, those thoughts were vain;

Faithless, ungrateful, cruel, though he be,
I still must love him.

Enter Charmion.

    Now, What news my *Charmion*? 35
Will he be kind? and, Will he not forsake me?
Am I to live, or dye? nay, Do I live?
Or am I dead? for, when he gave his answer,
Fate took the word, and then I liv'd, or dy'd.
Charmion. I found him, Madam ———
Cleopatra.   A long Speech preparing? 40
If thou bring'st comfort, hast, and give it me;
For never was more need.
Iras.   I know he loves you.
Cleopatra. Had he been kind, her eyes had told me so,
Before her tongue could speak it: now she studies,
To soften what he said; but give me death, 45
Just as he sent it, *Charmion*, undisguis'd,
And in the words he spoke.
Charmion.   I found him then
Incompass'd round, I think, with Iron Statues,
So mute, so motionless his Soldiers stood,
While awfully he cast his eyes about, 50
And ev'ry Leader's hopes or fears survey'd:
Methought he look'd resolv'd, and yet not pleas'd.
When he beheld me struggling in the croud,
He blush'd, and bade, make way.
Alexas.   There's comfort yet.
Charmion. Ventidius fixt his eyes upon my passage, 55
Severely, as he meant to frown me back,
And sullenly gave place: I told my message,
Just as you gave it, broken and disorder'd;
I numbred in it all your sighs and tears,
And while I mov'd your pitiful request, 60
That you but only beg'd a last farewel,
He fetch'd an inward groan, and ev'ry time
I nam'd you, sigh'd, as if his heart were breaking,
But shun'd my eyes, and guiltily look'd down;
He seem'd not now that awful *Antony* 65
Who shook an Arm'd Assembly with his Nod,
But making show as he would rub his eyes,
Disguis'd and blotted out a falling tear.
Cleopatra. Did he then weep? and, Was I worth a tear?
If what thou hast to say be not as pleasing, 70
Tell me no more, but let me dye contented.
Charmion. He bid me say, He knew himself so well,

He could deny you nothing, if he saw you;
And therefore ———
Cleopatra.   Thou would'st say, he wou'd not see me?
75   *Charmion.* And therefore beg'd you not to use a power,
   Which he could ill resist; yet he should ever
   Respect you as he ought.
   Cleopatra.   Is that a word
   For *Antony* to use to *Cleopatra*?
   Oh that faint word, Respect! how I disdain it!
80   Disdain my self, for loving after it!
   He should have kept that word for cold *Octavia*.
   Respect is for a Wife: Am I that thing,
   That dull insipid lump, without desires,
   And without pow'r to give 'em?
   Alexas.   You misjudge;
85   You see through Love, and that deludes your sight:
   As, what is strait, seems crooked through the Water;
   But I, who bear my reason undisturb'd,
   Can see this *Antony*, this dreaded Man,
   A fearful slave, who fain would run away,
90   And shuns his Master's eyes: if you pursue him,
   My life on't, he still drags a chain along,
   That needs must clog his flight.
   Cleopatra.   Could I believe thee! ———
   Alexas. By ev'ry circumstance I know he Loves.
   True, he's hard prest, by Intrest and by Honor;
95   Yet he but doubts, and parlyes, and casts out
   Many a long look for succor.
   Cleopatra.   He sends word,
   He fears to see my face.
   Alexas.   And would you more?
   He shows his weakness who declines the Combat;
   And you must urge your fortune. Could he speak
100   More plainly? To my ears, the Message sounds,
   Come to my rescue, *Cleopatra*, come;
   Come, free me from *Ventidius*; from my Tyrant:
   See me, and give me a pretence to leave him.
   I hear his Trumpets. This way he must pass.
105   Please you, retire a while; I'll work him first,
   That he may bend more easie.
   Cleopatra.   You shall rule me;
   But all, I fear, in vain.
                    Exit with Charmion *and* Iras.
   Alexas.   I fear so too;

84 *give*] cause others to have.

Though I conceal'd my thoughts, to make her bold:
But, 'tis our utmost means, and Fate befriend it.
                                        Withdraws.

Enter Lictors *with* Fasces; *one bearing the Eagle: then
Enter* Antony *with* Ventidius, *follow'd by other Commanders.*

Antony. Octavius is the Minion of blind Chance,   110
     But holds from Virtue nothing.
Ventidius.   Has he courage?
Antony. But just enough to season him from Coward.
     O, 'tis the coldest youth upon a Charge,
     The most deliberate fighter! if he ventures
     (As in *Illyria* once they say he did   115
     To storm a Town) 'tis when he cannot chuse,
     When all the World have fixt their eyes upon him;
     And then he lives on that for seven years after,
     But, at a close revenge he never fails.
Ventidius. I heard, you challeng'd him.
Antony.   I did, *Ventidius.*   120
     What think'st thou was his answer? 'twas so tame, ——
     He said he had more wayes than one to dye;
     I had not.
Ventidius.   Poor!
Antony.   He has more wayes than one;
     But he would chuse 'em all before that one.
Ventidius. He first would chuse an Ague, or a Fever. 125
Antony. No: it must be an Ague, not a Fever;
     He has not warmth enough to dye by that.
Ventidius. Or old Age, and a Bed.
Antony.   I, there's his choice.
     He would live, like a Lamp, to the last wink,
     And crawl upon the utmost verge of life: 130
     O *Hercules*! Why should a Man like this,
     Who dares not trust his fate for one great action,
     Be all the care of Heav'n? Why should he Lord it
     O're Fourscore thousand Men, of whom, each one
     Is braver than himself?
Ventidius.   You conquer'd for him: 135
     Philippi knows it; there you shar'd with him
     That Empire, which your Sword made all your own.
Antony. Fool that I was, upon my Eagle's Wings

111 *Virtue*] manliness.
114 *deliberate fighter*] thought to be a slur on Louis XIV, who had a
similar reputation.
119 *close*] secret.

225

140   I bore this Wren, till I was tir'd with soaring,
    And now he mounts above me.
    Good Heav'ns, Is this, is this the Man who braves me?
    Who bids my age make way: drives me before him,
    To the World's ridge, and sweeps me off like rubbish?
    Ventidius. Sir, we lose time; the Troops are mounted all.
145   *Antony.* Then give the word to March:
    I long to leave this Prison of a Town,
    To joyn thy Legions; and, in open Field,
    Once more to show my face. Lead, my Deliverer.

Enter Alexas.

    Alexas. Great Emperor,
150   In mighty Arms renown'd above Mankind,
    But, in soft pity to th'opprest, a God:
    This message sends the mournful *Cleopatra*
    To her departing Lord.
    Ventidius [aside].   Smooth Sycophant!
    Alexas. A thousand wishes, and ten thousand Prayers,
155   Millions of blessings wait you to the Wars,
    Millions of sighs and tears she sends you too,
    And would have sent
    As many dear embraces to your Arms,
    As many parting kisses to your Lips;
160   But those, she fears, have weary'd you already.
    Ventidius (aside). False Crocodyle!
    Alexas. And yet she begs not now, you would not leave her,
    That were a wish too mighty for her hopes,
    Too presuming
165   For her low Fortune, and your ebbing love,
    That were a wish for her more prosp'rous dayes,
    Her blooming beauty, and your growing kindness.
    Antony (aside). Well, I must Man it out; What would the
    Queen?
    Alexas. First, to these noble Warriors, who attend,
170   Your daring courage in the Chase of Fame,
    (Too daring, and too dang'rous for her quiet)
    She humbly recommends all she holds dear,
    All her own cares and fears, the care of you.
    Ventidius. Yes, witness *Actium*.
    Antony.   Let him speak, *Ventidius*.
175   *Alexas.* You, when his matchless valor bears him forward,
    With ardor too Heroick on his foes,

139 *I bore this Wren*] the fable of the wren who hid in the eagle's feathers and then surpassed the eagle (Noyes).

Fall down, as she would do, before his feet;
Lye in his way, and stop the paths of Death;
Tell him, this God is not invulnerable,
That absent *Cleopatra* bleeds in him;   180
And, that you may remember her Petition,
She begs you wear these Trifles, as a pawn,
Which, at your wisht return, she will redeem
     Gives Jewels to the Commanders.
With all the Wealth of *Ægypt*:
This, to the great *Ventidius* she presents,   185
Whom she can never count her Enemy,
Because he loves her Lord.
Ventidius.   Tell her I'll none on't;
 I'm not asham'd of honest Poverty:
 Not all the Diamonds of the East can bribe
 Ventidius from his faith. I hope to see   190
 These, and the rest of all her sparkling store,
 Where they shall more deservingly be plac'd.
Antony. And who must wear 'em then?
Ventidius.   The wrong'd *Octavia.*
Antony. You might have spar'd that word.
Ventidius.   And he that Bribe.
Antony. But have I no remembrance?
Alexas.   Yes, a dear one: 195
 Your slave, the Queen ———
Antony.   My Mistress.
Alexas.   Then your Mistress,
 Your Mistress would, she sayes, have sent her Soul,
 But that you had long since; she humbly begs
 This Ruby bracelet, set with bleeding hearts,
 (The emblems of her own) may bind your Arme.   200
     Presenting a Bracelet.
Ventidius. Now, my best Lord, in Honor's name, I ask you,
 For Manhood's sake, and for your own dear safety,
 Touch not these poyson'd gifts,
 Infected by the sender, touch 'em not,
 Miriads of blewest Plagues lye underneath 'em,   205
 And more than Aconite has dipt the Silk.
Antony. Nay, now you grow too Cynical, *Ventidius.*
 A Lady's favors may be worn with honor.
 What, to refuse her Bracelet! On my Soul,
 When I lye pensive in my Tent alone,   210
 'Twill pass the wakeful hours of Winter nights,
 To tell these pretty Beads upon my arm,

205 *blewest*] most livid.

To count for every one a soft embrace,
A melting kiss at such and such a time;
215 And now and then the fury of her love,
When ——— And what harm's in this?
Alexas. None, none my Lord,
But what's to her, that now 'tis past for ever.
Antony (*going to tye it*). We Soldiers are so aukward ———
help me tye it.
Alexas. In faith, my Lord, we Courtiers too are aukward
220 In these affairs: so are all Men indeed;
Ev'n I, who am not one. But shall I speak?
Antony. Yes, freely.
Alexas. Then, my Lord, fair hands alone
Are fit to tye it; she, who sent it, can.
Ventidius. Hell, Death; this Eunuch Pandar ruins you.
You will not see her?
Alexas whispers an Attendant, who goes out.
225 *Antony.* But to take my leave.
Ventidius. Then I have wash'd an *Æthiope.* Y'are undone;
Y'are in the Toils; y'are taken; y'are destroy'd:
Her eyes do *Cæsar's* work.
Antony. You fear too soon.
I'm constant to my self: I know my strength;
230 And yet she shall not think me Barbarous, neither,
Born in the depths of *Africk*: I'm a *Roman*,
Bred to the Rules of soft humanity.
A guest, and kindly us'd, should bid farewel.
Ventidius. You do not know
235 How weak you are to her, how much an Infant;
You are not proof against a smile, or glance;
A sigh will quite disarm you.
Antony. See, she comes!
Now you shall find your error. Gods, I thank you:
I form'd the danger greater than it was,
And, now 'tis near, 'tis lessen'd.
240 *Ventidius.* Mark the end yet.

Enter Cleopatra, Charmion *and* Iras.

Antony. Well, Madam, we are met.
Cleopatra. Is this a Meeting?
Then, we must part?
Antony. We must.
Cleopatra. Who sayes we must?
Antony. Our own hard fates.
Cleopatra. We make those Fates our selves.

Antony. Yes, we have made 'em; we have lov'd each other
   Into our mutual ruin.   245
Cleopatra. The Gods have seen my Joys with envious eyes;
   I have no friends in Heav'n; and all the World,
   (As 'twere the bus'ness of Mankind to part us)
   Is arm'd against my Love: ev'n you your self
   Joyn with the rest; you, you are arm'd against me.   250
Antony. I will be justify'd in all I do
   To late Posterity, and therefore hear me.
   If I mix a lye
   With any truth, reproach me freely with it;
   Else, favor me with silence.
Cleopatra.   You command me,   255
   And I am dumb:
Ventidius [aside]. I like this well: he shows Authority.
Antony. That I derive my ruin
   From you alone ———
Cleopatra.   O Heav'ns! I ruin you!
Antony. You promis'd me your silence, and you break it   260
   Ere I have scarce begun.
Cleopatra.   Well, I obey you.
Antony. When I beheld you first, it was in *Ægypt*,
   Ere *Cæsar* saw your Eyes; you gave me love,
   And were too young to know it; that I setled
   Your Father in his Throne, was for your sake,   265
   I left th'acknowledgment for time to ripen.
   Cæsar stept in, and with a greedy hand
   Pluck'd the green fruit, ere the first blush of red,
   Yet cleaving to the bough. He was my Lord,
   And was, beside, too great for me to rival,   270
   But, I deserv'd you first, though he enjoy'd you.
   When, after, I beheld you in *Cilicia*,
   An Enemy to *Rome*, I pardon'd you.
Cleopatra. I clear'd my self ———
Antony.   Again you break your Promise.
   I lov'd you still, and took your weak excuses,   275
   Took you into my bosome, stain'd by *Cæsar*,
   And not half mine: I went to *Ægypt* with you
   And hid me from the bus'ness of the World,
   Shut out enquiring Nations from my sight,
   To give whole years to you.   280
Ventidius (aside). Yes, to your shame be't spoken.
Antony.   How I lov'd
   Witness ye Dayes and Nights, and all your hours,
   That Danc'd away with Down upon your Feet,
   As all your bus'ness were to count my passion.

285 One day past by, and nothing saw but Love;
Another came, and still 'twas only Love:
The Suns were weary'd out with looking on,
And I untyr'd with loving.
I saw you ev'ry day, and all the day;
290 And ev'ry day was still but as the first:
So eager was I still to see you more.
Ventidius [*aside*]. 'Tis all too true.
Antony.   *Fulvia*, my Wife, grew jealous,
As she indeed had reason; rais'd a War
In *Italy*, to call me back.
Ventidius [*aside*].   But yet
You went not.
295 *Antony*.   While within your arms I lay,
The World fell mouldring from my hands each hour,
And left me scarce a grasp (I thank your love for't.)
Ventidius [*aside*]. Well push'd: that last was home.
Cleopatra.   Yet may I speak?
Antony. If I have urg'd a falshood, yes; else, not.
300 Your silence says I have not. *Fulvia* dy'd;
(Pardon, you gods, with my unkindness dy'd.)
To set the World at Peace, I took *Octavia*,
This *Cæsar's* Sister; in her pride of youth
And flow'r of Beauty did I wed that Lady,
305 Whom blushing I must praise, because I left her.
You call'd; my Love obey'd the fatal summons:
This rais'd the *Roman* Arms; the Cause was yours.
I would have fought by Land, where I was stronger;
You hindred it: yet, when I fought at Sea,
310 Forsook me fighting; and (Oh stain to Honor!
Oh lasting shame!) I knew not that I fled;
But fled to follow you.
Ventidius. What haste she made to hoist her purple Sails!
And, to appear magnificent in flight,
Drew half our strength away.
315 *Antony*.   All this you caus'd.
And, Would you multiply more ruins on me?
This honest Man, my best, my only friend,
Has gather'd up the Shipwrack of my Fortunes;
Twelve Legions I have left, my last recruits,
320 And you have watch'd the news, and bring your eyes
To seize them too. If you have ought to answer,
Now speak, you have free leave.
Alexas (*aside*).   She stands confounded:
Despair is in her eyes.
Ventidius. Now lay a Sigh i'th way, to stop his passage:

Prepare a Tear, and bid it for his Legions; 325
'Tis like they shall be sold.
Cleopatra. How shall I plead my cause, when you, my
Judge,
Already have condemn'd me? Shall I bring
The Love you bore me for my Advocate?
That now is turn'd against me, that destroys me; 330
For, love once past, is, at the best, forgotten;
But oftner Sours to hate: 'twill please my Lord
To ruine me, and therefore I'll be guilty.
But, could I once have thought it would have pleas'd
you,
That you would pry, with narrow searching eyes 335
Into my faults, severe to my destruction,
And watching all advantages with care,
That serve to make me wretched? Speak, my Lord,
For I end here. Though I deserve this usage,
Was it like you to give it?
Antony.   O you wrong me, 340
To think I sought this parting, or desir'd
To accuse you more than what will clear my self,
And justifie this breach.
Cleopatra.   Thus low I thank you.
And, since my innocence will not offend,
I shall not blush to own it.
Ventidius.   After this 345
I think she'll blush at nothing.
Cleopatra.   You seem griev'd,
(And therein you are kind) that *Cæsar* first
Enjoy'd my love, though you deserv'd it better:
I grieve for that, my Lord, much more than you;
For, had I first been yours, it would have sav'd 350
My second choice: I never had been his,
And ne'r had been but yours. But *Cæsar* first,
You say, possess'd my love. Not so, my Lord:
He first possess'd my Person; you my Love:
Cæsar lov'd me; but I lov'd *Antony.* 355
If I endur'd him after, 'twas because
I judg'd it due to the first name of Men;
And, half constrain'd, I gave, as to a Tyrant,
What he would take by force.
Ventidius.   O Syren! Syren!
Yet grant that all the love she boasts were true, 360
Has she not ruin'd you? I still urge that,
The fatal consequence.
Cleopatra.   The consequence indeed,

231

For I dare challenge him, my greatest foe,
To say it was design'd: 'tis true, I lov'd you,
365 And kept you far from an uneasie Wife,
(Such *Fulvia* was.)
Yes, but he'll say, you left *Octavia* for me; ———
And, Can you blame me to receive that love,
Which quitted such desert, for worthless me?
370 How often have I wish'd some other *Cæsar*,
Great as the first, and as the second young,
Would court my Love to be refus'd for you!
Ventidius. Words, words; but *Actium*, Sir, remember
    Actium.
Cleopatra. Ev'n there, I dare his malice. True, I Counsel'd
375 To fight at Sea; but, I betray'd you not.
I fled; but not to the Enemy. 'Twas fear;
Would I had been a Man, not to have fear'd,
For none would then have envy'd me your friendship,
Who envy me your Love.
Antony.   We're both unhappy:
380 If nothing else, yet our ill fortune parts us.
Speak; Would you have me perish, by my stay?
Cleopatra. If as a friend you ask my Judgment, go;
If as a Lover, stay. If you must perish:
'Tis a hard word; but stay.
385 *Ventidius.* See now th'effects of her so boasted love!
She strives to drag you down to ruine with her:
But, could she scape without you, oh how soon
Would she let go her hold, and haste to shore,
And never look behind!
Cleopatra. Then judge my love by this.
                      Giving Antony *a Writing.*
390   Could I have born
A life or death, a happiness or woe
From yours divided, this had giv'n me means.
Antony. By *Hercules*, the Writing of *Octavius*!
I know it well; 'tis that Proscribing hand,
395 Young as it was, that led the way to mine,
And left me but the second place in Murder. ———
See, see, *Ventidius*! here he offers *Ægypt*,
And joyns all *Syria* to it, as a present,
So, in requital, she forsake my fortunes,
And joyn her Arms with his.
400 *Cleopatra.*   And yet you leave me!

394 *Proscribing hand*] the hand that joined Antony in drawing
up a list of their enemies who should die, after the assassination of
Julius Caesar.

You leave me, *Antony*; and, yet I love you.
Indeed I do: I have refus'd a Kingdom,
That's a Trifle:
For I could part with life; with any thing,
But onely you. O let me dye but with you!   405
Is that a hard request?
Antony.   Next living with you,
'Tis all that Heav'n can give.
Alexas (aside).   He melts; We conquer.
Cleopatra. No: you shall go: your Int'rest calls you hence;
Yes; your dear interest pulls too strong, for these
Weak Armes to hold you here. ———
                          Takes his hand.
            Go; leave me, Soldier;   410
(For you're no more a Lover:) leave me dying:
Push me all pale and panting from your bosome,
And, when your March begins, let one run after
Breathless almost for Joy; and cry, she's dead:
The Souldiers shout; you then perhaps may sigh,   415
And muster all your *Roman* Gravity;
Ventidius chides; and strait your Brow cleares up,
As I had never been.
Antony.   Gods, 'tis too much;
Too much for Man to bear!
Cleopatra.   What is't for me then,
A weak forsaken Woman? and a Lover?———   420
Here let me breathe my last: envy me not
This minute in your Armes: I'll dye apace:
As fast as ere I can; and end your trouble.
Antony. Dye! Rather let me perish: looss'nd Nature
Leap from its hinges. Sink the props of Heav'n,   425
And fall the Skyes to crush the neather World.
My Eyes, my Soul; my all! ———   *Embraces her.*
Ventidius.   And what's this Toy
In ballance with your fortune, Honor, Fame?
Antony. What is't, *Ventidius?* it out-weighs 'em all;
Why, we have more than conquer'd *Cæsar* now: 430
My Queen's not only Innocent, but Loves me.
This, this is she who drags me down to ruin!
But, could she scape without me, with what haste
Would she let slip her hold, and make to shore,
And never look behind!   435
Down on thy knees, Blasphemer as thou art,
And ask forgiveness of wrong'd Innocence.
Ventidius. I'll rather dye, than take it. Will you go?
Antony. Go! Whither? go from all that's excellent!

440

Faith, Honor, Virtue, all good things forbid,
That I should go from her, who sets my love
Above the price of Kingdoms. Give, you Gods,
Give to your Boy, your *Cæsar*,
This Rattle of a Globe to play withal,

445

This Gu-gau World, and put him cheaply off:
I'll not be pleas'd with less than *Cleopatra*.
Cleopatra. She's wholly yours. My heart's so full of joy,
That I shall do some wild extravagance
Of Love, in publick; and the foolish World,

450

Which knows not tenderness, will think me Mad.
Ventidius. O Women! Women! Women! all the gods
Have not such pow'r of doing good to Man,
As you of doing harm.   *Exit.*
Antony.   Our Men are Arm'd.
Unbar the Gate that looks to *Cæsar's* Camp;

455

I would revenge the Treachery he meant me:
And long security makes Conquest easie.
I'm eager to return before I go;
For, all the pleasures I have known, beat thick
On my remembrance: how I long for night!

460

That both the sweets of mutual love may try,
And once Triumph o're *Cæsar* e're we dye.
                                       Exeunt.

ACT III

At one door, Enter Cleopatra, Charmion, Iras, *and* Alexas, *a Train of Ægyptians: at the other,* Antony *and* Romans. *The entrance on both sides is prepar'd by Musick; the Trumpets first sounding on* Antony's *part: then answer'd by Timbrels, &c. on* Cleopatra's. Charmion *and* Iras *hold a Laurel Wreath betwixt them. A Dance of Ægyptians. After the Ceremony,* Cleopatra *Crowns* Antony.

Antony. I thought how those white arms would fold me in,
And strain me close, and melt me into love;
So pleas'd with that sweet Image, I sprung forwards,
And added all my strength to every blow.

5

Cleopatra. Come to me, come, my Soldier, to my Arms,
You've been too long away from my embraces;
But, when I have you fast, and all my own,
With broken murmurs, and with amorous sighs,

447 She's] F; She Qq.   461 e're] Q2; *omit* Q1

461 *Triumph*] second syllable accented, as in Dryden's "Threnodia Augustalis" (l. 480), "His valor can triumph o'er land and main."

I'll say, you were unkind, and punish you,
And mark you red with many an eager kiss.   10
Antony. My Brighter *Venus!*
Cleopatra.   O my greater *Mars!*
Antony. Thou joinst us well, my Love!
Suppose me come from the *Phlegræan* Plains,
Where gasping Gyants lay, cleft by my Sword:
And Mountain tops par'd off each other blow,   15
To bury those I slew: receive me, goddess:
Let *Cæsar* spread his subtile Nets, like *Vulcan*;
In thy embraces I would be beheld
By Heav'n and Earth at once:
And make their envy what they meant their sport.   20
Let those who took us blush; I would love on
With awful State, regardless of their frowns,
As their superior god.
There's no satiety of Love, in thee;
Enjoy'd, thou still art new; perpetual Spring   25
Is in thy armes; the ripen'd fruit but falls,
And blossoms rise to fill its empty place;
And I grow rich by giving.

> *Enter* Ventidius, *and stands apart.*

Alexas. O, now the danger's past, your General comes.
He joyns not in your joys, nor minds your Triumphs;   30
But, with contracted brows, looks frowning on,
As envying your Success.
Antony. Now, on my Soul, he loves me; truely loves me;
He never flatter'd me in any vice,
But awes me with his virtue: ev'n this minute   35
Methinks he has a right of chiding me.
Lead to the Temple: I'll avoid his presence;
It checks too strong upon me.

> *Exeunt the rest.*
> *As* Antony *is going,* Ventidius *pulls him by the Robe.*

Ventidius.   Emperor.
Antony (looking back). 'Tis the old argument; I pr'ythee
        spare me.

13 *Phlegræan Plains*] in Macedonia, scene of the battle where the gods
subdued the titans.
15 *par'd off each other blow*] parried off every other blow of mine.
The titans tried to fend off Mars' blows by throwing mountain tops.
The *OED* does not list *par'd* as a spelling variant of *parried*, but this is a
clear case of elision.
18 *beheld*] When Mars and Venus were trapped in an iron net by
Vulcan, the Gods came to laugh. Mercury confessed, however, that
he would willingly trade places with Mars (*Odyssey*, VIII, 266–366).

Ventidius. But this one hearing, Emperor.
40 *Antony.*   Let go
    My Robe; or, by my Father *Hercules* ———
Ventidius. By *Hercules* his Father, that's yet greater,
    I bring you somewhat you would wish to know.
Antony. Thou see'st we are observ'd; attend me here,
45   And I'll return.   *Exit.*
Ventidius. I'm waining in his favor, yet I love him;
    I love this Man, who runs to meet his ruine;
    And, sure the gods, like me, are fond of him:
    His Virtues lye so mingled with his Crimes,
50   As would confound their choice to punish one,
    And not reward the other.

                    Enter Antony.

Antony. We can conquer, you see, without your aid.
    We have dislodg'd their Troops,
    They look on us at distance, and, like Curs
55 Scap'd from the Lion's paws, they bay far off,
    And lick their wounds, and faintly threaten War.
    Five thousand *Romans* with their faces upward,
    Lye breathless on the Plain.
Ventidius.   'Tis well: and he
    Who lost 'em, could have spar'd Ten thousand more.
60 Yet if, by this advantage, you could gain
    An easier Peace, while *Cæsar* doubts the Chance
    Of Arms! ———
Antony.   O think not on't, *Ventidius*;
    The Boy pursues my ruin, he'll no peace:
    His malice is considerate in advantage;
65 O, he's the coolest Murderer, so stanch,
    He kills, and keeps his temper.
Ventidius.   Have you no friend
    In all his Army, who has power to move him,
    Mæcenas, or *Agrippa* might do much.
Antony. They're both too deep in *Cæsar's* interests.
70   We'll work it out by dint of Sword, or perish.
Ventidius. Fain I would find some other.
Antony.   Thank thy love.
    Some four or five such Victories as this,
    Will save thy farther pains.
Ventidius. Expect no more; *Cæsar* is on his Guard:
75   I know, Sir, you have conquer'd against ods;

41 *my Father Hercules*] the traditional founder of his family,
Anton, was son of Hercules, according to Plutarch.
65 *stanch*] staunch.

But still you draw Supplies from one poor Town,
And of *Ægyptians*: he has all the World,
And, at his back, Nations come pouring in,
To fill the gaps you make. Pray think again.
Antony. Why dost thou drive me from my self, to search   80
  For Forreign aids? to hunt my memory,
  And range all o're a waste and barren place
  To find a Friend? The wretched have no Friends. ———
  Yet I had one, the bravest youth of *Rome*,
  Whom *Cæsar* loves beyond the love of Women;   85
  He could resolve his mind, as Fire does Wax,
  From that hard rugged Image, melt him down,
  And mould him in what softer form he pleas'd.
Ventidius. Him would I see; that man of all the world:
  Just such a one we want.
Antony.   He lov'd me too,   90
  I was his Soul; he liv'd not but in me:
  We were so clos'd within each other's brests,
  The rivets were not found that join'd us first.
  That does not reach us yet: we were so mixt,
  As meeting streams, both to our selves were lost;   95
  We were one mass; we could not give or take,
  But from the same; for he was I, I he.
Ventidius (aside). He moves as I would wish him.
Antony.   After this,
  I need not tell his name: 'twas *Dollabella*.
Ventidius. He's now in *Cæsar's* Camp.
Antony.   No matter where,   100
  Since he's no longer mine. He took unkindly
  That I forbade him *Cleopatra's* sight;
  Because I fear'd he lov'd her: he confest
  He had a warmth, which, for my sake, he stifled;
  For 'twere impossible that two, so one,   105
  Should not have lov'd the same. When he departed,
  He took no leave; and that confirm'd my thoughts.
Ventidius. It argues that he lov'd you more than her,
  Else he had staid; but he perceiv'd you jealous,
  And would not grieve his friend: I know he loves you.   110
Antony. I should have seen him then ere now.
Ventidius.   Perhaps
  He has thus long been lab'ring for your peace.
Antony. Would he were here.
Ventidius.   Would you believe he lov'd you?
  I read your answer in your eyes; you would.
  Not to conceal it longer, he has sent   115
  A Messenger from *Cæsar's* Camp, with Letters.

Antony. Let him appear.
Ventidius.   I'll bring him instantly.

Exit Ventidius, *and Re-enters immediately with* Dollabella.

Antony. 'Tis he himself, himself, by holy Friendship!
                              Runs to embrace him.
Art thou return'd at last, my better half?
Come, give me all my elf.
120   Let me not live,
If the young Bridegroom, longing for his night,
Was ever half so fond.
Dollabella. I must be silent; for my Soul is busie
About a nobler work: she's new come home,
125   Like a long-absent man, and wanders o'er
Each room, a stranger to her own, to look
If all be safe.
Antony.   Thou hast what's left of me.
For I am now so sunk from what I was,
Thou find'st me at my lowest water-mark.
130   The Rivers that ran in, and rais'd my fortunes,
Are all dry'd up, or take another course:
What I have left is from my native Spring;
I've still a heart that swells, in scorn of fate,
And lifts me to my banks.
135 *Dollabella.* Still you are Lord of all the World to me.
Antony. Why, then I yet am so; for thou art all.
If I had any joy when thou wert absent,
I grudg'd it to my self; methought I robb'd
Thee of thy part. But, Oh my *Dollabella*!
140   Thou hast beheld me other than I am.
Hast thou not seen my morning Chambers fill'd
With Scepter'd Slaves, who waited to salute me:
With Eastern Monarchs, who forgot the Sun,
To worship my uprising? Menial Kings
145   Ran coursing up and down my Palace-yard,
Stood silent in my presence, watch'd my eyes,
And, at my least command, all started out
Like Racers to the Goal.
Dollabella.   Slaves to your fortune.
Antony. Fortune is *Cæsar's* now; and what am I?
150 *Ventidius.* What you have made your self; I will not flatter.
Antony. Is this friendly done?
Dollabella. Yes, when his end is so; I must join with him,
Indeed I must, and yet you must not chide:
Why am I else your friend?
Antony.   Take heed, young man,

How thou upbraid'st my love: the Queen has eyes,   155
And thou too hast a Soul. Canst thou remember
When, swell'd with hatred, thou beheld'st her first
As accessary to thy Brother's death?
Dollabella. Spare my remembrance; 'twas a guilty day,
And still the blush hangs here.
Antony.   To clear her self,   160
For sending him no aid, she came from *Egypt.*
Her Gally down the Silver *Cydnos* row'd,
The Tackling Silk, the Streamers wav'd with Gold,
The gentle Winds were lodg'd in Purple sails:
Her Nymphs, like *Nereids,* round her Couch, were
plac'd;   165
Where she, another Sea-born *Venus,* lay.
Dollabella. No more: I would not hear it.
Antony.   O, you must!
She lay, and leant her cheek upon her hand,
And cast a look so languishingly sweet,
As if, secure of all beholders hearts,
Neglecting she could take 'em: Boys, like *Cupids,*   170
Stood fanning, with their painted wings, the winds
That plaid about her face: but if she smil'd,
A darting glory seem'd to blaze abroad:
That men's desiring eyes were never weary'd;   175
But hung upon the object: to soft Flutes
The Silver Oars kept time; and while they plaid,
The hearing gave new pleasure to the sight;
And both to thought: 'twas Heav'n, or somewhat more;
For she so charm'd all hearts, that gazing crowds   18(
Stood panting on the shore, and wanted breath
To give their welcome voice.
Then, *Dollabella,* where was then thy Soul?
Was not thy fury quite disarm'd with wonder?
Didst thou not shrink behind me from those eyes,   185
And whisper in my ear, Oh tell her not
That I accus'd her of my Brother's death?
Dollabella. And should my weakness be a plea for yours?
Mine was an age when love might be excus'd,
When kindly warmth, and when my springing youth   190
Made it a debt to Nature. Yours ——
Ventidius.   Speak boldly.
Yours, he would say, in your declining age,
When no more heat was left but what you forc'd,

162 *Cydnos*] now called the Tarsus river in southeast Turkey where
the meeting took place.

When all the sap was needful for the Trunk,
195   When it went down, then you constrain'd the course,
And robb'd from Nature, to supply desire;
In you (I would not use so harsh a word)
But 'tis plain dotage.

Antony.   Ha!

Dollabella.   'Twas urg'd too home.
But yet the loss was private that I made;
200   'Twas but my self I lost: I lost no Legions;
I had no World to lose, no people's love.

Antony. This from a friend?

Dollabella.   Yes, *Antony*, a true one;
A friend so tender, that each word I speak
Stabs my own heart, before it reach your ear.
205   O, judge me not less kind because I chide:
To *Cæsar* I excuse you.

Antony.   O ye Gods!
Have I then liv'd to be excus'd to *Cæsar*?

Dollabella. As to your equal.

Antony.   Well, he's but my equal:
While I wear this, he never shall be more.

Dollabella. I bring Conditions from him.
210   *Antony.*   Are they Noble?
Methinks thou shouldst not bring 'em else; yet he
Is full of deep dissembling; knows no Honour,
Divided from his Int'rest. Fate mistook him;
For Nature meant him for an Usurer,
215   He's fit indeed to buy, not conquer Kingdoms.

Ventidius. Then, granting this,
What pow'r was theirs who wrought so hard a temper
To honourable Terms!

Antony. It was my *Dollabella*, or some God.
220   *Dollabella.* Nor I; nor yet *Mæcenas*, nor *Agrippa*:
They were your Enemies; and I a Friend
Too weak alone; yet 'twas a *Roman's* deed.

Antony. 'Twas like a *Roman* done: show me that man
Who has preserv'd my life, my love, my honour;
Let me but see his face.
225   *Ventidius.*   That task is mine,
And, Heav'n thou know'st how pleasing.

                                Exit Ventidius.

Dollabella.   You'll remember
To whom you stand oblig'd?

Antony.   When I forget it,

209 *this*] his head.

Be thou unkind, and that's my greatest curse.
My Queen shall thank him too.
Dollabella.   I fear she will not.
Antony. But she shall do't: the Queen, my *Dollabella*!   230
Hast thou not still some grudgings of thy Fever?
Dollabella. I would not see her lost.
Antony.   When I forsake her,
Leave me, my better Stars; for she has truth
Beyond her beauty. *Cæsar* tempted her,
At no less price than Kingdoms, to betray me;   235
But she resisted all: and yet thou chid'st me
For loving her too well. Could I do so?
Dollabella. Yes, there's my reason.

> *Re-enter* Ventidius, *with* Octavia, *leading* Antony's
> *two little Daughters.*

Antony.   Where? —— *Octavia* there!
> *Starting back.*
Ventidius. What, is she poyson to you? a Disease?
Look on her, view her well; and those she brings: 240
Are they all strangers to your eyes? has Nature
No secret call, no whisper they are yours?
Dollabella. For shame, my Lord, if not for love, receive 'em
With kinder eyes. If you confess a man,
Meet 'em, embrace 'em, bid 'em welcome to you.   245
Your arms should open, ev'n without your knowledge,
To clasp 'em in; your feet should turn to wings,
To bear you to 'em; and your eyes dart out,
And aim a kiss ere you could reach the lips.
Antony. I stood amaz'd to think how they came hither.   250
Ventidius. I sent for 'em; I brought 'em in, unknown
To *Cleopatra's* Guards.
Dollabella.   Yet are you cold?
Octavia. Thus long I have attended for my welcome;
Which, as a stranger, sure I might expect.
Who am I?
Antony.   *Cæsar's* Sister.
Octavia.   That's unkind!   255
Had I been nothing more than *Cæsar's* Sister,
Know, I had still remain'd in *Cæsar's* Camp;
But your *Octavia*, your much injur'd Wife,
Tho' banish'd from your Bed, driv'n from your House,
In spight of *Cæsar's* Sister, still is yours.   260

231 *grudgings*] slight symptoms.
244 *confess*] acknowledge you are.

'Tis true, I have a heart disdains your coldness,
And prompts me not to seek what you should offer;
But a Wife's Virtue still surmounts that pride:
I come to claim you as my own; to show

265 My duty first, to ask, nay beg, your kindness:
Your hand, my Lord; 'tis mine, and I will have it.
                                        Taking his hand.
Ventidius. Do, take it, thou deserv'st it.
Dollabella.   On my Soul,
And so she does: she's neither too submissive,
Nor yet too haughty; but so just a mean,

270 Shows, as it ought, a Wife and *Roman* too.
Antony. I fear, *Octavia*, you have begg'd my life.
Octavia. Begg'd it, my Lord?
Antony.   Yes, begg'd it, my Ambassadress,
Poorly and basely begg'd it of your Brother.
Octavia. Poorly and basely I could never beg;

275 Nor could my Brother grant.
Antony. Shall I, who, to my kneeling Slave, could say,
Rise up, and be a King; shall I fall down
And cry, Forgive me, *Cæsar*? shall I set
A Man, my Equal, in the place of *Jove*,

280 As he could give me being?
No; that word, *Forgive*, would choke me up,
And die upon my tongue.
Dollabella.   You shall not need it.
Antony. I will not need it. Come, you've all betray'd me:
My Friend too! to receive some vile conditions.

285 My Wife has bought me, with her prayers and tears;
And now I must become her branded Slave:
In every peevish mood she will upbraid
The life she gave: if I but look awry,
She cries, I'll tell my Brother,
Octavia.   My hard fortune

290 Subjects me still to your unkind mistakes.
But the Conditions I have brought are such
You need not blush to take: I love your Honour,
Because 'tis mine; it never shall be said
Octavia's Husband was her Brother's Slave.

295 Sir, you are free; free, ev'n from her you loath;
For, tho' my Brother bargains for your love,
Makes me the price and cement of your peace,
I have a Soul like yours; I cannot take
Your love as alms, nor beg what I deserve.

300 I'll tell my Brother we are reconcil'd;
He shall draw back his Troops, and you shall march

To rule the East: I may be dropt at *Athens*;
No matter where, I never will complain,
But only keep the barren Name of Wife,
And rid you of the trouble.   305
Ventidius. Was ever such a strife of sullen Honour!
Both scorn to be oblig'd.
Dollabella. O, she has toucht him in the tender'st part;
See how he reddens with despight and shame
To be out-done in Generosity!   310
Ventidius. See how he winks! how he dries up a tear,
That fain would fall!
Antony. *Octavia*, I have heard you, and must praise
The greatness of your Soul;
But cannot yield to what you have propos'd: 315
For I can ne'er be conquer'd but by love;
And you do all for duty. You would free me,
And would be dropt at *Athens*; was't not so?
Octavia. It was, my Lord.
Antony.   Then I must be oblig'd
To one who loves me not, who, to her self,   320
May call me thankless and ungrateful **Man**:
I'll not endure it, no.
Ventidius. I'm glad it pinches there.
Octavia. Would you triumph o'er poor *Octavia's* Virtue?
That pride was all I had to bear me up;   325
That you might think you ow'd me for your life,
And ow'd it to my duty, not my love.
I have been injur'd, and my haughty Soul
Could brook but ill the Man who slights my Bed.
Antony. Therefore you love me not.
Octavia.   Therefore, my Lord,   330
I should not love you.
Antony.   Therefore you wou'd leave me?
Octavia. And therefore I should leave you ——— if I could.
Dollabella. Her Soul's too great, after such injuries,
To say she loves; and yet she lets you see it.
Her modesty and silence plead her cause.   335
Antony. O, *Dollabella*, which way shall I turn?
I find a secret yielding in my Soul;
But *Cleopatra*, who would die with me,
Must she be left? Pity pleads for *Octavia*;
But does it not plead more for *Cleopatra*?   340
Ventidius. Justice and Pity both plead for *Octavia*;
For *Cleopatra*, neither.
One would be ruin'd with you; but she first
Had ruin'd you: the other, you have ruin'd,

345   And yet she would preserve you.
In every thing their merits are unequal.
Antony. O, my distracted Soul!
Octavia.   Sweet Heav'n compose it.
Come, come, my Lord, if I can pardon you,
Methinks you should accept it. Look on these;
350   Are they not yours? Or stand they thus neglected
As they are mine? Go to him, Children, go;
Kneel to him, take him by the hand, speak to him;
For you may speak, and he may own you too,
Without a blush; and so he cannot all
355   His Children: go, I say, and pull him to me,
And pull him to your selves, from that bad Woman.
You, *Agrippina,* hang upon his arms;
And you, *Antonia,* clasp about his waste:
If he will shake you off, if he will dash you
360   Against the Pavement, you must bear it, Children;
For you are mine, and I was born to suffer.
                Here the Children go to him, &c.
Ventidius. Was ever sight so moving! Emperor!
Dollabella. Friend!
Octavia.   Husband!
Both Children.   Father!
Antony.   I am vanquish'd: take me,
Octavia; take me, Children; share me all.
                     Embracing them.
365   I've been a thriftless Debtor to your loves,
And run out much, in riot, from your stock;
But all shall be amended.
Octavia.   O blest hour!
Dollabella. O happy change!
Ventidius.   My joy stops at my tongue;
But it has found two chanels here for one,
370   And bubbles out above.
Antony (to Octavia). This is thy Triumph; lead me where
    thou wilt;
Ev'n to thy Brother's Camp.
Octavia.   All there are yours.

                Enter Alexas *hastily.*

Alexas. The Queen, my Mistress, Sir, and yours ———
Antony.   'Tis past.
Octavia, you shall stay this night; To morrow,

---

347 *distracted*] divided, drawn to different objects.
354–55 *all His Children*] He had children by Cleopatra.

Cæsar and we are one.   375
    Exit leading Octavia, Dollabella *and the Children follow.*
Ventidius. There's news for you; run, my officious Eunuch.
  Be sure to be the first; haste foreward:
  Haste, my dear Eunuch, haste.   *Exit,*
Alexas. This downright fighting Fool, this thick-scull'd
    Hero,
  This blunt unthinking Instrument of death,   380
  With plain dull Virtue, has out-gone my Wit:
  Pleasure forsook my early'st Infancy,
  The luxury of others robb'd my Cradle,
  And ravish'd thence the promise of a Man:
  Cast out from Nature, disinherited   385
  Of what her meanest Children claim by kind;
  Yet, greatness kept me from contempt: that's gone.
  Had *Cleopatra* follow'd my advice,
  Then he had been betray'd, who now forsakes.
  She dies for love; but she has known its joys: 390
  Gods, is this just, that I, who know no joys,
  Must die, because she loves?

       Enter Cleopatra, Charmion, Iras, *Train.*

  Oh, Madam, I have seen what blasts my eyes!
  Octavia's here!
Cleopatra.   Peace with that Raven's note.
  I know it too; and now am in   395
  The pangs of death.
Alexas.   You are no more a Queen;
  Egypt is lost.
Cleopatra.   What tell'st thou me of *Egypt*?
  My Life, my Soul is lost! *Octavia* has him!
  O fatal name to *Cleopatra's* love!
  My kisses, my embraces now are hers;   400
  While I ——— But thou hast seen my Rival; speak,
  Does she deserve this blessing? Is she fair,
  Bright as a Goddess? and is all perfection
  Confin'd to her? It is. Poor I was made
  Of that course matter which, when she was finish'd,   405
  The Gods threw by, for rubbish.
Alexas. She's indeed a very Miracle.
Cleopatra. Death to my hopes, a Miracle!
Alexas (bowing).   A Miracle;
  I mean of Goodness; for in Beauty, Madam,
  You make all wonders cease.

391 know] Q3; knows Q1–2

410 *Cleopatra.*   I was too rash:
Take this in part of recompence. But, Oh,
                              Giving a Ring.
I fear thou flatter'st me.
Charmion. She comes! she's here!
Iras.   Flie, Madam, *Cæsar's* Sister!
Cleopatra. Were she the Sister of the Thund'rer *Jove*,
415   And bore her Brother's Lightning in her eyes,
Thus would I face my Rival.

> *Meets* Octavia *with* Ventidius. Octavia *bears up to her.*
> *Their Trains come up on either side.*

Octavia. I need not ask if you are *Cleopatra*,
Your haughty carriage ————
Cleopatra.   Shows I am a Queen:
Nor need I ask you who you are.
Octavia.   A *Roman*:
420   A name that makes, and can unmake a Queen.
Cleopatra. Your Lord, the Man who serves me, is a *Roman*.
Octavia. He was a *Roman*, till he lost that name
To be a Slave in *Egypt*; but I come
To free him thence.
Cleopatra.   Peace, peace, my Lover's *Juno*.
425   When he grew weary of that Houshold-Clog,
He chose my easier bonds.
Octavia.   I wonder not
Your bonds are easie; you have long been practis'd
In that lascivious art: he's not the first
For whom you spread your snares: let *Cæsar* witness.
430 *Cleopatra.* I lov'd not *Cæsar*; 'twas but gratitude
I paid his love: the worst your malice can,
Is but to say the greatest of Mankind
Has been my Slave. The next, but far above him,
In my esteem, is he whom Law calls yours,
But whom his love made mine.
435 *Octavia* (*coming up close to her*).   I would view nearer
That face, which has so long usurp'd my right,
To find th'inevitable charms, that catch
Mankind so sure, that ruin'd my dear Lord.
Cleopatra. O, you do well to search; for had you known
440   But half these charms, you had not lost his heart.
Octavia. Far be their knowledge from a *Roman* Lady,
Far from a modest Wife. Shame of our Sex,
Dost thou not blush, to own those black endearments

424 *Lover's Juno*] hence Antony is her Jupiter.

That make sin pleasing?
Cleopatra.　　　　　　You may blush, who want 'em.
　If bounteous Nature, if indulgent Heav'n　　　　　　445
　Have giv'n me charms to please the bravest Man;
　Should I not thank 'em? should I be asham'd,
　And not be proud? I am, that he has lov'd me;
　And, when I love not him, Heav'n change this Face
　For one like that.
Octavia.　　　　　Thou lov'st him not so well.　　　　450
Cleopatra. I love him better, and deserve him more.
Octavia. You do not; cannot: you have been his ruine.
　Who made him cheap at *Rome*, but *Cleopatra*?
　Who made him scorn'd abroad, but *Cleopatra*?
　At *Actium*, who betray'd him? *Cleopatra.*　　　　　455
　Who made his Children Orphans? and poor me
　A wretched Widow? only *Cleopatra*!
Cleopatra. Yet she who loves him best is *Cleopatra*.
　If you have suffer'd, I have suffer'd more.
　You bear the specious Title of a Wife,　　　　460
　To guild your Cause, and draw the pitying World
　To favour it: the World contemns poor me;
　For I have lost my Honour, lost my Fame,
　And stain'd the glory of my Royal House,
　And all to bear the branded Name of Mistress.　　　465
　There wants but life, and that too I would lose
　For him I love.
Octavia.　　　Be't so then; take thy wish.
　　　　　　　　　　　　　Exit cum suis.
Cleopatra. And 'tis my wish,
　Now he is lost for whom alone I liv'd.
　My sight grows dim, and every object dances,　　　470
　And swims before me, in the maze of death.
　My spirits, while they were oppos'd, kept up;
　They could not sink beneath a Rival's scorn:
　But now she's gone they faint.
Alexas.　　　　　　　　Mine have had leisure
　To recollect their strength, and furnish counsel,　　475
　To ruine her; who else must ruine you.
Cleopatra. Vain Promiser!
　Lead me, my *Charmion*; nay, your hand too, *Iras*:
　My grief has weight enough to sink you both.
　Conduct me to some solitary Chamber,　　　480
　And draw the Curtains round;
　Then leave me to my self, to take alone

471 *maze*] delirium.

My fill of grief:
There I till death will his unkindness weep:
485   As harmless Infants moan themselves asleep.

Exeunt.

ACT IV

[*Enter*] Antony, Dollabella.

Dollabella. Why would you shift it from your self, on me?
Can you not tell her you must part?
Antony.   I cannot.
I could pull out an eye, and bid it go,
And t'other should not weep. Oh, *Dollabella*,
5   How many deaths are in this word *Depart*!
I dare not trust my tongue to tell her so:
One look of hers, would thaw me into tears
And I should melt till I were lost agen.
Dollabella. Then let *Ventidius*;
He's rough by nature.
10   *Antony.*   Oh, he'll speak too harshly;
He'll kill her with the news: Thou, only thou.
Dollabella. Nature has cast me in so soft a mould,
That but to hear a story feign'd for pleasure
Of some sad Lover's death, moistens my eyes,
15   And robs me of my Manhood.—I should speak
So faintly; with such fear to grieve her heart,
She'd not believe it earnest.
Antony.   Therefore; therefore
Thou only, thou art fit: think thy self me,
And when thou speak'st (but let it first be long)
20   Take off the edge from every sharper sound,
And let our parting be as gently made
As other Loves begin: wilt thou do this?
Dollabella. What you have said, so sinks into my Soul,
That, if I must speak, I shall speak just so.
25   *Antony.* I leave you then to your sad task: Farewel.
I sent her word to meet you.

Goes to the door, and comes back.

I forgot;
Let her be told, I'll make her peace with mine:
Her Crown and Dignity shall be preserv'd,
If I have pow'r with *Cæsar.* —— O, be sure
To think on that.
30   *Dollabella.*   Fear not, I will remember.

Antony *goes again to the door, and comes back.*

Antony. And tell her, too, how much I was constrain'd;

248

I did not this, but with extreamest force:
Desire her not to hate my memory,
For I still cherish hers; —— insist on that.
Dollabella. Trust me, I'll not forget it.
Antony.   Then that's all.   35
                        Goes out, and returns again.
Wilt thou forgive my fondness this once more?
Tell her, tho' we shall never meet again,
If I should hear she took another Love,
The news would break my heart.—Now I must go;
For every time I have return'd, I feel   40
My Soul more tender; and my next command
Would be to bid her stay, and ruine both.   *Exit.*
Dollabella. Men are but Children of a larger growth,
Our appetites as apt to change as theirs,
And full as craving too, and full as vain;   45
And yet the Soul, shut up in her dark room,
Viewing so clear abroad, at home sees nothing;
But, like a Mole in Earth, busie and blind,
Works all her folly up, and casts it outward
To the World's open view: thus I discover'd,   50
And blam'd the love of ruin'd *Antony*;
Yet wish that I were he, to be so ruin'd.

                    Enter Ventidius *above.*

Ventidius. Alone? and talking to himself? concern'd too?
Perhaps my ghess is right; he lov'd her once,
And may pursue it still.
Dollabella.   O Friendship! Friendship!   55
Ill canst thou answer this; and Reason, worse:
Unfaithful in th'attempt; hopeless to win;
And, if I win, undone: meer madness all.
And yet th'occasion's fair. What injury,
To him, to wear the Robe which he throws by?   60
Ventidius. None, none at all. This happens as I wish,
To ruine her yet more with *Antony*.

            Enter Cleopatra, *talking with* Alexas. Charmion, Iras
                        on the other side.

Dollabella. She comes! What charms have sorrow on that
    face!
Sorrow seems pleas'd to dwell with so much sweetness;
Yet, now and then, a melancholy smile   65
Breaks loose, like Lightning, in a Winter's night,
And shows a moment's day.
Ventidius. If she should love him too! Her Eunuch there!

That *Porcpisce* bodes ill weather. Draw, draw nearer,
Sweet Devil, that I may hear.

Dollabella *goes over to* Charmion *and* Iras; *seems to talk
with them.*

70   *Alexas.*   Believe me; try
    To make him jealous; jealousie is like
    A polisht Glass held to the lips when life's in doubt:
    If there be breath, 'twill catch the damp and show it.
  Cleopatra. I grant you jealousie's a proof of love,
75   But 'tis a weak and unavailing Med'cine;
    It puts out the disease, and makes it show,
    But has no pow'r to cure.
  Alexas. 'Tis your last remedy, and strongest too:
    And then this *Dollabella*, who so fit
80   To practice on? He's handsom, valiant, young,
    And looks as he were laid for Nature's bait
    To catch weak Women's eyes.
    He stands already more than half suspected
    Of loving you: the least kind word, or glance,
85   You give this Youth, will kindle him with love:
    Then, like a burning Vessel set adrift,
    You'll send him down amain before the wind,
    To fire the heart of jealous *Antony*.
  Cleopatra. Can I do this? Ah no; my love's so true,
90   That I can neither hide it where it is,
    Nor show it where it is not. Nature meant me
    A Wife, a silly harmless houshold Dove,
    Fond without art; and kind without deceit;
    But Fortune, that has made a Mistress of me,
95   Hast thrust me out to the wide World, unfurnish'd
    Of falshood to be happy.
  Alexas.   Force your self.
    Th'event will be, your Lover will return
    Doubly desirous to possess the good
    Which once he fear'd to lose.
  Cleopatra.   I must attempt it;
100   But Oh with what regret!
                Exit Alexas. *She comes up to* Dollabella.
  Ventidius. So, now the Scene draws near; they're in my
    reach.

69 *Porcpisce*] porpoise, the "messenger of tempests," a popular
substitution.
76 *puts out*] brings out.
97 *event*] outcome.

Cleopatra (to Dollabella). Discoursing with my Women!
   Might not I
   Share in your entertainment?
Charmion.   You have been
   The Subject of it, Madam.
Cleopatra.   How; and how?
Iras. Such praises of your beauty!
Cleopatra.   Meer Poetry.   105
   Your *Roman* Wits, your *Gallus* and *Tibullus*,
   Have taught you this from *Citheris* and *Delia*.
Dollabella. Those *Roman* Wits have never been in *Egypt*,
   Citheris and *Delia* else had been unsung:
   I, who have seen —— had I been born a Poet,   110
   Should chuse a nobler name.
Cleopatra.   You flatter me.
   But, 'tis your Nation's vice: all of your Country
   Are flatterers, and all false. Your Friend's like you.
   I'm sure he sent you not to speak these words.
Dollabella. No, Madam; yet he sent me ——
Cleopatra.   Well, he sent you ——   115
Dollabella. Of a less pleasing errand.
Cleopatra.   How less pleasing?
   Less to your self, or me?
Dollabella.   Madam, to both;
   For you must mourn, and I must grieve to cause it.
Cleopatra. You, *Charmion*, and your Fellow, stand at dis-
   tance.
   (*Aside*) Hold up, my Spirits. ——Well, now your
   mournful matter;   120
   For I'm prepar'd, perhaps can ghess it too.
Dollabella. I wish you would; for 'tis a thankless office
   To tell ill news: and I, of all your Sex,
   Most fear displeasing you.
Cleopatra.   Of all your Sex,
   I soonest could forgive you, if you should.   125
Ventidius. Most delicate advances! Woman! Woman!
   Dear damn'd, inconstant Sex!
Cleopatra.   In the first place,
   I am to be forsaken; is't not so?
Dollabella. I wish I could not answer to that question.
Cleopatra. Then pass it o'er, because it troubles you: 130
   I should have been more griev'd another time.
   Next, I'm to lose my Kingdom. —— Farewel, *Egypt*.

---

106 *Gallus and Tibullus*] Roman lyric poets who wrote of the
following named mistresses.

Yet, is there any more?
Dollabella.   Madam, I fear
Your too deep sense of grief has turn'd your reason.
135   *Cleopatra.* No, no, I'm not run mad; I can bear Fortune:
And Love may be expell'd by other Love,
As Poysons are by Poysons.
Dollabella.   You o'erjoy me, Madam,
To find your griefs so moderately born.
You've heard the worst; all are not false, like him.
Cleopatra. No; Heav'n forbid they should.
140   *Dollabella.*   Some men are constant.
Cleopatra. And constancy deserves reward, that's certain.
Dollabella. Deserves it not; but give it leave to hope.
Ventidius. I'll swear thou hast my leave. I have enough:
But how to manage this! Well, I'll consider.   *Exit.*
145   *Dollabella.* I came prepar'd,
To tell you heavy news; news, which I thought,
Would fright the blood from your pale cheeks to hear:
But you have met it with a cheerfulness
That makes my task more easie; and my tongue,
150   Which on another's message was employ'd,
Would gladly speak its own.
Cleopatra.   Hold, *Dollabella.*
First tell me, were you chosen by my Lord?
Or sought you this employment?
Dollabella. He pick'd me out; and, as his bosom-friend,
He charg'd me with his words.
155   *Cleopatra.*   The message then
I know was tender, and each accent smooth,
To mollifie that rugged word *Depart.*
Dollabella. Oh, you mistake: he chose the harshest words,
With fiery eyes, and with contracted brows,
160   He coyn'd his face in the severest stamp:
And fury, shook his Fabrick like an Earthquake;
He heav'd for vent, and burst like bellowing *Ætna*,
In sounds scarce humane, "Hence, away for ever:
Let her begone, the blot of my renown,
165   And bane of all my hopes:
Let her be driv'n as far as men can think
From Man's commerce: She'll poyson to the Center."

All the time of this speech, Cleopatra *seems more and more
concern'd, till she sinks quite down.*

Cleopatra. Oh, I can bear no more!   [*Faints.*]
Dollabella. Help, help: Oh Wretch! Oh cursed, cursed
Wretch!

What have I done?
Charmion.   Help, chafe her Temples, *Iras*.   170
Iras. Bend, bend her forward quickly.
Charmion.   Heav'n be prais'd,
  She comes again.
Cleopatra.   Oh, let him not approach me.
  Why have you brought me back to this loath'd Being,
  Th'abode of Falshood, violated Vows,
  And injur'd Love? For pity, let me go;   175
  For, if there be a place of long repose,
  I'm sure I want it. My disdainful Lord
  Can never break that quiet; nor awake
  The sleeping Soul, with hollowing in my Tomb
  Such words as fright her hence. Unkind, unkind.   180
Dollabella (kneeling). Believe me, 'tis against my self I speak,
  That sure deserves belief; I injur'd him:
  My Friend ne'er spoke those words. Oh, had you seen
  How often he came back, and every time
  With something more obliging and more kind,   185
  To add to what he said; what dear Farewels;
  How almost vanquisht by his love he parted,
  And lean'd to what unwillingly he left:
  I, Traitor as I was, for love of you,
  (But what can you not do, who made me false!)   190
  I forg'd that lye; for whose forgiveness kneels
  This self-accus'd, self-punish'd Criminal.
Cleopatra. With how much ease believe we what we wish!
  Rise, *Dollabella*; if you have been guilty,
  I have contributed, and too much love   195
  Has made me guilty too.
  Th'advance of kindness which I made, was feign'd,
  To call back fleeting love by jealousie;
  But 'twould not last. Oh, rather let me lose
  Than so ignobly trifle with his heart.   200
Dollabella. I find your breast fenc'd round from humane
    reach,
  Transparent as a Rock of solid Crystal;
  Seen through, but never pierc'd. My Friend, my Friend!
  What endless treasure hast thou thrown away,
  And scatter'd, like an Infant, in the Ocean,   205
  Vain sums of Wealth which none can gather thence.
Cleopatra. Could you not beg
  An hour's admittance to his private ear?
  Like one who wanders through long barren Wilds,
  And yet foreknows no hospitable Inn   210
  Is near to succour hunger,

253

Eats his fill, before his painful march:
So would I feed a while my famish'd eyes
Before we part; for I have far to go,
215   If death be far, and never must return.

               [*Enter*] Ventidius, *with* Octavia, *behind.*

Ventidius. From hence you may discover ———— Oh, sweet,
     sweet!
     Would you indeed? the pretty hand in earnest?
Dollabella (*takes her hand*). I will, for this reward. ————
                          Draw it not back,
     'Tis all I e'er will beg.
Ventidius. They turn upon us.
220   *Octavia.*   What quick eyes has guilt!
Ventidius. Seem not to have observ'd 'em, and go on.

                        They enter.

Dollabella. Saw you the Emperor, *Ventidius*?
Ventidius.   No.
     I sought him; but I heard that he was private,
     None with him, but *Hipparchus* his Freedman.
Dollabella. Know you his bus'ness?
225   *Ventidius.*   Giving him Instructions,
     And Letters, to his Brother *Cæsar.*
Dollabella.   Well,
     He must be found.
                Exeunt Dollabella *and* Cleopatra.
Octavia. Most glorious impudence!
Ventidius.   She look'd methought
     As she would say, Take your old man, *Octavia*;
     Thank you, I'm better here.
230   Well, but what use
     Make we of this discovery?
Octavia.   Let it die.
Ventidius. I pity *Dollabella*; but she's dangerous:
     Her eyes have pow'r beyond *Thessalian* Charms
     To draw the Moon from Heav'n; for Eloquence,
235   The Sea-green Syrens taught her voice their flatt'ry;
     And, while she speaks, Night steals upon the Day,
     Unmark'd of those that hear: Then she's so charming,
     Age buds at sight of her, and swells to youth:
     The holy Priests gaze on her when she smiles;
240   And with heav'd hands, forgetting gravity,

233 *Thessalian Charms*] Thessaly was the traditional home of
witchcraft.

They bless her wanton eyes: Even I who hate her,
With a malignant joy behold such beauty;
And, while I curse, desire it. *Antony*
Must needs have some remains of passion still,
Which may ferment into a worse relapse, 245
If now not fully cur'd. I know, this minute,
With *Cæsar* he's endeavouring her peace.
Octavia. You have prevail'd:—but for a farther purpose
                              Walks off.
I'll prove how he will relish this discovery.
What, make a Strumpet's peace! it swells my heart: 250
It must not, sha'not be.
Ventidius.   His Guards appear.
Let me begin, and you shall second me.

        Enter Antony.

Antony. Octavia, I was looking you, my love:
What, are your Letters ready? I have giv'n
My last Instructions.
Octavia.   Mine, my Lord, are written. 255
Antony. Ventidius!   *Drawing him aside.*
Ventidius.   My Lord?
Antony.   A word in private.
When saw you *Dollabella*?
Ventidius.   Now, my Lord,
He parted hence; and *Cleopatra* with him.
Antony. Speak softly. 'Twas by my command he went,
To bear my last farewel.
Ventidius (aloud).   It look'd indeed 260
Like your farewel.
Antony.   More softly. —— My farewel?
What secret meaning have you in those words
Of my Farewel? He did it by my Order.
Ventidius (aloud). Then he obey'd your Order. I suppose
You bid him do it with all gentleness, 265
All kindness, and all —— love.
Antony. How she mourn'd,
        The poor forsaken Creature!
Ventidius. She took it as she ought; she bore your parting
As she did *Cæsar's,* as she would another's,
Were a new Love to come.
Antony (aloud).   Thou dost belye her; 270
Most basely, and maliciously belye her.
Ventidius. I thought not to displease you; I have done.
Octavia (coming up). You seem disturb'd, my Lord.
Antony.   A very trifle.

Retire, my Love.

Ventidius.   It was indeed a trifle.

He sent ———

275   *Antony (angrily).* No more. Look how thou disobey'st me;
     Thy life shall answer it.

Octavia.   Then 'tis no trifle.

Ventidius (to Octavia). 'Tis less; a very nothing: you too saw it,
     As well as I, and therefore 'tis no secret.

Antony. She saw it!

Ventidius.   Yes: she saw young *Dollabella* ———

Antony. Young *Dollabella*!

280   *Ventidius.*   Young, I think him young,
     And handsom too; and so do others think him.
     But what of that? He went by your command,
     Indeed 'tis probable, with some kind message;
     For she receiv'd it graciously; she smil'd:

285   And then he grew familiar with her hand,
     Squeez'd it, and worry'd it with ravenous kisses;
     She blush'd, and sigh'd, and smil'd, and blush'd again;
     At last she took occasion to talk softly,
     And brought her cheek up close, and lean'd on his:

290   At which, he whisper'd kisses back on hers;
     And then she cry'd aloud, That constancy
     Should be rewarded.

Octavia.   This I saw and heard.

Antony. What Woman was it, whom you heard and saw
     So playful with my Friend!
                   Not *Cleopatra*?

295   *Ventidius.* Ev'n she, my Lord!

Antony. My *Cleopatra*?

Ventidius. Your *Cleopatra*;
     Dollabella's Cleopatra:
     Every Man's *Cleopatra*.

300   *Antony.* Thou ly'st.

Ventidius. I do not lye, my Lord.
     Is this so strange? Should Mistresses be left,
     And not provide against a time of change?
     You know she's not much us'd to lonely nights.

305   *Antony.* I'll think no more on't.
     I know 'tis false, and see the plot betwixt you.
     You needed not have gone this way, *Octavia*.
     What harms it you that *Cleopatra's* just?
     She's mine no more. I see; and I forgive:
     Urge it no farther, Love.

310   *Octavia.*   Are you concern'd

That she's found false?
Antony.   I should be, were it so;
For, tho 'tis past, I would not that the World
Should tax my former choice: That I lov'd one
Of so light note; but I forgive you both.
Ventidius. What has my age deserv'd, that you should
    think   315
    I would abuse your ears with perjury?
    If Heav'n be true, she's false.
Antony.   Tho Heav'n and Earth
Should witness it, I'll not believe her tainted.
Ventidius. I'll bring you then a Witness
From Hell to prove her so. Nay, go not back;   320
            Seeing Alexas *just entring, and starting back.*
For stay you must and shall.
Alexas.   What means my Lord?
Ventidius. To make you do what most you hate; speak
    truth.
You are of *Cleopatra's* private Counsel,
Of her Bed-Counsel, her lascivious hours;
Are conscious of each nightly change she makes,   325
And watch her, as *Chaldeans* do the Moon,
Can tell what Signs she passes through, what day.
Alexas. My Noble Lord ———
Ventidius.   My most Illustrious Pandar,
No fine set Speech, no Cadence, no turn'd Periods,
But a plain home-spun Truth, is what I ask: 330
I did, my self, o'erhear your Queen make love
To *Dollabella.* Speak; for I will know,
By your confession, what more past betwixt 'em;
How near the bus'ness draws to your employment;
And when the happy hour.   335
Antony. Speak truth, *Alexas,* whether it offend
Or please *Ventidius,* care not: justifie
Thy injur'd Queen from malice: dare his worst.
Octavia (aside). See, how he gives him courage! how he
    fears
To find her false! and shuts his eyes to truth,   340
Willing to be misled!
Alexas. As far as love may plead for Woman's frailty,
Urg'd by desert and greatness of the Lover;
So far (Divine *Octavia!*) may my Queen
Stand ev'n excus'd to you, for loving him,   345
Who is your Lord: so far, from brave *Ventidius,*

326 *Chaldeans*] astrologers and magicians.

May her past actions hope a fair report.

Antony. 'Tis well, and truly spoken: mark, *Ventidius.*

Alexas. To you, most Noble Emperor, her strong passion
350   Stands not excus'd, but wholly justifi'd.
    Her Beauty's charms alone, without her Crown,
    From *Ind* and *Meroe* drew the distant Vows
    Of sighing Kings; and at her feet were laid
    The Scepters of the Earth, expos'd on heaps,
355   To choose where she would Reign:
    She thought a *Roman* only could deserve her;
    And, of all *Romans*, only *Antony.*
    And, to be less than Wife to you, disdain'd
    Their lawful passion.
360 *Antony.* 'Tis but truth.

Alexas. And yet, tho love, and your unmatch'd desert,
    Have drawn her from the due regard of Honor,
    At last, Heav'n open'd her unwilling eyes
    To see the wrongs she offer'd fair *Octavia,*
365   Whose holy Bed she lawlesly usurpt:
    The sad effects of this improsperous War,
    Confirm'd those pious thoughts.

Ventidius (*aside*).   O, wheel you there?
    Observe him now; the Man begins to mend,
    And talk substantial reason. Fear not, Eunuch,
370   The Emperor has giv'n thee leave to speak.

Alexas. Else had I never dar'd t'offend his ears
    With what the last necessity has urg'd
    On my forsaken Mistress; yet I must not
    Presume to say her heart is wholly alter'd.

375 *Antony.* No, dare not for thy life, I charge thee dare not,
    Pronounce that fatal word.

Octavia (*aside*). Must I bear this? good Heav'n, afford me
    patience.

Ventidius. On, sweet Eunuch; my dear half man, proceed.

Alexas. Yet *Dollabella*
380   Has lov'd her long, he, next my God-like Lord,
    Deserves her best; and should she meet his passion,
    Rejected, as she is, by him she lov'd ———

Antony. Hence, from my sight; for I can bear no more:
    Let Furies drag thee quick to Hell; let all
385   The longer damn'd have rest; each torturing hand
    Do thou employ, till *Cleopatra* comes,
    Then joyn thou too, and help to torture her.
                      Exit Alexas, *thrust out by* Antony.

352 *Ind and Meroe*] India and upper Egypt.

Octavia. 'Tis not well,
    Indeed, my Lord, 'tis much unkind to me,
    To show this passion, this extream concernment   390
    For an abandon'd, faithless Prostitute.
Antony. Octavia, leave me: I am much disorder'd.
    Leave me, I say.
Octavia.   My Lord?
Antony.   I bid you leave me.
Ventidius. Obey him, Madam: best withdraw a while,
    And see how this will work.   395
Octavia. Wherein have I offended you, my Lord,
    That I am bid to leave you? Am I false,
    Or infamous? Am I a *Cleopatra*?
    Were I she,
    Base as she is, you would not bid me leave you;   400
    But hang upon my neck, take slight excuses,
    And fawn upon my falshood.
Antony.   'Tis too much,
    Too much, *Octavia*; I am prest with sorrows
    Too heavy to be born; and you add more:
    I would retire, and recollect what's left   405
    Of Man within, to aid me.
Octavia.   You would mourn
    In private, for your Love, who has betray'd you;
    You did but half return to me: your kindness
    Linger'd behind with her. I hear, my Lord,
    You make Conditions for her,   410
    And would include her Treaty. Wondrous proofs
    Of love to me!
Antony.   Are you my Friend, *Ventidius*?
    Or are you turn'd a *Dollabella* too,
    And let this Fury loose?
Ventidius.   Oh, be advis'd,
    Sweet Madam, and retire.   415
Octavia. Yes, I will go; but never to return.
    You shall no more be haunted with this Fury.
    My Lord, my Lord, love will not always last,
    When urg'd with long unkindness, and disdain;
    Take her again whom you prefer to me;   420
    She stays but to be call'd. Poor cozen'd Man!
    Let a feign'd parting give her back your heart,
    Which a feign'd love first got; for injur'd me,
    Tho' my just sense of wrongs forbid my stay,
    My duty shall be yours.   425
    To the dear pledges of our former love,
    My tenderness and care shall be transferr'd,

And they shall cheer, by turns, my Widow'd Nights:
So, take my last farewel; for I despair
430   To have you whole, and scorn to take you half.   *Exit.*
Ventidius. I combat Heav'n, which blasts my best designs:
My last attempt must be to win her back;
But Oh, I fear in vain.   *Exit.*
Antony. Why was I fram'd with this plain honest heart,
435   Which knows not to disguise its griefs and weakness,
But bears its workings outward to the World?
I should have kept the mighty anguish in,
And forc'd a smile at *Cleopatra's* falshood:
Octavia had believ'd it, and had staid;
440   But I am made a shallow-forded Stream,
Seen to the bottom: all my clearness scorn'd,
And all my faults expos'd! ——— See, where he comes

Enter Dollabella.

Who has prophan'd the Sacred Name of Friend,
And worn it into vileness!
445   With how secure a brow, and specious form
He guilds the secret Villain! Sure that face
Was meant for honesty; but Heav'n mis-match'd it,
And furnish'd Treason out with Nature's pomp,
To make its work more easie.
Dollabella.   O, my Friend!
450   *Antony.* Well, *Dollabella,* you perform'd my message?
Dollabella. I did, unwillingly.
Antony.   Unwillingly?
Was it so hard for you to bear our parting?
You should have wisht it.
Dollabella.   Why?
Antony.   Because you love me.
And she receiv'd my message, with as true,
455   With as unfeign'd a sorrow, as you brought it?
Dollabella. She loves you, ev'n to madness.
Antony.   Oh, I know it.
You, *Dollabella,* do not better know
How much she loves me. And should I
Forsake this Beauty? This all-perfect Creature?
Dollabella. I could not, were she mine.
460   *Antony.*   And yet you first
Perswaded me: how come you alter'd since?
Dollabella. I said at first I was not fit to go;
I could not hear her sighs, and see her tears,
But pity must prevail: and so, perhaps,

It may again with you; for I have promis'd   465
That she should take her last farewel: and, see,
She comes to claim my word.

        Enter Cleopatra.

Antony.   False *Dollabella*!
Dollabella. What's false, my Lord?
Antony.   Why, *Dollabella's* false,
And *Cleopatra's* false; both false and faithless.
Draw near, you well-join'd wickedness, you Serpents,   470
Whom I have, in my kindly bosom, warm'd
Till I am stung to death.
Dollabella.   My Lord, have I
Deserv'd to be thus us'd?
Cleopatra.   Can Heav'n prepare
A newer Torment? Can it find a Curse
Beyond our separation?
Antony.   Yes, if Fate   475
Be just, much greater: Heav'n should be ingenious
In punishing such crimes. The rowling Stone,
And gnawing Vulture, were slight pains, invented
When *Jove* was young, and no examples known
Of mighty ills; but you have ripen'd sin   480
To such a monstrous growth, 'twill pose the Gods
To find an equal Torture. Two, two such,
Oh there's no farther name, two such ——— to me,
To me, who lock'd my Soul within your breasts,
Had no desires, no joys, no life, but you;   485
When half the Globe was mine, I gave it you
In Dowry with my heart; I had no use,
No fruit of all, but you: a Friend and Mistress
Was what the World could give. Oh, *Cleopatra*!
Oh, *Dollabella*! how could you betray   490
This tender heart, which with an Infant-fondness
Lay lull'd betwixt your bosoms, and there slept
Secure of injur'd Faith?
Dollabella.   If she has wrong'd you,
Heav'n, Hell, and You revenge it.
Antony.   If she wrong'd me!
Thou wouldst evade thy part of guilt; but swear   495
Thou lov'st not her.
Dollabella.   Not so as I love you.

477–78 *rowling Stone . . . gnawing Vulture*] punishments of Sisyphus
and Tityus.
481 *pose*] perplex.
493 *Secure of*] safe from.

Antony. Not so! Swear, swear, I say, thou dost not love her.
Dollabella. No more than Friendship will allow.
Antony. No more?
   Friendship allows thee nothing: thou art perjur'd. ———
500   And yet thou didst not swear thou lov'dst her not;
   But not so much, no more. Oh trifling Hypocrite,
   Who dar'st not own to her thou dost not love,
   Nor own to me thou dost! *Ventidius* heard it;
   Octavia saw it.
Cleopatra. They are enemies.
505 *Antony.* *Alexas* is not so: he, he confest it;
   He, who, next Hell, best knew it, he avow'd it.
   (*To Dollabella*) Why do I seek a proof beyond your self?
   You whom I sent to bear my last Farewel,
   Return'd to plead her stay.
Dollabella. What shall I answer?
510   If to have lov'd be guilt, then I have sinn'd;
   But if to have repented of that love
   Can wash away my crime, I have repented.
   Yet, if I have offended past forgiveness,
   Let not her suffer: she is innocent.
515 *Cleopatra.* Ah, what will not a Woman do who loves!
   What means will she refuse, to keep that heart
   Where all her joys are plac'd! 'Twas I encourag'd,
   'Twas I blew up the fire that scorch'd his Soul,
   To make you jealous; and by that regain you.
520   But all in vain; I could not counterfeit:
   In spight of all the damms, my love broke o'er,
   And drown'd my heart again: Fate took th'occasion;
   And thus one minute's feigning has destroy'd
   My whole life's truth.
Antony. Thin Cobweb Arts of Falshood;
   Seen, and broke through at first.
525 *Dollabella.* Forgive your Mistress.
Cleopatra. Forgive your Friend.
Antony. You have convinc'd your selves,
   You plead each other's Cause: What Witness have you,
   That you but meant to raise my jealousie?
Cleopatra. Our selves, and Heav'n.
Antony. Guilt witnesses for guilt. Hence, Love and Friend-
530   ship;
   You have no longer place in humane breasts,
   These two have driv'n you out: avoid my sight;
   I would not kill the Man whom I have lov'd;

533 have] Congreve; *omit* Qq F
526 *convinc'd*] convicted.

And cannot hurt the Woman; but avoid me,
I do not know how long I can be tame;   535
For, if I stay one minute more to think
How I am wrong'd, my Justice and Revenge
Will cry so loud within me, that my pity
Will not be heard for either.
Dollabella.   Heav'n has but
Our sorrow for our sins; and then delights   540
To pardon erring Man: sweet Mercy seems
Its darling Attribute, which limits Justice;
As if there were degrees in Infinite;
And Infinite would rather want perfection
Than punish to extent.
Antony.   I can forgive   545
A Foe; but not a Mistress, and a Friend:
Treason is there in its most horrid shape,
Where trust is greatest: and the Soul resign'd
Is stabb'd by its own Guards: I'll hear no more;
Hence from my sight, for ever.
Cleopatra.   How? for ever!   550
I cannot go one moment from your sight,
And must I go for ever?
My joys, my only joys are center'd here:
What place have I to go to? my own Kingdom?
That I have lost for you: or to the *Romans*?   555
They hate me for your sake: or must I wander
The wide World o'er, a helpless, banish'd Woman,
Banish'd for love of you; banish'd from you;
I, there's the Banishment! Oh hear me; hear me,
With strictest Justice: for I beg no favour: 560
And if I have offended you, then kill me,
But do not banish me.
Antony.   I must not hear you.
I have a Fool within me takes your part;
But Honour stops my ears.
Cleopatra.   For pity hear me!
Wou'd you cast off a Slave who follow'd you,   565
Who crouch'd beneath your Spurn? ——— He has no
     pity!
See, if he gives one tear to my departure;
One look, one kind farewel: Oh Iron heart!
Let all the Gods look down, and judge betwixt us,
If he did ever love!

541–45] God is willing to limit his perfect justice rather than be un-
merciful and punish to the full extent of the law.
566 *Spurn*] literally, kick (Noyes).

570   *Antony.*   No more: *Alexas*!
         Dollabella. A perjur'd Villain!
         Antony (to Cleopatra).   Your *Alexas*; yours.
         Cleopatra. O 'twas his plot: his ruinous design
            T'ingage you in my love by jealousie.
            Hear him; confront him with me; let him speak.
         Antony. I have; I have.
575   *Cleopatra.*   And if he clear me not ——
         Antony. Your Creature! one who hangs upon your smiles!
            Watches your eye to say or to unsay
            Whate'er you please! I am not to be mov'd.
         Cleopatra. Then must we part? Farewel, my cruel Lord,
580   Th'appearance is against me; and I go
            Unjustifi'd, for ever from your sight.
            How I have lov'd, you know; how yet I love,
            My only comfort is, I know my self:
            I love you more, ev'n now you are unkind,
585   Than when you lov'd me most; so well, so truly,
            I'll never strive against it; but die pleas'd
            To think you once were mine.
         Antony. Good Heav'n, they weep at parting.
            Must I weep too? that calls 'em innocent.
590   I must not weep; and yet I must, to think
            That I must not forgive. ——
            Live; but live wretched, 'tis but just you shou'd,
            Who made me so: Live from each other's sight:
            Let me not hear you meet: Set all the Earth,
595   And all the Seas, betwixt your sunder'd Loves:
            View nothing common but the Sun and Skys:
            Now, all take several ways;
            And each your own sad fate with mine deplore;
            That you were false, and I could trust no more.
                                     Exeunt severally.

ACT V

[*Enter*] Cleopatra, Charmion, Iras.

         Charmion. Be juster, Heav'n: such virtue punish'd thus,
            Will make us think that Chance rules all above,
            And shuffles, with a random hand, the Lots
            Which Man is forc'd to draw.
5   *Cleopatra.* I cou'd tear out these eyes, that gain'd his heart,
            And had not pow'r to keep it. O the curse
            Of doting on, ev'n when I find it Dotage!
            Bear witness, Gods, you heard him bid me go;

You whom he mock'd with imprecating Vows
Of promis'd Faith. —— I'll die, I will not bear it.   10
     She pulls out her Dagger, and they hold her.
You may hold me ——
But I can keep my breath; I can die inward,
And choak this Love.

          Enter Alexas.

Iras.   Help, O *Alexas*, help!
The Queen grows desperate, her Soul struggles in her,
With all the Agonies of Love and Rage,   15
And strives to force its passage.
Cleopatra.   Let me go.
Art thou there, Traitor! —— O,
O, for a little breath, to vent my rage!
Give, give me way, and let me loose upon him.
Alexas. Yes, I deserve it, for my ill-tim'd truth.
Was it for me to prop   20
The Ruins of a falling Majesty?
To place my self beneath the mighty flaw,
Thus to be crush'd, and pounded into Atomes,
By its o'erwhelming weight? 'Tis too presuming
For Subjects, to preserve that wilful pow'r   25
Which courts its own destruction.
Cleopatra.   I wou'd reason
More calmly with you. Did not you o'er-rule,
And force my plain, direct, and open love
Into these crooked paths of jealousie?
Now, what's th'event? *Octavia* is remov'd;   30
But *Cleopatra*'s banish'd. Thou, thou, Villain,
Hast push'd my Boat, to open Sea; to prove,
At my sad cost, if thou canst steer it back.
It cannot be; I'm lost too far; I'm ruin'd:
Hence, thou Impostor, Traitor, Monster, Devil. ——   35
I can no more: thou, and my griefs, have sunk
Me down so low, that I want voice to curse thee.
Alexas. Suppose some shipwrack'd Seaman near the shore,
Dropping and faint, with climbing up the Cliff,
If, from above, some charitable hand   40
Pull him to safety, hazarding himself
To draw the other's weight; wou'd he look back
And curse him for his pains? The case is yours;
But one step more, and you have gain'd the heighth.   45
Cleopatra. Sunk, never more to rise.
Alexas. Octavia's gone, and *Dollabella* banish'd.

33 *Hast*]S-S; Has Qq F

265

Believe me, Madam, *Antony* is yours.
His heart was never lost; but started off
To Jealousie, Love's last retreat and covert:
Where it lies hid in Shades, watchful in silence,
And list'ning for the sound that calls it back.
Some other, any man, ('tis so advanc'd)
May perfect this unfinish'd work, which I
(Unhappy only to my self) have left
So easie to his hand.
Cleopatra.   Look well thou do't; else ———
Alexas. Else, what your silence threatens. ——— *Antony*
Is mounted up the *Pharos*; from whose Turret,
He stands surveying our *Egyptian* Gallies,
Engag'd with *Cæsar's* Fleet: now Death, or Conquest.
If the first happen, Fate acquits my promise:
If we o'ercome, the Conqueror is yours.
                   A distant Shout within.
Charmion. Have comfort, Madam: did you mark that
    Shout?
Iras. Hark; they redouble it.   *Second Shout nearer.*
Alexas.   'Tis from the Port.
    The loudness shows it near: good news, kind Heavens.
Cleopatra. Osiris make it so.
                Enter Serapion.
Serapion.   Where, where's the Queen?
Alexas. How frightfully the holy Coward stares!
As if not yet recover'd of th'assault,
When all his Gods, and what's more dear to him,
His Offerings were at stake.
Serapion.   O horror, horror!
    Egypt has been; our latest hour is come:
The Queen of Nations from her ancient seat,
Is sunk for ever in the dark Abyss:
Time has unrowl'd her Glories to the last,
And now clos'd up the Volume.
Cleopatra.   Be more plain:
    Say, whence thou com'st, (though Fate is in thy face,
Which from thy haggard eyes looks wildly out,
And threatens ere thou speak'st.)
Serapion.   I came from *Pharos*;
    From viewing (spare me and imagine it)
Our Land's last hope, your Navy ———
Cleopatra.   Vanquish'd?

58 *Pharos*] the lighthouse at Alexandria.
70–73 *O horror . . . Abyss*] recalling *Aeneid*, II, 324–26 (Brower).

Serapion.   No.   80
    They fought not.
Cleopatra.   Then they fled.
Serapion.   Nor that. I saw,
    With *Antony*, your well-appointed Fleet
    Row out; and thrice he wav'd his hand on high,
    And thrice with cheerful cries they shouted back:
    'Twas then, false Fortune, like a fawning Strumpet,   85
    About to leave the Bankrupt Prodigal,
    With a dissembled smile wou'd kiss at parting,
    And flatter to the last; the well-tim'd Oars
    Now dipt from every bank, now smoothly run
    To meet the Foe; and soon indeed they met,   90
    But not as Foes. In few, we saw their Caps
    On either side thrown up; th'*Egyptian* Gallies
    (Receiv'd like Friends) past through, and fell behind
    The *Roman* rear: and now, they all come forward,
    And ride within the Port.
Cleopatra.   Enough, *Serapion*:   95
    I've heard my doom. This needed not, you Gods:
    When I lost *Antony*, your work was done;
    'Tis but superfluous malice. Where's my Lord?
    How bears he this last blow?
Serapion. His fury cannot be express'd by words: 100
    Thrice he attempted headlong to have faln
    Full on his foes, and aim'd at *Cæsar's* Galley:
    With-held, he raves on you; cries, He's betray'd.
    Should he now find you ⸻
Alexas.   Shun him, seek your safety,
    Till you can clear your innocence.
Cleopatra.   I'll stay.   105
Alexas. You must not, haste you to your Monument,
    While I make speed to *Cæsar*.
Cleopatra.   *Cæsar*! No,
    I have no business with him.
Alexas.   I can work him
    To spare your life, and let this madman perish.
Cleopatra. Base fawning Wretch! wouldst thou betray him
      too?   110
    Hence from my sight, I will not hear a Traytor;
    'Twas thy design brought all this ruine on us;
    Serapion, thou art honest; counsel me:
    But haste, each moment's precious.
Serapion. Retire; you must not yet see *Antony*.   115
    He, who began this mischief,
    'Tis just he tempt the danger: let him clear you;

And, since he offer'd you his servile tongue,
To gain a poor precarious life from *Cæsar*,
120   Let him expose that fawning eloquence,
And speak to *Antony*.
Alexas.   O Heavens! I dare not,
I meet my certain death.
Cleopatra.   Slave, thou deserv'st it.
Not that I fear my Lord, will I avoid him;
I know him noble: when he banish'd me,
125   And thought me false, he scorn'd to take my life;
But I'll be justifi'd, and then die with him.
Alexas. O pity me, and let me follow you.
Cleopatra. To death, if thou stir hence. Speak, if thou canst,
Now for thy life, which basely thou wou'dst save;
130   While mine I prize at this. Come, good *Serapion*.
               Exeunt Cleopatra, Serapion, Charmion, Iras.
Alexas. O that I less cou'd fear to lose this being,
Which, like a Snow-ball, in my coward hand,
The more 'tis grasp'd, the faster melts away.
Poor Reason! what a wretched aid art thou!
135   For still, in spight of thee,
These two long Lovers, Soul and Body, dread
Their final separation. Let me think:
What can I say, to save my self from death?
No matter what becomes of *Cleopatra*.
Antony (*within*). Which way? where?
140   *Ventidius* (*within*).   This leads to th' Monument.
Alexas. Ah me! I hear him; yet I'm unprepar'd:
My gift of lying's gone;
And this Court-Devil, which I so oft have rais'd,
Forsakes me at my need. I dare not stay;
145   Yet cannot far go hence.   *Exit*.

          Enter Antony *and* Ventidius.

Antony. O happy *Cæsar*! Thou hast men to lead:
Think not 'tis thou hast conquer'd *Antony*;
But *Rome* has conquer'd *Egypt*. I'm betray'd.
Ventidius. Curse on this treach'rous Train!
150   Their Soil and Heav'n infect 'em all with baseness:
And their young Souls come tainted to the World
With the first breath they draw.
Antony. Th'original Villain sure no God created;
He was a Bastard of the Sun, by *Nile*,

154 *by Nile*] animals were thought to be bred out of the mud
left by the receding Nile flood.

Ap'd into Man; with all his Mother's Mud   155
Crusted about his Soul.
Ventidius.   The Nation is
One Universal Traitor; and their Queen
The very Spirit and Extract of 'em all.
Antony. Is there yet left
A possibility of aid from Valor?   160
Is there one God unsworn to my Destruction?
The least unmortgag'd hope? for, if there be,
Methinks I cannot fall beneath the Fate
Of such a Boy as *Cæsar*.
The World's one half is yet in *Antony*;   165
And, from each limb of it that's hew'd away,
The Soul comes back to me.
Ventidius.   There yet remain
Three Legions in the Town. The last assault
Lopt off the rest: if death be your design,
(As I must wish it now) these are sufficient   170
To make a heap about us of dead Foes,
An honest Pile for burial.
Antony.   They're enough.
We'll not divide our Stars; but side by side
Fight emulous: and with malicious eyes
Survey each other's acts: so every death   175
Thou giv'st, I'll take on me, as a just debt,
And pay thee back a Soul.
Ventidius. Now you shall see I love you. Not a word
Of chiding more. By my few hours of life,
I am so pleas'd with this brave *Roman* Fate,   180
That I wou'd not be *Cæsar*, to out-live you.
When we put off this flesh, and mount together,
I shall be shown to all th'Etherial crowd;
Lo, this is he who dy'd with *Antony*.
Antony. Who knows but we may pierce through all their
          Troops,   185
And reach my Veterans yet? 'Tis worth the tempting,
T'o'er-leap this Gulph of Fate,
And leave our wond'ring Destinies behind.

          Enter Alexas, *trembling.*

Ventidius. See, see, that Villain;
See *Cleopatra* stampt upon that face,   190
With all her cunning, all her arts of falshood!

155 *Ap'd*] counterfeited.
174 *emulous*] in rivalry.

269

How she looks out through those dissembling eyes!
How he has set his count'nance for deceit;
And promises a lye, before he speaks!
Let me dispatch him first.   *Drawing.*

195   *Alexas.*   O, spare me, spare me.
Antony. Hold; he's not worth your killing. On thy life,
(Which thou mayst keep, because I scorn to take it)
No syllable to justifie thy Queen;
Save thy base tongue its office.
Alexas.   Sir, she's gone,

200   Where she shall never be molested more
By Love, or you.
Antony.   Fled to her *Dollabella*!
Die, Traitor, I revoke my promise, die.
                       Going to kill him.
Alexas. O hold, she is not fled.
Antony.   She is: my eyes
Are open to her falshood; my whole life

205   Has been a golden dream, of Love and Friendship.
But, now I wake, I'm like a Merchant, rows'd
From soft repose, to see his Vessel sinking,
And all his Wealth cast o'er. Ingrateful Woman!
Who follow'd me, but as the Swallow Summer,

210   Hatching her young ones in my kindly Beams,
Singing her flatt'ries to my morning wake;
But, now my Winter comes, she spreads her wings,
And seeks the Spring of *Cæsar.*
Alexas.   Think not so:
Her Fortunes have, in all things, mixt with yours.

215   Had she betray'd her Naval force to *Rome,*
How easily might she have gone to *Cæsar,*
Secure by such a bribe!
Ventidius.   She sent it first,
To be more welcome after.
Antony.   'Tis too plain;
Else wou'd she have appear'd, to clear her self.

220   *Alexas.* Too fatally she has; she could not bear
To be accus'd by you; but shut her self
Within her Monument: look'd down, and sigh'd;
While, from her unchang'd face, the silent tears
Dropt, as they had not leave, but stole their parting.

225   Some undistinguish'd words she inly murmur'd;
At last, she rais'd her eyes; and, with such looks
As dying *Lucrece* cast, ———
Antony.   My heart forebodes ———
Ventidius. All for the best: go on.

Alexas.   She snatch'd her Ponyard,
  And, ere we cou'd prevent the fatal blow,
  Plung'd it within her breast: then turn'd to me,   230
  Go, bear my Lord (said she) my last Farewel;
  And ask him if he yet suspect my Faith.
  More she was saying, but death rush'd betwixt.
  She half pronounc'd your Name with her last breath,
  And bury'd half within her.
Ventidius.   Heav'n be prais'd.   235
Antony. Then art thou innocent, my poor dear Love?
  And art thou dead?
  O those two words! their sound shou'd be divided:
  Hadst thou been false, and dy'd; or hadst thou liv'd,
  And hadst been true —— But Innocence and Death!   240
  This shows not well above. Then what am I,
  The Murderer of this Truth, this Innocence!
  Thoughts cannot form themselves in words so horrid
  As can express my guilt!
Ventidius. Is't come to this? The Gods have been too
    gracious: 245
  And thus you thank 'em for't.
Antony (to Alexas).   Why stay'st thou here?
  Is it for thee to spy upon my Soul,
  And see its inward mourning? Get thee hence;
  Thou art not worthy to behold, what now
  Becomes a *Roman* Emperor to perform.   250
Alexas (aside). He loves her still:
  His grief betrays it. Good! The joy to find
  She's yet alive, compleats the reconcilement.
  I've saved my self, and her. But, Oh! the *Romans*!
  Fate comes too fast upon my Wit,   255
  Hunts me too hard, and meets me at each double.
                          Exit.
Ventidius. Wou'd she had dy'd a little sooner tho,
  Before *Octavia* went; you might have treated:
  Now 'twill look tame, and wou'd not be receiv'd.
  Come, rouze your self, and let's die warm together.   260
Antony. I will not fight: there's no more work for War.
  The bus'ness of my angry hours is done.
Ventidius. Cæsar is at your Gates.
Antony.   Why, let him enter;
  He's welcom now.
Ventidius. What Lethargy has crept into your Soul?   265
Antony. 'Tis but a scorn of life, and just desire

256 *double*] doubling back, as of a hunted hare.

To free my self from bondage.
Ventidius.   Do it bravely.
Antony. I will; but not by fighting. O, *Ventidius!*
    What shou'd I fight for now? My Queen is dead.
270 I was but great for her; my Pow'r, my Empire,
    Were but my Merchandise to buy her love;
    And conquer'd Kings, my Factors. Now she's dead,
    Let *Cæsar* take the World, ————
    An Empty Circle, since the Jewel's gone
275 Which made it worth my strife: my being's nauseous;
    For all the bribes of life are gone away.
Ventidius. Wou'd you be taken?
Antony.   Yes, I wou'd be taken;
    But, as a *Roman* ought, dead, my *Ventidius:*
    For I'll convey my Soul from *Cæsar's* reach,
280 And lay down life my self. 'Tis time the World
    Shou'd have a Lord, and know whom to obey.
    We two have kept its homage in suspence,
    And bent the Globe on whose each side we trod,
    Till it was dinted inwards: Let him walk
285 Alone upon't; I'm weary of my part.
    My Torch is out; and the World stands before me
    Like a black Desart, at th'approach of night:
    I'll lay me down, and stray no farther on.
Ventidius. I cou'd be griev'd,
290 But that I'll not out-live you: choose your death;
    For, I have seen him in such various shapes,
    I care not which I take: I'm only troubled
    The life I bear, is worn to such a rag,
    'Tis scarce worth giving. I cou'd wish indeed
295 We threw it from us with a better grace;
    That, like two Lyons taken in the Toils,
    We might at least thrust out our paws, and wound
    The Hunters that inclose us.
Antony.   I have thought on't.
    Ventidius, you must live.
Ventidius.   I must not, Sir.
300 *Antony.* Wilt thou not live, to speak some good of me?
    To stand by my fair Fame, and guard th'approaches
    From the ill Tongues of Men?
Ventidius.   Who shall guard mine,
    For living after you?
Antony.   Say, I command it.
Ventidius. If we die well, our deaths will speak themselves,
    And need no living witness.
305 *Antony.*   Thou hast lov'd me,

And fain I wou'd reward thee: I must die;
Kill me, and take the merit of my death
To make thee Friends with *Cæsar*.
Ventidius.   Thank your kindness.
You said I lov'd you; and, in recompence,
You bid me turn a Traitor: did I think
You wou'd have us'd me thus? that I shou'd die   310
With a hard thought of you?
Antony.   Forgive me, *Roman.*
Since I have heard of *Cleopatra's* death,
My reason bears no rule upon my tongue,
But lets my thoughts break all at random out: 315
I've thought better; do not deny me twice.
Ventidius. By Heav'n, I will not.
Let it not be t'out-live you.
Antony.   Kill me first,
And then die thou: for 'tis but just thou serve
Thy Friend, before thy self.
Ventidius.   Give me your hand.   320
We soon shall meet again. Now, Farewel, Emperor.
                                        Embrace.
Methinks that word's too cold to be my last:
Since Death sweeps all distinctions, Farewel, Friend.
That's all. ———
I will not make a bus'ness of a trifle: 325
And yet I cannot look on you, and kill you;
Pray turn your face.
Antony.   I do: strike home, be sure.
Ventidius. Home, as my Sword will reach.   *Kills himself.*
Antony.   O, thou mistak'st;
That wound was none of thine: give it me back:
Thou robb'st me of my death.
Ventidius.   I do indeed;   330
But, think 'tis the first time I e'er deceiv'd you;
If that may plead my pardon. And you, Gods,
Forgive me, if you will; for I die perjur'd,
Rather than kill my Friend.   *Dies.*
Antony. Farewel. Ever my Leader, ev'n in death!   335
My Queen and thou have got the start of me,
And I'm the lag of Honour. ——— Gone so soon?
Is death no more? He us'd him carelessly,
With a familiar kindness: ere he knock'd,
Ran to the door, and took him in his arms,   340
As who shou'd say, Y'are welcome at all hours,
A Friend need give no warning. Books had spoil'd him;
For all the Learn'd are Cowards by profession.

'Tis not worth

345   My farther thought; for death, for ought I know,
Is but to think no more. Here's to be satisfied.

                           Falls on his Sword.

I've mist my heart. O unperforming hand!
Thou never cou'dst have err'd in a worse time.
My Fortune jades me to the last; and death,

350   Like a great Man, takes state, and makes me wait
For my admittance. ———   *Trampling within.*

                Some perhaps from *Cæsar*:

If he shou'd find me living, and suspect
That I plaid booty with my life! I'll mend
My work, ere they can reach me.

                        Rises upon his knees.

Enter Cleopatra, Charmion, Iras.

Cleopatra. Where is my Lord? where is he?

355   *Charmion.*   There he lies,
And dead *Ventidius* by him.

Cleopatra. My fears were Prophets; I am come too late.
O that accurs'd *Alexas*!   *Runs to him.*

Antony.   Art thou living?
Or am I dead before I knew? and thou
The first kind Ghost that meets me?

360   *Cleopatra.*   Help me seat him.
Send quickly, send for help.

                  They place him in a Chair.

Antony.   I am answer'd.
We live both. Sit thee down, my *Cleopatra*:
I'll make the most I can of life, to stay
A moment more with thee.

Cleopatra. How is it with you?

365   *Antony.*   'Tis as with a man
Removing in a hurry; all pack'd up,
But one dear Jewel that his haste forgot;
And he, for that, returns upon the spur:
So I come back, for thee.

Cleopatra. Too long, you Heav'ns, you have been cruel to

370   me;
Now show your mended Faith, and give me back
His fleeting life.

Antony.   It will not be, my Love.
I keep my Soul by force.

---

353 *plaid booty*] as a gambler deliberately loses in order to swindle
a victim eventually.

Say but thou art not false.
Cleopatra.   'Tis now too late
  To say I'm true: I'll prove it, and die with you.   375
  Unknown to me, *Alexas* feign'd my death:
  Which, when I knew, I hasted, to prevent
  This fatal consequence. My Fleet betray'd
  Both you and me.
Antony.   And *Dollabella* ———
Cleopatra.   Scarce
  Esteem'd before he lov'd; but hated now.   380
Antony. Enough: my life's not long enough for more.
  Thou sayst thou wilt come after: I believe thee;
  For I can now believe whate'er thou sayst,
  That we may part more kindly.
Cleopatra.   I will come:
  Doubt not, my life, I'll come, and quickly too: 385
  Cæsar shall triumph o'er no part of thee.
Antony. But grieve not, while thou stay'st,
  My last disastrous times:
  Think we have had a clear and glorious day;
  And Heav'n did kindly to delay the storm   390
  Just till our close of ev'ning. Ten years love,
  And not a moment lost, but all improv'd
  To th'utmost joys: What Ages have we liv'd?
  And now to die each other's; and, so dying,
  While hand in hand we walk in Groves below,   395
  Whole Troops of Lovers Ghosts shall flock about us,
  And all the Train be ours.
Cleopatra. Your words are like the Notes of dying Swans,
  Too sweet to last. Were there so many hours
  For your unkindness, and not one for love?   400
Antony. No, not a minute. ——— This one kiss ———
  more worth
  Than all I leave to *Cæsar.*   *Dies.*
Cleopatra. O, tell me so again,
  And take ten thousand kisses, for that word.
  My Lord, my Lord: speak, if you yet have being;   405
  Sigh to me, if you cannot speak; or cast
  One look: Do any thing that shows you live.
Iras. He's gone too far, to hear you;
  And this you see, a lump of sensless Clay,
  The leavings of a Soul.
Charmion.   Remember, Madam,   410
  He charg'd you not to grieve.
Cleopatra.   And I'll obey him.
  I have not lov'd a *Roman* not to know

What should become his Wife; his Wife, my *Charmion*;
For 'tis to that high Title I aspire,
And now I'll not die less. Let dull *Octavia*
Survive, to mourn him dead: my Nobler Fate
Shall knit our Spousals with a tie too strong
For *Roman* Laws to break.
Iras.   Will you then die?
Cleopatra. Why shou'dst thou make that question?
Iras. Cæsar is merciful.
Cleopatra.   Let him be so
To those that want his mercy: my poor Lord
Made no such Cov'nant with him, to spare me
When he was dead. Yield me to *Cæsar's* pride?
What, to be led in triumph through the Streets,
A spectacle to base *Plebeian* eyes;
While some dejected Friend of *Antony's*,
Close in a corner, shakes his head, and mutters
A secret curse on her who ruin'd him?
I'll none of that.
Charmion.   Whatever you resolve,
I'll follow ev'n to death.
Iras.   I only fear'd
For you; but more shou'd fear to live without you.
Cleopatra. Why, now 'tis as it shou'd be. Quick, my Friends,
Dispatch; ere this, the Town's in *Cæsar's* hands:
My Lord looks down concern'd, and fears my stay,
Lest I shou'd be surpriz'd;
Keep him not waiting for his love too long.
You, *Charmion*, bring my Crown and richest Jewels,
With 'em the Wreath of Victory I made
(Vain Augury!) for him who now lies dead;
You, *Iras*, bring the cure of all our ills.
Iras. The Aspicks, Madam?
Cleopatra.   Must I bid you twice?
                    Exeunt Charmion *and* Iras.
'Tis sweet to die, when they wou'd force life on me,
To rush into the dark aboad of death,
And seize him first; if he be like my Love,
He is not frightful sure.
We're now alone, in secresie and silence;
And is not this like Lovers? I may kiss
These pale, cold lips; *Octavia* does not see me;

442 *'Tis sweet*] From this line to the end, there is greater debt to Samuel Daniel's *Cleopatra* than to Shakespeare. See Summers' or Arthur Sale's editions for parallels.

And, Oh! 'tis better far to have him thus,
Than see him in her arms. ——— O welcome, welcome.   450

Enter Charmion, Iras.

Charmion. What must be done?
Cleopatra.   Short Ceremony, Friends;
   But yet it must be decent. First, this Laurel
   Shall crown my Hero's Head: he fell not basely,
   Nor left his Shield behind him. Only thou
   Cou'dst triumph o'er thy self; and thou alone   455
   Wert worthy so to triumph.
Charmion.   To what end
   These Ensigns of your Pomp and Royalty?
Cleopatra. Dull, that thou art! why, 'tis to meet my Love;
   As when I saw him first, on *Cydnos* bank,
   All sparkling, like a Goddess; so adorn'd,   460
   I'll find him once again: my second Spousals
   Shall match my first, in Glory. Haste, haste, both,
   And dress the Bride of *Antony.*
Charmion.   'Tis done.
Cleopatra. Now seat me by my Lord. I claim this place;
   For I must conquer *Cæsar* too, like him,   465
   And win my share o'th'World. Hail, you dear Relicks
   Of my Immortal Love!
   O let no Impious hand remove you hence;
   But rest for ever here: let *Egypt* give
   His death that peace, which it deny'd his life.   470
   Reach me the Casket.
Iras. Underneath the fruit the Aspick lies.
Cleopatra (*putting aside the leaves*). Welcom, thou kind
      Deceiver!
   Thou best of Thieves; who, with an easie key,
   Dost open life, and, unperceiv'd by us,   475
   Ev'n steal us from our selves: discharging so
   Death's dreadful office, better than himself,
   Touching our limbs so gently into slumber,
   That Death stands by, deceiv'd by his own Image,
   And thinks himself but Sleep.
Serapion (*within*).   The Queen, where is she?   480
   The Town is yielded, *Cæsar's* at the Gates.
Cleopatra. He comes too late t'invade the Rights of Death.
   Haste, bare my Arm, and rouze the Serpent's fury.
               Holds out her Arm, and draws it back.
   Coward Flesh ———

459 *Cydnos*] See III.i.161–66.

485   Wou'dst thou conspire with *Cæsar*, to betray me,
         As thou wert none of mine? I'll force thee to't,
         And not be sent by him,
         But bring my self my Soul to *Antony*.
         Take hence; the work is done.
                 Turns aside, and then shows her Arm bloody.
         Serapion (*within*).   Break ope the door,
490   And guard the Traitor well.
         Charmion. The next is ours.
         Iras.   Now, *Charmion*, to be worthy
         Of our great Queen and Mistress.
                 They apply the Aspicks.
         Cleopatra. Already, Death, I feel thee in my Veins;
         I go with such a will to find my Lord,
495   That we shall quickly meet.
         A heavy numness creeps through every limb,
         And now 'tis at my head: my eye-lids fall,
         And my dear Love is vanish'd in a mist.
         Where shall I find him, where? O turn me to him,
500   And lay me on his breast. ——— *Cæsar*, thy worst;
         Now part us, if thou canst.   *Dies.*
         Iras *sinks down at her feet, and dies;* Charmion *stands*
                 behind her Chair, as dressing her head.

         Enter Serapion, *two Priests,* Alexas *bound,* Egyptians.

         2. Priests. Behold, *Serapion*, what havock Death has made!
         Serapion. 'Twas what I fear'd.
                 Charmion, is this well done?
         Charmion. Yes, 'tis well done, and like a Queen, the last
         Of her great Race: I follow her.   *Sinks down; Dies.*
505   *Alexas.*   'Tis true,
         She has done well: much better thus to die,
         Than live to make a Holy-day in *Rome*.
         Serapion. See, see how the Lovers sit in State together,
         As they were giving Laws to half Mankind.
510   Th'impression of a smile left in her face,
         Shows she dy'd pleas'd with him for whom she liv'd,
         And went to charm him in another World.
         Cæsar's just entring; grief has now no leisure.
         Secure that Villain, as our pledge of safety
515   To grace th'Imperial Triumph. Sleep, blest Pair,
         Secure from humane chance, long Ages out,
         While all the Storms of Fate fly o'er your Tomb;
         And Fame, to late Posterity, shall tell,
         No Lovers liv'd so great, or dy'd so well.
                         [Exeunt.]

Epilogue

Poets, like Disputants, when Reasons fail,
Have one sure Refuge left; and that's to rail.
Fop, Coxcomb, Fool, are thunder'd through the Pit;
And this is all their Equipage of Wit.
We wonder how the Devil this diff'rence grows,   5
Betwixt our Fools in Verse, and yours in Prose:
For, 'Faith, the quarrel rightly understood,
'Tis *Civil War* with their own Flesh and Blood.
The thread-bare Author hates the gawdy Coat;
And swears at the Guilt Coach, but swears a foot: 10
For 'tis observ'd of every Scribling Man,
He grows a Fop as fast as e'er he can;
Prunes up and asks his Oracle the Glass,
If Pink or Purple best become his face.
For our poor Wretch, he neither rails nor prays;   ⎫   15
Nor likes your Wit just as you like his Plays;   ⎬
He has not yet so much of Mr. *Bays*.   ⎭
He does his best; and, if he cannot please,
Wou'd quietly sue out his *Writ of Ease*.
Yet, if he might his own Grand Jury call,   20
By the Fair Sex he begs to stand or fall.
Let *Cæsar's* Pow'r the Men's ambition move,
But grace You him who lost the World for Love.
Yet if some antiquated Lady say,
The last Age is not Copy'd in his Play;   25
Heav'n help the Man who for that face must drudge,
Which only has the wrinkles of a Judge.
Let not the Young and Beauteous join with those;
For shou'd you raise such numerous Hosts of Foes,
Young Wits and Sparks he to his aid must call;   30
'Tis more than one Man's work to please you all.

17 *Mr. Bays*] the poet in *The Rehearsal*, representing Dryden.
19 *Writ of Ease*] certificate of discharge from employment.

CHANGES IN ACCIDENTALS

Preface 173 Would] would   179 scribble, . . .wantonness˯]~ ˯
. . .~,   205 *stifled*] stiffled   289 *Cygnum*,]~ ˯   318 pleasant,]~ ˯
I.20 clapt;] ~ ,   40 should] shonld   52 *Mæcenas*] *Mecænas*   381
equal,] ~ ;   389 y ou.] ~
II. 100 sounds,] ~ ˯   164–65 *one line in* Q1   176 Heroick ˯ . . .
foes,] ~ , . . . ~ ˯   215 love,] ~ .   230 neither,] ~ .
268 red,] ~ .   301 dy'd.] ~ ˯   303 *Cæsar's*] *Cesar's*   327
Judge,] ~ ˯   336 destruction,] ~ .   401 *Antony*] *Anthony*   417
up,] ~ .   418–19 *one line in* Q1
III.17 Nets,] ~ ;   17 *Vulcan*;] ~ ,   52 Q1 *lines:* We can conquer. /
You . . . aid   52 conquer,] ~ .   68 *Mæcenas*] *Mecænas*
83 Friends.] ~ ˯   152 so; . . . him,] ~ , . . . ~ ;   202 *Antony*]
Anthony   208 be] he   220 *Mæcenas*] *Mecænas*   280–81 Q1 *lines:*
As . . . word, / *Forgive* . . . up   284 to] To   373–74 *one line in* Q1
376 Q1 *lines:* There's . . . you; / Run . . . Eunuch   457 *Cleopatra*!]~ ?
IV.62.1 Alexas.] ~ ,   240 hands,] ~ ˯   243 *Antony*] *Anthony*
328 Lord—] ~ .   365 usurpt:] ~ ,   494 me!] ~ ,
V. 17 O,]~ ˯   103 betray'd.] ~ ˯   327 home,] ~ ˯   379–80 *One
line in* Q1

PRESS VARIANTS

Q1
Sheet b (outer forme)
Corrected: ICU
Uncorrected: NNP

Sig. b2ᵛ
Preface 128 proper,] proper;

Sheet B (inner forme)
Corrected: ICU, NNP
Uncorrected: Bodl

Sig. B2
I.72 perish, perish] perish, here

Sheet F (outer forme)
Corrected: ICU
Uncorrected: NNP

Sig. F1
III.117.1 *and*] omit

Sheet K (outer forme)
Corrected: BM¹, ICU
Uncorrected: BM²

Sig. K1
V.76 com'st] cam'st
79 spare] share
Sig. K2ᵛ
V.170 (As . . . now)] As . . . now,
176 giv'st] givest
177 back] in

Don Sebastian

In February, 1689, with the coming of William and Mary
to England, Dryden lost his position at court, and his post as
poet laureate was given to his enemy Thomas Shadwell. As
a Catholic he had to move at least ten miles out of London and
to pay double tax rates. His sympathy with James II reduced
his influence, and his income disappeared, causing him to
return to writing for the stage. The previous decade saw the
appearance of his major poems: *Absalom and Achitophel*,
Mac Flecknoe, *Religio Laici*, and the *Hind and the Panther*. Thus,
at the height of his powers, feeling isolated and ill-treated, he
turned to the subject of the almost mythical, ill-fated king of
Portugal, who was killed in battle against the Moors in 1578.
Sebastian had been a mystic who refused to marry but spent
all his time hunting and fighting. His great hope was to lead a
crusade against the Moors. After his death, rumors of the
"hidden king" persisted, and at least four pretenders came
forth to claim the throne. A political party, the Sebastianists,
comparable to the English Jacobites, emerged in Portugal.
Little wonder that an anonymous satirist saw analogies between *Don Sebastian* and Dryden's own predicament:

> Sebastian better does the trick,
> With Bobs and Innuendo's thick,
> Which Abdicated Laureat brings
> In praise of Abdicated Kings.[1]

Few passages outside the prologues seem to us as loaded with
innuendo, but it may be significant that Dryden has his
Sebastian abdicate the throne. Moreover, the presence of
occasional Miltonic diction, new in Dryden's plays, helps
remind us of an analogy with Milton, and it is fair to say that
Don Sebastian is to Dryden what *Samson Agonistes* is to Milton.
Both plays vigorously combine private and public emotions,
and both depict the hard struggle for self-respect against
isolation, guilt, and despair.

Scott thought *Don Sebastian* was undoubtedly Dryden's
best play, but Dr. Johnson expressed a more tempered judgment, when he said it was

> commonly esteemed either the first or second of his
> dramatick performances . . . and though it is not with-
> out sallies of frantick dignity, and more noise than

[1] From *The Late Revolution: or, The Happy Chance* (1690), cited by
Macdonald, p. 129.

meaning, yet as it makes approaches to the possibilities
of real life, and has some sentiments which leave a strong
impression, it continued long to attract attention. Amidst
the distresses of princes, and the vicissitudes of empire,
are inserted several scenes which the writer intended for
comick; but which, I suppose, that age did not much
commend, and this would not endure. There are, however, passages of excellence universally acknowledged;
the dispute and the reconciliation of Dorax and Sebastian
has always been admired.[2]

Having mentioned the themes of the main plot in the general introduction, we need to say something about the "several
scenes which the writer intended for comick." And since we
no longer worry greatly about the "purity" of dramatic
forms, we are in a better position than Johnson to appreciate
the subplot. We can see by the examples of George Bernard
Shaw and Sean O'Casey that comedy may be an essential
part of serious drama, for sometimes we laugh because life
would not be endurable otherwise. But whereas modern
plays unite comedy and tragedy, seventeenth-century drama
set parallel episodes next to each other. The two do not
necessarily deflate each other; rather they complement their
opposites to show a fuller range of human experience.[3] Hence
the comic scenes balance the serious ones. Immediately after
Sebastian and Almeyda leave the stage to find a priest and
Almeyda has asked for forgiveness for her frailty and her
fatal, unbounded love, Antonio begins his plans for an assignation with Johayma. Neither can restrain physical desire,
and the explicit parallel is made when Antonio says, "How
far a *Christian* shoul'd resist, I partly know; but how far a
lewd young *Christian* can resist is another question" (II.ii.79–
81). By choral juxtaposition, in the opening words of III.i the
non-Christian emperor admits he cannot resist his passion.
In the following scene (III.ii) Antonio pretends that he has a
qualm of conscience that will prevent his enjoying Johayma,
and Johayma pretends there is an attempted rape, similar to
the real attempt being made by the emperor, just off-stage.
The old woman teaches Antonio to bind a rose tree and myrtle
together (II.ii.65–66); Almeyda wishes to die "close embraced"
to Sebastian, and the emperor says he will untwist them
(III.i.195–96, 373). Antonio loves "playing in the dark"
(III.iii.197–98), but Sebastian and Almeyda confess their guilt

[2] *Lives of the Poets*, I, 362–63.
[3] See the introductions to *Secret Love* and *Marriage a-la-Mode* in the
companion volume: *John Dryden: Four Comedies* (1967).

from the deep pleasure of their night together, whose memory stays in the dark recesses of their souls (III.i.136, 156, 181). Dorax thought of himself as a fallen Lucifer, and Morayma plays at being Lucifer taking Antonio's soul to Hell (V.i.65–70). In the most outrageous parody, she jokes about giving birth to another man's child if Antonio goes astray. She will bear some young Antonio of another man's planting, just as Almeyda's mother bore the child of Sebastian's father.

Somewhat less obvious analogues may be seen between clusters of images in the serious and comic plots. The elaborate plays on garden, gardening, planting seeds, sowing lettuce, handling the pruning knife, and munching on melons may have been intended to complement the arid and destructive imagery of love in the main plot. At any rate, concealing and protective darkness in the subplot contrasts with the fearful and dark abyss of the main plot, and both are highly erotic. The problem remains, however, just how skillfully Dryden worked with the two aspects of his material. If we accept it in *The Spanish Friar* and *Marriage a-la-Mode*, I do not think we can object to the rather studied and deliberate patterning here, and self-conscious artifice is an attractive feature of *All for Love* and *Aureng-Zebe*. Something is wrong, nevertheless, and I am inclined to attribute it to Dryden's overwriting. If both plots were more economically handled, perhaps as Betterton cut them for the early performances, we might more easily see a graceful parallel of the themes.

The United Company with Thomas Betterton as Dorax produced *Don Sebastian* at Drury Lane in December, 1689; the queen occupied a box and paid for another box for her maids of honour on December 4, but the occasion may not have been the first performance. Another known acting date is May 26, 1697. I assume that our text is the uncut version, and the more than twelve hundred lines may have come out after an unsuccessful first night, as Ward thinks, or they may have been cut during rehearsal; the awkward length and repetition are so plain that the second possibility seems more likely.

Entered at the Stationers' Hall December 15, 1689, Q1 was dated 1690 (Macd. 89a, W & M 403) and advertised for sale in the first week of January, 1690. The copy-text for this edition has been the University of Chicago copy of Q1, compared with two British Museum copies (BM[1] 653.h.18(11) and BM[2] 644.g.71) and a University of Michigan copy. Q2 1692 contains two substantive corrections in the dialogue and one in the cast.

DON
SEBASTIAN,
𝕶ing of 𝕻o𝔷tugal :
A
TRAGEDY
Acted at the
Theatre Royal.

Written by Mr. *D R Y D E N.*

―――――*Nec tarda Senectus*
Debilitat vires animi, mutatque vigorem. Virgil.

L O N D O N :
Printed for *Jo. Hindmarsh,* at the *Golden Ball* in
Cornhil. M DC XC.

Title Page of the First Quarto, University of Chicago Copy

Nec . . . vigorem] Ev'n time that changes all, yet changes us in vain: /
The Body, not the Mind: Nor can controul / Th' immortal vigour, or
abate the Soul. (*Aeneid*, IX,610–11; 836–38 of Dryden's translation).

The Preface

Whether it happen'd through a long disuse of Writing, that I forgot the usual compass of a Play; or that by crowding it, with Characters and Incidents, I put a necessity upon my self of lengthning the main Action, I know not; but the first day's Audience sufficiently convinc'd me of my error; and that the Poem was insupportably too long. 'Tis an ill ambition of us Poets, to please an Audience with more than they can bear: And, supposing that we wrote as well, as vainly we imagin our selves to write; yet we ought to consider, that no man can bear to be long tickled. There is a nauseousness in a City feast when we are to sit four hours after we are cloy'd. I am, therefore, in the first place, to acknowledg with all manner of gratitude, their civility; who were pleas'd to endure it with so much patience, to be weary with so much good nature and silence, and not to explode an entertainment, which was design'd to please them; or discourage an Author, whose misfortunes have once more brought him against his will, upon the Stage. While I continue in these bad circumstances, (and truly I see very little probability of coming out:) I must be oblig'd to write, and if I may still hope for the same kind usage, I shall the less repent of that hard necessity. I write not this out of any expectation to be pityed; for I have Enemies enow to wish me yet in a worse condition; but give me leave to say, that if I can please by writing, as I shall endeavour it, the Town may be somewhat oblig'd to my misfortunes, for a part of their diversion. Having been longer acquainted with the Stage, than any Poet now living, and having observ'd how difficult it was to please; that the humours of Comedy were almost spent, that Love and Honour (the mistaken Topicks of Tragedy) were quite worn out; that the Theaters cou'd not support their charges, that the Audience forsook them, that young men without Learning set up for Judges, and that they talk'd loudest, who understood the least: all these discouragements had not only wean'd me from the Stage, but had also given me a loathing of it. But enough of this: the difficulties continue; they increase, and I am still condemn'd to dig in those exhausted Mines. Whatever fault I next commit, rest assur'd it shall not be that of too much length: Above twelve

5

10

15

20

25

30

35

15 *explode*] clap and hoot off the stage.

40 hunder'd lines have been cut off from this Tragedy, since it
was first deliver'd to the Actors. They were indeed so
judiciously lopt by Mr. *Betterton,* to whose care and excellent
action, I am equally oblig'd, that the connexion of the story
was not lost; but on the other side, it was impossible to pre-
45 vent some part of the action from being precipitated, and
coming on without that due preparation, which is requir'd to
all great events: as in particular, that of raising the Mobile,
in the beginning of the Fourth Act; which a Man of *Benducar's* cool Character, cou'd not naturally attempt, without
50 taking all those precautions, which he foresaw wou'd be
necessary to render his design successful. On this considera-
tion, I have replac'd those lines, through the whole Poem;
and thereby restor'd it, to that clearness of conception, and
(if I may dare to say it) that lustre, and masculine vigour,
55 in which it was first written. 'Tis obvious to every understanding Reader, that the most poetical parts, which are
Descriptions, Images, Similitudes, and Moral Sentences; are
those, which of necessity were to be par'd away, when the
body was swoln into too large a bulk for the representation
60 of the Stage. But there is a vast difference betwixt a publick
entertainment on the Theatre, and a private reading in the
Closet: In the first we are confin'd to time, and though we
talk not by the hour-glass, yet the Watch often drawn out of
the pocket, warns the Actors, that their Audience is weary;
65 in the last, every Reader is judge of his own convenience; he
can take up the book, and lay it down at his pleasure; and
find out those beauties of propriety, in thought and writing,
which escap'd him in the tumult and hurry of representing.
And I dare boldly promise for this Play, that in the roughness
70 of the numbers and cadences, (which I assure was not casual,
but so design'd) you will see somewhat more masterly
arising to your view, than in most, if not any of my former
Tragedies. There is a more noble daring in the Figures and
more suitable to the loftiness of the Subject; and besides this
75 some newnesses of *English,* translated from the Beauties of
Modern Tongues, as well as from the elegancies of the
Latin; and here and there some old words are sprinkled,
which for their significance and sound, deserv'd not to be
antiquated; such as we often find in *Salust* amongst the
80 *Roman* Authors, and in *Milton's Paradise* amongst ours;
though perhaps the latter instead of sprinkling, has dealt

47 *Mobile*] mob.
61 *on the Theatre*] on stage (*OED, cv* theatre 3a).
75 *newnesses*] This is itself the first use of *newnesses* recorded in the
OED.

them with too free a hand, even sometimes to the obscuring of his sense.

As for the story or plot of the Tragedy, 'tis purely fiction; for I take it up where the History has laid it down. We are assur'd by all Writers of those times, that *Sebastian* a young Prince of great courage and expectation, undertook that War partly upon a religious account, partly at the sollicitation of *Muley-Mahumet,* who had been driven out of his Dominions, by *Abdelmelech,* or as others call him *Muley-Moluch* his nigh Kinsman, who descended from the same Family of the *Xeriff's;* whose Fathers *Hamet* and *Mahomet* had conquer'd that Empire with joint Forces; and shar'd it betwixt them after their victory: That the body of *Don Sebastian* was never found in the Field of Battel; which gave occasion for many to believe, that he was not slain; that some years after, when the *Spaniards* with a pretended title, by force of Arms had Usurp'd the Crown of *Portugal,* from the House of *Braganza,* a certain Person who call'd himself *Don Sebastian,* and had all the marks of his body and features of his face, appear'd at *Venice,* where he was own'd by some of his Country-men; but being seiz'd by the *Spaniards* was first Imprison'd, then sent to the Gallies, and at last put to Death in private. 'Tis most certain, that the *Portugueses* expected his return for almost an Age together after that Battel; which is at least a proof of their extream love to his Memory; and the usage which they had from their new Conquerors, might possibly make them so extravagant in their hopes and wishes for their old Master.

This ground work the History afforded me, and I desire no better to build a Play upon it: For where the event of a great action is left doubtful, there the Poet is left Master: He may raise what he pleases on that foundation, provided he makes it of a piece, and according to the rule of probability. From hence I was only oblig'd, that *Sebastian* shou'd return to *Portugal* no more; but at the same time I had him at my own disposal, whether to bestow him in *Affrick,* or in any other corner of the World, or to have clos'd the Tragedy with his death; and the last of these was certainly the most easie, but for the same reason, the least artful; because as I have some-where said, the poyson and the dagger are still at hand, to

85

90

95

100

105

110

115

120

98 *Braganza*] After Henry II of Portugal died without heir, the Duke of Braganza claimed the crown of Portugal in opposition to Philip II of Spain.
99 *a certain Person*] Marco Tullio, an Italian peasant.
109 *old Master*] the closest Dryden comes to suggesting a parallel with James II of England, who abdicated in 1688.
120-21 *somewhere said*] in the dedication to *The Spanish Friar* (1681).

butcher a Heroe, when a Poet wants the brains to save him. It being therefore only necessary according to the Laws of the *Drama,* that *Sebastian* shou'd no more be seen upon the

125 Throne, I leave it for the World to judge, whether or no I have disposed of him according to art, or have bungled up the conclusion of his adventure. In the drawing of his character I forgot not piety, which any one may observe to be one principal ingredient of it; even so far as to be a habit in

130 him; though I show him once to be transported from it by the violence of a sudden passion, to endeavor a self murther. This being presuppos'd, that he was Religious, the horror of his incest, tho innocently committed, was the best reason which the Stage cou'd give for hind'ring his return. 'Tis true

135 I have no right to blast his Memory, with such a crime: but declaring it to be fiction, I desire my Audience to think it no longer true, than while they are seeing it represented: For that once ended, he may be a Saint for ought I know; and we have reason to presume he is. On this supposition, it was

140 unreasonable to have kill'd him; for the Learned Mr. *Rymer* has well observ'd, that in all punishments we are to regulate our selves by Poetical justice; and according to those measures an involuntary sin deserves not death; from whence it follows, that to divorce himself from the beloved object, to

145 retire into a desart, and deprive himself of a Throne, was the utmost punishment, which a Poet cou'd inflict, as it was also the utmost reparation, which *Sebastian* cou'd make. For what relates to *Almeyda,* her part is wholly fictitious: I know it is the surname of a noble Family in *Portugal,* which was very

150 instrumental in the Restoration of *Don John de Braganza,* Father to the most Illustrious and most Pious Princess our Queen *Dowager.* The *French* Author of a Novel, call'd *Don Sebastian,* has given that name to an *Affrican* Lady of his own invention, and makes her Sister to *Muley-Mahumet.* But I

155 have wholly chang'd the accidents, and borrow'd nothing but the supposition, that she was belov'd by the King of *Portugal.* Tho, if I had taken the whole story, and wrought it up into a Play, I might have done it exactly according to the practice of almost all the Ancients; who were never accus'd

160 of being Plagiaries, for building their Tragedies on known

140 *Mr. Rymer*] See the general introduction and the introduction to *All For Love* for comment on Thomas Rymer's influence.

150 *Don John de Braganza*] made king in 1641.

152–53 *a Novel*] *Don Sebastian, King of Portugal, an Historical Novel, in Four Parts,* translated by Ferraud Spence, 1683, treats events in the life of the pretender Marco Tullio Catizone.

160 *Plagiaries*] In 1687 Gerard Langbaine had accused Dryden of plagiarism.

288

Fables. Thus *Augustus Cæsar* wrote an *Ajax*, which was not
the less his own, because *Euripides* had written a Play before
him on that Subject. Thus of late years *Corneille* writ an
Oedipus after *Sophocles*; and I have design'd one after him,
which I wrote with Mr. *Lee*, yet neither the *French* Poet stole   165
from the *Greek*, nor we from the *French man*. 'Tis the contrivance, the new turn, and new characters, which alter the
property and make it ours. The *Materia Poetica* is as common
to all Writers, as the *Materia Medica* to all Physicians. Thus in
our *Chronicles, Daniel's* History is still his own, though   170
Matthew Paris, Stow and *Hollingshed* writ before him, otherwise we must have been content with their dull relations, if a
better Pen had not been allow'd to come after them, and
write his own account after a new and better manner.

I must farther declare freely, that I have not exactly kept   175
to the three Mechanick rules of unity: I knew them and had
them in my eye, but follow'd them only at a distance; for
the Genius of the *English* cannot bear too regular a Play; we
are given to variety, even to a debauchery of Pleasure. My
Scenes are therefore sometimes broken, because my Under-   180
plot requir'd them so to be; though the General Scene
remains of the same Castle; and I have taken the time of two
days, because the variety of accidents, which are here represented, cou'd not naturally be suppos'd to arrive in one: But
to gain a greater Beauty, 'tis lawful for a Poet to supersede   185
a less.

I must likewise own, that I have somewhat deviated from
the known History, in the death of *Muley-Moluch*, who, by
all relations, dyed of a feaver in the Battel, before his Army
had wholly won the Field; but if I have allow'd him another   190
day of life, it was because I stood in need of so shining a
Character of brutality, as I have given him; which is indeed
the same, with that of the present Emperor *Muley Ishmael*,
as some of our *English* Officers, who have been in his Court,
have credibly inform'd me.   195

I have been listning what objections had been made,
against the conduct of the Play, but found them all so trivial,
that if I shou'd name them, a true critick wou'd imagin that
I play'd booty, and only rais'd up fantoms for my self to
conquer. Some are pleas'd to say the Writing is dull; but   200

162 *Euripides*] a slip of the memory; Sophocles.
165 *Mr. Lee*] Nathaniel Lee and Dryden's *Oedipus* (1679).
170 *Daniel's History*] Samuel Daniel's *History of England*, 1612–
18(?).
199 *play'd booty*] in gambling, to lose intentionally in order to encourage large betting.

ætatem habet de se loquatur. Others that the double poyson is
unnatural; let the common received opinion, and *Ausonius*
his famous Epigram answer that. Lastly a more ignorant
sort of Creatures than either of the former, maintain that
205   the Character of *Dorax,* is not only unnatural, but inconsistent with it self; let them read the Play and think again,
and if yet they are not satisfied, cast their eyes on that Chapter
of the Wise *Montaigne,* which is intituled *de l'Inconstance des
actions humaines.* A longer reply, is what those Cavillers
210   deserve not; but I will give them and their fellows to understand, that the Earl of *Dorset,* was pleas'd to read the Tragedy
twice over before it was Acted; and did me the favour to
send me word, that I had written beyond any of my former
Plays; and that he was displeas'd any thing shou'd be cut
215   away. If I have not reason to prefer his single judgment to a
whole Faction, let the World be judge; for the opposition
is the same with that of *Lucan's* Heroe against an Army;
concurrere bellum, atque virum. I think I may modestly conclude,
that whatever errors there may be, either in the design, or
220   writing of this Play, they are not those which have been
objected to it. I think also, that I am not yet arriv'd to the
Age of doating; and that I have given so much application
to this Poem, that I cou'd not probably let it run into many
gross absurdities; which may caution my Enemies from too
225   rash a censure; and may also encourage my friends, who are
many more than I cou'd reasonably have expected, to
believe their kindness has not been very undeservedly
bestowed on me. This is not a Play that was huddled up in
hast; and to shew it was not, I will own, that beside the
230   general Moral of it, which is given in the four last lines,
there is also another Moral, couch'd under every one of the
principal Parts and Characters, which a judicious Critick will
observe, though I point not to it in this Preface. And there
may be also some secret Beauties in the decorum of parts,
235   and uniformity of design, which my puny judges will not
easily find out; let them consider in the last Scene of the

201 *ætatem habet de se loquatur*] John 9:21 ("*ipse de se*" Vulgate);
"He is of age, let him speak for himself," i.e., every man be his own
judge.
202–3 *Ausonius*] Epigram III, which tells of a wife who wished to be
sure that she would poison her husband, but the two ingredients in the
potion nullified each other.
208–9 *de l'Inconstance des actions humaines*] The title should be *De
l'inconstance de nos actions* (Montaigne's *Essays,* II.i).
211 *Earl of Dorset*] Charles Sackville (1638–1706).
218 *concurrere . . . virum*] Fortune sees a new pair meet in combat—a
man against an army (*Pharsalia,* VI, 191–92). The hero was Cato.

fourth Act, whether I have not preserv'd the rule of decency, in giving all the advantage to the Royal Character; and in making *Dorax* first submit: Perhaps too they may have thought, that it was through indigence of Characters, that I 240 have given the same to *Sebastian* and *Almeyda*; and consequently made them alike in all things but their Sex. But let them look a little deeper into the matter, and they will find that this identity of Character in the greatness of their Souls; was intended for a preparation of the final discovery, and 245 that the likeness of their nature, was a fair hint to the proximity of their blood.

To avoid the imputation of too much vanity (for all Writers, and especially Poets will have some) I will give but one other instance, in relation to the Uniformity of the 250 design. I have observ'd, that the *English* will not bear a thorough Tragedy; but are pleas'd, that it shou'd be lightned with underparts of mirth. It had been easie for me to have given my Audience a better course of Comedy, I mean a more diverting, than that of *Antonio* and *Morayma.* But I dare 255 appeal even to my Enemies, if I or any man cou'd have invented one, which had been more of a piece, and more depending, on the serious part of the design. For what cou'd be more uniform, than to draw from out of the members of a Captive Court, the Subject of a Comical entertainment? 260 To prepare this Episode, you see *Dorax* giving the Character of *Antonio,* in the beginning of the Play, upon his first sight of him at the Lottery; and to make the dependence, *Antonio* is ingag'd in the Fourth Act, for the deliverance of *Almeyda*; which is also prepar'd, by his being first made a Slave to the 265 Captain of the Rabble.

I shou'd beg pardon for these instances; but perhaps they may be of use to future Poets, in the conduct of their Plays: At least if I appear too positive; I am growing old, and thereby, in possession of some experience, which men in 270 years will always assume for a right of talking. Certainly, if a Man can ever have reason to set a value on himself, 'tis when his ungenerous Enemies are taking the advantage of the Times upon him, to ruin him in his reputation. And therefore for once, I will make bold to take the Counsel of 275 my Old Master *Virgil.*

Tu, ne cede malis; sed, contrà, audentior ito.

277 *Tu . . . ito*] But thou, secure of Soul, unbent with Woes, / The more thy Fortune frowns, the more oppose (*Aeneid,* VI, 95; 143–44 of Dryden's translation).

Persons Represented

Don Sebastian, King of Portugal.
Muley-Moluch, Emperor of Barbary.
Dorax, a Noble Portuguese now a Renegade, formerly *Don Alonzo de Sylvera Alcalde*, or Governor of Alcazar.
Benducar, Chief Minister and Favourite to the Emperor.
The Mufti *Abdalla*.
Muley-Zeydan, Brother to the Emperor.
Don Antonio, a Young Noble amorous Portuguese, now a Slave.
Don Alvarez, an old Counsellor to *Don Sebastian*, now a Slave also.
Mustafa, Captain of the Rabble.
Almeyda, a Captive Queen of Barbary.
Morayma, Daughter to the Mufti.
Johayma, Chief Wife to the Mufti.

> Two Merchants.
> Rabble.
> A Servant to *Benducar*.
> A Servant to the Mufti.

> Scene in the Castle of Alcazar.

Persons Represented] the cast as listed in Q1: *Sebastian*, Joseph Williams; *Muley Moluch*, Edward Kynaston; *Dorax*, Thomas Betterton; *Benducar*, Samuel Sandford; *Mufti*, Cave Underhill; *Muley Zeydan*, George Powell, Jr., *Antonio*, William Mountfort [a correction in Q2; Q1 gave this role to Betterton by mistake], *Alvarez*, John Bowman; *Mustapha*, Antony Leigh; *Almeyda*, Mrs. Elizabeth Barry; *Morayma*, Mrs. Susanna Mountfort; *Johayma*, Mrs. Elinor Leigh.

Prologue

to

DON SEBASTIAN King of *Portugal*.

Spoken by a Woman

The Judge remov'd, tho he's no more My Lord,
May plead at Bar, or at the Council-Board:
So may cast Poets write; there's no Pretension,
To argue loss of Wit from loss of Pension.
Your looks are cheerful; and in all this place   5
I see not one, that wears a damning face.
The *British* Nation, is too brave to show,
Ignoble vengeance, on a vanquish'd foe;
At least be civil to the Wretch imploring,
And lay your Paws upon him, without roaring: 10
Suppose our Poet was your foe before;
Yet now, the bus'ness of the Field is o'er;
'Tis time to let your Civil Wars alone,
When Troops are into Winter-quarters gone.
Jove was alike to *Latian* and to *Phrygian*;   15
And you well know, a Play's of no Religion.
Take good advice, and please your selves this day;
No matter from what hands you have the Play.
Among good Fellows ev'ry health will pass,
That serves to carry round another glass: 20
When, with full bowls of *Burgundy* you dine,   ⎫
Tho at the Mighty Monarch you repine,   ⎬
You grant him still most Christian, in his Wine.   ⎭

Thus far the Poet, but his brains grow Addle;
And all the rest is purely from this Noddle.   25
You've seen young Ladies at the Senate door,
Prefer Petitions, and your grace implore;
How ever grave the Legislators were,
Their Cause went ne'er the worse for being fair;

4 *loss of Pension*] See the introduction.
15 *Latian*] i.e., Latins and Carthaginians.
23 *most Christian*] The King of France had exclusive use of the
title *Rex Christianessimus*. The idea is that we enjoy French wine even
though we disapprove of the French.
24 *Addle*] simple.

30   Reasons as weak as theirs, perhaps I bring,
But I cou'd bribe you, with as good a thing.
I heard him make advances of good Nature;
That he for once, wou'd sheath his cutting Satyr:
Sign but his Peace, he vows he'll ne'er again
35   The sacred Names of Fops and Beaús profane.
Strike up the Bargain quickly; for I swear,
As Times go now, he offers very fair.
Be not too hard on him, with Statutes neither;
Be kind, and do not set your Teeth together,
40   To stretch the Laws, as Coblers do their Leather.
Horses, by Papists are not to be ridden;
But sure the Muse's Horse was ne'er forbidden.
For in no Rate-Book, it was ever found
That *Pegasus* was valued at Five-pound:
45   Fine him to daily Drudging and Inditing;
And let him pay his Taxes out, in Writing.

38 *Statutes*] laws passed in 1688 restricting the rights of Catholics, even so strict as to limit the ownership of horses to beasts worth less than five pounds.
46 *Taxes*] Catholics paid double taxes.

Don Sebastian, King of Portugal

ACT I. SCENE I

The Scene at Alcazar, *representing a Market-Place under the Castle.*

[*Enter*] Muley-Zeydan, Benducar.

Muley-Zeydan. Now *Affrica's* long Wars are at an end;
  And our parch'd earth is drench'd in Christian Blood,
  My conquering Brother will have Slaves enow,
  To pay his cruel Vows for Victory.
  What hear you of *Sebastian,* King of *Portugal*?   5
Benducar. He fell among a heap of slaughter'd *Moors*;
  Though yet his mangled Carcase is not found.
  The Rival of our threatned Empire, *Mahumet,*
  Was hot pursued; and in the general rout,
  Mistook a swelling Current for a Foord;   10
  And in *Mucazer's* Flood was seen to rise;
  Thrice was he seen; at length his Courser plung'd,
  And threw him off; the Waves whelm'd over him,
  And helpless in his heavy arms he drownd.
Muley-Zeydan. Thus, then, a doubtful Title is extinguish'd: 15
  Thus, *Moluch,* still the Favorite of Fate,
  Swims in a sanguine torrent to the Throne,
  As if our Prophet only work'd for him:
  The Heavens and all the Stars are his hir'd Servants,
  As *Muley-Zeydan* were not worth their care,   20
  And younger Brothers but the draff of Nature.
Benducar. Be still, and learn the soothing Arts of Court;
  Adore his fortune, mix with flattering Crowds,
  And when they praise him most, be you the loudest;
  Your Brother is luxurious, close, and cruel,   25
  Generous by fits, but permanent in mischief.
  The shadow of a discontent wou'd ruin us;
  We must be safe before we can be great:
  These things observ'd, leave me to shape the rest.
Muley-Zeydan. You have the Key, he opens inward to you.   30

11 *Mucazer's Flood*] the Makhazan River in northern Morocco,
near the site of the battle of Alcazar (or Al Kasr), 1578.
21 *draff*] dregs.
25 *luxurious*] lecherous.

Benducar. So often try'd, and ever found so true,
Has given me trust, and trust has given me means
Once to be false for all. I trust not him:
For now his ends are serv'd, and he grown absolute,
35 How am I sure to stand who serv'd those ends?
I know your nature open, mild, and grateful;
In such a Prince the People may be blest,
And I be safe.
Muley-Zeydan. My Father!   *Embracing him.*
40 *Benducar.* My future King! (auspicious *Muley-Zeydan*:)
Shall I adore you? No, the place is publick;
I worship you within; the outward act
Shall be reserv'd till Nations follow me,
And Heaven shall envy you the kneeling World.
45 You know th'Alcald of *Alcazar, Dorax*?
Muley-Zeydan. The gallant Renegade you mean?
Benducar.   The same:
That gloomy outside, like a rusty Chest,
Contains the shining Treasure of a Soul,
Resolv'd and brave; he has the Souldiers hearts,
And time shall make him ours.
50 *Muley-Zeydan.*   He's just upon us.
Benducar. I know him from a far, by the long stride
And by the sullen port: Retire my Lord.
Wait on your Brother's Triumph, yours is next,
His growth is but a wild and fruitless Plant,
55 I'll cut his barren branches to the stock,
And graft you on to bear.
Muley-Zeydan.   My Oracle!
                              Exit Muley-Zeydan.
Benducar. Yes, to delude your hopes, poor credulous Fool,
To think that I wou'd give away the Fruit
Of so much toil, such guilt, and such damnation;
60 If I am damn'd, it shall be for my self:
This easie Fool must be my Stale, set up
To catch the People's eyes; he's tame and merciful,
Him I can manage, till I make him odious
By some unpopular act, and then dethrone him.
                    Enter Dorax.
Now *Dorax*!

61 *Stale*] decoy.
62–64 *he's . . . him*] This and subsequent show of Benducar's
treachery leads John Robert Moore to identify him with the Earl
of Sunderland, the disastrous advisor to James II (*PMLA*, LXXIII
[1958], 39–41). The analogy breaks down when Moore identifies
the emperor with James II.

Dorax.   Well, *Benducar!*
Benducar.   Bare *Benducar!*   65
Dorax. Thou wouldst have Titles, take 'em then,
   Chief Minister, first Hangman of the State.
Benducar. Some call me Favourite.
Dorax.   What's that, his Minion?
   Thou art too old to be a Catamite!
   Now prithee tell me, and abate thy pride,   70
   Is not *Benducar* Bare, a better Name
   In a Friend's mouth, than all those gawdy Titles,
   Which I disdain to give the Man I love?
Benducar. But always out of humor, ———
Dorax.   I have cause:
   Tho all mankind is cause enough for Satyr.   75
Benducar. Why then thou hast reveng'd thee on mankind.
   They say in fight, thou hadst a thirsty Sword,
   And well 'twas glutted there.
Dorax. I spitted Frogs, I crush'd a heap of Emmets,
   A hundred of 'em to a single Soul,   80
   And that but scanty weight too: the great Devil
   Scarce thank'd me for my pains; he swallows Vulgar
   Like whip'd Cream, feels 'em not in going down.
Benducar. Brave Renegade! cou'dst thou not meet
      Sebastian?
   Thy Master had been worthy of thy Sword.   85
Dorax. My Master? By what title,
   Because I happen'd to be born where he
   Happen'd to be a King? And yet I serv'd him,
   Nay, I was fool enough to love him too.
   You know my story, how I was rewarded,   90
   For Fifteen hard Campaigns, still hoop'd in Iron,
   And why I turn'd Mahometan: I'm grateful,
   But whosoever dares to injure me,
   Let that man know, I dare to be reveng'd.
Benducar. Still you run off from biass; say what moves 95
   Your present spleen?
Dorax.   You mark'd not what I told you:
   I kill'd not one that was his Maker's Image;
   I met with none but vulgar two-leg'd Brutes.
   Sebastian was my aim; he was a Man:
   Nay, though he hated me, and I hate him,   100
   Yet I must do him right; he was a Man,

82 *Vulgar*] common people, the vulgar.
95 *off from biass*] out of a set course.
101–5 *he was . . . idoliz'd*] suggesting that Sebastian was a second
Aeneas (Brower).

297

Above man's height, ev'n towring to *Divinity*.
Brave, pious, generous, great, and liberal:
Just as the Scales of Heaven that weigh the Seasons,
105 He lov'd his People, him they idoliz'd:
And thence proceeds my mortal hatred to him,
That thus unblameable to all besides
He err'd to me alone:
His goodness was diffus'd to human kind,
110 And all his cruelty confin'd to me.
Benducar. You cou'd not meet him then?
Dorax.   No , though I sought
Where ranks fell thickest; 'twas indeed the place
To seek *Sebastian*: through a track of Death
I follow'd him, by Groans of dying Foes,
115 But still I came too late, for he was flown
Like Lightning, swift before me to new Slaughters.
I mow'd across, and made irregular Harvest,
Defac'd the pomp of Battel, but in vain,
For he was still supplying Death elsewhere:
120 This mads me that perhaps ignoble hands
Have overlaid him, for they cou'd not conquer:
Murder'd by Multitudes, whom I alone
Had right to slay; I too wou'd have been slain,
That catching hold upon his flitting Ghost
125 I might have robb'd him of his opening Heav'n;
And drag'd him down with me, spight of Predestination.
Benducar. 'Tis of as much import as *Affric*'s worth
To know what came of him, and of *Almeyda*,
The Sister of the Vanquish'd *Mahumet*,
130 Whose fatal Beauty to her Brother drew
The Land's third part, as *Lucifer* did Heav'n's.
Dorax. I hope she dy'd in her own Female calling,
Choak'd up with Man, and gorg'd with Circumcision.
As for *Sebastian* we must search the Field,
135 And where we see a Mountain of the Slain,
Send one to climb, and looking down below
There he shall find him at his Manly length
With his face up to Heav'n, in the red Monument,
Which his true Sword has digg'd.
140 *Benducar.* Yet we may possibly hear farther news;
For while our *Affricans* pursu'd the Chase,
The Captain of the Rabble issued out,
With a black shirt-less train to spoil the dead,
And seize the living.

131 *third part*] Satan's fall brought down "a third part of the
stars in heaven" *Revelation*, XII, 4.

Dorax.　　　　　　Each of 'em an Hoast,
　A Million strong of Vermine ev'ry Villain:　　　　　　145
　No part of Government, but Lords of Anarchy,
　Chaos of Power, and priviledg'd destruction.
Benducar. Yet I must tell you Friend, the Great must use
　'em,
　Sometimes as necessary tools of tumult.
Dorax. I wou'd use 'em　　　　　　　　　　　　　　150
　Like Dogs in times of Plague, out-laws of Nature,
　Fit to be shot and brain'd; without a process,
　To stop infection, that's their proper death.
Benducar. No more,
　Behold the Emperor coming to survey　　　　　　155
　The Slaves, in order to perform his Vow.

　Enter Muley-Moluch *the Emperor, with Attendants.*
　　[*After him*] *the* Mufty, *and* Muley-Zeydan.

Emperor. Our Armours now may rust, our idle scymitars
　Hang by our sides, for Ornament not use:
　Children shall beat our Atabals and Drums,
　And all the noisie trades of War, no more　　　　160
　Shall wake the peaceful morn: the *Xeriff's* blood
　No longer in divided Channels runs,
　The younger House took end in *Mahumet.*
　Nor shall *Sebastian's* formidable Name,
　Be longer us'd to lull the crying babe!　　　　165
Mufti. For this Victorious day our Mighty Prophet
　Expects your gratitude, the Sacrifice
　Of Christian Slaves, devoted, if you won.
Emperor. The purple present shall be richly paid:
　That Vow perform'd, fasting shall be abolish'd:　　170
　None ever serv'd Heav'n well with a starv'd face:
　Preach Abstinence no more; I tell thee *Mufty*
　Good feasting is devout: and thou our Head,
　Hast a Religious, ruddy Countenance:
　We will have learned Luxury; our lean Faith　　175
　Gives scandal to the *Christians*; they feed high:
　Then look for shoals of Converts, when thou hast
　Reform'd us into feasting.

159 *Atabals*] tabors.
163 *end in Mahumet*] descendants of Emperor Mahumet VIII, the
last of whom, Mahumet XI, took part in the battle of Alcazar. Sebastian
came to aid him against Abdel Malik. Since all three kings died in
battle, the throne was usurped by the Emperor of Barbary, Dryden's
Muley Moluch.
168 *devoted*] solemnly dedicated.

Mufti. Fasting is but the Letter of the Law:
180   Yet it shows well to Preach it to the Vulgar.
       Wine is against our Law, that's literal too,
       But not deny'd to Kings and to their Guides,
       Wine is a Holy Liquor, for the Great.
Dorax (aside). This *Mufti* in my conscience is some *English*
185   Renegade, he talks so savourly of toping.
Emperor. Bring forth th'unhappy Relicks of the War.

Enter Mustafa *Captain of the Rabble with his*
followers of the Black Guard, &c. and other Moors:
with them a Company of Portuguese *Slaves with-*
out any of the chief Persons.

Emperor. These are not fit to pay an Emperor's Vow;
       Our Bulls and Rams had been more noble Victims;
       These are but garbidge, not a Sacrifice.
190 *Mufti.* The Prophet must not pick and choose his Offrings;
       Now he has giv'n the Day, 'tis past recalling:
       And he must be content with such as these.
Emperor. But are these all? Speak you who are their
       Masters.
Mustafa. All upon my Honour: If you'll take 'em as their
195   Fathers got 'em, so. If not, you must stay till they get a
       better generation: These *Christians* are mere bunglers;
       they procreate nothing but out of their own Wives;
       And these have all the looks of Eldest Sons.
Emperor. Pain of your lives let none conceal a Slave.
200 *Mustafa.* Let every Man look to his own Conscience, I am
       sure mine shall never hang me.
Benducar. Thou speak'st as thou wert privy to conceal-
       ments:
       Then thou art an Accomplice.
Mustafa. Nay if Accomplices must suffer, it may go hard
205   with me; but here's the Devil on't, there's a Great Man
       and a Holy Man too, concern'd with me. Now if I con-
       fess, he'll be sure to scape between his Greatness and his
       Holiness, and I shall be murder'd, because of my Poverty
       and Rascality.
Mufti (winking at him). Then if thy silence save the Great
210   and Holy,
       'Tis sure thou shalt go straight to Paradise.
Mustafa. 'Tis a fine place they say; but Doctor I am not
       worthy on't: I am contented with this homely World,
       'tis good enough for such a poor rascally Musulman as
215   I am: Besides I have learnt so much good manners,
       Doctor, as to let my Betters be serv'd before me.

Emperor. Thou talk'st as if the *Mufty* were concern'd.

Mustafa. Your Majesty may lay your Soul on't: but for my
part, though I am a plain Fellow, yet I scorn to be
trick'd into Paradise, I wou'd he shou'd know it. The   220
troth on't is an't like you, His reverence bought of me
the flower of all the Market; these ——— these are but
Dog's meat to 'em, and a round price he pay'd me too
I'll say that for him; but not enough for me to venture
my neck for: If I get Paradice when my time comes I   225
can't help my self; but I'll venture nothing before-hand,
upon a blind Bargain.

Emperor. Where are those Slaves? produce 'em.
One goes out to fetch them.

Mufti. They are not what he says.

Emperor. No more excuses. Know thou may'st better dally   230
With a dead Prophet, than a living King.

Mufti. I but reserv'd 'em to present thy Greatness
An Off'ring worthy thee.

Mustafa. By the same token there was a dainty Virgin,
(Virgin said I! but I won't be too positive of that   235
neither) with a roguish leering eye! he paid me down for
her upon the nail a thousand golden *Sultanins*; or he had
never had her I can tell him that: Now is it very likely
he would pay so dear for such a delicious Morsel, and
give it away out of his own mouth; when it had such   240
a farewel with it too?

Enter Sebastian *conducted in mean habit, with* Alvarez,
Antonio, *and* Almeyda: *her face veil'd with a* Barnus.

Emperor. Ay; These look like the Workmanship of Heav'n:
This is the porcelain clay of human kind,
And therefore cast into these noble moulds.
Dorax *aside while the Emperor whispers* Benducar.

Dorax. By all my wrongs   245
'Tis he: damnation seize me but 'tis he!
My heart heaves up and swells; he's poyson to me;
My injur'd honour, and my ravish'd love,
Bleed at their Murderer's sight.
Benducar *to* Dorax *aside.*

Benducar. The Emperor wou'd learn these Pris'ners names;   250
You know 'em?

Dorax. Tell him, no.

---

237 *Sultanins*] gold Turkish coins, valued at a little more than a
dollar.
241.2 *Barnus*] burnoose, a hooded cloak.

301

And trouble me no more. ——— (*aside*) I will not know
'em.
Shall I trust Heav'n, that Heav'n which I renounc'd,
255   With my revenge? then, where's my satisfaction?
No, it must be my own; I scorn a Proxy.
Emperor. 'Tis decreed,
These of a better aspect, with the rest
Shall share one common Doom, and Lots decide it.
260   For ev'ry number'd Captive put a ball
Into an Urn; three only black be there,
The rest, all white, are safe.
Mufti. Hold Sir, the Woman must not draw.
Emperor.   O *Mufti.*
We know your reason, let her share the danger.
265   *Mufti.* Our Law says plainly Women have no Souls.
Emperor. 'Tis true; their Souls are mortal, set her by:
Yet were *Almeyda* here, though Fame reports her
The fairest of her Sex, so much unseen,
I hate the Sister of our Rival House,
270   Ten thousand such dry Notions of our *Alcoran*
Shou'd not protect her life; if not Immortal:
Dye as she cou'd, all of a piece, the better,
That none of her remain.

> *Here an Urn is brought in: The Pris'ners approach with
> great concernment; and among the rest* Sebastian,
> Alvarez *and* Antonio; *who come more chearfully.*

Dorax (*aside*). Poor abject Creatures how they fear to dye!
275   These never knew one happy hour in life,
Yet shake to lay it down: is load so pleasant?
Or has Heav'n hid the happiness of Death
That Men may bear to live? ——— Now for our
Heroes.   *The three approach.*
O, these come up with Spirits more resolv'd!
280   Old venerable *Alvarez*, well I know him,
The Fav'rite once of this *Sebastian's* Father;
Now Minister; (too honest for his Trade)
Religion bears him out, a thing taught young,
In Age ill practis'd, yet his prop in Death.
285   O, he has drawn a black; and smiles upon't,
As who shou'd say my Faith and Soul are white
Tho my Lot swarthy: Now if there be hereafter
He's blest; if not, well cheated, and dyes pleas'd.
                    Antonio *holding his Lot in his clench'd hand.*
Antonio. Here I have thee,

Be what thou wilt: I will not look too soon.   290
Thou hast a colour; if thou prov'st not right,
I have a minute good ere I behold thee.
Now, Let me rowl, and grubble thee,
Blind Men say white feels smooth, and black feels rough;
Thou hast a rugged skin; I do not like thee.   295
Dorax. There's th'Amorous airy spark, *Antonio*;
The wittiest Woman's toy in *Portugal*.
Lord what a loss of Treats and Serenades!
The whole She Nation will b'in mourning for him.
Antonio. I've a moist sweaty palm; the more's my Sin;   300
If it be black, yet only dy'd, not odious
Damn'd Natural Ebony, there's hope in rubbing
To wash this Ethiope white. —— (*Looks*) Pox of the
     Proverb!
As black as Hell: another lucky saying!
I think the Devil's in me: —— good again,   305
I cannot speak one syllable, but tends
To Death or to Damnation.   *Holds up his ball.*
Dorax (*aside*). He looks uneasie at his future Journey:
And wishes his Boots off again; for fear
Of a bad Road, and a worse Inn at night.   310
Go to bed fool, and take secure repose
For thou shalt wake no more.
                    Sebastian *comes up to draw.*
Emperor (*to Benducar*). Mark him who now approaches to
     the Lott'ry,
He looks secure of Death, superior greatness,
Like *Jove* when he made Fate, and said thou art   315
The Slave of my Creation; I admire him.
Benducar. He looks as Man was made, with face erect,
That scorns his brittle Corps, and seems asham'd
He's not all spirit, his eyes with a dumb Pride,
Accusing Fortune that he fell not warm: 320
Yet now disdains to live.
                    Sebastian *draws a black.*
Emperor.   He has his wish;
And I have fail'd of mine!
Dorax (*aside*). Robb'd of my Vengeance, by a trivial
     chance!
Fine work above, that their anointed care
Shou'd dye such little Death: or did his Genius   325
Know mine the stronger *Demon*, fear'd the grapple,

293 *grubble*] feel blindly, grope; a new word.
300 *moist sweaty palm*] signifying an amorous nature.
303 *wash this Ethiope*] i.e., to labor in vain, a proverb (Tilley, E186).

303

And looking round him, found this nook of fate
To skulk behind my Sword; shall I discover him?
Still he wou'd dye not mine: no thanks to my
330   Revenge: reserv'd but to more royal shambles.
'Twere base too; and below those Vulgar Souls,
That shar'd his danger, yet not one disclos'd him:
But struck with Rev'rence kept an awful silence.
I'll see no more of this: Dog of a Prophet!
                                      Exit Dorax.

335   *Emperor.* One of these Three is a whole Hecatomb;
And therefore only one of 'em shall dye.
The Rest are but mute Cattle; and when Death
Comes, like a rushing Lion, couch like Spaniels,
With lolling tongues, and tremble at the paw,
340   Let Lots again decide it.

      The Three draw again: and the Lot falls on Sebastian.

Sebastian. Then there's no more to manage! if I fall
It shall be like my self; a setting Sun
Shou'd leave a track of Glory in the Skies.
Behold *Sebastian* King of *Portugal.*
345   *Emperor. Sebastian*! ha! it must be he; no other
Cou'd represent such suff'ring Majesty:
I saw him, as he terms himself, a Sun
Strugling in dark Eclipse, and shooting day
On either side of the black Orb that veil'd him.
350   *Sebastian.* Not less ev'n in this despicable now,
Than when my Name fill'd *Affrick* with affrights,
And froze your hearts beneath your torrid Zone.
Benducar (to Emperor). Extravagantly brave! ev'n to an
    Impudence
Of Greatness.
Sebastian.   Here satiate all your fury;
355   Let fortune empty her whole Quiver on me,
I have a Soul, that like an ample Shield
Can take in all; and verge enough for more.
I wou'd have conquer'd you; and ventur'd only
A narrow neck of Land for a third World;
360   To give my loosen'd Subjects room to play.
Fate was not mine,
Nor am I Fate's: Now I have pleas'd my longing,
And trod the ground which I beheld from far,
I beg no pity for this mouldring Clay:

330 *shambles*] carnage.
338 *couch*] lie in their dens.
357 *verge*] space, a new word in this sense.

Don Sebastian, Act I. Scene 1

For if you give it burial there it takes   365
  Possession of your Earth:
  If burnt and scatter'd in the air: the Winds
  That strow my dust, diffuse my royalty,
  And spread me o'er your Clime: for where one Atome
  Of mine shall light; know there *Sebastian* Reigns.   370
Emperor. What shall I do to conquer thee?
Sebastian.   Impossible!
  Souls know no Conquerors.
Emperor. I'll show thee for a Monster through my *Affrick.*
Sebastian. No thou canst only show me for a Man:
  Affrick is stor'd with Monsters; Man's a Prodigy   375
  Thy Subjects have not seen.
Emperor.   Thou talk'st as if
  Still at the head of Battel.
Sebastian.   Thou mistak'st,
  For then I would not talk.
Benducar.   Sure he wou'd sleep.
Sebastian. Till Dooms-day; when the Trumpet sounds to
    rise;
  For that's a Soldier's call.
Emperor.   Thou'rt brave too late: 380
  Thou shou'dst have dy'd in battel, like a Soldier.
Sebastian. I fought and fell like one, but Death deceiv'd
    me,
  I wanted weight of feeble *Moors* upon me,
  To crush my Soul out.
Emperor.   Still untameable!
  In what a ruine has thy head-strong Pride,   385
  And boundless thirst of Empire plung'd thy People.
Sebastian. What say'st thou, ha! No more of that.
Emperor.   Behold,
  What Carcases of thine thy Crimes has strew'd,
  And left our *Affric* Vultures to devour.
Benducar. Those Souls were those thy God intrusted with
    thee,   390
  To cherish not destroy.
Sebastian. Witness, O Heaven, how much
  This sight concerns me! Wou'd I had a Soul
  For each of these: How gladly wou'd I pay
  The Ransom down: But since I have but one,   395
  'Tis a King's life, and freely 'tis bestow'd.
  Not your false Prophet, but eternal Justice
  Has destin'd me the Lot, to dye for these:
  'Tis fit a Sovereign so shou'd pay such Subjects;
  For Subjects such as they are seldom seen,   400

305

Who not forsook me at my greatest need;
Nor for base lucre sold their Loyalty,
But shar'd my dangers to the last event,
And fenc'd 'em with their own: These thanks I pay you:
        Wipes his Eyes.
405 And know, that when *Sebastian* weeps, his Tears
Come harder than his Blood.
Emperor.   They plead too strongly
To be withstood: My Clouds are gath'ring too,
In kindly mixture with this Royal showr:
Be safe, and owe thy Life, not to my gift,
410 But to the greatness of thy mind, *Sebastian*:
Thy Subjects too shall live; a due reward
For their untainted Faith, in thy concealment.
        A general shout.
Mufti. Remember, Sir, your Vow.
Emperor.   Do thou remember
Thy Function, Mercy, and provoke not blood.
Muley-Zeydan (aside to Benducar). One of his generous Fits,
415 too strong to last.
Benducar (to him). The *Mufti* reddens, mark that holy
 Cheek.
He frets within, froths Treason at his mouth,
And churns it through his teeth; leave me to work him.
Sebastian. A mercy unexpected, undesir'd,
420 Surprizes more: You've learnt the art to vanquish:
You cou'd not (give me leave to tell you Sir)
Have giv'n me life but in my Subjects safety:
Kings, who are Fathers, live but in their People.
Emperor. Still great, and grateful, that's thy character.
425 Unveil the Woman; I wou'd view the Face
That warm'd our *Mufti's* Zeal:
These pious Parrots peck the fairest Fruit:
Such Tasters are for Kings.
     Officers go to Almeyda *to unveil her.*
Almeyda. Stand off ye Slaves, I will not be unveil'd.
Emperor. Slave is thy Title: Force her.
430 *Sebastian.*   On your lives,
 Approach her not.
Emperor. How's this!
Sebastian.   Sir pardon me,
 And hear me speak. ——
Almeyda.   Hear me; I will be heard:
I am no Slave; the noblest blood of *Affric*

428 *Tasters*] royal tasters, who tasted the king's food before it
came to his table.

Runs in my Veins; a purer stream than thine;
For, though deriv'd from the same Source, thy Current   435
Is puddl'd, and defil'd with Tyranny.
Emperor. What Female Fury have we here!
Almeyda.   I shou'd be one,
Because of kin to thee: Wou'dst thou be touch'd
By the presuming hands of sawcy Grooms?
The same respect, nay more, is due to me: 440
More for my Sex; the same for my descent.
These hands are only fit to draw the Curtain.
Now, if thou dar'st, behold *Almeyda's* face.
                                    Unveils her self.
Benducar (*aside*). Wou'd I had never seen it!
Almeyda. She whom thy *Mufti* tax'd to have no Soul;   445
Let *Affric* now be judg;
Perhaps thou think'st I meanly hope to 'scape,
As did *Sebastian* when he own'd his greatness.
But to remove that scruple know, base Man,
My murther'd Father, and my Brother's Ghost   450
Still haunt this Brest, and prompt it to revenge.
Think not I cou'd forgive nor dare thou pardon.
Emperor. Wou'dst thou revenge thee, Trait'ress, hadst thou
   pow'r?
Almeyda. Traitor, I wou'd; the Name's more justly thine:
Thy Father was not more than mine, the Heir   455
Of this large Empire; but with arms united
They fought their way, and seiz'd the Crown by force:
And equal as their danger was their share:
For where was Eldership, where none had right,
But that which Conquest gave? 'Twas thy ambition   460
Pull'd from my peaceful Father what his Sword
Help'd thine to gain: Surpriz'd him and his Kingdom,
No provocation given, no War declar'd.
Emperor. I'll hear no more.
Almeyda. This is the living Coal that burning in me   465
Wou'd flame to vengeance, cou'd it find a vent.
My Brother too, that lies yet scarcely cold
In his deep watry bed: My wandring Mother,
Who in exile died.
O that I had the fruitful Heads of *Hydra*,   470
That one might bourgeon where another fell!
Still wou'd I give thee work; still, still, thou Tyrant,
And hiss thee with the last.
Emperor. Something, I know not what, comes over me:
Whether the Toyls of Battel, unrepaird   475
With due repose, or other sudden qualm.

307

Benducar do the rest.

Goes off, the Court follows him.

Benducar. Strange; in full health! This pang is of the Soul;
The Body's unconcern'd: I'll think hereafter.

480   Conduct these Royal Captives to the Castle;
Bid *Dorax* use 'em well, till farther order.

Going off, stops.

The inferior Captives their first owners take,
To sell, or to dispose. ——— You, *Mustafa*,
Set ope the Market for the sale of Slaves.

Exit Benducar. [Sebastian *and* Almeyda *led off.*]

*The Masters and Slaves come forward, and Buyers of
several Qualities come in and chaffer about the several
Owners, who make their Slaves do Tricks.*

485   *Mustafa.* My Chattels are come into my hands again, and
my Conscience will serve me to sell 'em twice over;
any price now, before the *Mufti* comes to claim 'em.

1st Merchant (to Mustafa). What do'st hold that old Fellow
at? *Pointing to* Alvarez.

490   He's tough, and has no service in his limbs.

Mustafa. I confess he's somewhat tough; but I suppose you
wou'd not boyl him. I ask for him a thousand Crowns.

1st Merchant. Thou mean'st a thousand Marvedi's.

Mustafa. Prithee Friend, give me leave to know my own

495   meaning.

1st Merchant. What virtues has he to deserve that price?

Mustafa. Marry come up Sir! Virtues quoth a! I took
him in the King's Company; he's of a great Family,
and rich. What other Virtues wou'dst thou have in a

500   Noble-man?

1st Merchant. I buy him with another man's Purse, that's
my comfort.

My Lord *Dorax*, the Governor, will have him at any
rate:—

505   There's Handsel.

Come, old Fellow, to the Castle.

Alvarez (aside). To what is miserable Age reserv'd!
But oh the King! And oh the fatal Secret!
Which I have kept thus long, to time it better,

510   And now I wou'd disclose, 'tis past my pow'r.

Exit with his Master.

493 *Marvedi's*] Spanish coins of small worth.
505 *Handsel*] earnest money.

Mustafa. Something of a Secret, and of the King I heard
 him mutter: A Pimp I warrant him, for I am sure he is
 an old Courtier.
 Now to put off t'other remnant of my Merchan-
 dize, ———   515
 (*To* Antonio). Stir up, Sirrah.
Antonio. Dog, what wou'dst thou have!
Mustafa. Learn better manners, or I shall serve you a Dog-
 trick; come, down upon all four immediately;
 I'll make you know your Rider.   520
Antonio. Thou wilt not make a Horse of me?
Mustafa. Horse or Ass, that's as thy Mother made thee:
 ——— But take earnest in the first place for thy Sawcy-
 ness.   *Lashes him with his Whip.*
 Be advis'd Friend, and buckle to thy Geers: Behold my   525
 Ensign of Royalty display'd over thee.
Antonio. I hope one day to use thee worse in *Portugal.*
Mustafa. Ay, and good reason, Friend, if thou catchest me
 a conquering on thy side of the water, lay me on
 lustily, I'll take it as kindly as thou dost this. ———   530
                                              Holds up his Whip.
Antonio (*lying down*). Hold my dear Thrum-cap: I obey
 thee chearfully,
 I see the Doctrine of Non-Resistance is never practis'd
 thoroughly but when a Man can't help himself.

                Enter a Second Merchant.

2d Merchant. You, Friend, I wou'd see that Fellow do his   535
 Postures.
Mustafa. Now Sirrah follow, for you have rope enough:
                                         Bridling Antonio.
 To your paces Villain, amble, trot, and gallop: ———
 Quick, about there.— Yeap, the more Money's bidden
 for you, the more your credit.   540

Antonio *follows at the end of the Bridle on his hands and
              feet, and does all his Postures.*

2d Merchant. He's well chin'd, and has a tolerable good
 back; that's half in half. (*To* Mustafa) I wou'd see him
 strip, has he no Diseases about him?

518–19 *Dog-trick*] a low or scurvy trick.
525 *Geers*] harness of a riding horse.
531 *Thrum-cap*] a rough shaggy cap.
539 *Yeap*] possibly a variation on "hip," or "giddiap."
541 *chin'd*] with meat along the backbone.
542 *half in half*] half the total.

Mustafa. He's the best piece of Man's flesh in the Market,
545   not an Eye-sore in his whole body: Feel his Legs,
Master, neither Splint, Spavin, nor Wind-gall.

Claps him on the shoulder.

*Merchant feeling about him, and then putting his hand
to his side.*

2d Merchant. Out upon him, how his flank heaves! The
Whorson's broken-winded.

Mustafa. Thick breath'd a little: Nothing but a sorry cold
550   with lying out a nights in Trenches;—but sound Wind
and Limb, I warrant him.

Try him at a loose trot a little.

Puts the Bridle into his hand, he strokes him.

Antonio. For Heaven's sake Owner spare me; you know
I am but new broken.

555   *2d Merchant.* 'Tis but a washy Jade, I see: What do you ask
for this Bauble?

Mustafa. Bauble do you call him; he's a substantial true-
bred Beast; bravely forehanded; mark but the clean-
ness of his shapes too; his Dam may be a Spanish Gennet,
560   but a true Barb by the Sire, or I have no skill in Horse-
flesh. ———

Marry I ask Six Hundred Xeriffs for him.

Enter Mufti.

Mufti. What's that you are asking, Sirrah?

Mustafa. Marry, I ask your Reverence Six Hundred
565   Pardons; I was doing you a small piece of service here,
putting off your Chattel for you.

Mufti. And putting the Mony into your own Pocket.

Mustafa. Upon vulgar reputation, no my Lord, it was for
your profit and emolument. What, wrong the Head of
570   my Religion? I was sensible you wou'd have damn'd
me, or any man that shou'd have injur'd you in a single
Farthing; for I knew that was Sacrifice.

Mufti. Sacriledge you mean, Sirrah,—and damning shall
be the least part of your punishment; I have taken you
575   in the manner, and will have the Law upon you.

555 *washy*] weak.
558 *bravely forehanded*] has a good neck, chest, and shoulders.
559 *Gennet*] a small Spanish horse.
560 *Barb*] Barbary horse, noted for speed and endurance.
562 *Xeriffs*] coins formerly used in the Levant, valued at about
a dollar.
574–75 *taken you in the manner*] caught you in the act, or in
a habitual act(?).

Mustafa. Good my Lord, take pity upon a poor man in
this World, and damn me in the next.

Mufti. No Sirrah, so you may repent, and scape punishment: Did not you sell this very Slave amongst the rest
to me, and take Mony for him.   580

Mustafa. Right my Lord.

Mufti. And selling him again? Take Mony twice for the
same Commodity? Oh, Villain!
But did you not know him to be my Slave, Sirrah?

Mustafa. Why shou'd I lye to your Honor, I did know   585
him; and thereupon, seeing him wander about; I took
him up for a stray, and impounded him, with intention
to restore him to the right Owner.

Mufti. And yet at the same time was selling him to another:
How rarely the Story hangs together.   590

Mustafa. Patience, my Lord.
I took him up, as your Heriot, with intention to have
made the best of him, and then have brought the whole
product of him in a Purse to you; for I know you wou'd
have spent half of it upon your pious Pleasures, have   595
hoarded up the other half, and given the remainder in
Charities to the Poor.

Mufti. And what's become of my other Slave? Thou hast
sold him too I have a villainous suspicion.

Mustafa. I know you have, my Lord; but while I was   600
managing this young robustous Fellow, that old Spark
who was nothing but Skin and Bone, and by consequence, very nimble, slipt through my fingers like an
Eel, for there was no hold fast of him, and ran away to
buy himself a new Master.   605

Mufti (to Antonio). Follow me home, Sirrah: *(to Mustafa)* I
shall remember you some other time.

Exit Mufti *with* Antonio.

Mustafa. I never doubted your Lordship's memory, for an
ill turn: And I shall remember him too in the next rising
of the Mobile, for this act of Resumption; and more   610
especially for the Ghostly Counsel he gave me before
the Emperor, to have hang'd my self in silence, to have
sav'd his Reverence. The best on't is, I am beforehand
with him, for selling one of his Slaves twice over. ———

587 *stray*] Stray cattle were to be held and advertised in the market
place until the rightful owner claimed them.
   592 *Heriot*] the best beast given as a payment by a tenant to a feudal
lord.
   610 *Mobile*] mob.
   610 *Resumption*] recovering a gift, a royal prerogative.

615
And if he had not come just in the nick, I might have pocketed up t'other: For what should a poor Man do, that gets his living by hard labor, but pray for bad times when he may get it easily. O, for some incomparable Tumult! Then shou'd I naturally wish, that the

620
beaten Party might prevail, because we have plundered t'other side already, and there's nothing more to get of 'em.

Both rich and poor for their own interest pray, ⎫
'Tis ours to make our Fortunes while we may; ⎬
625
For Kingdoms are not conquer'd every day. ⎭

Exit Mustafa.

ACT II. Scene 1 ˙

Suppos'd to be a terrace Walk, on the side of the Castle of Alcazar.

[*Enter*] Emperor [Muley-Moloch *and*] Benducar.

Emperor. And thinkest thou not it was discovered?
Benducar.   No:
The thoughts of Kings are like religious Groves,
The Walks of muffled Gods: Sacred retreat,
Where none but whom they please t'admit, approach.
5
Emperor. Did not my conscious Eyes flash out a Flame
To lighten those brown horrors, and disclose
The secret path I trod?
Benducar. I cou'd not find it, 'till you lent a Clue
To that close Labarynth; how then shou'd they?
10
Emperor. I wou'd be loth they shou'd: it breeds contempt
For Herds to listen, or presume to pry,
When the hurt Lion groans within his Den:
But is 't not strange?
Benducar. To love? not more than 'tis to live; a Tax
15
Impos'd on all by Nature, paid in kind,
Familiar as our being.
Emperor.   Still 'tis strange
To me: I know my Soul as wild as winds,
That sweep the Desarts of our moving Plains;
Love might as well be sow'd upon our Sands,
20
As in a brest so barren:
To love an Enemy, the only One
Remaining too, whom yester Sun beheld,
Must'ring her charms, and rolling as she past
By every Squadron her alluring eyes:

To edge her Champions Swords, and urge my ruin.   25
The shouts of Soldiers, and the burst of Cannon,
Maintain ev'n still a deaf and murm'ring noise;
Nor is Heav'n yet recover'd of the sound
Her Battel rows'd: Yet spight of me I love.
Benducar. What then controuls you?   30
  Her Person is as prostrate as her Party.
Emperor. A thousand things controul this Conqueror,
  My native pride to own th'unworthy passion,
  Hazard of Int'rest, and my People's love:
  To what a Storm of Fate am I expos'd!   35
  What if I had her murder'd? 'tis but what
  My Subjects all expect, and she deserves.
  Wou'd not th'impossibility
  Of ever, ever seeing, or possessing,
  Calm all this rage, this Hurrican of Soul?   40
Benducar. That ever, ever,
  I mark'd the double, shows extream reluctance
  To part with her for ever.
Emperor.   Right, thou hast me,
  I wou'd, but cannot kill: I must enjoy her:
  I must, and what I must be sure I will.   45
  What's Royalty but pow'r to please my self?
  And if I dare not, then am I the Slave,
  And my own Slaves the Sovereigns, ——— 'tis resolv'd,
  Weak Princes flatter when they want the pow'r
  To curb their People; tender Plants must bend,   50
  But when a Government is grown to strength,
  Like some old Oak, rough with its armed Bark,
  It yields not to the tug, but only nods,
  And turns to sullen State.
Benducar.   Then you resolve
  T'implore her pity, and to beg relief?   55
Emperor. Death, must I beg the pity of my Slave?
  Must a King beg? Yes, Love's a greater King;
  A Tyrant, nay a Devil that possesses me:
  He tunes the Organs of my voice, and speaks
  Unknown to me within me; pushes me,   60
  And drives me on by force. ———
  Say I shou'd wed her, wou'd not my wise Subjects
  Take check, and think it strange? perhaps revolt?
Benducar. I hope they wou'd not.
Emperor. Then thou doubt'st they wou'd?
Benducar.   To whom?

54 *sullen*] solemn.

65

Emperor.   To her
    Perhaps, or to my Brother, or to Thee.
Benducar (in disorder). To me! me did you mention? how I
    tremble!
    The name of Treason shakes my honest Soul.
    If I am doubted, Sir,

70

    Secure your self this moment, take my life.
Emperor. No more: if I suspected thee—I wou'd.
Benducar (aside). I thank your kindness: Guilt had almost
    lost me!
Emperor. But clear my doubts: think'st thou they may rebel?
Benducar (aside). This goes as I wou'd wish:—(to th'Emperor)
    'Tis possible.

75

    A secret Party still remains, that lurks
    Like Embers rak'd in ashes—wanting but
    A breath to blow aside th'involving dust,
    And then they blaze abroad.
Emperor. They must be trampled out.
Benducar.   But first be known.

80

Emperor. Torture shall force it from 'em.
Benducar. You wou'd not put a Nation to the rack?
Emperor. Yes, the whole World; so I be safe, I care not.
Benducar. Our Limbs and Lives
    Are yours, but mixing Friends with Foes is hard.
Emperor. All may be foes; or how to be distinguish'd,

85

    If some be friends?
Benducar.   They may with ease be winnow'd:
    Suppose some one, who has deserv'd your trust,
    Some one who knows Mankind, shou'd be employ'd
    To mix among 'em, seem a Malcontent,

90

    And dive into their breasts, to try how far
    They dare oppose your love?
Emperor. I like this well: 'Tis wholesom wickedness.
Benducar. Whomever he suspects, he fastens there,
    And leaves no cranny of his Soul unsearch'd:

95

    Then, like a Bee bag'd with his honey'd venome,
    He brings it to your Hive: if such a Man
    So able, and so honest, may be found;
    If not, my project dyes. ———
Emperor. By all my hopes thou hast describ'd thy self:—

100

    Thou, thou alone art fit to play that Engine,
    Thou only cou'dst contrive.
Benducar.   Sure I cou'd serve you:
    I think I cou'd: ——— but here's the difficulty,

77 *involving*] surrounding.

I'm so entirely yours,
That I shou'd scurvily dissemble hate;
The cheat wou'd be too gross.
Emperor.   Art thou a Statesman   105
And canst not be a Hypocrite? Impossible:
Do not distrust thy Vertues.
Benducar. If I must personate this seeming Villain,
Remember 'tis to serve you.
Emperor.   No more words:
Love goads me to *Almeyda*, all affairs   110
Are troublesom but that; and yet that most.
Bid *Dorax* treat *Sebastian* like a King;   *Going.*
I had forgot him;—but this Love marrs all,
And takes up my whole brest.   *Exit* Emperor.
Benducar (to the Emperor).   Be sure I'll tell him. ——
With all the aggravating Circumstances   *Alone.*   115
I can, to make him swell at that Command.
The Tyrant first suspected me:
Then, with a sudden gust, he whirld about,
And trusted me too far: Madness of Pow'r!
Now, by his own consent, I ruin him.   120
For, shou'd some feeble Soul, for fear or gain
Bolt out t'accuse me, ev'n the King is cozen'd,
And thinks he's in the secret.
How sweet is Treason when the Traytor's safe!

Sees the Mufti *and* Dorax *entring and seeming to confer.*

The *Mufti*, and with him my sullen *Dorax*,   125
That first is mine already.
'Twas easie work to gain a cov'tous mind,
Whom rage to loose his Pris'ners had prepar'd:
Now, caught himself,
He wou'd seduce another; I must help him: 130
For Church-men, though they itch to govern all,
Are silly, woful, awkard Politicians;
They make lame mischief, though they mean it well:
Their Int'rest is not finely drawn, and hid,
But seams are coarsly bungled up, and seen.   135
Mufti. He'll tell you more.
Dorax.   I've heard enough already
To make me loath thy Morals.
Benducar (to Dorax).   You seem warm:
The good Man's zeal, perhaps has gon too far.
Dorax. Not very far; not farther than zeal goes

---

135 *bungled up*] made unskillfully.

315

140   Of course; a small day's journey short of Treason.
        Mufti. By all that's Holy, Treason was not nam'd:
        I spar'd the Emperor's broken Vows to save
        The Slaves from Death; though it was cheating Heav'n,
        But I forgave him that.
        Dorax (scornfully).   And slighted o'er
145   The wrongs himself sustain'd in property:
        When his bought Slaves were seiz'd by force, no loss
        Of his consider'd, and no cost repaid.
        Mufti. Not wholly slighted o'er, not absolutely:
        Some modest hints of private wrongs I urg'd.
150   *Dorax.* Two thirds of all he said: there he began;
        To shew the fulness of his heart, there ended:
        Some short excursions of a broken Vow,
        He made indeed, but flat insipid stuff:
        But when he made his loss the Theme, he flourish'd,
155   Reliev'd his fainting Rhetorick with new Figures,
        And thunder'd at oppressing Tyranny.
        Mufti. Why not, when Sacrilegious Pow'r wou'd seize
        My Property, 'tis an affront to Heav'n,
        Whose Person, though unworthy, I sustain.
160   *Dorax.* You've made such strong Alliances above,
        That 'twere Profaneness in us Laiety
        To offer earthly Aid.
        I tell thee, *Mufti,* if the World were wise,
        They wou'd not wag one finger in your quarrels.
165   Your Heav'n you promise, but our Earth you covet.
        The Phaethons of mankind, who fire that World,
        Which you were sent by Preaching but to warm.
        Benducar. This goes beyond the mark.
        Mufti.   No, let him rail;
        His Prophet works within him;
        He's a rare Convert.
170   *Dorax.*   Now his Zeal yearns,
        To see me burnt; he damns me from his Church,
        Because I wou'd restrain him to his Duty;
        Is not the care of Souls a load sufficient?
        Are not your holy stipends pay'd for this?
175   Were you not bred apart from worldly noise,
        To study Souls, their Cures and their Diseases?
        If this be so, we ask you but our own:
        Give us your whole Employment, all your care:
        The Province of the Soul is large enough
180   To fill up every Cranny of your time,
        And leave you much to answer, if one Wretch
        Be damn'd by your neglect.

Benducar (to the Mufti).   He speaks but reason.
Dorax. Why then these forein thoughts of State-Employ-
       ments,
   Abhorrent to your Function and your Breeding?
   Poor droaning Truants of unpractis'd Cells,   185
   Bred in the Fellowship of bearded Boys,
   What wonder is it if you know not Men?
   Yet there, you live demure, with down-cast Eyes,
   And humble as your Discipline requires:
   But, when let loose from thence to live at large,   190
   Your little tincture of Devotion dies:
   Then Luxury succeeds, and set agog
   With a new Scene of yet untasted Joys,
   You fall with greedy hunger to the Feast.
   Of all your College Vertues, nothing now   195
   But your Original Ignorance remains:
   Bloated with Pride, Ambition, Avarice,
   You swell, to counsel Kings and govern Kingdoms.
Mufti. He prates as if Kings had not Consciences,
   And none requir'd Directors but the Crowd.   200
Dorax. As private men they want you, not as Kings;
   Nor wou'd you care t'inspect their publick Conscience,
   But that it draws dependencies of Pow'r,
   And Earthly Interest which you long to sway.
   Content you with monopolizing Heav'n,   205
   And let this little hanging Ball alone;
   For give you but a foot of Conscience there,
   And you, like *Archimedes,* toss the Globe.
   We know your thoughts of us that Laymen are:
   Lag Souls, and rubbish of remaining Clay,   210
   Which Heav'n, grown weary of more perfect work,
   Set upright with a little puff of breath,
   And bid us pass for Men.
Mufti.   I will not answer,
   Base foul mouth'd Renegade; but I'll pray for thee
   To shew my Charity.   *Exit* Mufti.   215
Dorax. Do; but forget not him who needs it most:
   Allow thy self some share: He's gone too soon;
   I had to tell him of his holy jugglings;
   Things that wou'd startle Faith, and make us deem
   Not this or that, but all Religions false.   220
Benducar (aside). Our Holy Oratour has lost the Cause:
   But I shall yet redeem it.—*(to Dorax)* Let him go;
   For I have secret Orders from the Emperour,

195 *College*] cloistered and clerical.
210 *Lag*] of the lowest class.

Which none but you must hear: I must confess
225   I cou'd have wish'd some other hand had brought 'em.
When did you see your Pris'ner Great *Sebastian*?
Dorax. You might as well have ask'd me when I saw
A crested Dragon, or a Basilisk;
Both are less Poison to my Eyes and Nature.
230   He knows not I am I; nor shall he see me
Till time has perfected a lab'ring thought,
That rouls within my brest.
Benducar.   'Twas my mistake:
I guess'd indeed that time, and his misfortunes,
And your returning duty had effac'd
235   The mem'ry of past wrongs; they wou'd in me;
And I judg'd you as tame and as forgiving.
Dorax. Forgive him! no, I left my foolish Faith
Because it wou'd oblige me to forgiveness.
Benducar. I can but grieve to find you obstinate:
240   For you must see him; 'tis our Emp'rour's will,
And strict Command.
Dorax.   I laugh at that Command.
Benducar. You must do more than see; serve, and respect
     him.
Dorax. See, serve him, and respect, and after all
My yet uncancell'd wrongs, I must do this!
But I forget my self.
245 *Benducar.*   Indeed you do.
Dorax. The Emp'rour is a stranger to my wrongs;
I need but tell my story, to revoke
This hard Commission.
Benducar.   Can you call me Friend,
And think I cou'd neglect to speak, at full,
250   Th'Affronts you had from your ungrateful Master?
Dorax. And yet enjoyn'd my Service, and Attendance?
Benducar. And yet enjoyn'd 'em both: wou'd that were all;
He scru'd his Face into a harden'd smile,
And said, *Sebastian* knew to govern Slaves.
255 *Dorax.* Slaves are the growth of *Africk*, not of *Europe*:
By Heav'n I will not lay down my Commission;
Not at his foot, I will not stoop so low;
But if there be a part in all his Face
More sacred than the rest, I'll throw it there.
260 *Benducar.* You may; but then you lose all future means
Of Vengeance on *Sebastian*, when no more
Alcalde of this Fort.
Dorax.   That thought escap'd me.
Benducar. Keep your Command; and be reveng'd on both:

Nor sooth your self; you have no pow'r t'affront him:
The Emp'rour's love protects him from insults.   265
And he, who spoke that proud ill-natur'd word,
Following the bent of his impetuous temper,
May force your reconcilement to *Sebastian*:
Nay bid you kneel, and kiss th'offending foot,
That kick'd you from his Presence.   270
But think not to divide their punishment;
You cannot touch a hair of loath'd *Sebastian*,
While *Muley-Moluch* lives.
Dorax.   What means this Riddle?
Benducar. 'Tis out: there needs no *Oedipus* to solve it.
Our Emp'rour is a Tyrant, fear'd and hated;   275
I scarce remember in his Reign, one day
Pass guiltless o'er his execrable head.
He thinks the Sun is lost that sees not bloud:
When none is shed we count it Holiday.
We, who are most in favour, cannot call   280
This hour our own! ——— you know the younger
    Brother,
Mild *Muley Zeydan* ———
Dorax.   Hold and let me think.
Benducar. The Soldiers Idolize you,
He trusts you with the Castle,
The Key of all his Kingdom.   285
Dorax. Well; and he trusts you too.
Benducar.   Else I were mad,
To hazard such a daring Enterprize.
Dorax. He trusts us both; mark that, shall we betray him?
A Master who reposes Life and Empire
On our fidelity: I grant he is a Tyrant,   290
That hated name my nature most abhors;
More, as you say, has loaded me with scorn:
Ev'n with the last contempt, to serve *Sebastian*.
Yet more, I know he vacates my revenge;
Which, but by this revolt I cannot compass: 295
But, while he trusts me, 'twere so base a part
To fawn and yet betray, I shou'd be hiss'd
And whoop'd in Hell for that Ingratitude.
Benducar. Consider well what I have done for you.
Dorax. Consider thou what thou woud'st have me do.   300
Benducar. You've too much honour for a Renegade.
Dorax. And thou too little faith to be a Fav'rite.
Is not the bread thou eat'st, the Robe thou wear'st,

294 *vacates*] renders it inoperative.
298 *whoop'd*] hooted at.

Thy Wealth, and Honours, all the pure indulgence
305   Of him thou wou'dst destroy?
And wou'd his Creature, nay his Friend betray him?
Why then no Bond is left on human kind:
Distrusts, debates, immortal strifes ensue;
Children may murder Parents, Wives their Husbands;
310   All must be Rapine, Wars, and Desolation,
When trust and gratitude no longer bind.
   Benducar. Well have you argued in your own defence:
You, who have burst asunder all those bonds,
And turn'd a Rebel to your Native Prince.
315   *Dorax.* True, I rebell'd: but when did I betray?
Indignities, which Man cou'd not support,
Provok'd my vengeance to this noble Crime.
But he had strip'd me first of my Command,
Dismiss'd my Service, and absolv'd my Faith;
320   And, with disdainful Language, dar'd my worst.
I but accepted War, which he denounc'd.
Else had you seen, not *Dorax,* but *Alonzo,*
With his couch'd Lance against your foremost *Moors:*
Perhaps too turn'd the fortune of the day;
325   Made *Affrick* mourn, and *Portugal* triumph.
   Benducar. Let me embrace thee.
   Dorax.   Stand off Sycophant,
And keep Infection distant.
   Benducar.   Brave and honest.
   Dorax. In spight of thy Temptations.
   Benducar.   Call 'em Trials:
They were no more: thy faith was held in Balance,
330   And nicely weigh'd by jealousie of Pow'r;
Vast was the trust of such a Royal Charge;
And our wise Emperour, might justly fear
Sebastian might be freed and reconcil'd,
By new Obligements to thy former love.
335   *Dorax.* I doubt thee still; thy reasons were too strong,
And driv'n too near the head, to be but Artifice.
And after all, I know thou art a Statesman,
Where truth is rarely found.
   Benducar.   Behold the Emperour;

Enter Emperor, Sebastian *and* Almeyda.

Ask him, I beg thee, to be justify'd,
340   If he employ'd me not to foord thy Soul,

322 *not Dorax, but Alonzo*] i.e., he would have been a faithful follower of Sebastian, under his former name, Alonzo.
323 *couch'd*] lowered into the position of attack.

And try the footing whether false or firm.
Dorax. Death to my Eyes, I see *Sebastian* with him!
  Must he be serv'd! avoid him, if we meet,
  It must be like the crush of Heav'n and Earth,
  T'involve us both in ruin.   *Exit* Dorax.   345
Benducar. 'Twas a bare saving game I made with *Dorax,*
  But better so than lost; he cannot hurt me,
  That I precaution'd: I must ruin him.
  But now this Love; Ay, there's the gath'ring storm!
  The Tyrant must not wed *Almeyda*; no,   350
  That ruins all the Fabrick I am raising.
  Yet seeming to approve it, gave me time,
  And gaining time gains all.

         Benducar *goes and waits behind the* Emperour.
    The Emperour; Sebastian *and* Almeyda *advance to the*
          front of the Stage. Guards and Attendants.

Emperor (to Sebastian). I bad 'em serve you, and if they obey
    not,
  I keep my Lions keen within their Dens,   355
  To stop their maws with disobedient Slaves.
Sebastian. If I had Conquer'd,
  They cou'd not have with more observance waited:
  Their eyes, hands, feet,
  Are all so quick they seem t'have but one motion,   360
  To catch my flying words. Onely the *Alcayde*
  Shuns me, and with a grim Civility,
  Bows, and declines my Walks.
Emperor.   A Renegade:
  I know not more of him: but that he's brave,
  And hates your Christian Sect. If you can frame   365
  A farther wish, give wing to your desires,
  And name the thing you want.
Sebastian.   My Liberty:
  For were ev'n Paradise it self my Prison,
  Still I shou'd long to leap the Chrystal walls.
Emperor. Sure our two Souls have somewhere been
    acquainted   370
  In former beings; or, struck out together,
  One spark to *Africk* flew, and one to *Portugal.*
  Expect a quick deliverance: *(turning to Almeyda)* here's a
    third,

346 *bare saving game*] not turning to loss though not gainful (Dr.
Johnson's *Dictionary*); in gambling, to set part of a bet against another,
to hedge (Farmer).
355 *keen*] savage.

Of kindred Soul to both: pity our Stars
375 Have made us Foes! I shou'd not wish her death.
Almeyda. I ask no pity; if I thought my Soul
Of kin to thine, soon wou'd I rend my heart-strings,
And tear out that Alliance: but thou Viper
Hast cancell'd kindred, made a rent in Nature,
380 And through her holy bowels gnaw'd thy way,
Through thy own Bloud to Empire.
Emperor. This again: ———
And yet she lives; and only lives t'upbraid me.
Sebastian. What honour is there in a Woman's death!
Wrong'd as she says, but helpless to revenge;
385 Strong in her Passion, impotent of Reason,
Too weak to hurt, too fair to be destroy'd.
Mark her Majestick Fabrick; She's a Temple
Sacred by birth, and built by Hands Divine;
Her Soul's the Deity, that lodges there:
390 Nor is the Pile unworthy of the God.
Emperor. She's all that thou canst say or I can think.
But the perverseness of her clam'rous Tongue
Strikes Pity deaf.
Sebastian. Then onely hear her Eyes;
Though they are mute they plead; nay more, command;
395 For beauteous Eyes have Arbitrary Power.
All Females have prerogative of Sex,
The Shes ev'n of the salvage herd are safe;
And when they snarl or bite, have no return
But Courtship from the Male.
400 *Emperor.* Were She not She, and I not *Muley-Moluch*,
She's Mistress of unevitable Charms,
For all but me; nor am I so exempt,
But that—I know not what I was to say—
But I am too obnoxious to my Friends;
And sway'd by your Advice.
405 *Sebastian.* Sir, I advis'd not.
By Heav'n, I never counsell'd Love but Pity.
Emperor. By Heav'n thou didst: deny it not, thou didst:
For what was all that Prodigality
Of praise, but to enflame me? ———
Sebastian. Sir, ———
Emperor. No more:
410 Thou hast convinc'd me, that she's worth my Love.
Sebastian (aside). Was ever Man so ruin'd by himself!

397 *salvage*] savage.
401 *unevitable*] inevitable.
404 *obnoxious*] exposed to the influence of.

Almeyda. Thy Love; that odious Mouth was never fram'd
　To speak a word so soft:
　Name Death again, for that thou canst pronounce
　With horrid grace, becoming of a Tyrant.　　　　　　　415
　Love is for human hearts, and not for thine,
　Where the brute Beast extinguishes the Man.
Emperor. Such if I were, yet rugged Lions love,
　And grapple, and compel their savage Dames.———
　　　　　　　　　　　　　　　　　She frowns.
　Mark my *Sebastian*, how that sullen frown,　　　　　　420
　Like flashing Lightning, opens angry Heaven;
　And while it kills, delights. But yet, insult not
　Too soon, proud Beauty, I confess no love.
Sebastian. No Sir, I said so, and I witness for you;
　Not love, but noble pity mov'd your mind:　　　　　　425
　Int'rest might urge you too to save her life;
　For those who wish her party lost, might murmur
　At shedding Royal Blood.
Emperor.　　　　　　　Right, thou instruct'st me;
　Int'rest of State requires not Death, but Marriage;
　T'unite the jarring Titles of our Line.　　　　　　　430
Sebastian (aside). Let me be dumb for ever, all I plead,
　Like Wild-fire thrown against the Wind, returns
　With double force to burn me.
Emperor. Cou'd I but bend to make my beauteous Foe
　The Partner of my Throne, and of my Bed ———　　435
Almeyda. Still thou dissemblest, but I read thy heart,
　And know the power of my own Charms; thou lov'st,
　And I am pleas'd for my revenge thou dost.
Emperor. And thou hast cause.
Almeyda. I have; for I have pow'r to make thee wretched.　440
　Be sure I will, and yet despair of freedom.
Emperor. Well then, I love, ———
　And 'tis below my greatness to disown it:
　Love thee implacably, yet hate thee too;
　Wou'd hunt thee bare-foot, in the mid-day Sun,　　　445
　Through the parch'd Desarts, and the scorching Sands,
　T'enjoy thy Love, and once enjoy'd to kill thee.
Almeyda. 'Tis a false Courage, when thou threat'nest me;
　Thou canst not stir a hand to touch my Life:
　Do not I see thee tremble while thou speak'st?　　　450
　Lay by the Lion's Hide, vain Conqueror,
　And take the Distaff; for thy Soul's my Slave.
Emperor. Confusion! How thou viewest my very Heart!

451 *Lion's Hide*] as Hercules did when he was a prisoner of love to
Omphale.

455

I cou'd as soon,
Stop a Spring-tide, blown in, with my bare hand,
As this impetuous Love: ——— Yes, I will wed thee;
In spight of thee, and of my self, I will.

Almeyda. For what? To people *Affric* with new Monsters,
Which that unnatural mixture must produce?

460

No, were we joyn'd, e'vn tho it were in death,
Our Bodies burning in one Funeral Pile,
The Prodigy of *Thebes* wou'd be renew'd,
And my divided flame shou'd break from thine.

Emperor. Serpent, I will engender Poyson with thee;

465

Joyn Hate with Hate, add Venom to the birth;
Our Off-spring, like the seed of Dragons Teeth,
Shall issue arm'd, and fight themselves to death.

Almeyda. I'm calm again; thou canst not marry me.

Emperor. As gleams of Sun-shine soften storms to show'rs,

470

So, if you smile, the loudness of my rage
In gentle Whispers shall return, but this, ———
That nothing can divert my Love, but Death.

Almeyda. See how thou art deceiv'd, I am a *Christian*;
'Tis true, unpractis'd in my new Belief,

475

Wrongs I resent, nor pardon yet with ease:
Those Fruits come late, and are of slow increase
In haughty Hearts, like mine: Now, tell thy self
If this one word destroy not thy designs:
Thy Law permits thee not to marry me.

480

Emperor. 'Tis but a specious Tale, to blast my hopes,
And baffle my pretensions. Speak, *Sebastian,*
And, as a King, speak true.

Sebastian.   Then, thus adjur'd,
On a King's word 'tis truth, but truth ill tim'd;
For her dear Life is now expos'd anew;

485

Unless you wholly can put on Divinity,
And graciously forgive.

Almeyda.   Now learn by this,
The little value I have left for life,
And trouble me no more.

Emperor.   I thank thee Woman;

462 *Prodigy of Thebes*] When the bodies of Polynices and Eteocles were placed upon one funeral pyre, the flames divided and blazed separately; for as the two brothers had been enemies in life, so they were also separated in death (Summers).

466 *seed of Dragons Teeth*] Since this alludes to Ovid's tale of Cadmus, Addison objected that "The Emperor of *Barbary* shows himself acquainted with the *Roman* Poets as well as either of his Prisoners ... Ovid seems to have been Muley Molock's Favorite Author." *The Guardian,* no. 110, Friday, July 17, 1713.

Thou hast restor'd me to my native Rage;
And I will seize my happiness by force.   490
Sebastian. Know *Muley-Moluch* when thou dar'st attempt—
Emperor. Beware, I wou'd not be provok'd to use
  A Conqueror's right, and therefore charge thy silence.
  If thou wou'dst merit to be thought my Friend,
  I leave thee to perswade her to compliance: 495
  If not, there's a new gust in Ravishment,
  Which I have never try'd.
Benducar (*aside*).   They must be watch'd;
  For something I observ'd creates a doubt.
                   Exeunt Emperour *and* Benducar.
Sebastian. I've been too tame, have basely born my
    Wrongs,
  And not exerted all the King, within me;   500
  I heard him, O sweet Heavens, he threat'ned Rape;
  Nay insolently urg'd me to perswade thee,
  Ev'n thee, thou Idol of my Soul and Eyes;
  For whom I suffer Life, and drag this being.
Almeyda. You turn my Prison to a Paradise;   505
  But I have turn'd your Empire to a Prison:
  In all your Wars good fortune flew before you;
  Sublime you sate in Triumph on her Wheel;
  Till in my fatal Cause your Sword was drawn;
  The weight of my misfortunes drag'd you down.   510
Sebastian. And is't not strange, that Heav'n shou'd bless
    my Arms
  In common Causes, and desert the best?
  Now in your greatest, last extremity,
  When I wou'd ayd you most, and most desire it,
  I bring but Sighs, the succors of a Slave.   515
Almeyda. Leave then the luggage of your fate behind,
  To make your flight more easie, leave *Almeyda.*
  Nor think me left a base ignoble Prey,
  Expos'd to this inhuman Tyrant's lust;
  My Virtue is a guard beyond my strength,   520
  And Death, my last defence, within my call.
Sebastian. Death may be call'd in vain, and cannot come;
  Tyrants can tye him up from your relief:
  Nor has a Christian privilege to dye.
  Alas thou art too young in thy new Faith;   525
  Brutus and *Cato* might discharge their Souls,
  And give 'em Furlo's for another World:

---

498 *something I observ'd*] see III.i.30.
527 *Furlo's*] i.e., furloughs, passports.

But we, like Centry's, are oblig'd to stand
In starless Nights, and wait the pointed hour.
530 *Almeyda.* If shunning ill be good, then Death is good
To those who cannot shun it but by Death:
Divines but peep on undiscover'd Worlds,
And draw the distant Landshape as they please:
But who has e'er return'd from those bright Regions,
535 To tell their Manners, and relate their Laws?
I'll venture landing on that happy shoar
With an unsully'd Body, and white Mind;
If I have err'd, some kind Inhabitant
Will pity a stray'd Soul, and take me home.
540 *Sebastian.* Beware of Death, thou canst not dye unperjur'd,
And leave an unaccomplish'd Love behind:
Thy Vows are mine; nor will I quit my claim:
The tye of Minds are but imperfect Bonds,
Unless the Bodies joyn to seal the Contract.
545 *Almeyda.* What Joys can you possess or can I give?
Where groans of Death succeed the sighs of Love.
Our Hymen has not on his Saffron Robe;
But muffled up in Mourning, downward holds
His dropping Torch, extinguish'd with his Tears.
550 *Sebastian.* The God of Love stands ready to revive it
With his etherial breath.
Almeyda. 'Tis late to joyn, when we must part so soon.
Sebastian. Nay rather let us haste it, ere we part:
Our Souls, for want of that acquaintance here,
555 May wander in the starry Walks above,
And, forc'd on worse Companions, miss our selves.
Almeyda. The Tyrant will not long be absent hence;
And soon I shall be ravish'd from your arms.
Sebastian. Wilt thou thy self become the greater Tyrant,
560 And give not Love, while thou hast Love to give?
In dang'rous days, when Riches are a Crime,
The wise betimes make over their Estates:
Make o'er thy Honour, by a deed of trust,
And give me seizure of the mighty wealth.
565 *Almeyda.* What shall I do! O teach me to refuse!
I wou'd; and yet I tremble at the grant.
For dire presages fright my Soul by day,
And boding Visions haunt my Nightly Dreams:
Sometimes, methinks, I hear the groans of Ghosts;
570 Thin, hollow sounds, and lamentable screams;

533 *Landshape*] i.e., landscape.
547 *Saffron*] Hymen is so described by Ovid, *Metamorphoses*,
X.i, possibly because saffron is used in love potions.

Then, like a dying Eccho, from afar,
My Mother's Voice, that cries, Wed not *Almeyda*!
Forewarn'd *Almeyda*, Marriage is thy Crime.
Sebastian. Some envious *Demon*, to delude our joys;
   Love is not Sin, but where 'tis sinful Love.   575
Almeyda. Mine is a flame so holy, and so clear,
   That the white taper leaves no soot behind;
   No smoak of Lust; but chast as Sisters love,
   When coldly they return a Brother's kiss,
   Without the zeal that meets at lovers mouths.   580
Sebastian. Laugh then at fond presages; I had some;
   Famed *Nostradamus*, when he took my Horoscope,
   Foretold my Father I shou'd wed with Incest:
   Ere this unhappy War my Mother dy'd;
   And Sisters I had none; vain Augury!   585
   A long Religious Life, a Holy Age,
   My Stars assign'd me too; impossible.
   For how can Incest suit with Holiness,
   Or Priestly Orders with a Princely State?
Almeyda (sighing). Old venerable *Alvarez*! ———   590
Sebastian. But why that sigh in naming that good Man?
Almeyda. Your Father's Counsellor and Confident ———
Sebastian. He was; and, if he lives, my second Father.
Almeyda. Mark'd our farewel, when going to the fight,
   You gave *Almeyda* for the word of Battel;   595
   'Twas in that fatal Moment, he discover'd
   The Love that long we labour'd to conceal.
   I know it; though my eyes stood full of tears,
   Yet, through the mist, I saw him stedfast gaze:
   Then knock'd his Aged breast, and inward groan'd;   600
   Like some sad Prophet, that foresaw the doom
   Of those whom best he lov'd, and cou'd not save.
Sebastian. It startles me! and brings to my remembrance,
   That, when the shock of Battel was begun,
   He wou'd have much complain'd (but had not time)   605
   Of our hid passion; then, with lifted hands,
   He beg'd me by my Father's Sacred Soul,
   Not to espouse you, if he dy'd in fight:
   For if he liv'd, and we were Conquerors,
   He had such things to urge against our Marriage,   610
   As, now declar'd, wou'd blunt my sword in Battel;
   And dastardize my Courage.

582 *Nostradamus*] astrologer, after Michel de Nostredame (1503–66),
the French physician famous for his prophecies.
  612 *dastardize*] terrify, cow.

Almeyda.   My blood cruddles;
And cakes about my heart.
Sebastian. I'll breath a sigh, so warm into thy bosom,
615   Shall make it flow again. My Love, he knows not
Thou art a *Christian*; that produc'd his fear:
Lest thou shoud'st sooth my Soul with charms so strong,
That Heav'n might prove too weak.
Almeyda.   There must be more:
This cou'd not blunt your Sword.
620   *Sebastian.* Yes, if I drew it, with a curst intent,
To take a Misbeliever to my Bed;
It must be so.
Almeyda.   Yet ———
Sebastian.   No, thou shalt not plead
With that fair mouth, against the Cause of Love.
Within this Castle is a Captive Priest,
625   My Holy Confessor, whose free access
Not ev'n the barb'rous Victors have refus'd;
This happy hour his hands shall make us one.
Almeyda. I go; with Love and Fortune, two blind Guides,
To lead my way: half loth and half consenting.
630   If, as my Soul fore-bodes, some dire event
Pursue this Union, or some Crime unknown,
Forgive me Heav'n; and all ye Blest above,
Excuse the frailty of unbounded Love.
                                        Exeunt Ambo.

[ACT II.] Scene 2

*Suppos'd a Garden; with Lodging Rooms behind it;
or on the sides.*

Enter Mufti; Antonio *as a Slave; and* Johayma *the
Mufti's Wife.*

Mufti. And how do you like him, look upon him well;
he's a personable Fellow of a Christian Dog. Now I
think you are fitted, for a Gardiner: Ha what say'st thou
Johayma?
5   *Johayma.* He may make a shift to sow lettice, raise Melons,
and water a Garden plat.
But otherwise a very filthy Fellow; how odiously he

612 *cruddles*] curdles.
3 *Gardiner*] Since a garden was a conventional metaphor for
the female pudendum, the "gardener" became the male, and in-
tercourse was "greens" (Farmer). See Shakespeare's Sonnet 16, "Now
stand you on the top of happy hours, / And many maiden gardens,
yet unset, / With virtuous wish would bear your living flowers."

smells of his Country garlike! fugh, how he stinks of
Spain.

Mufti. Why honey-bird I bought him a purpose for thee;   10
didst not thou say thou long'dst for a Christian Slave?

Johayma. Ah, but the sight of that loathsom creature has
almost cur'd me; And how can I tell that he's a *Christian*? and he were well search'd he may prove a *Jew* for
ought I know.   15
And besides I have always long'd for an Eunuch; for
they say that's a Civil Creature, and almost as harmless
as your self, Husband: speak fellow, are not you such a
kind of peaceable thing?

Antonio. I was never taken for one in my own Country;   20
and not very peaceable neither, when I am well provok'd.

Mufti. To your Occupation, Dog; bind up the Jessamines
in yond Arbor, and handle your pruning knife with
dexterity; tightly I say, go tightly to your business; you   25
have cost me much; and must earn it in your work;
here's plentiful provision for you, rascal, sallating in the
Garden, and water in the tank, and on Holydays the
licking of a platter of Rice, when you deserve it.

Johayma. What have you been bred up to Sirrah, and what   30
can you perform to recommend you to my service?

Antonio (making legs). Why Madam, I can perform as much
as any Man, in a fair Ladies Service.
I can play upon the Flute, and Sing; I can carry your
Umbrella, and fan your Ladyship, and cool you when   35
you are too hot: in fine, no Service either by day or by
night shall come amiss to me; and besides am of so
quick an apprehension, that you need but wink upon
me at any time, to make me understand my duty.

                              She winks at him.

Antonio (aside). Very fine, she has tipt the wink already.   40
———

Johayma. The Whelp may come to something in time,
when I have enter'd him into his business.

Mufti. A very malapert Cur, I can tell him that; I do not
like his fawning, you must be taught your distance   45
Sirrah.   *Strikes him.*

Johayma. Hold, hold. ———
He ha's deserv'd it I confess; but for once let his ignorance plead his pardon; we must not discourage a

---

27 *sallating*] herbs and vegetables for salads.
32 *making legs*] bowing.

50   beginner. Your Reverence has taught us Charity ev'n
to Birds and Beasts: here you filthy brute you:—take
this little Alms, to buy you plaisters.

                        Gives him a piece of money.

Antonio (*aside*). Money and a Love-pinch in the inside of
my palm into the bargain.

                  Enter a Servant.

55   Servant. Sir, my Lord *Benducar* is coming to wait on you,
and is already at the Palace Gate.

Mufti. Come in *Johayma*, regulate the rest of my Wives
and Concubines, and leave the Fellow to his work.

Johayma. Look how stupidly he stares about him, like a
60   Calf new come into the World: I shall teach you Sirrah
to know your business, a little better. —— This way
you awkard rascal, here lyes the Arbour, must I be
showing you eternally?   *Turning him about.*

Mufti. Come away Minion; you shall show him nothing.
65   Johayma. I'll but bring him into the Arbor, where a Rose-
tree and a Myrtle are just falling for want of a prop; if
they were bound together they wou'd help to keep up
one another: —— He's a raw Gardiner, and 'tis but
Charity to teach him.

70   Mufti. No more deeds of Charity to day; come in, or I
shall think you a little better dispos'd than I cou'd wish
you.

Johayma. Well, go before, I will follow my Pastor.

Mufti. So you may cast a sheep's eye behind you: In before
75   me. And you, sawciness, mind your pruning knife; or
I may chance to use it for you.

               Exeunt Mufti *and* Johayma.

Antonio (*alone*). Thank you for that; but I am in no such
hast to be made a Musulman. For his Wedlock, with all
her haughtiness, I find her coming. How far a *Christian*
80   shou'd resist, I partly know; but how far a lewd young
Christian can resist is another question. She's tolerable,
and I am a poor Stranger, far from better Friends, and
in a bodily necessity: Now have I a strange temptation
to try what other Females are belonging to this Family:
85   I am not far from the Women's apartment I am sure;
and if these Birds are within distance, here's that will
chuckle 'em together. (*Pulls out his Flute.*) If there be
variety of *Moor's* flesh in this Holy Market 'twere
madness to lay out all my money upon the first bargain.

                            He plays.

87 *chuckle*] to call with a cackle.

A Grate opens and Morayma *the* Mufti's *Daughter appears at it.*

Antonio. Ay there's an Apparition! This is a Morsel worthy   90
of a *Mufti*; this is the relishing bit in secret; this is the
Mystery of his Alcoran, that must be reserv'd from the
knowledg of the profane Vulgar. This is his Holyday
Devotion; see, she beckons too. ———
                                        She beckons to him.
Morayma. Come a little nearer and speak softly.   95
Antonio. I come, I come I warrant thee; the least twinckle
had brought me to thee; such another kind syllable or
two, wou'd turn me to a Meteor and draw me up to
thee.
Morayma. I dare not speak, for fear of being over-heard;   100
but if you think my Person worth your hazard, and can
deserve my love ——— the rest this Note shall tell you.
——— (*Throws down a handkerchief.*) No more, my
heart goes with you.   *Exit from the Grate.*
Antonio. O thou pretty little heart; art thou flown hither, 105
I'll keep it warm I warrant it, and brood upon it in the
new nest: but now for my Treasure trove, that's wrapt
up in the handkerchief: No peeping here, though I long
to be spelling her Arabick scrawls and pot-hooks. But I
must carry off my prize, as Robbers do; and not think   110
of sharing the booty, before I am free from danger,
and out of eye-shot from the other Windows. If her wit
be as poynant as her Eyes, I am a double Slave. Our
Northern Beauties are meer dough to these: Insipid
white Earth, meer Tobaccopipe-clay; With no more   115
Soul and Motion in 'em, than a Fly in Winter.
Here the warm Planet ripens, and sublimes
The well bak'd Beauties of the Southern Climes;
Our Cupid's but a bungler in his Trade;
His keenest Arrows are in *Affrick* made.   120
                              Exit Antonio.

ACT III. Scene 1

*A Terrace-walk; or some other publick place in the
Castle of* Alcazar.

[*Enter*] *Emperor* Muley-Moluch; Benducar.

Emperor. Marry'd! I'll not believe it; 'tis imposture;
Improbable they shou'd presume t'attempt,

97 *syllable*] i.e., monosyllable, the pudendum (Farmer).

Impossible they shou'd effect their wish.

Benducar. Have patience till I clear it.

Emperor.   I have none:

5   Go bid our moving Plains of Sand lye still,
And stir not, when the stormy South blows high:
From top to bottom thou hast toss'd my Soul,
And now 'tis in the madness of the Whirl,
Requir'st a sudden stop? unsay thy lye:
That may in time do somewhat.

10   *Benducar.*   I have done:
For, since it pleases you it shou'd be forg'd,
'Tis fit it shou'd: far be it from your Slave,
To raise disturbance in your Sacred brest.

Emperor. Sebastian is my Slave as well as thou;

15   Nor durst offend my love by that presumption.

Benducar. Most sure he ought not.

Emperor.   Then all means were wanting;
No Priest, no Ceremonies of their Sect;
Or, grant we these defects cou'd be supply'd,
How cou'd our Prophet do an Act so base,

20   So to resume his gifts, and curse my Conquests
By making me unhappy! No, the Slave
That told thee so absurd a story, ly'd.

Benducar. Yet, till this moment I have found him faithful:
He said he saw it too.

Emperor.   Dispatch; what saw he?

25   *Benducar.* Truth is, considering with what earnestness,
Sebastian pleaded for *Almeyda's* life,
Inhanc'd her beauty, dwelt upon her praise, ———

Emperor. O stupid, and unthinking as I was!
I might have mark'd it too: 'twas gross and palpable!

30   *Benducar.* Methought I trac'd a Lover ill disguis'd;
And sent my spy, a sharp observing Slave,
T'inform me better, if I guess'd aright.
He told me, that he saw *Sebastian's* Page
Run cross the Marble Square; who soon return'd,

35   And after him there lag'd a puffing Fryar;
Close wrap'd he bore some secret Instrument
Of Christian Superstition in his hand:
My servant follow'd fast, and through a chink,
Perceiv'd the Royal Captives hand in hand:

40   And heard the hooded Father mumbling charms,
That make those Misbelievers Man and Wife.
Which done, the Spouses kiss'd with such a fervour,
And gave such furious earnest of their flames,
That their eyes sparkled, and their mantling blood

Flew flushing o'er their faces.
Emperor.   Hell confound 'em!   45
Benducar. The Reverend Father, with a Holy leer,
    Saw he might well be spar'd, and soon withdrew:
    This forc'd my Servant to a quick retreat,
    For fear to be discover'd; guess the rest.
Emperor. I do. My fancy is too exquisite,   50
    And tortures me with their imagin'd bliss.
    Some Earthquake shou'd have ris'n, and rent the ground,
    Have swallow'd him, and left the longing Bride,
    In Agony of unaccomplish'd Love.
                                Walks disorderly.
                    Enter the Mufti.

Benducar (aside). In an unlucky hour
    That Fool intrudes, raw in this great affair,   55
    And uninstructed how to stem the tide.
                        Coming up to the Mufti *aside.*
    The Emp'ror must not marry, nor enjoy;
    Keep to that point; stand firm, for all's at stake.
Emperor (seeing him). You, Druggerman of Heaven, must I
        attend
    Your droaning Prayers? Why came you not before?   60
    Do'st thou not know the Captive King has dar'd
    To wed *Almeyda*? Cancel me that Marriage,
    And make her mine; about the business, quick,
    Expound thy *Mahomet*; make him speak my sense,
    Or he's no Prophet here, and thou no *Mufti*,   65
    Unless thou know'st the trick of thy vocation,
    To wrest and rend the Law to please thy Prince.
Mufti. Why, verily the Law is monstrous plain:
    There's not one doubtful Text in all the Alchoran,
    Which can be wrench'd in favor to your Project.   70
Emperor. Forge one, and foist it into some by-place,
    Of some old rotten Roll; do't, I command thee:
    Must I teach thee thy Trade?
Mufti.   It cannot be.
    For Matrimony being the dearest point
    Of Law, the People have it all by heart: 75
    A Cheat on Procreation will not pass.
    Besides th'offence is so exorbitant,   *In a higher tone.*
    To mingle with a misbelieving Race,
    That speedy Vengeance wou'd pursue your Crime,
    And holy *Mahomet* launch himself from Heav'n,   80
    Before th'unready Thunderbolt were form'd.

60 *Druggerman*] dragoman, interpreter.

333

Emperor *taking him by the Throat with one hand, snatches out his Sword with the other, and points it to his Brest.*

Emperor. Slave, have I rais'd thee to this pomp and pow'r,
  To preach against my Will? Know I am Law;
85 And thou, not *Mahomet's* Messenger, but mine:
  Make it, I charge thee, make my pleasure lawful:
  Or first I strip thee of thy ghostly greatness,
  Then send thee post, to tell thy Tale above;
  And bring thy vain Memorials to thy Prophet
90 Of Justice done below for Disobedience.
Mufti. For Heaven's sake hold, the respite of a moment,—
  To think for you.
Emperor.   And for thy self. ———
Mufti.   For both.
Benducar (aside). Disgrace, and Death, and Avarice have lost
  him!
Mufti. 'Tis true, our Law forbids to wed a *Christian*;
95 But it forbids you not to ravish her.
  You have a Conqueror's right upon your Slave;
  And then, the more despight you do a *Christian,*
  You serve the Prophet more who loaths that Sect.
Emperor. Oh now it mends; and you talk reason, *Mufti.*
100 But stay! I promis'd freedom to *Sebastian*:
  Now shou'd I grant it, his revengeful Soul
  Wou'd ne'er forgive his violated Bed.
Mufti. Kill him, for then you give him liberty:
  His Soul is from his earthly Prison freed.
105 *Emperor.* How happy is the Prince who has a Churchman
  So learn'd and pliant to expound his Laws.
Benducar. Two things I humbly offer to your prudence.
Emperor. Be brief; but let not either thwart my love.
Benducar. First, since our holy Man has made Rape lawful,
110 Fright her with that: proceed not yet to force:
  Why shou'd you pluck the green distastful Fruit
  From the unwilling Bough,
  When it may ripen of it self and fall?
Emperor. Grant her a day; tho that's too much to give
115 Out of a Life which I devote to Love.
Benducar. Then next, to bar
  All future hopes of her desir'd *Sebastian,*
  Let *Dorax* be enjoyn'd to bring his head.

83 *rais'd thee*] A mufti was appointed by the government and asked to give opinions on difficult questions of law.

Emperor (to the Mufti). Go *Mufti*, call him to receive his
    Orders.   *Exit* Mufti.
  I taste thy Counsel, her desires new rowz'd,   120
  And yet unslak'd, will kindle in her fancy,
  And make her eager to renew the Feast.
Benducar (aside). *Dorax*, I know before, will disobey:
  There's a Foe's Head well cropt. ———
  But this hot love precipitates my Plot;   125
  And brings it to projection ere its time.

    Enter Sebastian *and* Almeyda *hand in hand; upon
    sight of the* Emperor, *they separate and seem disturb'd.*

Almeyda. He breaks, at unawares, upon our Walks,
  And like a mid-night Wolf invades the Fold:
  Make speedy preparation of your Soul,
  And bid it arm apace: He comes for answer,   130
  And brutal mischief sits upon his brow.
Sebastian. Not the last sounding, cou'd surprize me more,
  That summons drowzy Mortals to their doom,
  When call'd in haste, they fumble for their Limbs,
  And tremble unprovided for their charge: 135
  My sense has been so deeply plung'd in Joys,
  The Soul out-slept her hour; and, scarce awake,
  Wou'd think too late, and cannot! But brave Minds
  At worst can dare their Fate.———
                Emperor *coming up to them.*
Emperor.   Have you perform'd
  Your Embassy, and treated with success?   140
Sebastian. I had not time.
Emperor.   No, not for my Affairs,
  But for your own too much.
Sebastian. You talk in Clouds, explain your meaning, Sir.
Emperor. Explain yours first: What meant you hand in
    hand,
  And when you saw me, with a guilty start,   145
  You loos'd your hold, affrighted at my presence?
Sebastian. Affrighted?
Emperor.   Yes, astonish'd, and confounded.
Sebastian. What mak'st thou of thy self, and what of me?
  Art thou some Ghost, some Demon, or some God?
  That I shou'd stand astonish'd at thy sight?   150
  If thou cou'dst deem so meanly of my Courage,
  Why didst thou not engage me man for man,
  And try the virtue of that *Gorgon* Face,

126 *projection*] the twelfth and last process in alchemy.

335

To stare me into statue?

155   *Emperor.* Oh, thou art now recover'd, but by Heav'n,
Thou wert amaz'd at first, as if surpriz'd
At unexpected baseness brought to light.
For know, ungrateful man, that Kings, like Gods,
Are every where; walk in th'abyss of minds,
160   And view the dark recesses of the Soul.
    Sebastian. Base and ungrateful never was I thought;
Nor till this turn of fate, durst thou have call'd me;
But, since thou boast'st th'omniscience of a God,
Say, in what cranny of *Sebastian's* Soul,
165   Unknown to me, so loath'd a Crime is lodg'd?
    Emperor. Thou hast not broke my trust repos'd in thee?
    Sebastian. Impos'd, but not receiv'd: Take back that false-
       hood.
    Emperor. Thou art not marry'd to *Almeyda*?
    Sebastian.   Yes.
    Emperor. And own'st the usurpation of my Love?
170   *Sebastian.* I own it in the face of Heav'n and thee
No Usurpation; but a lawful claim,
Of which I stand possest.
    Emperor.   Sh'has chosen well,
Betwixt a Captive and a Conqueror.
    Almeyda. Betwixt a Monster and the best of Men.
175   He was the envy of his neighb'ring Kings;
For him their sighing Queens despis'd their Lords,
And Virgin Daughters blush'd when he was nam'd.
To share his noble Chains is more to me,
Than all the salvage greatness of thy Throne.
180   *Sebastian.* Were I to choose again, and knew my fate,
For such a night I wou'd be what I am.
The Joys I have possest are ever mine;
Out of thy reach behind Eternity,
Hid in the sacred treasure of the past;
185   But bless'd remembrance bring's 'em hourly back.
    Emperor. Hourly indeed, who hast but hours to live:
O mighty purchase of a boasted bliss!
To dream of what thou hadst one fugitive night,
And never shalt have more.
190   *Sebastian.* Barbarian, thou canst part us but a mo-
       ment; ———
We shall be one again in thy despight:
Life is but air,
That yields a passage to the whistling Sword,
And closes when 'tis gone.
195   *Almeyda.* How can we better dye than close embrac'd,

Sucking each other's Souls while we expire?
Which so transfus'd, and mounting both at once,
The Saints deceiv'd, shall by a sweet mistake,
Hand up thy Soul for mine, and mine for thine.
Emperor. No, I'll untwist you: 200
I have occasion for your stay on earth:
Let him mount first, and beat upon the Wing,
And wait an Age for what I here detain.
Or sicken at immortal Joys above,
And languish for the Heav'n he left below.   205
Almeyda. Thou wilt not dare to break what Heav'n has
    joyn'd?
Emperor. Not break the Chain, but change a rotten link,
And rivet one to last.
Think'st thou I come to argue right and wrong?
Why lingers *Dorax* thus? Where are my Guards,   210
To drag that Slave to death?   *Pointing to* Sebastian.
        Benducar *goes out for the Guards, and returns.*
                Now storm and rage,
Call vainly on thy Prophet, then defie him
For wanting power to save thee.
Sebastian. That were to gratifie thy Pride: I'll shew thee
How a Man shou'd, and how a King dare dye: 215
So even, that my Soul shall walk with ease
Out of its flesh, and shut out Life as calmly
As it does words; without a Sigh, to note
One struggle in the smooth dissolving frame.
Almeyda (*to the* Emperor). Expect revenge from Heav'n,   220
    inhuman Wretch;
Nor hope t'ascend *Sebastian's* holy Bed.
Flames, Daggers, Poysons, guard the sacred steps:
Those are the promis'd Pleasures of my love.
Emperor. And these might fright another, but not me.
Or me, if I design'd to give you pleasure;   225
I seek my own, and while that lasts, you live.

            Enter two of the Guards.

Go, bear the Captive to a speedy death,
And set my Soul at ease.
Almeyda. I charge you hold, ye Ministers of death:
Speak my *Sebastian*;   230

196 *Sucking each other's Souls*] suggesting the belief that the soul at
death left the body by way of the mouth. The custom of kissing dead
relatives, as the biblical Joseph kissed his father, has been interpreted as
an attempt to catch the souls of the dying as they escape through the
mouth (*Dictionary of Folklore*, II, 583).

Plead for thy life: Oh ask it of the Tyrant;
'Tis no dishonour, trust me, Love, 'tis none:
I wou'd die for thee, but I cannot plead;
My haughty heart disdains it, ev'n for thee.
235   Still silent! Will the King of *Portugal*
Go to his death, like a dumb Sacrifice?
Beg him to save my life in saving thine.
Sebastian. Farewel, my life's not worth another word.
Emperor (to the Guards). Perform your Orders.
240 *Almeyda.* Stay, take my farewel too:
Farewel the greatness of *Almeyda's* Soul!
Look, Tyrant, what excess of love can do,
It pulls me down thus low, as to thy feet;
                               Kneels to him.
Nay to embrace thy Knees with loathing hands,
245   Which blister when they touch thee: Yet ev'n thus,
Thus far I can to save *Sebastian's* life.
Emperor. A secret pleasure trickles through my Veins:
It works about the inlets of my Soul,
To feel thy touch; and pity tempts the pass;
250   But the tough metal of my heart resists;
'Tis warm'd with the soft fire, not melted down.
Almeyda. A flood of scalding Tears will make it run,
Spare him, Oh spare; can you pretend to love,
And have no pity? Love and that are Twins.
255   Here will I grow;
Thus compass you with these supplanting Cords,
And pull so long till the proud Fabrick falls.
Emperor. Still kneel, and still embrace; 'tis double pleasure
So to be hugg'd, and see *Sebastian* dye.
260 *Almeyda.* Look Tyrant, when thou nam'st *Sebastian's* death,
Thy very Executioners turn pale;
Rough as they are, and harden'd in the trade
Of Death, they start at an anointed Head,
And tremble to approach: ——— He hears me not;
265   Nor minds th'impression of a God on Kings;
Because no stamp of Heav'n was on his Soul:
But the resisting Mass drove back the Seal.
Say, though thy heart be rock of Adamant,
Yet Rocks are not impregnable to Bribes:

---

249 *touch*] concern, interest.
249 *pass*] passage, a navigable channel, especially as a river's mouth.
269 *Rocks are not impregnable to Bribes*] Hearing Orpheus's complaints for his lost Erydice, "The rocks were mov'd to pity with his moan" (Virgil, *Georgics*, IV, 739, Dryden's translation).

Instruct me how to bribe thee: Name thy price;   270
Lo, I resign my Title to the Crown;
Send me to exile with the Man I love,
And banishment is Empire.
Emperor.   Here's my claim;
And this extinguish'd thine; thou giv'st me nothing.
                        Clapping his hand to his Sword.
Almeyda. My Father's, Mother's, Brother's death I pardon: 275
That's somewhat sure; a mighty Sum of Murther,
Of innocent and kindred blood strook off.
My Prayers and Penance shall discount for these,
And beg of Heav'n to charge the Bill on me:
Behold what price I offer, and how dear   280
To buy *Sebastian's* life.
Emperor. Let after reck'nings trouble fearful fools;
I'll stand the tryal of those trivial Crimes:
But, since thou beg'st me to prescribe my terms,
The only I can offer are thy love;   285
And this one day of respite to resolve.
Grant or deny, for thy next word is Fate;
And Fate is deaf to Pray'r.
Almeyda.   May Heav'n be so
                                      Rising up.
At thy last breath to thine: I curse thee not,
For who can better curse the Plague or Devil,   290
Than to be what they are? That Curse be thine.
Now, do not speak *Sebastian*, for you need not,
But dye, for I resign your Life: Look Heav'n,
Almeyda dooms her dear *Sebastian's* death!
But is there Heav'n, for I begin to doubt;   295
The Skyes are hush'd; no grumbling Thunders roul:
Now take your swing, ye impious; Sin unpunish'd;
Eternal providence seems overwatch'd,
And with a slumb'ring Nod assents to Murther.

                Enter Dorax *attended by three Soldiers.*

Emperor. Thou mov'st a Tortoise pace to my relief.   300
Take hence that, once a King; that sullen pride
That swells to dumbness; lay him in the Dungeon,
And sink him deep with Irons; that when he wou'd,
He shall not groan to hearing: when I send
The next Commands are death.   305
Almeyda. Then Prayers are vain as Curses.
Emperor.   Much at one

298 *overwatch'd*] weary with too much watching.

339

In a Slave's mouth, against a Monarch's Pow'r.
This day thou hast to think;
At night, if thou wilt curse, thou shalt curse kindly;
Then I'll provoke thy lips; lay siege so close,
That all thy sallying breath shall turn to Blessings.
Make haste, seize, force her, bear her hence.
Almeyda. Farewel, my last *Sebastian!*
I do not beg, I challenge Justice now;
O Pow'rs, if Kings be your peculiar care,
Why plays this Wretch with your Prerogative?
Now flash him dead, now crumble him to ashes;
Or henceforth live confin'd in your own Palace;
And look not idely out upon a World
That is no longer yours.
　　She is carried off strugling, Emperour *and* Benducar
　　　　　　　　　　　　　　　　follow.

Sebastian struggles in his Guards Arms, and shakes off one of *them, but two others come in, and hold him; he speaks not all the while.*

Dorax (aside). I find I'm but a half-strain'd Villain yet;
But mungril, mischievous; for my Blood boyl'd,
To view this brutal act; and my stern Soul
Tug'd at my arm to draw in her defence.
Down thou rebelling *Christian* in my heart;
Redeem thy fame on this *Sebastian* first;
Then think on others wrongs, when thine are righted.
　　　　　　　　　　　　　　　Walks a turn.
But how to right 'em? on a Slave disarm'd,
Defenceless, and submitted to my rage?
A base revenge is vengeance on my self!
　　　　　　　　　　　　　　　Walks again.
I have it; and I thank thee, honest head,
Thus present to me at my great necessity:—
　　　　　　　　　　　Comes up to Sebastian.
You know me not?
Sebastian.　　　　　I hear Men call thee *Dorax.*
Dorax. 'Tis well, you know enough for once: you speak too;
You were struck mute before.
Sebastian. Silence became me then.
Dorax. Yet we may talk hereafter.
Sebastian. Hereafter is not mine: ———

311 *sallying*] attacking, satirical.
321 *half-strain'd*] half-breed (the four examples in the *OED* come from Dryden).

Dispatch thy work, good Executioner.

Dorax. None of my blood were hangmen; add that
    falshood   340
    To a long Bill that yet remains unreckon'd.

Sebastian. A King and thou can never have a reck'ning.

Dorax. A greater summ perhaps than you can pay.
    Mean time I shall make bold t'increase your debt,
    Take this, and use it at your greatest need.   345
                         Gives him his Sword.

Sebastian. This hand and this, have been acquainted well;
                              Looks on it.
    It shou'd have come before into my grasp,
    To kill the Ravisher.

Dorax. Thou heardst the Tyrant's orders; Guard thy life
    When 'tis attack'd, and guard it like a Man.   350

Sebastian. I'm still without thy meaning but I thank thee.

Dorax. Thank me when I ask thanks; thank me with that.

Sebastian. Such surly kindness did I never see!

Dorax (*to the Captain of his Guards*). *Muza*, draw out a file,
    pick man by man,
    Such who dare dye, and dear will sell their death.   355
    Guard him to th'utmost; now conduct him hence,
    And treat him as my Person.

Sebastian.   Something like
    That voice methinks I shou'd have somewhere heard:
    But floods of woes have hurry'd it far off;
    Beyond my kenn of Soul.   360
              Exit Sebastian *with the Soldiers.*

Dorax (*solus*). But I shall bring him back, ungrateful Man,
    I shall, and set him full before thy sight,
    When I shall front thee, like some staring Ghost,
    With all my wrongs about me. ——— What so soon
    Return'd? This hast is boding.   365

      Enter to him Emperor, Benducar, Mufti.

Emperor. She's still inexorable, still Imperious;
    And loud, as if like *Bacchus* born in thunder.
    Be quick, ye false Physicians of my mind,
    Bring speedy Death or Cure.

Benducar. What can be counsell'd while *Sebastian* lives?   370
    The Vine will cling, while the tall poplar stands:
    But that cut down creeps to the next support,
    And twines as closely there.

---

367 *born in thunder*] as son of Zeus by Semele, who was consumed
by Zeus' fire.

Emperor. That's done with ease, I speak him dead: proceed.

375   *Mufti.* Proclaim your Marriage with *Almeyda* next,
That Civil Wars may cease; this gains the Crowd;
Then you may safely force her to your will:
For People side with violence and injustice,
When done for publick good.
     Emperor.   Preach thou that doctrine.

380   *Benducar (aside).* Th'unreasonable fool has broach'd a truth
That blasts my hopes; but since 'tis gone so far,
He shall divulge *Almeyda* is a *Christian*:
If that produce no tumult I despair.
     Emperor. Why speaks not *Dorax*?

385   *Dorax.* Because my Soul abhors to mix with him.
Sir, let me bluntly say, you went too far
To trust the Preaching pow'r on State Affairs,
To him or any Heavenly Demagogue.
'Tis a limb lopt from your Prerogative,

390   And so much of Heav'n's Image blotted from you.
     Mufti. Sure thou hast never heard of Holy Men
(So *Christians* call 'em) fam'd in State Affairs;
Such as in *Spain Ximenes, Albornoz,*
In *England Woolsey*; match me these with Laymen.

395   *Dorax.* How you triumph in one or two of these,
Born to be Statesmen, hap'ning to be Church-men:
Thou callst 'em holy; so their function was;
But tell me, *Mufti*, which of 'em were Saints?
Next, Sir, to you; the summ of all is this;

400   Since he claims pow'r from Heav'n, and not from Kings,
When 'tis his int'rest, he can int'rest Heav'n
To preach you down; and Ages oft depend
On hours, uninterrupted, in the Chair.
     Emperor. I'll trust his Preaching while I rule his pay.

405   And I dare trust my *Affricans*, to hear
Whatever he dare Preach.
     Dorax.   You know 'em not.
The genius of your *Moors* is mutiny;
They scarcely want a Guide to move their madness:
Prompt to rebel on every weak pretence,

410   Blustring when courted, crouching when opprest.

393 *Ximenes*] Cardinal Francisco Ximenes (1436–1517), who for
a time was regent of Spain.
393 *Albornoz*] Gil Alvarez de Albornoz, fourteenth-century cardinal, soldier, and diplomat.
394 *Woolsey*] cardinal and lord chancellor under Henry VIII.
403 *Chair*] the seat of ecclesiastical authority; from which a
mufti might depose a Mohammedan ruler.

Wise to themselves, and fools to all the World.
Restless in change, and perjur'd to a Proverb.
They love Religion sweetn'd to the sense;
A good, luxurious, palatable faith.
Thus Vice and Godliness, prepost'rous pair,   415
Ride cheek by joul; but Churchmen hold the Reins.
And, when ere Kings wou'd lower Clergy greatness,
They learn too late what pow'r the Preachers have,
And whose the Subjects are; the *Mufti* knows it;
Nor dares deny what pass'd betwixt us two.   420
Emperor. No more; what ere he said was by Command.
Dorax. Why then no more, since you will hear no more;
     Some Kings are resolute to their own ruin.
Emperor. Without your medling where you are not ask'd,
     Obey your Orders, and dispatch *Sebastian*.   425
Dorax. Trust my revenge; be sure I wish him dead.
Emperor. What mean'st thou! what's thy wishing to my
     will;
     Dispatch him, rid me of the Man I loath.
Dorax. I hear you Sir, I'll take my time and do't ———
Emperor. Thy time? what's all thy time, what's thy whole
     life   430
     To my one hour of ease? no more replies,
     But see thou do'st it; Or ———
Dorax. Choak in that threat: I can say Or, as loud.
Emperor. 'Tis well, I see my words have no effect,
     But I may send a Message to dispose you.   *Is going off.* 435
Dorax. Expect an answer worthy of that Message.
Mufti (aside). The Prophet ow'd him this:
     And thank'd be Heav'n, he has it.
Benducar. By Holy *Alha*, I conjure you stay,
     And judge not rashly of so brave a Man.   440
          Draws the Emperor *aside and whispers him.*
     I'll give you reasons why he cannot execute
     Your Orders now, and why he will hereafter.
Mufti (aside). *Benducar* is a fool to bring him off,
     I'll work my own revenge, and speedily.
Benducar. The Fort is his, the Soldiers hearts are his;   445
     A thousand Christian Slaves are in the Castle,
     Which he can free to reinforce his pow'r;
     Your Troops far off, beleaguering *Larache*,
     Yet in the *Christians* hands.
Emperor.   I grant all this;
     But grant me he must dye.

448 *Larache*] El Araish, a city in northern Morocco.

343

450   *Benducar.*   He shall; by poyson:
       'Tis here, the deadly drug prepar'd in powder,
       Hot as Hell fire: ———— then, to prevent his Soldiers
       From rising to revenge their Gen'ral's death,
       While he is struggling with his Mortal pangs,
455   The Rabble on the sudden may be rais'd
       To seize the Castle.
       Emperor.   Do't; 'tis left to thee.
       Benducar. Yet more; but clear your brow; for he observes.
                         They whisper again.
       Dorax (*aside*). What, will the Fav'rite prop my falling
          fortunes,
          O Prodigie of Court!
                 Emperor and Benducar *return to* Dorax.
460   *Emperor.* Your Friend has fully clear'd your Innocence;
       I was too hasty to condemn unheard,
       And you perhaps too prompt in your replies.
       As far as fits the Majesty of Kings,
       I ask excuse.
       Dorax.   I'm sure I meant it well.
465   *Emperor.* I know you did:—this to our love renew'd.—
                          Emperor drinks.
         Benducar, fill to *Dorax.*
              Benducar turns and mixes a powder in it.
       Dorax. Let it go round for all of us have need
         To quench our heats; 'tis the King's health *Benducar.*—
                         He drinks.
       And I wou'd pledge it though I knew 'twere poyson.
470   *Benducar.* Another Bowl, for what the King has touch'd,
       And you have pledg'd, is sacred to your loves.————
                   Drinks out of another Bowl.
       Mufti. Since Charity becomes my calling, thus
         Let me provoke your friendship: and heav'n bless it
         As I intend it well. ————

       Drinks; and turning aside pours some drops out of a little
             Vial into the Bowl; then presents it to Dorax.

       Dorax.   Heav'n make thee honest,
475   On that condition we shall soon be friends.—   *Drinks.*
       Mufti (*aside*). Yes, at our meeting in another World;
         For thou hast drunk thy passport out of this.
         Not the Nonacrian fount, nor Lethe's Lake,
         Cou'd sooner numb thy nimble faculties

---

478 *Nonacrian*] the river Styx, identified with a water-fall near
Nonacris, regarded as poisonous.

Than this, to sleep eternal.   480
Emperor. Now farewel *Dorax*; this was our first quarrel,
  And I dare prophesie will prove our last.
            Exit Emperor *with* Benducar *and the* Mufti.
Dorax. It may be so: I'm strangely discompos'd;
  Quick shootings through my limbs, and pricking pains,
  Qualms at my heart, Convulsions in my nerves,   485
  Shiv'rings of cold, and burnings of my entrails
  Within my little World make medley War,
  Lose and regain, beat and are beaten back;
  As momentary Victors quit their ground.
  Can it be poyson! poyson's of one tenour,   490
  Or hot or cold; this neither, and yet both.
  Some deadly Draught, some enemy of life
  Boils in my bowels, and works out my Soul.
  Ingratitude's the growth of ev'ry Clime;
  Affrick, the Scene remov'd, is *Portugal*.   495
  Of all Court-service learn the common lot;
  To day 'tis done, to morrow 'tis forgot.
  Oh were that all! my honest Corps must lye
  Expos'd to scorn, and publick Infamy:
  My shameful Death will be divulg'd alone;   500
  The worth and honour of my Soul unknown.
                        Exit.

[ACT III.] SCENE 2

Is a Night Scene of the Mufti's *Garden where an Arbour
is discover'd.*

Enter Antonio.

Antonio. She names her self *Morayma*; the *Mufti's* only
  Daughter, and a Virgin! This is the time and place that
  she appointed in her letter, yet she comes not. Why
  thou sweet delicious Creature, why to torture me with
  thy delay! dar'st thou be false to thy Assignation?   5
  What, in the cool and silence of the night, and to a new
  Lover? Pox on the Hypocrite thy Father, for instructing
  thee so little in the sweetest point of his Religion.
  Hark, I hear the rustling of her Silk Mantle. Now she
  comes; now she comes; no, hang't, that was but the   10
  whistling of the wind through the *Orange* Trees. Now
  again, I hear the pit a pat of a pretty foot through the
  dark Alley: No, 'tis the Son of a Mare that's broken
  loose and munching upon the Melons: ——— Oh the
  misery of an expecting Lover! Well I'll e'en despair, go   15

into my Arbour, and try to sleep; in a dream I shall
enjoy her in despight of her.

Goes into the Arbour and lyes down.

Enter Johayma *wrapt up in a Moorish Mantle.*

Johayma. Thus far my love has carry'd me, almost without
my knowledg whither I was going: Shall I go on,
shall I discover my self! ———— What an injury am I
doing to my old Husband! ———— Yet what injury,
since he's old, and has three Wives and six Concubines
besides me! 'Tis but stealing my own Tythe from him.

She comes a little nearer the Arbour.
Antonio *raising himself a little and looking.*

Antonio. At last 'tis she: this is no illusion I am sure; 'tis a
true She-devil of Flesh and Blood; and she cou'd never
have taken a fitter time to tempt me. ————

Johayma. He's young and handsome. ————

Antonio (aside). Yes, well enough I thank nature.

Johayma. And I am yet neither old nor ugly: sure he will
not refuse me.

Antonio (aside). No, thou mayst pawn thy Maiden-head
upon't he wonnot.

Johayma. The *Mufti* wou'd feast himself upon other
Women, and keep me fasting.

Antonio (aside). O, the holy Curmudgeon!

Johayma. Wou'd Preach abstinence, and practice luxury!
but I thank my Stars, I have edify'd more by his example
than his precept.

Antonio (aside). Most divinely argu'd; she's the best Casuist
in all *Affrick.* *He rushes out and embraces her.*
I can hold no longer from embracing thee my dear
Morayma: the old unconscionable Whorson thy Father,
cou'd he expect cold chastity from a Child of his
begetting?

Johayma. What nonsense do you talk? do you take me for
the *Mufti's* Daughter?

Antonio. Why are you not, Madam?

Throwing off her Barnus.

Johayma. I find you had an appointment with *Morayma*.

Antonio (aside). By all that's good, the nauseous Wife.

Johayma. What, you are confounded and stand mute?

Antonio. Somewhat nonplust I confess; to hear you deny
your name so positively; why, are not you *Morayma*
the *Mufti's* Daughter? Did not I see you with him, did

47.1 *Barnus*] i.e., burnoose.

346

not he present me to you? Were you not so charitable
as to give me Money? Ay and to tread upon my foot,   55
and squeeze my hand too, if I may be so bold to
remember you of past favours.

Johayma. And you see I am come to make 'em good, but I
am neither *Morayma* nor the *Mufti's* Daughter.

Antonio. Nay, I know not that: but I am sure he is old   60
enough to be your Father: and either Father, or
Reverend Father, I heard you call him.

Johayma. Once again, how came you to name *Morayma*?

Antonio. Another damn'd mistake of mine: For, asking one
of my fellow Slaves, who were the chief Ladies about   65
the house; he answer'd me *Morayma* and *Johayma*; but
she it seems is his Daughter, with a Pox to her, and you
are his beloved Wife.

Johayma. Say your beloved Mistris, if you please; for that's
the Title I desire. This Moon-shine grows offensive to   70
my Eyes, come, shall we walk into the Arbor? There
we may rectifie all mistakes.

Antonio. That's close and dark.

Johayma. And are those faults to Lovers?

Antonio. But there I cannot please my self, with the sight   75
of your beauty.

Johayma. Perhaps you may do better.

Antonio. But there's not a breath of air stirring.

Johayma. The breath of Lovers is the sweetest air; but you
are fearful.   80

Antonio. I am considering, indeed, that if I am taken with
you ———

Johayma. The best way to avoid it, is to retire, where we
may not be discover'd.

Antonio. Where lodges your Husband?   85

Johayma. Just against the face of this open Walk.

Antonio. Then he has seen us already, for ought I know.

Johayma. You make so many Difficulties, I fear I am displeasing to you.

Antonio (*aside*). If *Morayma* comes and takes me in the Arbor   90
with her, I have made a fine exchange of that Diamond
for this Pebble.

Johayma. You are much fall'n off, let me tell you, from the
fury of your first embrace.

Antonio. I confess, I was somewhat too furious at first, but   95
you will forgive the transport of my passion; now I have
consider'd it better, I have a qualm of Conscience.

Johayma. Of Conscience! Why, what has Conscience to do
with two young Lovers that have opportunity?

347

100   *Antonio.* Why truly Conscience is something to blame for interposing in our matters: But how can I help it, if I have a Scruple to betray my Master?

     Johayma. There must be something more in it; for your Conscience was very quiet when you took me for
105   *Morayma.*

     Antonio. I grant you, Madam, when I took you for his Daughter: For then I might have made you an honorable amends by Marriage.

     Johayma. You *Christians* are such peeking Sinners, you
110   tremble at a Shadow in the Moon-shine.

     Antonio. And you *Affricans* are such Termagants, you stop at nothing. I must be plain with you, you are married, and to a Holy Man, the Head of your Religion: Go back to your Chamber, go back, I say, and consider of
115   it for this night; as I will do on my part: I will be true to you, and invent all the Arguments I can to comply with you; and who knows, but at our next meeting, the sweet Devil may have more power over me: I am true flesh and blood, I can tell you that for your comfort.

120   *Johayma.* Flesh without blood I think thou art; or if any, 'tis as cold as that of Fishes. But I'll teach thee, to thy cost, what Vengeance is in store for refusing a Lady, who has offer'd thee her Love: ——— Help, Help, there; will no body come to my assistance?

125   *Antonio.* What do you mean, Madam, for Heaven's sake peace; your Husband will hear you; think of your own danger, if you will not think of mine.

     Johayma. Ingrateful Wretch, thou deserv'st no pity: Help, Help, Husband, or I shall be ravish'd: The Villain will
130   be too strong for me. Help, help, for pity of a poor distressed Creature.

     Antonio. Then I have nothing but impudence to assist me: I must drown her clamor what e'er comes on't.

          He takes out his Flute, and plays as loud as he can possibly,
                              and she continues crying out.

        Enter the Mufti *in his Night-gown, and two Servants.*

     Mufti. O thou Villain, what horrible impiety art thou com-
135   mitting? What, ravishing the Wife of my Bosom? Take him away, ganch him, impale him, rid the World of such a Monster.   *Servants seize him.*

109 *peeking*] sickly, pining.
111 *Termagants*] tyrants.
136 *ganch*] impale upon sharp hooks or stakes as a means of execution.

Antonio. Mercy, dear Master, Mercy: Hear me first, and
after, if I have deserved hanging, spare me not: What
have you seen to provoke you to this cruelty?   140
Mufti. I have heard the out-crys of my Wife; the bleatings
of the poor innocent Lamb: Seen nothing, say'st thou?
If I see the Lamb lye bleeding, and the Butcher by her
with his Knife drawn and bloody, is not that evidence
sufficient of the Murther? I come too late, and the   145
Execution is already done.
Antonio. Pray think in reason, Sir, is a Man to be put to
death for a similitude? No Violence has been committed; none intended: The Lamb's alive; and if I durst
tell you so, no more a Lamb than I am a Butcher.   150
Johayma. How's that, Villain, dar'st thou accuse me?
Antonio. Be patient Madam, and speak but truth, and I'll
do any thing to serve you: I say again, and swear it too,
I'll do any thing to serve you.
Johayma (aside). I understand him; but I fear, 'tis now too   155
late to save him: ——— Pray hear him speak, Husband;
perhaps he may say something for himself; I know not.
Mufti. Speak thou, has he not violated my Bed and thy
Honor?
Johayma. I forgive him freely; for he has done nothing: 160
What he will do hereafter, to make me satisfaction,
himself best knows.
Antonio. Any thing, any thing, sweet Madam: I shall refuse
no drudgery.
Mufti. But, did he mean no mischief? Was he endeavouring   165
nothing?
Johayma. In my Conscience, I begin to doubt he did not.
Mufti. 'Tis impossible: Then what meant all those out-
crys?
Johayma. I heard Musick in the Garden, and at an un-   170
seasonable time of night; and I stole softly out of my
Bed, as imagining it might be he.
Mufti. How's that *Johayma*? Imagining it was he, and yet
you went?
Johayma. Why not, my Lord? Am not I the Mistris of the   175
Family? And is it not my place to see good Orders kept
in it? I thought he might have allur'd some of the Shee-
slaves to him; and was resolv'd to prevent what might
have been betwixt him and them; when on the sudden
he rush'd out upon me, caught me in his arms, with   180
such a fury ———
Mufti. I have heard enough, away with him. ———
Johayma. Mistaking me, no doubt, for one of his fellow

349

185

Slaves: With that, affrighted as I was, I discover'd my
self, and cry'd aloud: But as soon as ever he knew me,
the Villain let me go, and I must needs say, he started
back, as if I were some Serpent; and was more afraid
of me than I of him.

190

Mufti. O thou corrupter of my Family, that's cause enough
of death; once again, away with him.

Johayma. What, for an intended Trespass? No harm has
been done, whatever may be. He cost you five hundred
Crowns I take it.———

195

Mufti. Thou say'st true, a very considerable Sum: He shall
not dye, tho he had committed folly with a Slave; 'tis
too much to lose by him.

Antonio. My only fault has ever been to love playing in the
dark, and the more she cry'd, the more I play'd; that it
might be seen I intended nothing to her.

200

Mufti. To your Kennel, Sirrah, mortifie your flesh, and
consider in whose Family you are.

Johayma. And one thing more; remember from henceforth
to obey better.

205

Mufti (aside). For all her smoothness, I am not quite cur'd
of my Jealousie; but I have thought of a way that will
clear my doubts.

Exit Mufti *with* Johayma *and Servants.*

Antonio. I am mortify'd sufficiently already, without the
help of his ghostly Counsel. Fear of Death has gone
farther with me in two Minutes, than my Conscience

210

wou'd have gone in two Months. I find my self in a very
dejected condition, all over me; poor Sin lyes dormant,
Concupiscence is retir'd to his winter quarters; and if
Morayma shou'd now appear, I say no more, but alas
for her and me!

Morayma *comes out of the Arbour; she steals behind him,*
and claps him on the back.

215

Morayma. And if *Morayma* shou'd appear, as she does
appear, alas you say for her and you!

Antonio. Art thou there, my sweet temptation! my Eyes,
my Life, my Soul, my all!

220

Morayma. A mighty Complement, when all these, by your
own Confession, are just nothing.

Antonio. Nothing, till thou cam'st to new create me; thou
dost not know the power of thy own Charms: let me
embrace thee, and thou shalt see how quickly I can turn
wicked.

225

Morayma (stepping back). Nay, if you are so dangerous, 'tis

best keeping you at a distance; I have no mind to warm
a frozen Snake in my bosom; he may chance to recover,
and sting me for my pains.

Antonio. Consider what I have suffer'd for thy sake already;
and make me some amends: two disappointments in a   230
night, O cruel Creature!

Morayma. And you may thank your self for both: I came
eagerly to the Charge, before my time, through the
back walk behind the Arbour; and you, like a fresh-
water Soldier, stood guarding the Pass before: if you   235
miss'd the Enemy, you may thank your own dulness.

Antonio. Nay, if you will be using stratagems, you shall
give me leave to make use of my advantages, now I have
you in my power: we are fairly met; I'll try it out, and
give no quarter.   240

Morayma. By your favour, Sir, we meet upon treaty now,
and not upon defiance.

Antonio. If that be all, you shall have *Carte blanche* immediately; for I long to be ratifying.

Morayma. No, now I think on't, you are already enter'd   245
into Articles with my Enemy *Johayma:* Any thing to
serve you Madam; I shall refuse no drudgery: whose
words were those, Gentleman? was that like a Cavalier
of honour?

Antonio. Not very heroick; but self preservation is a point   250
above Honour and Religion too. —— *Antonio* was a
Rogue I must confess; but you must give me leave to
love him.

Morayma. To beg your life so basely; and to present your
Sword to your Enemy; Oh Recreant!   255

Antonio. If I had died honourably, my fame indeed wou'd
have sounded loud, but I shou'd never have heard the
blast: Come, don't make your self worse natur'd than
you are: to save my life, you wou'd be content I shou'd
promise any thing.   260

Morayma. Yes, if I were sure you wou'd perform nothing.

Antonio. Can you suspect I wou'd leave you for *Johayma?*

Morayma. No; but I can expect you wou'd have both of
us: Love is covetous, I must have all of you; heart for
heart is an equal truck. In short, I am younger; I think   265
handsomer; and am sure I love you better. She has been
my step-mother these fifteen years: you think that's her
face you see, but 'tis only a dawb'd Vizard: she wears

234–35 *a fresh-water Soldier*] a raw recruit (Farmer).
265 *truck*] commodity for barter.

270 an Armour of proof upon't: an inch thick of Paint, besides the Wash: her Face is so fortifi'd that you can make no approaches to it, without a Shovel. But for her constancy, I can tell you for your comfort, she will love till death, I mean till yours: for when she has worn you out, she will certainly dispatch you to another world,

275 for fear of telling tales; as she has already serv'd three Slaves, your Predecessors of happy memory in her favours. She has made my pious Father a three pil'd Cuckold to my knowledg: and now she wou'd be robbing me of my single Sheep too.

280 *Antonio.* Prithee prevent her then; and at least take the shearing of me first.

Morayma. No; I'll have a Butcher's Pen'worth of you; first secure the Carcass, and then take the fleece into the bargain.

285 *Antonio.* Why sure, you did not put your self and me to all this trouble, for a dry come off: by this hand ———

Taking it.

Morayma. Which you shall never touch; but upon better assurances than you imagine. *Pulling her hand away.*

Antonio. I'll marry thee, and make a *Christian* of thee thou

290 pretty damn'd Infidel.

Morayma. I mean you shall: but no earnest, till the bargain be made before witness: there's love enough to be had, and as much as you can turn you to; never doubt it, but all upon honourable terms.

295 *Antonio.* I vow and swear by Love; and he's a Deity in all Religions.

Morayma. But never to be trusted in any: he has another name too, of a worse sound. Shall I trust an Oath, when I see your Eyes languishing, your Cheeks flushing, and

300 can hear your heart throbbing? no, I'll not come near you: He's a foolish Physitian who will feel the pulse of a Patient, that has the Plague-spots upon him.

Antonio. Did one ever hear a little Moppet, argue so perversly against so good a Cause! Come, prithee, let me

305 anticipate a little of my Revenue.

Morayma. You wou'd feign be fingring your Rents beforehand; but that makes a man an ill Husband ever after. Consider, Marriage is a painful Vocation, as you shall

277–78 *three pil'd*] Three-pile cloth uses an extra thread, therefore more wool must be sheared from sheep.

282 *Butcher's Pen'worth*] what's owing and more but paid in flesh.

286 *a dry come off*] probably like a "dry bob," coition without emission (Farmer).

prove it; manage your Incomes as thriftily as you can,
you shall find a hard task on't, to make even at the
year's end, and yet to live decently.

Antonio. I came with a Christian intention, to revenge my
self upon thy Father; for being the head of a false
Religion.

Morayma. And so you shall; I offer you his Daughter for
your Second: but since you are so pressing, meet me
under my Window, to morrow night, body for body,
about this hour; I'll slip down out of my Lodging, and
bring my Father in my hand.

Antonio. How, thy Father!

Morayma. I mean all that's good of him; his Pearls, and
Jewels, his whole contents, his heart, and Soul; as much
as ever I can carry. I'll leave him his Alchoran; that's
revenue enough for him: every page of it is Gold and
Diamonds. He has the turn of an Eye, a demure Smile,
and a godly Cant, that are worth Millions to him. I
forgot to tell you, that I will have a Slave prepar'd at
the Postern gate, with two Horses ready sadled: no
more, for I fear, I may be miss'd; and think I hear
'em calling for me,—if you have constancy and
Courage ———

Antonio. Never doubt it: and love, in abundance to wander
with thee all the World over.

Morayma. The value of twelve hundred thousand Crowns
in a Casket!———

Antonio. A heavy burden Heaven knows! but we must
pray for patience to support it.

Morayma. Besides a willing Titt that will venture her Corps
with you:—Come, I know you long to have a parting blow with me; and therefore to shew I am in
Charity ———   *He kisses her.*

Antonio. Once more, for pity; that I may keep the flavour
upon my lips till we meet again.

Morayma. No; frequent Charities make bold Beggars: and
besides I have learnt of a Falconer, never to feed up a
Hawk when I wou'd have him fly: that's enough ———
but if you will be nibling, here's a hand to stay your
stomach.   *Kissing her hand.*

Antonio. Thus Conquer'd Infidels, that Wars may cease,
Are forc'd to give their hands, and sign the Peace.

Morayma. Thus *Christians* are outwitted by the Foe;

310

315

320

325

330

335

340

345

350

317 *body for body*] person to person.
338 *Titt*] girl, hussy.

You had her in your Pow'r, and let her go.
If you release my hand, the fault's not mine;
You shou'd have made me seal, as well as sign.
She runs off, he follows her to the door; then comes back
again, and goes out at the other.

ACT IV. Scene 1

Benducar's Pallace in the Castle of Alcazar.

Benducar (solus). My future Fate, the colour of my life,
My all depends on this important hour:
This hour my Lott is weighing in the Scales,
And Heav'n, perhaps, is doubting what to do.
5   *Almeyda* and a Crown, have push'd me forward;
'Tis fix'd, the Tyrant must not ravish her:
He and *Sebastian* stand betwixt my hopes;
He most; and therefore first to be dispatch'd.
These and a thousand things are to be done
10   In the short compass of this rowling Night,
And nothing yet perform'd,
None of my Emissaries yet return'd.

Enter Haly—First Servant.

Oh *Haly*, thou hast held me long in pain.
What hast thou learnt of *Dorax*? is he dead?
15   *Haly.* Two hours I warily have watch'd his Palace;
All doors are shut, no Servant peeps abroad;
Some Officers with striding hast pass'd in,
While others outward went on quick dispatch;
Sometimes hush'd silence seem'd to reign within;
20   Then Cries confus'd, and a joint clamour follow'd;
Then Lights went gliding by, from room to room,
And shot like thwarting Meteors cross the house:
Not daring farther to enquire, I came
With speed, to bring you this imperfect news.
25   *Benducar.* Hence I conclude him either dead or dying:
His mournful Friends, summon'd to take their leaves,
Are throng'd about his Couch, and sit in Council;
What those Caballing Captains may design,
I must prevent, by being first in Action.
30   To *Muley-Zeydan* fly with speed, desire him
To take my last instructions; tell th'importance

10 *rowling*] elapsing.
22 *thwarting Meteors*] meteors passing crosswise.
31 *take*] undertake and perform.

354

And hast his presence here.　　　　　　*Exit* Haly.
How has this Poison lost its wonted way?
It shou'd have burnt its passage, not have linger'd
In the blind Labyrinths and crooked turnings　　　　　35
Of human Composition; now it moves
Like a slow Fire that works against the Wind,
As if his stronger Stars had interpos'd.

　　　　　Enter Hamet.

Well *Hamet*, are our Friends the Rabble rais'd?
From *Mustafa*, what Message?
Hamet.　　　　　　　　　What you wish:　　　　40
　The streets are thicker in this noon of Night
Than at the Mid-day Sun: a drowzy horrour
Sits on their Eyes, like fear not well awake,
All crowd in heaps, as at a Night Alarm
The Bees drive out upon each other's backs,　　　　45
T'imboss their Hives in clusters; all ask news:
Their busie Captain runs the weary round
To whisper Orders; and commanding silence
Makes not noise cease; but deafens it to murmurs.
Benducar. Night wasts apace: when, when will he appear?　50
Hamet. He only waits your Summons.
Benducar.　　　　　　　Hast their coming.
　Let secrecy and silence be enjoin'd
In their close march: what news from the Lieutenant?
Hamet. I left him at the Gate, firm to your Interest,
　T'admit the Townsmen at their first appearance.　　55
Benducar. Thus far 'tis well: go hasten *Mustafa*.
　　　　　　　　　　　Exit Hamet.

　　　Enter Orchan *the Third Servant.*

O, *Orchan*, did I think thy diligence
Wou'd lag behind the rest? what from the *Mufti*?
Orchan. I sought him round his Palace; made enquiry
Of all the Slaves: in short, I us'd your name　　　　60
And urg'd th'importance home; but had for answer
That since the shut of Evening none had seen him.
Benducar. O the curst fate of all Conspiracies!
They move on many Springs, if one but fail
The restiff *Machine* stops.—In an ill hour he's absent;　65
'Tis the first time, and sure will be the last
That e'er a *Mufti* was not in the way,

---

32 *hast*] hasten.
44–46 *All . . . clusters*] recalling Virgil's *Georgics*, IV, 67–87 (Brower).

When Tumult and Rebellion shou'd be broach'd.
Stay by me; thou art resolute and faithful;
70   I have Employment worthy of thy Arm.   *Walks.*

Enter Muley-Zeydan.

Muley-Zeydan. You see me come impatient of my hopes,
    And eager as the Courser for the Race:
    Is all in readiness?
Benducar.   All but the *Mufti.*
Muley-Zeydan. We must go on without him.
Benducar.   True we must;
75   For 'tis ill stopping in the full Career,
    How e'er the leap be dangerous and wide.
Orchan (looking out). I see the blaze of Torches from afar;
    And hear the trampling of thick beating feet;
    This way they move.
Benducar.   No doubt the Emperour.
80   We must not be surpriz'd in Conference.
    Trust to my management the Tyrant's death;
    And hast your self to join with *Mustafa.*
    The Officer who guards the Gate is yours;
    When you have gain'd that Pass, divide your Force;
85   Your self in Person head one chosen half,
    And march t'oppress the Faction in Consult
    With dying *Dorax*: Fate has driv'n 'em all
    Into the Net: you must be bold and sudden:
    Spare none, and if you find him strugling yet
90   With pangs of Death, trust not his rowling Eyes
    And heaving gasps; for Poison may be false.
    The home-thrust of a friendly Sword is sure.
Muley-Zeydan. Doubt not my Conduct: they shall be
        surpriz'd;
    Mercy may wait without the Gate one Night,
    At Morn I'll take her in. ———
95   *Benducar.*   Here lies your way,
    You meet your Brother there.
Muley-Zeydan.   May we ne'er meet:
    For, like the Twins of *Leda*, when I mount
    He gallops down the Skies. ———
                              Exit Muley-Zeydan.
    Benducar.   He comes: now Heart

97 *Twins of Leda*] Castor and Pollux. According to some versions
of the legend they trade places in heaven and hell on alternate
days, i.e., the Morning and Evening Star. As one rises the other
sets. (Servius's commentary on *Aeneid*, VI, 121, cited by Sir J. G.
Frazer, *The Fasti of Ovid*, IV, 116–17, 1929).

Be rib'd with Iron for this one attempt:
Set ope thy Sluces, send the vigorous bloud   100
Through every active Limb for my relief:
Then, take thy rest within thy quiet Cell,
For thou shalt drum no more.

Enter Muley-Moluch [*the Emperor*] *and Guards
attending him.*

Emperor. What news of our Affairs, and what of *Dorax*?
Is he no more? say that, and make me happy.   105
Benducar. May all your Enemies be like that Dog,
Whose parting Soul is lab'ring at the Lips.
Emperor. The People, are they rais'd?
Benducar.   And Marshall'd too;
Just ready for the March.
Emperor.   Then I'm at ease.
Benducar. The Night is yours, the glitt'ring Hoast of
Heav'n   110
Shines but for you; but most the Star of Love,
That twinckles you to fair *Almeyda's* Bed.
Oh there's a joy, to melt in her embrace,
Dissolve in pleasures;
And make the gods curse Immortality,   115
That so they cou'd not dye.
But haste, and make 'em yours.
Emperor.   I will; and yet
A kind of weight hangs heavy at my Heart;
My flagging Soul flyes under her own pitch;
Like Fowl in air too damp, and lugs along,   120
As if she were a body in a body,
And not a mounting substance made of Fire.
My Senses too are dull and stupifi'd,
Their edge rebated; sure some ill approaches,
And some kind Spirit knocks softly at my Soul,   125
To tell me Fate's at hand.
Benducar.   Mere Fancies all.
Your Soul has been beforehand with your Body,
And drunk so deep a Draught of promis'd bliss,
She slumbers o'er the Cup; no danger's near,
But of a Surfeit at too full a Feast.   130
Emperor. It may be so; it looks so like the Dream
That overtook me at my waking hour
This Morn; and Dreams they say are then divine,
When all the balmy Vapors are exhal'd,
And some o'er-pow'ring God continues sleep.   135
'Twas then methought *Almeyda*, smiling, came

357

Attended with a Train of all her Race,
Whom in the rage of Empire I had murther'd.
But now, no longer Foes, they gave me Joy
140   Of my new Conquest, and with helping hands
Heav'd me into our Holy Prophet's arms,
Who bore me in a purple Cloud to Heav'n.
Benducar. Good Omen, Sir, I wish you in that Heaven
Your Dream portends you.
        (*Aside*) Which presages death. ———
145 *Emperor.* Thou too wert there;
And thou methought didst push me from below,
With thy full force to Paradise.
Benducar.   Yet better.
Emperor. Ha! What's that grizly Fellow that attends thee?
Benducar. Why ask you Sir?
Emperor.   For he was in my Dream;
And help'd to heave me up.
150 *Benducar.*   With Pray'rs and Wishes;
For I dare swear him honest.
Emperor.   That may be;
But yet he looks Damnation.
Benducar.   You forget,
The Face wou'd please you better: Do you love,
And can you thus forbear?
Emperor.   I'll head my People;
155   Then think of dalliance, when the danger's o'er.
My warlike Spirits work now another way;
And my Soul's tun'd to Trumpets.
Benducar. You debase your self,
To think of mixing with th'ignoble Herd.
160   Let such perform the servile Work of War,
Such who have no *Almeyda* to enjoy.
What, shall the People know their God-like Prince
Skulk'd in a nightly Skirmish? Stole a Conquest,
Headed a Rabble, and profan'd his Person,
165   Shoulder'd with Filth, born in a tide of Ordure,
And stifled with their rank offensive Sweat?
Emperor. I am off again: I will not prostitute
The Regal Dignity so far, to head 'em.
Benducar. There spoke a King.
170   Dismiss your Guards to be employ'd elsewhere
In ruder Combats: You will want no Seconds
In those Alarms you seek.

137–38 *Attended . . . murther'd*] a curious recollection of the spirits
who appear in *Richard III*, V.iii.204–33. They damn Richard for
murdering them, and they cry victory over Richmond.

Emperor (to the Guards).   Go joyn the Crowd;
Benducar, thou shalt lead 'em, in my place.
                                        Exeunt Guards.
The God of Love once more has shot his Fires
Into my Soul; and my whole Heart receives him.   175
Almeyda now returns with all her Charms;
I feel her as she glides along my Veins,
And dances in my Blood: So when our Prophet
Had long been ham'ring in his lonely Cell,
Some dull, insipid, tedious Paradise,   180
A brisk Arabian Girl came tripping by;
Passing she cast at him a side-long glance,
And look'd behind in hopes to be pursu'd:
He took the hint, embrac'd the flying Fair;
And having found his Heav'n, he fix'd it there.   185
                                        Exit Emperor.
Benducar. That Paradise thou never shalt possess.
His death is easie now, his Guards are gone;
And I can sin but once to seize the Throne.
All after Acts are sanctify'd by pow'r.
Orchan. Command my Sword and Life.
Benducar.   I thank thee *Orchan*,   190
And shall reward thy Faith: This Master Key
Frees every Lock, and leads us to his Person:
And shou'd we miss our blow, as Heav'n forbid,
Secures retreat: Leave open all behind us;
And first set wide the *Mufti's* Garden Gate,   195
Which is his private passage to the Palace:
For there our Mutineers appoint to meet,
And thence we may have aid. Now sleep ye Stars
That silently o'erwatch the fate of Kings;
Be all propitious Influences barr'd,   200
And none but murd'rous Planets mount the Guard.
                                        Exit with Orchan.

ACT IV. SCENE 2

A Night Scene of the Mufti's *Garden*

Enter the Mufti *alone, in a Slave's habit, like that of*
Antonio.

Mufti. This 'tis to have a sound Head-piece; by this I have
got to be chief of my Religion; that is, honestly speaking, to teach others what I neither know nor believe my

---

184 *flying Fair*] fleeing woman.

359

5

self. For what's *Mahomet* to me, but that I get by him?
Now for my Policy of this night: I have mew'd up my
suspected Spouse in her Chamber. No more Embassies
to that lusty young Stallion of a Gardiner. Next my
habit of a Slave; I have made my self as like him as I
can, all but his youth and vigor; which when I had, I

10

pass'd my time as well as any of my Holy Predecessors.
Now walking under the Windows of my Seraglio, if
Johayma look out, she will certainly take me for *Antonio*,
and call to me; and by that I shall know what Concupiscence is working in her; she cannot come down to

15

commit Iniquity, there's my safety; but if she peep, if
she put her Nose abroad, there's demonstration of her
pious Will: And I'll not make the first precedent for a
Church-man to forgive Injuries.

Enter Morayma *running to him with a Casket in her
hand, and embracing him.*

Morayma. Now I can embrace you with a good Con-

20

science; here are the Pearls and Jewels, here's my Father.
Mufti. I am indeed thy Father; but how the Devil didst
thou know me in this disguise? And what Pearls and
Jewels dost thou mean?
Morayma (going back). ——— What have I done, and what

25

will now become of me!
Mufti. Art thou mad, *Morayma?*
Morayma. I think you'll make me so.
Mufti. Why, what have I done to thee? Recollect thy self,
and speak sense to me.

30

Morayma. Then give me leave to tell you, you are the
worst of Fathers.
Mufti. Did I think I had begotten such a Monster? Proceed
my dutiful Child, proceed, proceed.
Morayma. You have been raking together a mass of Wealth,

35

by indirect and wicked means; the Spoils of Orphans
are in these Jewels, and the Tears of Widows in these
Pearls.
Mufti. Thou amazest me!
Morayma. I wou'd do so. This Casket is loaded with your

40

Sins; 'tis the Cargo of Rapines, Simony, and Extortions;
the Iniquity of thirty Years Muftiship, converted into
Diamonds.
Mufti. Wou'd some rich rayling Rogue would say as
much to me, that I might squeeze his Purse for scandal.

45

Morayma. No Sir, you get more by pious Fools than
Raylers, when you insinuate into their Families, manage

their Fortunes while they live, and beggar their Heirs by
getting Legacies when they dye. And do you think I'll
be the receiver of your Theft? I discharge my Conscience of it: Here take again your filthy Mammon, and
restore it you had best to the true Owners.

Mufti. I am finely documented by my own Daughter.

Morayma. And a great credit for me to be so: Do but think
how decent a Habit you have on, and how becoming
your Function to be disguis'd like a Slave, and eves-
dropping under the Women's Windows, to be saluted,
as you deserve it richly, with a Piss-pot: If I had not
known you casually by your shambling gate, and a certain
reverend awkardness that is natural to all of your
Function, here you had been expos'd to the laughter of
your own Servants; who have been in search of you
through your whole Seraglio, peeping under every
Petticoat to find you.

Mufti. Prithee Child reproach me no more of human
Failings; they are but a little of the pitch and spots of the
World that are still sticking on me; but I hope to scour
'em out in time: I am better at bottom than thou
think'st; I am not the Man thou tak'st me for.

Morayma. No, to my sorrow Sir you are not.

Mufti. It was a very odd beginning, tho methought, to see
thee come running in upon me with such a warm
embrace; prithee what was the meaning of that violent
hot Hug?

Morayma. I am sure I meant nothing by it, but the zeal and
affection which I bear to the Man of the World, whom
I may love lawfully.

Mufti. But thou wilt not teach me at this age the nature of
a close Embrace?

Morayma. No indeed; for my Mother in Law complains,
that you are past teaching: But if you mistook my
innocent Embrace for Sin, I wish heartily it had been
given where it wou'd have been more acceptable.

Mufti. Why, this is as it shou'd be now: Take the Treasure
again, it can never be put into better hands.

Morayma. Yes, to my knowledg but it might. I have confess'd my Soul to you, if you can understand me rightly;
I never disobey'd you till this night, and now since
through the violence of my Passion, I have been so
unfortunate, I humbly beg your pardon, your blessing,
and your leave, that upon the first opportunity I may

52 *documented*] instructed in an imperious way.

361

go for ever from your sight; for Heaven knows, I never
desire to see you more.

Mufti (wiping his eyes). Thou mak'st me weep at thy
unkindness; indeed dear Daughter we will not part.

95 *Morayma.* Indeed dear Daddy but we will.

Mufti. Why if I have been a little pilfering, or so, I take it
bitterly of thee to tell me of it; since it was to make thee
rich; and I hope a Man may make bold with his own
Soul, without offence to his own Child: Here take the

100 jewels again, take 'em I charge thee upon thy Obedience.

Morayma. Well then, in vertue of Obedience I will take
'em; but on my Soul, I had rather they were in a better
hand.

Mufti. Meaning mine, I know it.

105 *Morayma.* Meaning his whom I love better than my life.

Mufti. That's me again.

Morayma. I wou'd have you think so.

Mufti. How thy good nature works upon me; well I can
do no less than venture damning for thee, and I may put

110 fair for it, if the Rabble be order'd to rise to Night.

Enter Antonio *in an* Affrican *rich habit.*

Antonio. What do you mean my Dear, to stand talking in
this suspicious place, just underneath *Johayma's* Window?
(*To the Mufti*) You are well met Comerade, I know you
are the friend of our flight? are the horses ready at the

115 postern gate?

Mufti. Antonio, and in disguise! now I begin to smell a rat.

Antonio. And I another, that out-stinks it; false *Morayma*,
hast thou thus betray'd me to thy Father!

Morayma. Alas, I was betray'd my self: He came disguis'd

120 like you, and I poor Innocent ran into his hands.

Mufti. In good time you did so; I laid a trap for a Bitch
Fox, and a worse Vermine has caught himself in it: you
wou'd fain break loose now, though you left a limb
behind you; but I am yet in my own Territories and in

125 call of Company, that's my comfort.

Antonio (taking him by the throat). No; I have a trick left to
put thee past thy squeeking: I have giv'n thee the
quinzey; that ungracious tongue shall Preach no more
false Doctrin.

130 *Morayma.* What do you mean? you will not throttle him?
consider he's my Father.

Antonio. Prithee let us provide first for our own safety; if

128 *quinzey*] tonsillitis.

I do not consider him, he will consider us with a
vengeance afterwards.

Morayma. You may threaten him for crying out, but for 135
my sake give him back a little cranny of his Wind-pipe,
and some part of Speech.

Antonio. Not so much as one single Interjection: Come
away Father-in-Law, this is no place for Dialogues:
when you are in the Mosque you talk by hours, and 140
there no Man must interrupt you; this is but like for
like, good Father-in-Law; now I am in the Pulpit 'tis
your turn to hold your tongue. *He struggles.*
Nay if you will be hanging back, I shall take care you
shall hang forward. 145

Pulls him along the Stage; with his Sword at his reins.

Morayma. T'other way, to the Arbour with him; and make
hast before we are discover'd.

Antonio. If I only bind and gag him there, he may commend me hereafter for civil usage; he deserves not so
much favour by any action of his life. 150

Morayma. Yes, pray bate him one, for begetting your
Mistress.

Antonio. I wou'd, if he had not thought more of thy
Mother than of thee; once more come along in silence,
my Pythagorean Father-in-Law. 155

Johayma (at the balcony).—A Bird in a Cage may peep at
least; though she must not fly; what bustle's there
beneath my Window? *Antonio* by all my hopes, I know
him by his habit; but what makes that Woman with
him, and a Friend, a Sword drawn, and hasting hence? 160
this is no time for silence: Who's within, call there,
where are the Servants, why *Omar, Abedin, Hassan* and
the rest, make hast and run into the Garden; there are
Thieves and Villains; arm all the Family, and stop 'em.

Antonio (turning back). O that Schriech Owl at the Window! 165
we shall be pursu'd immediatly; which way shall we
take?

Morayma (giving him the Casket). 'Tis impossible to escape
them; for the way to our Horses lyes back again by the
House; and then we shall meet 'em full in the teeth; 170
here take these Jewels; thou may'st leap the Walls and
get away.

Antonio. And what will become of thee then poor kind
Soul?

Morayma. I must take my fortune; when you are got safe 175

155 *Pythagorean*] mute, as Pythagoreans were contemplative.

into your own Country, I hope you will bestow a sigh
on the memory of her who lov'd you!

Antonio. It makes me mad, to think how many a good night
will be lost betwixt us! take back thy Jewels; 'tis an
180   empty Casket without thee; besides I shou'd never leap
well with the weight of all thy Father's sins about me,
thou and they had been a bargain.

Morayma. Prithee take 'em, 'twill help me to be reveng'd
on him.

185 *Antonio.* No; they'll serve to make thy peace with him.

Morayma. I hear 'em coming; shift for your self at least;
remember I am yours for ever.

    Servants crying this way, this way, *behind the Scenes.*

Antonio. And I but the empty shadow of my self without
thee! farewel Father-in-Law, that shou'd have been, if I
190   had not been curst in my Mother's belly.——— Now
which way fortune.———

    Runs amazedly backwards and forwards.

Servants (within). Follow, follow, yonder are the Villains.

Antonio. O here's a gate open; but it leads into the Castle;
yet I must venture it.   *Going out.*

    A shout behind the Scenes where Antonio *is going out.*

195 *Antonio.* There's the Rabble in a Mutiny; what, is the Devil
up at Midnight! ——— however 'tis good herding in a
Crowd.   *Runs out.*

    Mufti *runs to* Morayma *and lays hold on her, then
snatches away the Casket.*

Mufti. Now, to do things in order, first I seize upon the
Bag, and then upon the Baggage: for thou art but my
200   flesh and blood, but these are my Life and Soul.

Morayma. Then let me follow my flesh and blood, and
keep to your self your Life and Soul.

Mufti. Both or none; come away to durance.

Morayma. Well, if it must be so, agreed; for I have another
205   trick to play you; and thank your self for what shall
follow.

                         Enter Servants.

Johayma (from above). One of them took through the
private way into the Castle; follow him be sure, for
these are yours already.

210 *Morayma.* Help here quickly *Omar, Abedin*; I have hold on
the Villain that stole my jewels; but 'tis a lusty Rogue,
and he will prove too strong for me; what, help I say,
do you not know your Master's Daughter?

Mufti. Now if I cry out they will know my voice; and

then I am disgrac'd for ever: O thou art a venomous   215
Cockatrice!
Morayma. Of your own begetting.
                                    The Servants seize him.
1st Servant. What a glorious deliverance have you had
Madam from this bloody-minded *Christian*!
Morayma. Give me back my Jewels, and carry this notorious   220
Malefactor to be punish'd by my Father.
I'll hunt the other dry-foot.
    Takes the Jewels and runs out after Antonio *at the same*
                                                Passage.
1st Servant. I long to be handselling his hide, before we
bring him to my Master.
2d Servant. Hang him, for an old Covetous Hypocrite: 225
he deserves a worse punishment himself for keeping us
so hardly.
1st Servant. Ay, wou'd he were in this Villain's place; thus
I wou'd lay him on, and thus.   *Beats him.*
2d Servant. And thus wou'd I revenge my self of my last   230
beating.   *He beats him too, and then the rest.*
Mufti. Oh, oh, oh!
1st Servant. Now supposing you were the *Mufti*, Sir,———
                                    Beats him again.
Mufti. The Devil's in that supposing, Rascal; I can bear no
more; and I am the *Mufti*: Now suppose your selves my   235
Servants, and hold your hands; an anointed halter take
you all.
1st Servant. My Master! you will pardon the excess of
our zeal for you, Sir, indeed we all took you for a
Villain, and so we us'd you.   240
Mufti. Ay so I feel you did; my back and sides are abun-
dant testimonies of your zeal. Run Rogues, and bring
me back my Jewels, and my Fugitive Daughter: run I
say.
    They run to the Gate and the first Servant runs back again.
1st Servant. Sir, the Castle is in a most terrible combustion;   245
you may hear 'em hither.
Mufti. 'Tis a laudable commotion: The voice of the
Mobile is the voice of Heaven. I must retire a little, to
strip me of the Slave, and to assume the *Mufti*; and
then I will return: for the piety of the People must be   250

222 *dry-foot*] by scent of the foot.
223 *handselling*] inaugurating with some ceremony, here ironically.
236 *annointed halter*] a halter rope for hanging, here, by ecclesiastical
decree.
248 *Mobile*] *Vox populi, vox Dei.*

encouraged; that they may help me to recover my
Jewels, and my Daughter.
Exit Mufti *and Servants.*

Scene changes to the Castle-yard, and discovers Antonio,
Mustafa, *and the Rabble shouting, they come forward.*

255 *Antonio.* And so at length, as I inform'd you, I escap'd out
of his covetous clutches; and now fly to your illustrious
feet for my protection.

Mustafa. Thou shalt have it, and now defie the *Mufti.* 'Tis
the first Petition that has been made to me since my
exaltation to Tumult; in this second Night of the Month
260 *Abib,* and in the year of the *Hegyra;* the Lord knows
what year; but 'tis no matter; for when I am settled,
the Learned are bound to find it out for me: for I am
resolv'd to date my Authority over the Rabble, like
other Monarchs.

265 *Antonio.* I have always had a longing to be yours again;
though I cou'd not compass it before, and had design'd
you a Casket of my Master's jewels too; for I knew the
Custom, and wou'd not have appear'd before a Great
Person, as you are, without a present: But he has
270 defrauded my good intentions, and basely robb'd you
of 'em, 'tis a prize worth a Million of Crowns, and you
carry your Letters of mark about you.

Mustafa. I shall make bold with his Treasure, for the
support of my New Government.
The People gather about him.
What do these vile Ragga-muffins so near our Person?
275 your savour is offensive to us; bear back there, and make
room for honest Men to approach us; these fools and
knaves are always impudently crowding next to Princes,
and keeping off the more deserving, bear back I say.
They make a wider Circle.
That's dutifully done; now shout to show your Loyalty.
280 (*A great shout.*) Hear'st thou that, Slave *Antonio?* these
obstreperous Villains shout, and know not for what they
make a noise. You shall see me manage 'em, that you

259 *Abib*] the month when the Children of Israel came out of
Egypt, hence the first month in the Jewish religious year.
259 *Hegyra*] dating from the year that Mohammed fled from
Mecca (July 16, A.D. 622), beginning the Mohammedan era.
262–63 *date my Authority*] fix the date, reckon my reign as beginning from. This may allude to the anti-Catholic rioting in London,
December, 1688, when Prince William of Orange approached the
city.
271 *Letters of mark*] letters attesting to your authority.

may judge what ignorant Beasts they are. For whom do
you shout now? who's to Live and Reign? tell me that,
the wisest of you.   285
1st Rabble. Even who you please Captain.
Mustafa. La you there; I told you so.
2d Rabble. We are not bound to know who is to Live and
   Reign; our business is only to rise upon command, and
   plunder.   290
3d Rabble. Ay, the Richest of both Parties; for they are
   our Enemies.
Mustafa. This last Fellow is a little more sensible than the
   rest; he has enter'd somewhat into the merits of the
   Cause.   295
1st Rabble. If a poor Man may speak his mind, I think,
   Captain, that your self are the fittest to Live and Reign,
   I mean not over, but next and immediatly under the
   People; and thereupon I say, *A Mustafa, A Mustafa.*
All Cry. A Mustafa, A Mustafa.   300
Mustafa. I must confess the sound is pleasing, and tickles
   the ears of my Ambition; but alas good People, it must
   not be: I am contented to be a poor simple Vice-Roy;
   but Prince *Muley-Zeydan* is to be the Man: I shall take
   care to instruct him in the arts of Government; and in   305
   his duty to us all: and therefore mark my Cry: *A Muley-
   Zeydan, A Muley-Zeydan.*
All Cry. A Muley-Zeydan, A Muley-Zeydan.
Mustafa. You see Slave *Antonio,* what I might have been.
Antonio. I observe your Modesty.   310
Mustafa. But for a foolish promise I made once to my
   Lord *Benducar,* to set up any one he pleas'd.

   Re-enter the Mufti *with his Servants.*

Antonio. Here's the Old Hypocrite again; now stand your
   ground, and bate him not an inch. Remember the
   Jewels, the Rich and Glorious Jewels; they are destin'd   315
   to be yours, by virtue of Prerogative.
Mustafa. Let me alone to pick a quarrel, I have an old
   grudge to him upon thy account.
          Mufti, *making up to the Mobile.*
Mufti. Good People, here you are met together.
1st Rabble. Ay, we know that without your telling, but   320
   why are we met together, Doctor? for that's it which
   no body here can tell.
2d Rabble. Why, to see one another in the Dark; and to
   make Holy-day at Midnight.
Mufti. You are met, as becomes good Musulmen; to settle   325

the Nation; for I must tell you, that though your
Tyrant is a lawful Emperor, yet your lawful Emperor
is but a Tyrant.

Antonio. What stuff he talks!

330 *Mustafa.* 'Tis excellent fine matter indeed, Slave *Antonio*; he
has a rare tongue; Oh, he wou'd move a Rock of
Elephant!

Antonio (aside). What a Block have I to work upon.
(*To him*) But still remember the Jewels, Sir, the Jewels.

335 *Mustafa.* Nay that's true on t'other side: the Jewels must
be mine; but he has a pure fine way of talking; my
Conscience goes along with him, but the Jewels have
set my heart against him.

Mufti. That your Emperor is a Tyrant is most manifest;
340 for you were born to be *Turks*, but he has play'd the
Turk with you; and is taking your Religion away.

2d Rabble. We find that in our decay of Trade; I have
seen for these hunder'd years, that Religion and Trade
always go together.

345 *Mufti.* He is now upon the point of Marrying himself,
without your Sovereign consent; and what are the
effects of Marriage?

3d Rabble. A scoulding, domineering Wife, if she prove
honest; and if a Whore, a fine gawdy Minx, that robs
350 our Counters every Night, and then goes out, and spends
it upon our Cuckold-makers.

Mufti. No, the natural effects of Marriage are Children:
Now on whom wou'd he beget these Children? Even
upon a *Christian*! Oh horrible; how can you believe
355 me, though I am ready to swear it upon the Alcoran!
Yes, true Believers, you may believe me, that he is
going to beget a Race of Misbelievers.

Mustafa. That's fine, in earnest; I cannot forbear hearkening
to his enchanting Tongue.

360 *Antonio.* But yet remember ———

Mustafa. Ay, Ay, the Jewels! Now again I hate him; but
yet my Conscience makes me listen to him.

Mufti. Therefore to conclude all, Believers, pluck up your
Hearts, and pluck down the Tyrant: Remember the

331–32 *Rock of Elephant*] a rock of ivory. "Heavy Gold and
polished elephant" (*Aeneid*, III, 595, Dryden's translation).

350 *Counters*] tables or places where money is kept and
counted.

352–57 *No ... Misbelievers*] an allusion to objections that had
been made to James II's marriage to a Catholic, Mary of Modena
(John Robert Moore, *PMLA*, LXXIII [1958], 42).

Courage of your Ancestors; remember the Majesty of 365
the People; remember your selves, your Wives and
Children; and lastly, above all, remember your Religion,
and our holy *Mahomet*; all these require your timous
assistance; shall I say they beg it? No, they claim it of
you, by all the nearest and dearest Tyes of these three 370
P's Self-Preservation, our Property, and our Prophet.
Now answer me with an unanimous chearful Cry, and
follow me, who am your Leader to a glorious Deliverance.

All cry, A Mufti, A Mufti, and are following him off the
Stage.

Antonio. Now you see what comes of your foolish Qualms 375
of Conscience: The Jewels are lost, and they are all
leaving you.
Mustafa. What, am I forsaken of my Subjects? Wou'd the
Rogue purloin my liege People from me! I charge you
in my own Name come back ye Deserters; and hear me 380
speak.
1st Rabble. What, will he come with his Balderdash, after
the *Mufti's* eloquent Oration?
2d Rabble. He's our Captain, lawfully pick'd up, and
elected upon a Stall; we will hear him. 385
Omnes. Speak Captain, for we will hear you.
Mustafa. Do you remember the glorious Rapines and
Robberies you have committed? Your breaking open
and gutting of Houses, your rummaging of Cellars, your
demolishing of Christian Temples, and bearing off in 390
triumph the superstitious Plate and Pictures, the Orna-
ments of their wicked Altars, when all rich Moveables
were sentenc'd for idolatrous, and all that was idolatrous
was seiz'd? Answer first for your remembrance, of all
these sweetnesses of Mutiny; for upon those Grounds 395
I shall proceed.
Omnes. Yes we do remember, we do remember.
Mustafa. Then make much of your retentive Faculties.
And who led you to those Hony-Combs? Your *Mufti*?
No, Believers, he only preach'd you up to it; but durst 400
not lead you; he was but your Counsellor, but I was

368 *timous*] timeous, early.
382 *Balderdash*] senseless jumble of words.
385 *Stall*] a seat of office.
390 *Christian Temples*] suggesting the pillaging of Roman Catholic
churches in London, upon the flight of James II (see Evelyn's *Diary*,
Dec. 13, 1688).

your Captain; he only lood you, but 'twas I that led you.

Omnes. That's true, that's true.

405 *Antonio.* There you were with him for his Figures.

Mustafa. I think I was, Slave *Antonio*. Alas I was ignorant of my own Talent.—Say then, Believers, will you have a Captain for your *Mufti*? Or a *Mufti* for your Captain? And further to instruct you how to Cry, Will you have

410 a *Mufti*, or no *Mufti*?

Omnes. No *Mufti*, no *Mufti*.

Mustafa. That I laid in for 'em, Slave *Antonio*. ———
Do I then spet upon your Faces? Do I discourage Rebellion, Mutiny, Rapine, and Plundering? You may

415 think I do, Believers, but Heaven forbid: No, I encourage you to all these laudable Undertakings; you shall plunder, you shall pull down the Government; but you shall do this upon my Authority, and not by his wicked Instigation.

420 *3d Rabble.* Nay, when his turn is serv'd, he may preach up Loyalty again, and Restitution, that he might have another Snack among us.

1st Rabble. He may indeed; for 'tis but his saying 'tis Sin, and then we must restore; and therefore I wou'd have a

425 new Religion, where half the Commandments shou'd be taken away, the rest mollifi'd, and there shou'd be little or no Sin remaining.

Omnes. Another Religion, a new Religion, another Religion.

430 *Mustafa.* And that may easily be done, with the help of a little Inspiration: For I must tell you, I have a Pigeon at home, of *Mahomet's* own breed; and when I have learnt her to pick Pease out of my Ear, rest satisfi'd 'till then, and you shall have another. But now I think on't, I am

435 inspir'd already, that 'tis no Sin to depose the *Mufti*.

402 *lood*] urged on, as hunters incite dogs to chase. The prologue to Shadwell's *Bury Fair* (1689): "If any Noble Patriot did excel / His own, and Country's Rights defending well / These yelping Currs were straight loo'd on the bark" (Summers).

405 *with him for his Figures*] under the spell of Mufti's rhetoric, and recognizing the crowd's identity with hound dogs.

412 *laid in for*] exerted myself in order to gain.

413 *spet*] i.e., spit.

422 *Snack*] share of the booty.

431–32 *Pigeon at home*] "*Mohamets* pigeon, which would resort unto him being in the middest of his campe, and picke a pease out of his eare; in such sort that manie of the people thought that the Holie-ghost came and told him a tale in his eare" (Reginald Scot, *The Discoverie of Witchcraft* [1584; 1930 edition], p. 144).

Antonio. And good reason; for when Kings and Queens
  are to be discarded, what shou'd Knaves do any longer
  in the pack?
Omnes. He is depos'd, he is depos'd, he is depos'd.
Mustafa. Nay, if he and his Clergy will needs be preaching   440
  up Rebellion, and giving us their Blessing, 'tis but
  justice they shou'd have the first fruits of it.—Slave
  Antonio, take him into custody; and does thou hear,
  Boy, be sure to secure the little transitory Box of
  Jewels: If he be obstinate, put a civil Question to him   445
  upon the Rack, and he squeaks I warrant him.
Antonio (seizing the Mufti). Come my *quondam* Master, you
  and I must change Qualities.
Mufti. I hope you will not be so barbarous to torture me,
  we may preach Suffering to others, but alas, holy Flesh   450
  is too well pamper'd to endure Martyrdom.
Mustafa. Now, late *Mufti*, not forgetting my first Quarrel
  to you, we will enter our selves with the Plunder of
  your Palace: 'tis good to sanctifie a Work, and begin a
  God's name.   455
1st Rabble. Our Prophet let the Devil alone with the last
  Mob.
Mustafa. But he takes care of this himself.

As they are going out enter Benducar *leading* Almeyda: *He
  with a Sword in one hand;* Benducar's *Slave follows with*
  Muley-Moluch's *Head upon a Spear.*

Not so much hast Masters; come back again: you are
  so bent upon mischief, that you take a man upon the   460
  first word of Plunder. Here's a sight for you: the
  Emperour is come upon his head to visit you. *(bowing)*
  Most Noble Emperour, now I hope you will not hit
  us in the teeth, that we have pull'd you down, for we
  can tell you to your face, that we have exalted you.   465
                                        They all shout.
Benducar (to Almeyda apart). Think what I am, and what
  your self may be,
  In being mine: refuse not proffer'd Love
  That brings a Crown.
Almeyda (to him). I have resolv'd,   470
  And these shall know my thoughts.
Benducar (to her).   On that I build. ——
                  He comes up to the Rabble.

448 *Qualities*] positions or ranks.
454–55 *a God's*] in God's.
463–64 *hit us in the teeth*] reproach.

Joy to the People for the Tyrant's Death!
Oppression, Rapine, Banishment and Bloud
Are now no more; but speechless as that tongue
475   That lyes for ever still.
How is my grief divided with my joy,
When I must own I kill'd him! bid me speak,
For not to bid me, is to disallow
What for your sakes is done.
480   *Mustafa.* In the name of the People we command you
speak: But that pretty Lady shall speak first; for we
have taken somewhat of a likeing to her Person. Be not
afraid Lady to speak to these rude Ragga-muffians:
there's nothing shall offend you, unless it be their
485   stink, and please you.   *Making a Legg.*
Almeyda. Why shou'd I fear to speak who am your
Queen?
My peacefull Father sway'd the Scepter long;
And you enjoy'd the Blessings of his Reign,
While you deserv'd the name of *Affricans.*
490   Then not commanded, but commanding you,
Fearless I speak: know me for what I am.
Benducar (aside). How she assumes! I like not this beginning.
Almeyda. I was not born so base, to flatter Crowds,
And move your pitty by a whining tale:
495   Your Tyrant would have forc'd me to his Bed;
But in th'attempt of that foul brutal Act,
These Loyall Slaves secur'd me by his Death.
                              Pointing to Benducar.
Benducar (aside). Makes she no more of me then of a Slave?
(*To* Almeyda) Madam, I thought I had instructed you
500   To frame a Speech more suiting to the times:
The Circumstances of that dire design,
Your own despair, my unexpected ayd,
My Life endanger'd by his bold defence,
And after all, his Death, and your Deliv'rance,
505   Were themes that ought not to be slighted o're.
Mustafa. She might have pass'd over all your petty busi-
nesses and no great matter: But the Raising of my
Rabble is an Exploit of consequence; and not to be
mumbled up in silence for all her pertness.
510   *Almeyda.* When force invades the gift of Nature, Life,
The eldest Law of nature bids defend:
And if in that defence, a Tyrant fall,
His Death's his Crime, not ours:

485 *Making a Legg*] bowing.

Suffice it that he's Dead: all wrongs dye with him;
When he can wrong no more I pardon him: 515
Thus I absolve my self: and him excuse,
Who sav'd my life, and honour; but praise neither.
Benducar. 'Tis cheap to pardon, whom you would not pay;
But what speak I of payment and reward?
Ungratefull Woman, you are yet no Queen;   520
Nor more than a proud haughty *Christian* slave:
As such I seize my right.   *Going to lay hold on her.*
Almeyda (drawing a Dagger).   Dare not to approach me;
Now *Affricans,*
He shows himself to you; to me he stood
Confest before, and own'd his Insolence   525
T'espouse my person, and assume the Crown,
Claym'd in my Right: for this he slew your Tyrant;
Oh no, he only chang'd him for a worse;
Imbas'd your Slavery by his own vileness,
And loaded you with more ignoble bonds: 530
Then think me not ungratefull, not to share,
Th'Imperial Crown with a presuming Traytor.
He says I am a *Christian*; true I am,
But yet no Slave: If *Christians* can be thought,
Unfit to govern those of other Faith,   535
'Tis left for you to judge.
Benducar. I have not patience; she consumes the time
In Idle talk, and owns her false Belief:
Seize her by force, and bear her hence unheard.
Almeyda (to the People). No, let me rather dye your sacrifice   540
Than live his Tryumph;
I throw my self into my People's armes;
As you are Men compassionate my wrongs,
And as good men Protect me.
Antonio (aside). Something must be done to save her.   545
(*To Mustafa*) This is all address'd to you Sir: She
singled you out with her eye, as Commander in chief
of the Mobility.
Mustafa. Think'st thou so Slave *Antonio*?
Antonio. Most certainly Sir; and you cannot in honour but   550
protect her. Now look to your hits, and make your
fortune.
Mustafa. Methought indeed she cast a kind leer towards
me: Our Prophet was but just such another Scoundrell
as I am, till he rais'd himself to power, and consequently   555

529 *Imbas'd*] humiliated.
551 *hits*] lucky chances, scores made in dice play.

373

to Holyness, by marrying his master's Widow: I am resolved I'le put forward for my self: for why should I be my Lord *Benducar's* Fool and Slave, when I may be my own fool and his Master?

560 *Benducar.* Take her into possession, *Mustafa*.

Mustafa. That's better Counsell than you meant it: Yes I do take her into possession, and into protection too: what say you, Masters, will you stand by me?

Omnes. One and all; One and all.

565 *Benducar.* Hast thou betray'd me Traytor?

Mufti speak and mind 'em of Religion.

Mufti *shakes his head.*

Mustafa. Alas the poor Gentleman has gotten a cold, with a Sermon of two hours long, and a prayer of four: and besides, if he durst speak, mankind is grown wiser at

570 this time of day, than to cut one another's throats about Religion. Our *Mufti* is a Green coat, and the *Christian's* is a black coat; and we must wisely go together by the ears, whether green or black shall sweep our spoils.

Drums within and shouts.

Benducar. Now we shall see whose numbers will prevail:

575 The Conquering Troups of *Muley-Zeydan*, come To crush Rebellion, and espouse my Cause.

Mustafa. We will have a fair Tryall of Skill for't, I can tell him that. When we have dispatch'd with *Muley-Zeydan*, your Lordship shall march in equall pro-

580 portions of your body, to the four gates of the City: and every Tower shall have a Quarter of you.

Antonio *draws them up and takes* Almeyda *by the hand.*

Shouts again and Drums.

Enter Dorax *and* Sebastian *attended by* Affrican *Soldiers and* Portugueses. Almeyda *and* Sebastian *run into each other's armes and both speak together.*

Sebastian and Almeyda. My *Sebastian*! My *Almeyda*!

Almeyda. Do you then live?

Sebastian.   And live to love thee ever.

Benducar. How! *Dorax* and *Sebastian* still alive!

585 The *Moors* and *Christians* joyn'd! I thank thee Prophet.

Dorax. The Citadell is ours; and *Muley-Zeydan*

556 *his master's widow*] Mohammed was thought to have been bonded to a merchant and to have married his master's widow, a woman twenty years his senior.

571 *Green coat*] noblemen, emirs, descendents of the prophet, who wore green clothes, sashes, and turbans.

572 *black coat*] a parson.

Safe under Guard, but as becomes a Prince.
Lay down your armes: such base Plebeian bloud
Would only stain the brightness of my Sword,
And blunt it for some nobler work behind.   590
Mustafa. I suppose you may put it up without offence to
  any man here present? For my part, I have been Loyall
  to my Soveraign Lady: though that Villain *Benducar*,
  and that Hypocrite the *Mufti*, would have corrupted me;
  but if those two scape publick Justice, then I and all my   595
  late honest Subjects here, deserve hanging.
Benducar (to Dorax). I'm sure I did my part to poyson thee,
  What Saint soe're has Sodder'd thee again.
  A Dose less hot had burst through ribs of Iron.
Mufti. Not knowing that, I poyson'd him once more,   600
  And drench'd him with a draught so deadly cold
  That, had'st not thou prevented, had congeal'd
  The channell of his bloud, and froze him dry.
Benducar. Thou interposing Fool, to mangle mischief,
  And think to mend the perfect work of Hell.   605
Dorax. Thus, when Heaven pleases, double poysons cure.
  I will not tax thee of Ingratitude
  To me thy Friend, who hast betray'd thy Prince:
  Death he deserv'd indeed, but not from thee.
  But fate it seems reserv'd the worst of men   610
  To end the worst of Tyrants.
  Go bear him to his fate.
  And send him to attend his Master's Ghost.
  Let some secure my other poys'ning Friend,
  Whose double dilligence preserv'd my life.   615
Antonio. You are fall'n into good hands, Father in law;
  your sparkling Jewells, and *Morayma's* eyes may prove
  a better bail than you deserve.
Mufti. The best that can come of me, in this condition, is
  to have my life begg'd first, and then to be begg'd for a 620
  Fool afterwards.
     Exit Antonio *with the* Mufti, *and at the same time*
                      Benducar *is carry'd off.*
Dorax (to Mustafa). You and your hungry herd depart
  untouch'd;
  For Justice cannot stoop so low, to reach
  The groveling sin of Crowds: but curst be they

590 *behind*] later.
598 *Sodder'd*] patched up.
606 *double poysons cure*] See the note to Dryden's preface, 202–203
620–21 *begg'd for a Fool*] the former practice of asking the king to give
guardianship of an idiot and his estate to one of the courtiers.

625   Who trust revenge with such mad Instruments,
Whose blindfold bus'ness is but to destroy:
And like the fire Commission'd by the Winds,
Begins on sheds, but rouling in a round,
On Pallaces returns. Away ye skum,
630   That still rise upmost when the Nation boyls:
Ye mungrill work of Heaven, with humane shapes,
Not to be damn'd, or sav'd, but breath, and perish,
That have but just enough of sence, to know
The master's voice, when rated, to depart.
                               Exeunt Mustafa *and* Rabble.
Almeyda (kneeling to him). With gratitude as low, as knees
635   can pay
To those blest holy Fires, our Guardian Angells,
Receive these thanks; till Altars can be rais'd.
Dorax (raising her up). Arise fair Excellence; and pay no
thanks,
Till time discover what I have deserv'd.
640   *Sebastian*. More then reward can answer.
If *Portugall* and *Spain* were joyn'd to *Affrique*,
And the main Ocean crusted into Land,
If Universall Monarchy were mine,
Here should the gift be plac'd.
645   *Dorax*. And from some hands I shou'd refuse that gift:
Be not too prodigall of Promises;
But stint your bounty to one only grant,
Which I can ask with honour.
Sebastian.   What I am
Is but thy gift, make what thou canst of me.
Secure of no Repulse.
650   *Dorax (to Sebastian)*.   Dismiss your Train.
     (*To Almeyda*) You, Madam, please one moment to
retire.

     Sebastian *signes to the* Portugueses *to go off.* Almeyda
       bowing to him, goes off also: The Affricans *follow her.*

Dorax (to the Captain of his Guard). With you one word in
private.   *Goes out with the Captain.*
Sebastian (solus). Reserv'd behaviour, open Nobleness,
A long misterious Track of a stern bounty.
655   But now the hand of Fate is on the Curtain,
And draws the Scene to sight.

     Re-enter Dorax, *having taken off his Turbant and put
on a Peruque, Hat and Crevat.*

634 *rated*] chided, also driven off, especially with reference to dogs.

Dorax. Now do you know me?
Sebastian.　　　　　　　　Thou shouldst be *Alonzo*.
Dorax. So you shou'd be *Sebastian*:
　But when *Sebastian* ceas'd to be himself,
　I ceas'd to be *Alonzo.*
Sebastian.　　　　　As in a Dream　　　　　　　660
　I see thee here, and scarce believe mine eyes.
Dorax. Is it so strange to find me, where my wrongs,
　And your Inhumane Tyranny have sent me?
　Think not you dream: or, if you did, my Injuries
　Shall call so loud, that Lethargy should wake;　　665
　And Death should give you back to answer me.
　A Thousand Nights have brush'd their balmy wings
　Over these eyes, but ever when they clos'd,
　Your Tyrant Image forc'd 'em ope again,
　And dry'd the dewes they brought.　　　　　　670
　The long expected hour is come at length,
　By manly Vengence to redeem my fame;
　And that once clear'd, eternall sleep is welcome.
Sebastian. I have not yet forgot I am a King;
　Whose Royall Office is redress of Wrongs:　　675
　If I have wrong'd thee, charge me face to face;
　I have not yet forgot I am a Soldier.
Dorax. 'Tis the first Justice thou hast ever done me.
　Then, though I loath this Woman's War of tongues,
　Yet shall my Cause of Vengeance first be clear:　680
　And, Honour, be thou Judge.
Sebastian. Honour befriend us both.
　Beware, I warn thee yet, to tell thy griefs
　In terms becoming Majesty to hear:
　I warn thee thus, because I know thy temper　　685
　Is Insolent and haughty to Superiours:
　How often hast thou brav'd my peacefull Court,
　Fill'd it with noisy brawls, and windy boasts;
　And, with past service, nauseously repeated,
　Reproach'd ev'n me thy Prince?　　　　　　690
Dorax. And well I might, when you forgot reward,
　The part of Heav'n in Kings: for punishment
　Is Hangman's work, and drudgery for Devils.
　I must and will reproach thee with my service,
　Tyrant, (it irks me so to call my Prince.)　　695
　But just resentment and hard usage coyn'd
　Th'unwilling word; and grating as it is
　Take it, for 'tis thy due.
Sebastian.　　　　　How, Tyrant?
Dorax.　　　　　　　　Tyrant.

377

700

705

710

715

720

725

730

735

740

Sebastian. Traytour! that name thou canst not Eccho back:
That Robe of Infamy, that Circumcision
Ill hid beneath that Robe, proclaim thee Traytor:
And, if a Name
More foul than Traytor be, 'tis Renegade.
Dorax. If I'm a Traytor, think and blush, thou Tyrant,
Whose Injuries betray'd me into treason.
Effac'd my Loyalty, unhing'd my Faith,
And hurryed me from hopes of Heaven to Hell.
All these, and all my yet unfinish'd Crimes,
When I shall rise to plead before the Saints,
I charge on thee, to make thy damning sure.
Sebastian. Thy old presumptuous Arrogance again,
That bred my first dislike, and then my loathing.
Once more be warn'd, and know me for thy King.
Dorax. Too well I know thee; but for King no more:
This is not *Lisbonne*, nor the Circle this,
Where, like a Statue, thou hast stood besieg'd,
By Sycophants and Fools, the growth of Courts:
Where thy gull'd eyes, in all the gawdy round,
Met nothing but a lye in every face;
And the gross flattery of a gaping Crowd,
Envious who first should catch, and first applaud
The Stuff of Royall Nonsense: when I spoke,
My honest homely words were carp'd, and censur'd,
For want of Courtly Stile: related Actions,
Though modestly reported, pass'd for boasts:
Secure of Merit, if I ask'd reward
Thy hungry Minions thought their rights invaded,
And the bread snatch'd from Pimps and Parasits.
Enriquez answer'd, with a ready lye,
To save his King's, the boon was begg'd before.
Sebastian. What sayst thou of *Enriquez*? now by Heaven
Thou mov'st me more by barely naming him,
Than all thy foul unmanner'd scurril taunts.
Dorax. And therefore 'twas to gaul thee, that I nam'd him:
That thing, that nothing, but a cringe and smile;
That Woman, but more dawb'd; or if a man,
Corrupted to a Woman: thy Man Mistress.
Sebastian. All false as Hell or thou.
Dorax.   Yes; full as false
As that I serv'd thee fifteen hard Campaignes,
And pitch'd thy Standard in these Forreign Fields:

715 *the Circle*] an assembly surrounding the principal person
in a court.

By me thy greatness grew; thy years grew with it,
But thy Ingratitude outgrew 'em both.
Sebastian. I see to what thou tend'st, but tell me first
   If those great Acts were done alone for me;
   If love produc'd not some, and pride the rest?   745
Dorax. Why Love does all that's noble here below;
   But all th'advantage of that love was thine.
   For, coming fraughted back, in either hand
   With Palm and Olive, Victory and Peace,
   I was indeed prepar'd to ask my own: 750
   (For *Violante's* vows were mine before:)
   Thy malice had prevention, ere I spoke;
   And ask'd me *Violante* for *Enriquez.*
Sebastian. I meant thee a reward of greater worth.
Dorax. Where justice wanted, could reward be hop'd?   755
   Could the robb'd Passenger expect a bounty,
   From those rapacious hands who stript him first?
Sebastian. He had my promise, e're I knew thy love.
Dorax. My Services deserv'd thou should'st revoke it.
Sebastian. Thy Insolence had cancell'd all thy Service: 760
   To violate my Laws, even in my Court,
   Sacred to peace, and safe from all affronts;
   E'ven to my face, as done in my despight,
   Under the wing of awfull Majesty
   To strike the man I lov'd!   765
Dorax. Even in the face of Heaven, a place more Sacred,
   Would I have struck the man, who propt by power,
   Would Seize my right, and rob me of my Love:
   But, for a blow provok'd by thy Injustice,
   The hasty product of a just despair,   770
   When he refus'd to meet me in the field,
   That thou shoud'st make a Coward's Cause thy own!
Sebastian. He durst; nay more, desir'd and begg'd with
     tears,
   To meet thy Challenge fairly: 'twas thy fault
   To make it publique; but my duty, then,   775
   To interpose; on pain of my displeasure,
   Betwixt your Swords.
Dorax.   On pain of Infamy
   He should have disobey'd.
Sebastian. Th'Indignity thou didst, was ment to me;
   Thy gloomy eyes were cast on me, with scorn,   780
   As who should say the blow was there intended;
   But that thou didst not dare to lift thy hands
   Against Annointed power: so was I forc'd
   To do a Soveraign justice to my self;

      And spurn thee from my presence.

785 *Dorax.*   Thou hast dar'd
      To tell me, what I durst not tell my self:
      I durst not think that I was spurn'd, and live;
      And live to hear it boasted to my face.
      All my long Avarice of honour lost,
790   Heap'd up in Youth, and hoarded up for Age;
      Has honour's Fountain then suck'd back the stream?
      He has; and hooting Boys, may dry-shod pass,
      And gather pebbles from the naked Foord.
      Give me my Love, my Honour; give 'em back: ———
795   Give me revenge; while I have breath to ask it. ———
  Sebastian. Now, by this honour'd Order which I wear,
      More gladly would I give, than thou dar'st ask it:
      Nor shall the Sacred Character of King
      Be urg'd, to shield me from thy bold appeal.
800   If I have injur'd thee, that makes us equall:
      The wrong, if done, debas'd me down to thee.
      But thou hast charg'd me with Ingratitude:
      Hast thou not charg'd me; speak?
  Dorax.   Thou know'st I have:
      If thou disown'st that Imputation, draw,
805   And prove my Charge a lye.
  Sebastian. No; to disprove that lye, I must not draw:
      Be conscious to thy worth, and tell thy Soul
      What thou hast done this day in my defence:
      To fight thee, after this, what were it else,
810   Than owning that Ingratitude thou urgest?
      That *Isthmus* stands betwixt two rushing Seas;
      Which, mounting, view each other from afar;
      And strive in vain to meet.
  Dorax.   I'le cut that *Isthmus*.
      Thou know'st I meant not to preserve thy Life,
815   But to reprieve it, for my own revenge.
      I sav'd thee out of honourable malice:
      Now draw; I should be loath to think thou dar'st not:
      Beware of such another vile excuse.
  Sebastian. O patience Heaven!
  Dorax.   Beware of Patience too;
820   That's a Suspicious word: it had been proper
      Before thy foot had spurn'd me; now 'tis base:
      Yet, to disarm thee of thy last defence,
      I have thy Oath for my security:
      The only boon I begg'd was this fair Combat:
825   Fight or be Perjur'd now; that's all thy choice.

Sebastian (*drawing*). Now I can thank thee as thou wouldst
    be thank'd:
    Never was vow of honour better pay'd,
    If my true Sword but hold, than this shall be.
    The sprightly Bridegroom, on his Wedding Night,
    More gladly enters not the lists of Love. 830
    Why 'tis enjoyment to be summon'd thus.
    Go: bear my Message to *Enriquez* Ghost;
    And say his Master and his Friend reveng'd him.
Dorax. His Ghost! then is my hated Rivall dead?
Sebastian. The question is beside our present purpose; 835
    Thou seest me ready; we delay too long.
Dorax. A minute is not much in either's Life,
    When their's but one betwixt us; throw it in,
    And give it him of us, who is to fall.
Sebastian. He's dead: make hast, and thou mayst yet o're
    take him. 840
Dorax. When I was hasty, thou delay'st me longer.
    I prethee let me hedge one moment more
    Into thy promise; for thy life preserv'd:
    Be kind: and tell me how that Rivall dy'd,
    Whose Death next thine I wish'd. 845
Sebastian. If it would please thee thou should'st never
    know:
    But thou, like Jealousy, enquir'st a truth,
    Which, found, will torture thee: He dy'd in Fight:
    Fought next my person; as in Consort fought:
    Kept pace for pace, and blow for every blow; 850
    Save when he heav'd his Shield in my defence;
    And on his naked side receiv'd my wound.
    Then, when he could no more, he fell at once:
    But rowl'd his falling body cross their way;
    And made a Bulwark of it for his Prince. 855
Dorax. I never can forgive him such a death!
Sebastian. I prophecy'd thy proud Soul could not bear it.
    Now, judge thy self, who best deserv'd my Love.
    I knew you both; (and durst I say) as Heaven
    Foreknew among the shining Angell host 860
    Who would stand firm, who fall.
Dorax. Had he been tempted so, so had he fall'n;
    And so, had I been favour'd, had I stood.
Sebastian. What had been is unknown; what is appears:
    Confess he justly was preferr'd to thee. 865
Dorax. Had I been born with his indulgent Stars,
    My fortune had been his, and his been mine.
    O, worse than Hell! what Glory have I lost,

And what has he acquir'd, by such a death!
870   I should have fallen by *Sebastian's* side;
      My Corps had been the Bulwark of my King.
      His glorious end was a patch'd work of fate,
      Ill sorted with a soft effeminate life:
      It suited better with my life than his
875   So to have dy'd: mine had been of a peice,
      Spent in your service, dying at your feet.
Sebastian. The more effeminate and soft his life,
      The more his fame, to struggle to the field,
      And meet his glorious fate: Confess, proud Spirit,
880   (For I will have it from thy very mouth)
      That better he deserv'd my love than thou.
Dorax. O, whether would you drive me! I must grant,
      Yes I must grant, but with a swelling Soul,
      Enriquez had your Love with more desert:
885   For you he fought, and dy'd; I fought against you;
      Through all the mazes of the bloudy field,
      Hunted your Sacred life; which that I miss'd
      Was the propitious errour of my fate,
      Not of my Soul; my Soul's a Regicide.
Sebastian (more calmly). Thou might'st have given it a more
890   gentle name:
      Thou meant'st to kill a Tyrant, not a King:
      Speak didst thou not, *Alonzo?*
Dorax.   Can I speak!
      Alas, I cannot answer to *Alonzo*:
      No, *Dorax* cannot answer to *Alonzo*:
895   *Alonzo* was too kind a name for me.
      Then, when I fought and conquer'd with your Armes,
      In that blest Age I was the man you nam'd:
      Till rage and pride debas'd me into *Dorax*;
      And lost like *Lucifer*, my name above.
900 *Sebastian.* Yet, twice this day I ow'd my life to *Dorax*.
Dorax. I sav'd you but to kill you; there's my grief.
Sebastian. Nay, if thou can'st be griev'd, thou can'st repent:
      Thou coud'st not be a Villain, though thou woud'st:
      Thou own'st too much, in owning thou hast err'd;
905   And I too little, who provok'd thy Crime.
Dorax. O stop this headlong Torrent of your goodness:
      It comes too fast upon a feeble Soul,
      Half drown'd in tears, before; spare my confusion:
      For pitty spare, and say not, first, you err'd.
910   For yet I have not dar'd, through guilt and shame,
      To throw my self beneath your Royall feet.
                                        Falls at his feet.

Now spurn this Rebell, this proud Renegade:
'Tis just you should, nor will I more complain.
Sebastian (taking him up). Indeed thou shoud'st not ask
   forgiveness first,
But thou preventst me still, in all that's noble.   915
Yet I will raise thee up with better news:
Thy *Violante's* heart was ever thine;
Compell'd to wed, because she was my Ward,
Her Soul was absent when she gave her hand:
Nor could my threats, or his pursuing Courtship,   920
Effect the Consummation of his Love:
So, still indulging tears, she pines for thee,
A Widdow and a Maid.
Dorax. Have I been cursing Heav'n while Heaven blest
   me?
I shall run mad with extasy of joy: 925
What, in one moment, to be reconcil'd
To Heaven, and to my King, and to my Love!
But pitty is my Friend, and stops me short,
For my unhappy Rivall: poor *Enriquez!*
Sebastian. Art thou so generous too, to Pitty him?   930
Nay, then I was unjust to love him better.
Here let me ever hold thee in my arms:
                     Embracing him.
And all our quarrells be but such as these,
Who shall love best, and closest shall embrace:
Be what *Enriquez* was; be my *Alonzo.*   935
Dorax. What, my *Alonzo* sayd you? my *Alonzo!*
Let my tears thank you; for I cannot speak:
And if I cou'd,
Words were not made to vent such thoughts as mine.
Sebastian. Thou canst not speak, and I can ne're be silent. 940
Some Strange reverse of Fate must, sure attend
This vast profusion, this extravagance
Of Heaven, to bless me thus. 'Tis Gold so pure
It cannot bear the Stamp, without allay.
Be kind, ye Powers, and take but half away: 945
With ease the gifts of Fortune I resign;
But, let my Love, and Friend, be ever mine.
                            Exeunt.

ACT V. [SCENE 1]

The Scene is a Room of State

Enter Dorax *and* Antonio.

Dorax. Joy is on every face, without a Cloud:
　　As, in the Scene of opening Paradice,
　　The whole Creation danc'd at their new being:
　　Pleas'd to be what they were; pleas'd with each other.
5　　Such Joy have I, both in my self, and Friends:
　　And double Joy, that I have made 'em happy.
Antonio. Pleasure has been the bus'ness of my life;
　　And every change of Fortune easy to me,
　　Because I still was easy to my self.
10　　The loss of her I lov'd would touch me nearest;
　　Yet, if I found her, I might love too much;
　　And that's uneasy Pleasure.
Dorax. 　　　　　　　　　If she be fated
　　To be your Wife, your fate will find her for you:
　　Predestinated ills are never lost.
15 *Antonio.* I had forgot
　　T'Enquire before, but long to be inform'd,
　　How, poison'd and betray'd, and round beset,
　　You could unwind your self from all these dangers;
　　And move so speedily to our relief!
20 *Dorax.* The double poisons, after a short Combat,
　　Expell'd each other in their Civill War,
　　By nature's benefit: and rows'd my thoughts
　　To Guard that life which now I found Attack'd.
　　I summon'd all my Officers in hast,
25　　On whose experienc'd Faith I might rely:
　　All came; resolv'd to dye in my defence,
　　Save that one Villain who betray'd the Gate.
　　Our diligence prevented the surprize
　　We justly fear'd: so, *Muley-Zeydan* found us
30　　Drawn-up in Battle, to receive the charge.
Antonio. But how the *Moors* and *Christian* slaves were
　　joyn'd,
　　You have not yet unfolded.
Dorax. 　　　　　　　　That remains.
　　We knew their Int'rest was the same with ours:
　　And though I hated more than Death, *Sebastian*;
35　　I could not see him dye by Vulgar hands:
　　But prompted by my Angell, or by his,
　　Freed all the Slaves, and plac'd him next my self,
　　Because I would not have his Person known.

I need not tell the rest, th'event declares it.

Antonio. Your Conquest came of course; their men were
    raw,   40
    And yours were disciplin'd: one doubt remains,
    Why you industriously conceal'd the King,
    Who, known, had added Courage to his Men?

Dorax. I would not hazard civill broils, betwixt
    His Friends and mine: which might prevent our Com-
    bat: 45
    Yet, had he fall'n, I had dismiss'd his Troops;
    Or, if Victorious, order'd his escape.
    But I forgot a new increase of Joy,
    To feast him with surprize; I must about it:
    Expect my swift return.   *Exit* Dorax.   50

         Enter a Servant to Antonio.

Servant. Here's a Lady at the door, that bids me tell you,
    she is come to make an end of the game, that was
    broken off betwixt you.

Antonio. What manner of Woman is she? Does she not
    want two of the four Elements? has she any thing about   55
    her but ayr and fire?

Servant. Truly, she flys about the room, as if she had
    wings instead of legs; I believe she's just turning into a
    bird: a house-bird I warrant her: and so hasty to fly to
    you, that, rather than fail of entrance, she wou'd come   60
    tumbling down the Chimney, like a Swallow.

         Enter Morayma.

      Antonio *running to her and Embracing her.*

Antonio. Look if she be not here already: what, no deniall
    it seems will serve your turn? why! thou little dun, is
    thy debt so pressing?

Morayma. Little Devill if you please: your lease is out,   65
    good Master Conjurer; and I am come to fetch you Soul
    and Body; not an hour of lewdness longer in this world
    for you.

Antonio. Where the Devill hast thou been? and how the
    Devill didst thou find me here?   70

Morayma. I follow'd you into the Castle-yard: but there
    was nothing but Tumult, and Confusion: and I was
    bodily afraid of being pick'd up by some of the Rabble:
    considering I had a double charge about me, ——— my
    Jewells and my Mayden-head.   75

Antonio. Both of 'em intended for my Worship's sole use
    and Property.

Morayma. And what was poor little I among 'em all?

Antonio. Not a mouthfull a piece: 'twas too much odds in
80   Conscience.
Morayma. So seeking for shelter, I naturally ran to the old
     place of Assignation, the Garden-house: where for want
     of instinct, you did not follow me.
Antonio. Well, for thy Comfort, I have secur'd thy Father;
85   and I hope thou hast secur'd his effects for us.
Morayma. Yes truly I had the prudent foresight to consider
     that when we grow old, and weary of Solacing one
     another, we might have, at least, wherewithall to make
     merry with the World; and take up with a worse plea-
90   sure of eating and drinking, when we were disabled for
     a better.
Antonio. Thy fortune will be e'en too good for thee: for
     thou art going into the Country of Serenades, and
     Gallantries; where thy street will be haunted every
95   Night, with thy foolish Lovers, and my Rivals; who
     will be sighing, and singing under thy inexorable
     windows, lamentable ditties, and call thee Cruell, and
     Goddess, and Moon, and Stars, and all the Poeticall
     names of wicked rhyme: while thou and I, are minding
100   our bus'ness, and jogging on, and laughing at 'em; at
     leisure-minuts, which will be very few, take that by way
     of threatning.
Morayma. I am afraid you are not very valiant, that you
     huff so much before hand: but, they say, your Churches
105   are fine places for Love-devotion: many a she-Saint is
     there worship'd.
Antonio. Temples are there, as they are in all other Coun-
     tries, good conveniences for dumb enterviews: I hear
     the Protestants an't much reform'd in that point neither;
110   for their Sectaries call their Churches by the naturall
     name of Meeting-houses. Therefore I warn thee in good
     time, not more of devotion than needs must, good
     future Spowse; and allways in a veile; for those eyes of
     thine are damn'd enemies to mortification.
115 *Morayma.* The best thing I have heard of Christendom, is
     that we women are allow'd the priviledge of having
     Souls; and I assure you, I shall make bold to bestow
     mine, upon some Lover, when ever you begin to go
     astray, and, if I find no Convenience in a Church, a
120   private Chamber will serve the turn.
Antonio. When that day comes, I must take my revenge
     and turn Gardener again: for I find I am much given to
     Planting.
     123 *Planting*] copulating (Farmer).

Morayma. But take heed, in the mean time, that some
  young *Antonio* does not spring up in your own Family;   125
  as false as his Father, though of another man's planting.

Reenter Dorax *with* Sebastian *and* Almeyda. Sebastian *enters
speaking to* Dorax, *while in the mean time* Antonio *presents*
Morayma *to* Almeyda.

Sebastian. How fares our Royall Pris'ner, *Muley-Zeydan?*
Dorax. Dispos'd to grant whatever I desire,
  To gain a Crown, and Freedom: well I know him,
  Of easy temper, naturally good,   130
  And faithfull to his word.
Sebastian.   Yet one thing wants,
  To fill the measure of my happiness:
  I'm still in pain for poor *Alvarez's* life.
Dorax. Release that fear; the good old man is safe:
  I pay'd his ransome: 135
  And have already order'd his Attendance.
Sebastian. O bid him enter for I long to see him.

    Enter Alvarez *with a Servant, who departs when*
        Alvarez *is enter'd.*

    Alvarez *falling down and embracing the King's knees.*
Alvarez. Now by my Soul, and by these hoary hairs,
  I'm so ore-whelm'd with pleasure, that I feel
  A latter spring within my with'ring limbs,   140
  That Shoots me out again.
Sebastian (raising him).   Thou good old Man!
  Thou hast deceiv'd me into more, more joys;
  Who stood brim-full before.
Alvarez.   O my dear Child!
  I love thee so, I cannot call thee King,
  Whom I so oft have dandled in these arms!   145
  What, when I gave thee lost to find thee living!
  'Tis like a Father, who himself had scap'd
  A falling house, and after anxious search,
  Hears from afar, his only Son within:
  And digs through rubbish, till he drags him out   150
  To see the friendly light.
  Such is my hast, so trembling is my joy
  To draw thee forth from underneath thy Fate.
Sebastian. The Tempest is ore-blown; the Skys are clear,
  And the Sea, charm'd into a Calm so still,   155
  That not a wrinkle ruffles her smooth face.
Alvarez. Just such she shows before a rising storm:
  And therefore am I come, with timely speed,

To warn you into Port.
Almeyda (aside).   My Soul fore-bodes
160   Some dire event involv'd in those dark words;
    And just disclosing, in a birth of fate.
Alvarez. Is there not yet an Heir of this vast Empire,
    Who still Survives, of *Muley-Moluch's* branch?
Dorax. Yes such an one there is, a Captive here,
    And Brother to the Dead.
165 *Alvarez.*   The Power's above
    Be prais'd for that: My prayers for my good Master
    I hope are heard.
Sebastian.   Thou hast a right in Heav'n,
    But why these prayers for me?
Alvarez. A door is open yet for your deliv'rance,
170   Now you my Country-men, and you *Almeyda*,
    Now all of us, and you (my all in one)
    May yet be happy in that Captive's life.
Sebastian. We have him here an honourable Hostage
    For terms of peace: what more he can Contribute
    To make me blest, I know not.
175 *Alvarez.*   Vastly more:
    Almeyda may be settled in the Throne;
    And you review your Native Clime with fame:
    A firm Alliance, and eternall Peace,
    (The glorious Crown of honourable War,)
180   Are all included in that Prince's life:
    Let this fair Queen be giv'n to *Muley-Zeydan*;
    And make her love the Sanction of your League.
Sebastian. No more of that: his life's in my dispose;
    And Pris'ners are not to insist on terms.
185   Or if they were, yet he demands not these.
Alvarez. You shou'd exact 'em.
Almeyda.   Better may be made;
    These cannot: I abhor the Tyrant's race;
    My Parents Murtherers, my Throne's Usurpers.
    But, at one blow to cut off all dispute,
190   Know this, thou busy, old, officious Man,
    I am a *Christian*; now be wise no more;
    Or if thou woud'st be still thought wise, be silent.
Alvarez. O! I perceive you think your Int'rest touch'd:
    'Tis what before the Battail I observ'd:
    But I must speak, and will.
195 *Sebastian.*   I prethee peace;
    Perhaps she thinks they are too near of bloud.
Alvarez. I wish she may not wed to bloud more near.
Sebastian. What if I make her mine?

Alvarez.   Now Heav'n forbid!
Sebastian. Wish rather Heav'n may grant.
  For, if I cou'd deserve, I have deserv'd her: 200
  My toyls, my hazards, and my Subjects lives,
  (Provided she consent) may claim her love:
  And, that once granted, I appeal to these,
  If better, I cou'd chuse a beauteous Bride.
Antonio. The fairest of her Sex.
Morayma.   The pride of Nature.   205
Dorax. He only merits her; she only him.
  So payr'd, so suited in their minds and Persons,
  That they were fram'd the Tallyes for each other.
  If any Alien love had interpos'd
  It must have been an eyesore to beholders,   210
  And to themselves a Curse.
Alvarez.   And to themselves
  The greatest Curse that can be, were to joyn.
Sebastian. Did I not love thee, past a change to hate,
  That word had been thy ruine; but no more,
  I charge thee on thy life, perverse old man.   215
Alvarez. Know, Sir, I wou'd be silent if I durst:
  But, if on Shipbord, I shou'd see my Friend,
  Grown frantique in a raging Calenture,
  And he, imagining vain flowry fields,
  Wou'd headlong plunge himself into the deep,   220
  Shou'd I not hold him from that mad attempt,
  Till his sick fancy were by reason cur'd?
Sebastian. I pardon thee th'effects of doting Age;
  Vain doubts, and idle cares, and over-caution;
  The second Non-age of a Soul, more wise;   225
  But now decay'd, and sunk into the Socket,
  Peeping by fits and giving feeble light.
Alvarez. Have you forgot?
Sebastian.   Thou mean'st my Father's Will,
  In bar of Marriage to *Almeyda's* bed:
  Thou seest my faculties are still entire,   230
  Though thine are much impair'd. I weigh'd that Will,
  And found 'twas grounded on our diff'rent Faiths;
  But, had he liv'd to see her happy change,
  He wou'd have cancell'd that harsh Interdict,
  And joyn'd our hands himself.
Alvarez.   Still had he liv'd   235
  And seen this change, he still had been the Same.

218 *Calenture*] a disease of sailors, characterized by delirium, in which the patient fancies the sea to be green fields and desires to leap into it.

Sebastian. I have a dark remembrance of my Father;
   His reas'nings and his Actions both were just;
   And, granting that, he must have chang'd his measures.
240 *Alvarez.* Yes, he was just, and therefore cou'd not change.
Sebastian. 'Tis a base wrong thou offer'st to the Dead.
Alvarez. Now Hea'vn forbid,
   That I shou'd blast his pious Memory:
   No, I am tender of his holy Fame:
245   For, dying he bequeath'd it to my charge.
   Believe I am; and seek to know no more,
   But pay a blind obedience to his will.
   For to preserve his Fame I wou'd be silent.
Sebastian. Craz'd fool, who woud'st be thought an Oracle,
250   Come down from off thy Tripos, and speak plain;
   My Father shall be justify'd, he shall:
   'Tis a Son's part to rise in his defence;
   And to confound thy malice, or thy dotage.
Alvarez. It does not grieve me that you hold me craz'd;
255   But, to be clear'd at my dead Master's cost,
   O there's the wound! but let me first adjure you,
   By all you owe that dear departed Soul,
   No more to think of Marriage with *Almeyda*.
Sebastian. Not Hea'vn and Earth combin'd, can hinder it.
260 *Alvarez.* Then, witness Hea'vn and Earth, how loath I am
   To say, you must not, nay you cannot wed.
   And since not only a dead Father's fame,
   But more, a Ladies honour must be touch'd,
   Which nice as Ermines will not bear a Soil;
265   Let all retire; that you alone may hear
   What ev'n in whispers I wou'd tell your ear.
                        All are going out.
Almeyda. Not one of you depart; I charge you stay.
   And, were my voice a Trumpet loud as Fame,
   To reach the round of Hea'vn, and Earth, and Sea,
270   All Nations shou'd be Summon'd to this place.
   So little do I fear that Fellow's charge:
   So shou'd my honour like a rising Swan,
   Brush with her wings, the falling drops away,
   And proudly plough the waves.
275 *Sebastian.* This noble Pride becomes thy Innocence:
   And I dare trust my Father's memory,
   To stand the charge of that foul forging tongue.
Alvarez. It will be soon discover'd if I forge:
   Have you not heard your Father in his youth,

250 *Tripos*] an oracle sat on a three-legged stool.

When newly marry'd, travel'd into *Spain*,   280
And made a long abode in *Phillip's* Court?
Sebastian. Why so remote a question? which thy self
  Can answer to thy self, for thou wert with him,
  His Fav'rite, as I oft have heard thee boast:
  And nearest to his Soul.   285
Alvarez. Too near indeed, forgive me Gracious Heaven
  That ever I should boast I was so near.
  The Confident of all his young Amours.
  (*To Almeyda*) And have not you, unhappy beauty,
    heard,
  Have you not often heard, your Exil'd Parents   290
  Were refug'd in that Court, and at that time?
Almeyda. 'Tis true: and often since, my Mother own'd
  How kind that Prince was, to espouse her cause;
  She Counsell'd, nay, Enjoyn'd me on her blessing
  To seek the Sanctuary of your Court: 295
  Which gave me first encouragement to come,
  And, with my Brother, beg *Sebastian's* aid.
Sebastian (*to Almeyda*). Thou help'st me well, to justify my
    War:
  My dying Father swore me, then a Boy;
  And made me kiss the Cross upon his Sword,   300
  Never to sheath it, till that exil'd Queen
  Were by my Arms restor'd.
Alvarez.   And can you finde
  No mistery, couch'd in this excess of kindness?
  Were Kings e're known, in this degenerate Age,
  So passionately fond of noble Acts,   305
  Where Interest shar'd not more than half with honour?
Sebastian. Base groveling Soul, who know'st not honour's
    worth;
  But weigh'st it out in mercenary Scales;
  The Secret pleasure of a generous Act,
  Is the great mind's great bribe.   310
Alvarez. Show me that King, and I'le believe the Phœnix.
  But knock at your own breast, and ask your Soul
  If those fair fatall eyes, edg'd not your Sword,
  More than your Father's charge, and all your vows?
  If so; and so your silence grants it is,   315
  Know King, your Father had, like you, a Soul;
  And Love is your Inheritance from him.
  Almeyda's Mother too had eyes, like her,
  And not less charming, and were charm'd no less
  Than your's are now with her, and her's with you.   320
Almeyda. Thou ly'st Imposter, Perjur'd Fiend thou ly'st.

Sebastian. Wa'st not enough to brand my Father's fame,
But thou must load a Ladies memory?
O Infamous base, beyond repair.
325 And, to what end this ill concerted lye,
Which, palpable and gross, yet granted true,
It barrs not my Inviolable vows.
Alvarez. Take heed and double not your Father's crimes;
To his Adult'ry, do not add your Incest.
330 Know, she is the product of unlawfull Love:
And 'tis your Carnall Sister you wou'd wed.
Sebastian. Thou shallt not say thou wert Condemn'd
unheard.
Else, by my Soul, this moment were thy last.
Almeyda. But think not Oaths shall justify thy charge,
335 Nor Imprecations on thy cursed head;
For who dares lye to Heaven, thinks Heaven a Jest.
Thou hast confess'd thy self the Conscious Pandar
Of that pretended passion:
A Single Witness, infamously known,
340 Against two Persons of unquestion'd fame.
Alvarez. What Int'rest can I have, or what delight
To blaze their shame, or to divulge my own?
If prov'd you hate me, if unprov'd Condemn?
Not Racks or Tortures could have forc'd this secret,
345 But too much care, to save you from a Crime,
Which would have sunk you both. For let me say,
Almeyda's beauty well deserves your love.
Almeyda. Out, base Impostor, I abhor thy praise.
Dorax. It looks not like Imposture: but a truth,
350 On utmost need reveal'd.
Sebastian. Did I expect from *Dorax*, this return?
Is this the love renew'd?
Dorax.   Sir, I am silent;
Pray Heav'n my fears prove false.
Sebastian. Away; you all combine to make me wretched.
355 *Alvarez.* But hear the story of that fatall Love;
Where every Circumstance shall prove another;
And truth so shine, by her own native light,
That if a Lye were mixt, it must be seen.
Sebastian. No; all may still be forg'd, and of a piece.
360 No; I can credit nothing thou can'st say.
Alvarez. One proof remains; and that's your Father's hand;
Firm'd with his Signet: both so fully known,
That plainer Evidence can hardly be,
Unless his Soul wou'd want her Hea'vn a while,
And come on Earth to swear.

Sebastian.   Produce that Writing.   365
Alvarez (to Dorax). Alonzo has it in his Custody.
  The same, which when his nobleness redeem'd me,
  And in a friendly visit own'd himself,
  For what he is, I then deposited:
  And had his Faith to give it to the King.   370
            Dorax *giving a seal'd Paper to the King.*
Dorax. Untouch'd, and Seal'd as when intrusted with
  me,
  Such I restore it, with a trembling hand,
  Lest ought within disturb your peace of Soul.
            Sebastian *tearing open the Seals.*
Sebastian. Draw near *Almeyda*: thou are most concern'd.
  For I am most in Thee.   375
  Alonzo, mark the Characters:
  Thou know'st my Father's hand, observe it well:
  And if th'Impostor's Pen, have made one slip,
  That shows it Counterfeit, mark that and save me.
Dorax. It looks, indeed, too like my Master's hand: 380
  So does the Signet; more I cannot say;
  But wish 'twere not so like.
Sebastian.   Methinks it owns
  The black Adult'ry, and *Almeyda's* birth;
  But such a mist of grief comes o're my eyes,
  I cannot, or I wou'd not read it plain.   385
Almeyda. Hea'vn cannot be more true, than this is false.
Sebastian. O Coud'st thou prove it, with the same assur-
  ance!
  Speak, hast thou ever seen my Father's hand?
Almeyda. No; but my Mother's honour has been read
  By me, and by the world, in all her Acts;   390
  In Characters more plain, and legible
  Then this dumb Evidence, this blotted lye.
  Oh that I were a man, as my Soul's one,
  To prove thee, Traytor, an Assassinate
  Of her fair fame: thus wou'd I tear thee, thus—   395
            Tearing the Paper.
  And scatter, o're the field, thy Coward limbs,
  Like this foul offspring of thy forging brain.
            Scatt'ring the Paper.
Alvarez. Just so, shalt thou be torn from all thy hopes.
  For know proud Woman, know in thy despight,
  The most Authentique proof is still behind.   400
  Thou wear'st it on thy finger: 'tis that Ring,
  Which match'd with that on his, shall clear the doubt.
  'Tis no dumb forgery: for that shall speak;

And sound a rattling peal to either's Conscience.

405   *Sebastian.* This Ring indeed, my Father, with a cold
And shaking hand, just in the pangs of Death,
Put on my finger; with a parting sigh,
And wou'd have spoke; but falter'd in his speech,
With undistinguish'd sounds.

   Alvarez.   I know it well:

410   For I was present: Now, *Almeyda,* speak:
And, truly tell us, how you come by yours?

   Almeyda. My Mother, when I parted from her sight,
To go to *Portugall,* bequeath'd it to me,
Presaging she shou'd never see me more:

415   She pull'd it from her finger, shed some tears,
Kiss'd it, and told me 'twas a pledge of Love;
And hid a Mistery of great Importance
Relating to my Fortunes.

   Alvarez.   Mark me now,
While I disclose that fatall Mistery.

420   Those rings, when you were born, and thought another's,
Your Parents, glowing yet in sinfull love,
Bid me bespeak: a Curious Artist wrought 'em:
With joynts so close, as not to be perceiv'd;
Yet are they both each other's Counterpart.

425   Her part had *Juan* inscrib'd, and his had *Zayda.*
(You know those names are theirs:) and in the midst,
A heart divided in two halves was plac'd.
Now if the rivets of those Rings, inclos'd,
Fit not each other, I have forg'd this lye:

430   But if they joyn, you must for ever part.

   Sebastian. Now life, or death.

   Almeyda.   And either thine, or ours.

       Sebastian *pulling off his Ring.* Almeyda *does the same,*
         and gives it to Alvarez *who unscrues both the Rings*
         and fits one half to the other.

   Almeyda. I'm lost for ever. ———   *Swoons.*
       The Women and Morayma, *take her up and carry her off.*
       Sebastian *here stands amaz'd without motion, his eyes*
                         fixt upward.

   Sebastian. Look to the Queen my Wife; For I am past
All Pow'r of Aid, to her or to my self.

435   *Alvarez.* His Wife, said he, his Wife! O fatall sound!
For, had I known it, this unwelcome news
Had never reach'd their ears.
So they had still been blest in Ignorance,

---

404 *rattling*] full of scolding or reproof.

And I alone unhappy.
Dorax. I knew it, but too late: and durst not speak.   440
Sebastian (starting out of his amazement). I will not live: no
    not a moment more;
    I will not add one moment more to Incest.
    I'le cut it off, and end a wretched being.
    For, should I live, my Soul's so little mine,
    And so much hers, that I should still enjoy.   445
    Ye Cruell Powers
    Take me as you have made me, miserable;
    You cannot make me guilty; 'twas my fate
    And you made that, not I.   *Draws his Sword.*
    Antonio *and* Alvarez *lay hold on him, and* Dorax
        wrests the Sword out of his hand.
Antonio. For Heav'n's sake hold, and recollect your mind.   450
Alvarez. Consider whom you punish, and for what;
    Your self? unjustly: You have charg'd the fault,
    On Heav'n that best may bear it.
    Though Incest is indeed a deadly Crime,
    You are not guilty, since, unknown 'twas done,   455
    And, known, had been abhorr'd.
Sebastian. By Heaven y're Traytours, all, that hold my
    hands,
    If death be but cessation of our thought,
    Then let me dye for I would think no more.
    I'le boast my Innocence above;   460
    And let 'em see a Soul they cou'd not sully:
    I shall be there before my Father's Ghost;
    That yet must languish long, in frosts and fires,
    For making me unhappy by his Crime:
               Struggling again.
    Stand off and let me take my fill of death;   465
    For I can hold my breath in your despight,
    And swell my heaving Soul out, when I please.
Alvarez. Heav'n comfort you!
Sebastian.   What, art thou giving comfort!
    Wou'dst thou give comfort, who hast giv'n despair?
    Thou seest *Alonzo* silent; he's a man.   470
    He knows, that men abandon'd of their hopes
    Shou'd ask no leave, nor stay for sueing out
    A tedious Writ of ease, from lingring Heaven,
    But help themselves, as timely as they cou'd,

468 giving] Q2 given Q1
463 *frosts and fires*] the temporal punishments of purgatory (Summers).
473 *Writ of ease*] a certificate of discharge from employment.

And teach the fates their duty.

475 *Dorax (to Alvarez and Antonio).*   Let him go:
He is our King; and he shall be obey'd.
Alvarez. What to destroy himself, O Parricide!
Dorax. Be not Injurious in your foolish zeal,
But leave him free; or by my sword I swear,
480 To hew that Arm away, that stops the passage
To his Eternal rest.
Antonio (letting go his hold). Let him be Guilty of his own
death if he pleases: for I'le not be guilty of mine; by
holding him.
The King shakes off Alvarez.
485 *Alvarez (to Dorax).* Infernal Fiend,
Is this a Subject's part?
Dorax.   'Tis a Friend's Office.
He has convinc'd me that he ought to dye.
And, rather than he should not, here's my sword
To help him on his Journey.
490 *Sebastian.* My last, my only Friend, how kind art thou
And how Inhuman these!
Dorax. To make the trifle death, a thing of moment!
Sebastian. And not to weigh th'Important cause I had,
To rid my self of life?
Dorax.   True; for a Crime,
495 So horrid in the face of Men and Angells,
As wilfull Incest is!
Sebastian.   Not wilfull neither.
Dorax. Yes, if you liv'd and with repeated Acts,
Refresh'd your Sin, and loaded crimes with crimes,
To swell your scores of Guilt.
Sebastian. True; if I liv'd.
500 *Dorax.*   I said so, if you liv'd.
Sebastian. For hitherto 'twas fatall ignorance:
And no intended crime.
Dorax.   That you best know.
But the Malicious World will judge the worst.
Alvarez. O what a Sophister has Hell procur'd,
To argue for Damnation!
505 *Dorax.*   Peace, old Dotard.
Mankind that always judge of Kings with malice,
Will think he knew this Incest, and pursu'd it.
His only way to rectify mistakes,
And to redeem her honour, is to dye.

485 *Infernal Fiend*] probably intended as a continuation of line
481.

Sebastian. Thou hast it right, my dear, my best *Alonzo*!   510
  And that, but petty reparation too;
  But all I have to give.
Dorax.   Your pardon, Sir;
  You may do more, and ought.
Sebastian.   What, more than death?
Dorax. Death? Why that's Children's sport: a Stage-Play,
    Death.
  We Act it every Night we go to bed.   515
  Death to a Man in misery is sleep:
  Wou'd you, who perpetrated such a Crime,
  As frighten'd nature, made the Saints above
  Shake Heav'n's Eternal pavement with their trembling,
  To view that act, wou'd you but barely dye?   520
  But stretch your limbs, and turn on t'other side,
  To lengthen out a black voluptuous slumber,
  And dream you had your Sister in your arms.
Sebastian. To expiate this, can I do more then dye?
Dorax. O yes: you must do more; you must be damn'd: 525
  You must be damn'd to all Eternity.
  And, sure, self-Murder is the readiest way.
Sebastian. How, damn'd?
Dorax.   Why, is that News?
Alvarez.   O, horrour! horrour!
Dorax. What, thou a Statesman,
  And make a bus'ness of Damnation?   530
  In such a World as this, why 'tis a trade.
  The Scriv'ner, Usurer, Lawyer, Shop-keeper,
  And Soldier, cannot live, but by damnation.
  The Polititian does it by advance:
  And gives all gone before-hand.   535
Sebastian. O thou hast giv'n me such a glimse of Hell,
  So push'd me forward, even to the brink,
  Of that irremeable burning Gulph,
  That looking in th'*Abyss*; I dare not leap.
  And now I see what good thou meanst my Soul,   540
  And thank thy pious fraud: Thou hast indeed,
  Appear'd a Devill, but didst an Angell's work.
Dorax. 'Twas the last Remedy, to give you leisure.
  For, if you cou'd but think, I knew you safe.
Sebastian. I thank thee, my *Alonzo*: I will live: 545
  But never more to *Portugall* return:
  For, to go back and reign, that were to show
  Triumphant Incest, and pollute the Throne.

538 *irremeable*] from the Latin *irremeabilis*, admitting of no return.

Alvarez. Since Ignorance ——

Sebastian.   O, palliate not my wound:

550 When you have argu'd all you can, 'tis Incest:
No, 'tis resolv'd, I charge you plead no more;
I cannot live without *Almeyda's* sight,
Nor can I see *Almeyda* but I sin.
Heav'n has inspir'd me with a Sacred thought,

555 To live alone to Hea'vn: and dye to her.

Dorax. Mean you to turn an Anchoret?

Sebastian.   What else?

The world was once too narrow for my mind,
But one poor little nook will serve me now;
To hide me from the rest of humane kinde.

560 *Affrique* has desarts wide enough to hold
Millions of Monsters, and I am, sure, the greatest.

Alvarez. You may repent, and wish your Crown too late.

Sebastian. O never, never: I am past a Boy,
A Scepter's but a play thing, and a Globe

565 A bigger bounding Stone. He who can leave
Almeyda, may renounce the rest with ease.

Dorax. O Truly great!
A Soul fix'd high, and capable of Hea'vn.
Old as he is, your Uncle Cardinall

570 Is not so far enamour'd of a Cloyster,
But he will thank you, for the Crown you leave him.

Sebastian. To please him more, let him believe me dead:
That he may never dream I may return.
Alonzo, I am now no more thy King,

575 But still thy Friend, and by that holy Name,
Adjure thee, to perform my last request.
Make our Conditions with yon Captive King,
Secure me but my Solitary Cell;
'Tis all I ask him for a Crown restor'd.

580 *Dorax.* I will do more:
But fear not *Muley-Zeydan*; his soft mettall
Melts down with easy warmth; runs in the mould,
And needs no farther forge.   *Exit* Dorax.

Re-enter Almeyda, *led by* Morayma, *and followd
by her Attendants.*

563–65 *Boy . . . Stone*] echoing Antony's memorable lines in *All
For Love*, III.i.443–45.

565 *bounding Stone*] nuts or cherry stones used in street games
(Norman Douglas, *London Street Games* [1916], pp. 18–19).

569 *your Uncle Cardinall*] Cardinal Prince Henry who reigned
as Henry I, 1578–80.

Sebastian. See where she comes again.
  By Heav'n when I behold those beauteous eyes,   585
  Repentance laggs and Sin comes hurrying on.
Almeyda. This is too cruell!
Sebastian. Speak'st thou of Love, of Fortune, or of Death,
  Or double Death, for we must part *Almeyda.*
Almeyda. I speak of all.   590
  For all things that belong to us are cruell.
  But what's most cruell, we must love no more.
  O 'tis too much that I must never see you,
  But not to love you is impossible:
  No, I must love you: Heav'n may bate me that;   595
  And charge that Sinfull Sympathy of Souls,
  Upon our Parents, when they lov'd too well.
Sebastian. Good Heav'n, thou speakst my thoughts, and I
    speak thine.
  Nay then there's Incest in our very Souls.
  For we were form'd too like.
Almeyda.   Too like indeed,   600
  And yet not for each other.
  Sure when we part (for I resolv'd it too
  Tho' you propos'd it first,) however distant,
  We shall be ever thinking of each other.
  And, the same moment, for each other pray.   605
Sebastian. But if a wish shou'd come a thwart our prayers!
Almeyda. It wou'd do well to curb it: if we cou'd.
Sebastian. We cannot look upon each other's face,
  But, when we read our love, we read our guilt.
  And yet methinks I cannot chuse but love.   610
Almeyda. I wou'd have ask'd you, if I durst for shame,
  If still you lov'd? you gave it Air before me.
  Ah why were we not born both of a Sex;
  For then we might have lov'd, without a Crime!
  Why was not I your Brother? though that wish   615
  Involv'd our Parents guilt, we had not parted;
  We had been Friends, and Friendship is not Incest.
Sebastian. Alas, I know not by what name to call thee!
  Sister and Wife are the two dearest Names;
  And I wou'd call thee both; and both are Sin.   620
  Unhappy we! that still we must confound
  The dearest Names, into a common Curse.
Almeyda. To love, and be belov'd, and yet be wretched!
Sebastian. To have but one poor night of all our lives;
  It was indeed a glorious; guilty night: 625
  So happy, that, forgive me Heav'n, I wish
  With all its guilt, it were to come again.

Why did we know so soon, or why at all,
That Sin cou'd be conceal'd in such a blisse?
630   *Almeyda.* Men have a larger priviledge of words,
Else I shou'd speak: but we must part, *Sebastian*,
That's all the name that I have left to call thee.
I must not call thee by the name I wou'd;
But when I say *Sebastian*, dear *Sebastian*,
635   I kiss the name I speak.
    Sebastian. We must make hast, or we shall never part.
I wou'd say something that's as dear as this;
Nay, wou'd do more than say: one moment longer,
And I shou'd break through Laws Divine, and Humane;
640   And think 'em Cobwebs, spred for little man,
Which all the bulky herd of nature breaks.
The vigorous young world, was ignorant
Of these restrictions, 'tis decrepit now;
Not more devout, but more decay'd, and cold.
645   All this is impious; therefore we must part:
For, gazing thus, I kindle at thy sight,
And, once burnt down to tinder, light again
Much sooner then before.

Re-enter Dorax.

    Almeyda. Here comes the sad denouncer of my fate,
650   To toul the mournfull knell of Seperation:
While I, as on my Death-bed, hear the sound,
That warns me hence for ever.
    Sebastian (to Dorax).   Now be brief,
And I will try to listen.
And share the minute that remains, betwixt
655   The care I owe my Subjects and my Love.
    Dorax. Your fate has gratify'd you all she can;
Gives easy misery, and makes Exile pleasing.
I trusted *Muley-Zeydan*, as a friend,
But swore him first to Secresy: he wept
660   Your fortune, and with tears, not squeez'd by Art,
But shed from nature, like a kindly shower:
In short, he proffer'd more than I demanded:
A safe retreat, a gentle Solitude,
Unvex'd with noise, and undisturb'd with fears:
I chose you one ———
665   *Almeyda.*   O do not tell me where:
For if I knew the place of his abode,
I shou'd be tempted to pursue his steps,
And then we both were lost.
    Sebastian.   Ev'n past redemption.

For, if I knew thou wert on that design,
(As I must know, because our Souls are one,)   670
I shou'd not wander, but by sure Instinct
Shou'd meet thee just half-way in pilgrimage,
And close for ever: for I know my love
More strong than thine, and I more frail than thou.
Almeyda. Tell me not that: for I must boast my Crime,   675
   And cannot bear that thou shoud'st better love.
Dorax. I may inform you both: for you must go,
   Where Seas, and winds, and Desarts will divide you.
   Under the ledge of *Atlas*, lyes a Cave,
   Cut in the living Rock, by Nature's hands: 680
   The Venerable Seat of holy Hermites.
   Who there, secure in separated Cells,
   Sacred ev'n to the *Moors*, enjoy Devotion:
   And from the purling Streams and savage fruits,
   Have wholesome bev'rage, and unbloudy feasts.   685
Sebastian. 'Tis pennance too Voluptuous, for my Crime.
Dorax. Your Subjects conscious of your life are few:
   But all desirous to partake your Exile:
   And to do office to your Sacred Person.
   The rest who think you dead, shall be dismiss'd,   690
   Under safe Convoy till they reach your Fleet.
Almeyda. But how am wretched I to be dispos'd?
   A vain Enquiry, since I leave my Lord:
   For all the world beside is Banishment!
Dorax. I have a Sister, Abbesse in *Tercera's*,   695
   Who lost her Lover on her Bridall day. ———
Almeyda. There, fate provided me a fellow-Turtle;
   To mingle sighs with sighs, and tears with tears.
Dorax. Last, for my self, if I have well fullfill'd
   My sad Commission, let me beg the boon,   700
   To share the sorrows of your last recess:
   And mourn the Common losses of our loves.
Alvarez. And what becomes of me? must I be left,
   (As Age and time had worn me out of use?)
   These Sinews are not yet so much unstrung,   705
   To fail me when my Master shou'd be serv'd:
   And when they are, then will I steal to death:
   Silent, and unobserv'd, to save his tears.
Sebastian. I've heard you both: *Alvarez* have thy wish.
   But thine *Alonzo*, thine, is too unjust.   710
   I charge thee with my last Commands, return,
   And bless thy *Violante* with thy vows.

695 *Tercera's*] in the Azores.

        Antonio, be thou happy too, in thine.
        Last, let me swear you all to Secresy;
715   And to conceal my shame conceal my life.
Dorax, Antonio, Morayma. We swear to keep it secret.
Almeyda. Now I wou'd speak the last farewell, I cannot.
        It wou'd be still farewell, a thousand times:
        And, multiply'd in Eccho's, still farewell.
720   I will not speak; but think a thousand thousand;
        And be thou silent too, my last *Sebastian;*
        So let us part in the dumb pomp of grief.
        My heart's too great; or I wou'd dye this moment:
        But Death I thank him, in an hour, has made
725   A mighty journey, and I hast to meet him.
                   She staggers and her Women hold her up.
Sebastian. Help to support this feeble, drooping flower:
        This tender Sweet, so shaken by the storm.
        For these fond arms must, thus be stretch'd in vain,
        And never, never must embrace her more.
        Tis past: ——— my Soul goes in that word; ———
730   farewell.
        Alvarez *goes with* Sebastian *to one end of the Stage.*
                Women *with* Almeyda *to the other.*

        Dorax, *coming up to* Antonio *and* Morayma, *who stand*
                 on the Middle of the Stage.
Dorax. Hast to attend *Almeyda:* for your sake
        Your Father is forgiven: but to *Antonio*
        He forfeits half his Wealth: be happy both:
        And let *Sebastian* and *Almeyda's* Fate,
735   This dreadfull Sentence to the World relate,
        That unrepented Crimes of Parents dead,
        Are justly punish'd on their Children's head.

---

   730 Soul] Q2; Souls Q1
   721 *my last Sebastian*] my last farewell, Sebastian.

Epilogue

Don Sebastian, King of Portugall

Spoken betwixt Antonio *and* Morayma.

Morayma. I quak'd at heart for fear the Royal Fashion
  Shou'd have seduc'd Us two to Separation:
  To be drawn in, against our own desire,
  Poor I to be a Nun, poor You a Fryar.
Antonio. I trembled when the Old Man's hand was in,   5
  He would have prov'd we were too near of kin:
  Discovering old Intrigues of Love, like t'other, ⎤
  Betwixt my Father and thy sinfull Mother; ⎬
  To make Us Sister Turk and Christian Brother. ⎦
Morayma. Excuse me there; that League shou'd have been
    rather   10
  Betwixt your Mother and my *Mufti*-Father;
  'Tis for my own and my Relations Credit
  Your Friends shou'd bear the Bastard, mine shou'd get it.
Antonio. Suppose us two *Almeyda* and *Sebastian* ⎤
  With Incest prov'd upon us: ——— ⎬
Morayma.   Without question ⎬   15
  Their Conscience was too queazy of digestion. ⎦
Antonio. Thou woud'st have kept the Councell of thy
    Brother
  And sinn'd till we repented of each other.
Morayma. Beast as you are on Nature's Laws to trample;
  'Twere fitter that we follow'd their Example   20
  And since all Marriage in Repentance ends,
  'Tis good for us to part while we are Friends.
  To save a Maid's remorses and Confusions
  E'en leave me now before We try Conclusions.
Antonio. To copy their Example first make certain   25
  Of one good hour like theirs before our parting;
  Make a debauch o're Night of Love and Madness;
  And marry when we wake in sober sadness.
Morayma. I'le follow no new Sects of your inventing,
  One Night might cost me nine long months repenting: 30
  First wed, and if you find that life a fetter,
  Dye when you please, the sooner Sir the better:

---

5 *hand was in*] while Alvarez was having a run of luck, finally able
to tell his story of Almeyda's birth.

My wealth wou'd get me love e're I cou'd ask it:
Oh there's a strange Temptation in the Casket:
35   All these Young Sharpers wou'd my grace importune,
And make me thundring Votes of lives and fortune.

36 *Votes of lives and fortune*] Scott thought this alluded to public
addresses upon the Revolution of 1688.

Prologue

*Sent to the Author by an unknown hand,
and propos'd to be spoken*

By Mrs. Montford *drest like an Officer.*

Bright Beauties who in awfull Circle sit,
And yon grave Synod of the dreadfull Pit,
And you the Upper-tire of pop-gun wit.

Pray ease me of my wonder if you may;
Is all this Crowd barely to see the play,   5
Or is't the Poet's Execution day?

His breath is in your hands I will presume,
But I advise you to deferr his doom:
Till you have got a better in his room.

And don't maliciously combine together,   10
As if in spight and spleen you were come hither,
For he has kept the Pen tho' lost the feather.

And on my Honour Ladies I avow,
This Play was writ in Charity to you,
For such a dearth of Wit whoever knew?   15

Sure 'tis a Judgment on this Sinfull Nation
For the abuse of so great Dispensation:
And therefore I resolv'd to change Vocation.

For want of Petty-coat I've put on buff,
To try what may be got by lying rough: 20
How think you Sirs, is it not well enough?

0.1 *by an unknown hand*] thought to be by Sir Harry Sheeres, a
Jacobite friend of Dryden. The humor of the prologue turns on "the
unwillingness displayed to attend King William into Ireland by many
of the nobility and gentry, who had taken arms at the Revolution"
(Scott). James II, with French aid, was trying to recover his throne in an
Irish campaign in 1689.
  0.3 *By Mrs. Montford*] i.e., Morayma.
  3 *Upper-tire*] upper balcony.
  12 *feather*] i.e., the laureatship.
  19 *buff*] clothes of a soldier.
  20 *lying rough*] lying in one's clothes all night.

Of Bully Criticks I a Troup wou'd lead;
But one reply'd, thank you there's no such need,
I at Groom-Porter's Sir can safer bleed.

25 Another who the name of danger loaths,
Vow'd he would go, and swore me Forty Oaths,
But that his Horses were in body-cloaths.

A third cry'd, Dam my bloud, I'de be content
To push my Fortune, if the Parliament
30 Would but recall Claret from Banishment.

A Fourth (and I have done) made this excuse,
I'de draw my Sword in *Ireland* Sir to chuse:
Had not their Women gouty leggs and wore no shoes!

Well, I may march thought I and fight and trudge,
35 But of these blades the Devill a man will budge,
They there would fight e'n just as here they judge.

Here they will pay for leave to find a fault,
But when their Honour calls they can't be bought,
Honour in danger, bloud and wounds is sought.

40 Lost Virtue whether fled, or where's thy dwelling,
Who can reveal, at least 'tis past my telling,
Unless thou art Embarkt for *Iniskelling*.

On Carrion tits those Sparks denounce their rage
In boot of wisp and Leinster freese ingage,
45 What would you do in such an Equipage?

The Siege of *Derry* does you Gallants threaten:
Not out of Errant shame of being beaten,
As fear of wanting meat or being eaten.

24 *Groom-Porter's*] offices in the Royal Household, in charge of gambling.
30 *Claret from Banishment*] In 1689 Parliament prohibited trade with France, because France and England were at war.
40 *whether*] i.e., whither.
42 *Iniskelling*] Enniskillen, in Ireland, where English horsemen behaved courageously against the forces of King James.
43 *Carrion tits*] small horse carcasses.
44 *boot of wisp*] boots of straw.
44 *Leinster freese*] rough Irish cloth, associated with peasantry.
46 *Derry*] Londonderry, one of the main strongholds of King William, which suffered a severe food shortage under siege in 1689.

Were Wit like honour to be won by fighting
How few just Judges would there be of writing,   50
Then you would leave this Villanous back-biting.

Your Talents lye how to express your spight,
But where is he knows how to praise aright,
You praise like Cowards but like Criticks fight.

Ladies be wise, and wean these yearling Calves   55
Who in your Service too are meer faux-braves,
They Judge and write and fight, and—Love by halves.

Preface 4 lengthning] lenghthning   31 out;] ~,   180 Under- /
plot] Under-plot   189 relations,] ~ ₍
Prologue 8 foe;] ~,   9 imploring,] ~ ;   28 were,] ~.   29 fair;] ~,
30 bring,] ~ ;   38 neither;] ~,   39 kind,] ~ ;
I.i.17 Throne,] ~.   19 Servants,] ~.   51–52 Q *lines:* I . . . far, /
By . . . port: / Retire . . .   65 Well,] ~ ₍   65 *Benducar . . . Ben-*
ducar] Bemboucar   66–67 Q *lines:* Thou . . .Minister, / First . . .
76 mankind.] ~,   116 Lightning] Ligtning   116 Slaughters.] ~,
128 *Almeyda,*] ~ ₍   148 Friend,] ~ ₍   157 *Emperor.*] Q *prefix*
throughout Moluch   181 that's] thar's   189 garbidge,] ~ ₍
230 Q *lines:* No . . . excuses. / Know . . .   251 'em?] ~.   375
Prodigy ₍] ~,   443 dar'st,] ~ ₍   497 a] ah   499 rich.] ~,
560 Horse- / flesh] Horse-flesh
II.i.23 past ₍] ~,   43 Right,] ~ ₍   73 rebel?] ~.   101 cou'dst]
coudst   116 Command.] ~,   209 are:] ~,   249 full,] ~ ₍
281 own!] ~ ?   281 Brother,] ~ ₍   294 more,] ~ ₍   332 our]
onr   339 thee,] ~ ₍   370 acquainted ₍] ~ :   422 kills,] ~ ₍
424 you;] ~,   425 love,] ~ ;   514 wou'd ₍] ~,   578 Sisters]
Sister's
II.ii.18 self,] ~ ₍   23 Occupation,] ~ ₍
III.i.9 lye:] ~,   87 thee] the   229 death:] ~,   261 pale;] ~,
304 hearing:] ~,   330 self!] ~ ?   361 back,] ~ ₍   458 What,]
~ ₍   466 *Benducar,*] ~ ₍
III.ii.47 not,] ~ ₍   50 What,] ~ ₍   52 why,] ~ ₍   135 What,]
~ ₍   234 fresh- / water] fresh-water   266 better. She] better,
she   306 before- / hand] before-hand   309 it;] ~,
IV.i.23 enquire,] ~ :   27 Council;] ~,   41 Night ₍] ~ :   162
What,] ~ ₍
IV.ii.55 eves- / dropping] eves-dropping   139 Dialogues:] ~,   146
way,] ~ ₍   195 what,] ~ ₍   234 supposing,] ~ ₍   252.2
Antonio,] ~ ₍   284 that,] ~ ₍   323 Why,] ~ ₍   333 upon.] ~,
378 What,] ~ ₍   382 What,] ~ ₍   482 Person. Be] Person, be
512–13 *one line in* Q   513 Crime,] ~ ₍   551 her.] ~,   656.2
Peruque,] ~ ₍   698 How,] ~ ₍   726 Merit, . . . reward ₍] ~ ₍
. . . ~,   773 more,] ~ ₍   924 Heaven blest] Heav'n blest
V.i.84 Well,] ~ ₍   111 Therefore] therefore   132 happiness:] ~ ₍
152 hast,] ~ ₍   231 impair'd.] ~,   235–36 Q *lines:* Still . . .
change, / He . . .   263 more,] ~ ₍   314 Father's] Fashers   334
charge;] ~ ;   335 head;] ~,   361 hand;] ~ :   362 Signet:] ~ ;
377 hand,] ~ ₍   395 thus— ₍] ~ —:   420 Those] Yhose   421
Your] Tour   468 What,] ~ ₍   494 Crime,] ~.   528 Why,]
~ ₍   569 is, . . . Cardinall ₍] ~ ₍ . . . ~,   648.1 *Re-enter*]
Reenter   671 wander, . . . Instinct ₍] ~ ₍ . . . ~,   672 half-way ₍
. . . pilgrimage,] ~, . . . ~ ₍   687 Subjects ₍] ~,
Prologue 0.3 Montford] Monford   4 may;] ~ ₍   7 presume,] ~ ₍
28 Dam my] Dammy   31 excuse,] ~ ₍   33 shoes!] ~.

Bibliography

ALSSID, MICHAEL. "The Design of Dryden's *Aureng-Zebe*," *Journal of English and Germanic Philology*, LXIV (1965), 452–69.

——. "The Perfect Conquest: A Study of Theme and Structure in Dryden's *The Indian Emperour*," *Studies in Philology*, LIX (1962), 539–59.

AVERY, EMMETT L., SCOUTEN, ARTHUR H., VAN LENNEP, WILLIAM, et al. *The London Stage 1660–1800: A Calendar of Plays*. 8 vols. published. Carbondale, Ill., 1960—.

BEHN, APHRA. *Plays, Histories, and Novels of Mrs. Aphra Behn*. 6 vols. London, 1871.

BERNIER, FRANÇOIS. *Histoire de la dernière révolution des États du Grand Mogol*. English translation. London, 1671.

BOWERS, FREDSON. "Current Theories of Copy-Text, with an Illustration from Dryden," *Modern Philology*, XLVIII (1950), 12–20.

——. *A Supplement to the Woodward and McManaway Check List of English Plays 1641–1700*. Charlottesville, Va., 1949.

——. "Textual Criticism," in *The Aims and Methods of Scholarship in Modern Languages and Literature*. Edited by James Thorpe. New York, 1964.

——. "The 1665 Manuscript of Dryden's *Indian Emperour*," *Studies in Philology*, XLVIII (1950), 738–60.

——. "The Text of This Edition," *The Dramatic Works in the Beaumont and Fletcher Canon*. Vol. I. Cambridge, 1966.

——. "Variants in Early Editions of Dryden Plays," *Harvard Library Bulletin*, III (1949), 278–88.

BROOKS, CLEANTH. *Modern Poetry and the Tradition*. Chapel Hill, N.C., 1939.

BROWER, REUBEN. "Dryden's Epic Manner and Virgil," *PMLA*, LV (1940), 119–38.

CIBBER, COLLEY. *An Apology for the Life of Mr. Colley Cibber, Comedian*. Edited by Robert W. Lowe. 2 vols. London, 1889.

DEARING, VINTON A. "The Use of Computer in Analyzing Dryden's Spelling," *Literary Data Processing Conference Proceedings, September 9, 10, 11, 1964*, pp. 200–10. [Armonk, N.Y., 1964.]

DENNIS, JOHN. *Critical Works*. Edited by Edward Niles Hooker. 2 vols. Baltimore, 1939–43.

DOBRÉE, BONAMY. "Milton and Dryden: A Comparison and Contrast in Poetic Ideas and Poetic Method," *ELH: A Journal of English Literary History*, III (1936), 83–100.

——. *Restoration Tragedy 1660–1720*. Oxford, 1929.

DOUGLAS, NORMAN. *London Street Games*. London, 1916.

DOWNES, JOHN. *Roscius Anglicanus; or, An Historical Review of the Stage from 1660–1706*. Edited by Montague Summers. London, [1928].

DRYDEN, JOHN. *All for Love*. Edited by R. J. Kaufmann. San Francisco, 1962.

——. *All for Love*. Edited by Arthur Sale. London, 1957.

Bibliography

DRYDEN, JOHN. *Of Dramatic Poesy and Other Critical Essays*. Edited by George Watson. 2 vols. New York, 1962.

————. *Dryden: The Dramatic Works*. Edited by Montague Summers. 6 vols. London, 1931–32.

————. *The Poems of John Dryden*. Edited by James Kinsley. 4 vols. Oxford, 1958.

————. *The Selected Dramas of John Dryden*. Edited by George R. Noyes. Chicago, 1910.

————. *The Songs of John Dryden*. Edited by Cyrus Lawrence Day. Cambridge, Mass., 1932.

————. *The Works of John Dryden*. Edited by Sir Walter Scott, revised and corrected by George Saintsbury. 18 vols. Edinburgh, 1882–93.

————. *The Works of John Dryden*. Vol. IX. Edited by John Loftis and Vinton A. Dearing. Berkeley and Los Angeles, 1966.

ELIOT, T. S. "John Dryden" in *Homage to John Dryden*. London, 1924.

————. *John Dryden: The Poet, The Dramatist, The Critic*. New York, 1932.

EVELYN, JOHN. *Diary*. Edited by E. S. de Beer. 6 vols. Oxford, 1955.

FARMER, JOHN S. and HENLEY, W. E. *Slang and Its Analogues*. 7 vols. London, 1890–1904.

FELTHAM, OWEN. *Resolves, Divine, Morall, Politicall*. Third edition. London, 1628.

FRAZER, JAMES GEORGE. *The Golden Bough: A Study in Magic and Religion*. Third edition. 12 vols. London, 1911–15.

FUJIMURA, THOMAS H. "The Appeal of Dryden's Heroic Plays," *PMLA*, LXXV (1960), 868–83.

GAGEN, JEAN. "Love and Honor in Dryden's Heroic Plays," *PMLA*, LXXVII (1962), 208–20.

GOGGIN, L. P. "This Bow of Ulysses," *Essays and Studies in Language and Literature*. Duquesne Studies: Philological Series, no. 5, pp. 49–86. Pittsburgh, 1964.

GÓMARA, FRANCISCO LÓPEZ DE. *The Conquest of the Weast India* (*1578*). Edited by Herbert Ingram Priestley. New York, 1940.

GREG, W. W. "The Rationale of Copy-Text," *Studies in Bibliography*, III (1950–51), 19–36.

HARBAGE, ALFRED. *Cavalier Drama*. New York, 1936.

HARTSOCK, MILDRED E. "Dryden's Plays: A Study of Ideas," *Seventeenth Century Studies*. Edited by Robert Shafer, 2d series, pp. 71–176. Princeton, 1937.

HEYWOOD, THOMAS. *An Apology for Actors* (*1612*). Edited by R. H. Perkinson. New York, 1941.

HORACE. *Satires, Epistles, Ars Poetica*. Translated by H. R. Fairclough. London, 1929.

HUGHES, MERRITT Y. "Dryden as a Statist," *Philological Quarterly*, VI (1927), 335–50.

HUNTLEY, FRANK L. "Dryden, Rochester, and The Eighth Satire of Juvenal," *Philological Quarterly*, XVIII (1939), 281–82.

JEFFERSON, D. W. "Aspects of Dryden's Imagery," *Essays in Criticism*, IV (1954), 20–41.

JEFFERSON, D. W. "The Significance of Dryden's Heroic Plays," *Proceedings of the Leeds Philosophical and Literary Society*, V (1940), 125–39.

JOHNSON, SAMUEL. *A Dictionary of the English Language*. 4 vols. London, 1805.

———. *Lives of the English Poets*. Edited by George Birkbeck Hill. 3 vols. London, 1905.

JUVENAL. *Juvenal and Persius*. Translated by G. G. Ramsay. London, 1912.

KING, BRUCE. "Dryden's Intent in *All for Love*," *College English*, XXIV (1963), 267–71.

———. *Dryden's Major Plays*. Edinburgh, 1966.

KIRSCH, ARTHUR *Dryden's Heroic Drama*. Princeton, 1965.

LEACH, MARIA (ed.). *Standard Dictionary of Folklore, Mythology, and Legend*. 2 vols. New York, 1949.

LEAVIS, F. R. " 'Antony and Cleopatra' and 'All for Love,' " *Scrutiny*, V (1940), 158–69.

LEECH, CLIFFORD. "Restoration Tragedy: A Reconsideration," *Durham University Journal*, XLII (1950), 106–15.

LUCAN. *The Civil War, books I–X*. Translated by J. D. Duff. London, 1928.

MACDONALD, HUGH. *John Dryden: A Bibliography of Early Editions and of Drydeniana*. Oxford, 1939.

MACMILLAN, DOUGALD. "The Sources of Dryden's *The Indian Emperour*," *The Huntington Library Quarterly*, XIII (1950), 353–70.

MARTIAL. *Epigrams*. Translated by W. C. A. Ker. 2 vols. London, 1919–20.

MONK, SAMUEL. *John Dryden: A List of Critical Studies*. Minneapolis, 1950.

MONTAIGNE, MICHAEL. *The Essayes of Michael, Lord of Montaigne*. Translated by John Florio. 3 vols. London, 1928.

MOORE, John R. "Political Allusions in Dryden's Later Plays," *PMLA*, LXXIII (1958), 36–41.

MUIR, KENNETH. "The Imagery of 'All for Love,' " *Proceedings of the Leeds Philosophical and Literary Society*, V (1938–43), 140–49.

NICOLL, ALLARDYCE. *A History of English Drama 1660–1900*, vol. I. (*Restoration Drama, 1660–1700.*) Fourth edition, revised. Cambridge, 1952.

OSBORNE, JAMES M. *John Dryden: Some Biographical Facts and Problems*. Revised edition. Gainsville, Fla., 1965.

———. "Macdonald's Bibliography of Dryden," *Modern Philology*, XXXIX (1941–42), 69–98, 197–212, 313–19.

OSBORNE, SCOTT C. "Heroical Love in Dryden's Heroic Drama," *PMLA*, LXXIII (1958), 480–90.

OVID. *Publii Ovidii Nasonis: Fastorum Libro Sex*. Edited by Sir James George Frazer. 5 vols. London, 1929.

———. *Metamorphoses*. Translated by Frank Justus Miller. 2 vols. London, 1916.

———. *Tristia, Ex Ponto*. Translated by Arthur Leslie Wheeler. London, 1924.

Bibliography

PENDLEBURY, B. J. *Dryden's Heroic Plays, a Study of the Origins.* London, 1923.

PEPYS, SAMUEL. *The Diary of Samuel Pepys.* Transcribed by Rev. Mynors Bright, edited with additions by Henry B. Wheatley. 10 vols. London, 1893–99.

PRIOR, MOODY. *The Language of Tragedy.* New York, 1947.

———. "Poetic Drama: An Analysis and a Suggestion," *English Institute Essays 1949.* New York, 1950.

QUINTILIAN. *The Institutio Oratoria.* Edited and translated by H. E. Butler. 4 vols. London, 1920.

REINERT, OTTO. "Passion and Pity in *All for Love*," in *The Hidden Sense and Other Plays.* Norwegian Studies in English, no. 9, pp. 159–95. Oslo, 1963.

SCOTT, REGINALD. *The Discoverie of Witchcraft.* Introduction by Montague Summers. London, 1930.

SENECA. *Epistulae Morales.* Edited by L. D. Reynolds. 2 vols. Oxford, 1965.

STECK, JAMES S. "Dryden's *Indian Emperour*: The Early Editions and Their Relation to the Text," *Studies in Bibliography*, II (1949–50), 139–52.

TEETER, LEWIS. "The Dramatic Use of Hobbes's Political Ideas," *ELH: A Journal of English Literary History*, III (1936), 140–69.

TILLEY, MORRIS PALMER. *A Dictionary of Proverbs in England in the Sixteenth and Seventeenth Centuries.* Ann Arbor, 1950.

TROWBRIDGE, HOYT. "The Place of Rules in Dryden's Criticism," *Modern Philology*, XLIV (1946), 84–96.

VOLTAIRE, FRANÇOIS MARIE AROUET DE. *Essai sur les mœurs et l'esprit des nations.* Edited by René Pomeau. 2 vols. Paris, 1963.

WAITH, EUGENE M. *The Herculean Hero in Marlowe, Chapman, Shakespeare, and Dryden.* London, 1962.

WALLERSTEIN, RUTH. "Dryden and the Analysis of Shakespeare's Techniques," *Review of English Studies*, XIX (1942), 165–85.

WARD, CHARLES E. *The Life of John Dryden.* Chapel Hill, N.C., 1961.

WILSON, JOHN HAROLD. *All the King's Ladies: Actresses of the Restoration.* Chicago, 1958.

———. *A Preface to Restoration Drama.* Boston, 1965.

WINTERBOTTOM, JOHN. "The Place of Hobbesian Ideas in Dryden's Tragedies," *The Journal of English and Germanic Philology*, LVII (1958), 665–83.

WOODWARD, GERTRUDE L. and MCMANAWAY, JAMES G. *A Check List of English Plays 1641–1700.* Chicago, 1945.